NINETEENTH-CENTURY GALLERY

By the same author

PORTRAITS OF POWER

An Introduction to
Twentieth-century History

THE GEORGIAN CENTURY
(1714–1837)

NINETEENTH-CENTURY GALLERY

Portraits of Power and Rebellion

S. E. AYLING

SOMETIME SCHOLAR OF EMMANUEL COLLEGE CAMBRIDGE
AND GOLDSMITHS' COMPANY'S EXHIBITIONER
FORMERLY SENIOR HISTORY MASTER
SANDOWN GRAMMAR SCHOOL ISLE OF WIGHT

BARNES & NOBLE, INC.
New York, New York

Published in the United States, 1970
by BARNES & NOBLE, INC.

© *S. E. Ayling* 1970
Copyright. All rights reserved

SBN 389 01248 3

Made in Great Britain

PREFACE

This book somewhat resembles its predecessor, *Portraits of Power*, which, perhaps over-ambitiously, bore the sub-title *An Introduction to Twentieth-century History*. Like that earlier book, this is not a textbook in the sense of trying to 'get everything in'; but it also, through short lives of outstanding figures, does attempt a similar view of some of the preceding century's most significant events.

I should like to thank Mr Charles Bawdon for much useful criticism and assistance. I am particularly in his debt for Chapter Four on Andrew Jackson.

The illustrations for Metternich, Bolívar, Jackson, Palmerston, Thiers, the Tsars Nicholas I and Alexander II, and the first of the two Gladstone portraits are from the Mansell Collection; those for Lincoln and Kaiser William II from Paul Popper, Ltd.

S.E.A.

CONTENTS

CONTENTS

ILLUSTRATIONS

MAPS

I

NAPOLEON I

(1769-1821)

The Turmoil and Aftermath of Revolution

Napoleon Bonaparte, France's man of destiny, the heir and destroyer of the French Revolution and the greatest of modern military conquerors, was a Frenchman by only the narrowest of margins. He was born on August 15th, 1769; only the year before, the Republic of Genoa, unable to subdue the long-lived rebellion of the islanders under Paoli, had sold out their Corsican rights to France.

Both parents of Napoleon came from leading Corsican families. "We thought ourselves as good as the Bourbons," he once said; "in the island we really were." Carlo Buonaparte, his father, had fought under Paoli, but transferred his allegiance to France and was admitted to the French nobility in 1770. He was thus able to place four of his children at schools in France, among them the nine-year-old Napoleon at Brienne, where there was one of the newly founded military academies for the sons of noblemen. Carlo's wife, Letizia, destined to become mother of the kings of half Europe,[1] always remained most at ease when speaking the Corsican *patois*; and all his life Napoleon retained his Corsican accent.

Intelligence, industry, and in particular proficiency at mathe-

[1] Her eight surviving children were Joseph, later King successively of Naples and of Spain; Napoleon, Emperor of the French and King of Italy; Lucien; Elise; Louis, later King of Holland; Pauline; Caroline, later Queen of Naples, married to Murat; and Jerome, later King of Westphalia.

This impressively sensible matriarch ('Madame Mère') once rapped the knuckles of her emperor son when he held out his hand for her to kiss. Awarded by him a handsome income and estate, she hoarded her francs. "One day," she said, "I may have to find bread for all these kings I have borne"; and, indeed, after the collapse of the Empire she gave away to various members of her family nearly ten million francs. She survived, blind in her old age, until 1836, fifteen years after Napoleon's death and fifty-one after her husband Carlo's.

matics took him after five years at Brienne to the Ecole Militaire in
Paris, where his bookishness, his shy aggressiveness, and his half-
foreign uncouthness kept him something of an outsider among his
aristocratic fellow-cadets; but he distinguished himself in his
examinations and became a very youthful, as well as expert,
lieutenant of artillery. While his wealthier fellows pursued their
amours, he went to bed at ten (by his own account), rose at four,
ate once a day, but fed voraciously on a varied diet composed
of the French classics, Rousseau and the new political philosophers,
Ossian and the romantic poets, and a wide range of works upon
geography, science, and history. History especially; he himself
aspired to write a history of Corsica and its struggle for freedom.
In these early days of the Revolution, with turbulence in Paris and
anarchy in the provinces, the young Napoleon's principal political
interest still lay in his home island. He managed to stay there for
most of the time between September 1789 and May 1792, outstaying
at last his already extended leave to the point of forfeiting his commission. The name Buonaparte counted in Corsica, and Napoleon
brought with him a breath of metropolitan radicalism, as well as a
supply of tricolours for distribution; but the old leader, Paoli,
having been deliriously welcomed back from exile, did not propose
to have any truck with such 'Jacobins' as Napoleon or his firebrand
brother Lucien. After a series of failures to gain control of Ajaccio
in the name of the National Convention, Napoleon and the whole
Buonaparte family were obliged to leave Corsica in 1793.

To Paoli Napoleon may have seemed a Jacobin, and his loyalty
to the revolutionary régime was sufficient to ensure his military
reinstatement and advancement; but Napoleon, though he was an
open republican and readily adopted the current phraseology of
the Revolution, was always authoritarian by conviction and temper.
He despised and feared the rabble. He had seen them in action in
the murderous riots of 1792, running loose in Paris with heads
impaled on their pikes. He had watched "decently dressed women"
doing violence to the corpses of the King's Swiss Guard. Napoleon
must have expressed some forceful views upon "the sovereign
people" to his brother Lucien, for already in June 1792 this democratic seventeen-year-old was noting ominously his elder brother's
"*ambition tout à fait égoiste. . . .*" "I am convinced that he is a
dangerous man in a free country. . . . He seems to have strong
leanings towards tyranny."

By now revolutionary France was at war with Austria and Prussia. In September 1792 she turned back their invading armies, and was soon on the offensive against them. By January 1793 the revolutionaries had guillotined Louis XVI. The ancient English and European fear of French aggression was joined now by fear of a democratic revolutionary crusade, for the Jacobins preached revolution and war against tyranny everywhere. The following month they were at war with Britain too. France itself was torn by bloody dissension between the political factions. The Reign of Terror began, and two-thirds of the French départements were affected by civil war. Among the royalists of La Vendée resistance was most bitter; in the south Lyons, Marseilles, and Toulon were all for a time in counter-revolutionary hands. The effective rulers of revolutionary France were by this time the Committee of Public Safety, a ten-man dictatorship savagely engaged in making war upon the "enemies of the people". Dominating this Committee was the tyrant Robespierre; but among the ten was one whose work was of more enduring importance: Lazare Carnot, engineer, politician, and soldier, the "organizer of victory". The army that Carnot fashioned out of the raw young conscripts (already 800,000 strong by the end of 1794), each brigade stiffened with a battalion of veterans and indoctrinated by a political representative (*député en mission*), was soon to prove more than a match for the troops of the *ancien régime*. This revolutionary army was the weapon which later in Napoleon's hands cut a path of conquest through Europe.

The good fortune that stayed with him almost to the end was already manifest. The revolutionary levies took Marseilles and pressed on to Toulon, where the counter-revolutionaries had opened the harbour to the British and Spanish fleets. When the chief officer of the artillery was wounded Napoleon was brought in to take command in his place, being recommended by a fellow-Corsican, one of the *députés en mission*. After a long siege Toulon fell (December 1793); it was Napoleon's heavy guns that had played a big part in the success. In the assault itself he received a thigh wound from a British bayonet, the only wound of his whole career; but this was nothing to the bouquets of praise that his military superiors and the *députés en mission* combined to give him. One of these Deputies at Toulon was Robespierre's brother Augustin; he wrote to Paris of Napoleon's "transcendent merit".

Still only twenty-four, Napoleon was promoted to brigadier-general, and by mid-1794 was, with Augustin Robespierre, in charge of military planning on the Southern (Italian) front.

This lucky friendship served its purpose for him; but it well might have ended in disaster with Maximilien Robespierre's fall in July (Thermidor[2]) 1794, when a halt was called at last to the mounting political slaughter. Within the space of two days Robespierre, the last, most high-minded, and bloodiest of the dictators of the Terror, was shouted down in the Convention, arrested, and executed with his chief associates. Napoleon might well have disappeared with them if he had been nearer to the hub of affairs. As it was, he escaped with a short period of arrest; in political intrigues he had not, after all, been personally involved, and he still had influential friends.

After the anti-Robespierre *coup* of Thermidor and the execution of the last of the executioners, a more relaxed and fluid state of affairs prevailed. Primarily, the 'reaction of Thermidor' was a protest of the middle classes against the intolerable excesses of the reign of 'Virtue and Terror'. There were many who had made money during the years of revolution, war, and inflation; the period of Thermidor and of the five-man Directory that followed it (1795–99) marks the successful overturn of the Revolution by the new rich. This was the period in which Napoleon climbed to the top. It was a time of extremes—the rich grew richer and the poor poorer. It was a time for extravagance and ostentation, for frivolity and licence. It was a time to be anything but Jacobin; a time, therefore, for the ex-Jacobins to change their political clothes and for opportunists to seize their political chances.

Two of the leaders of this unprincipled, pagan world of the Thermidorians were men who had led the revolt against Robespierre—the ex-Jacobins Tallien, briefly President of the Convention in 1794, and Barras, soon the most powerful figure in France. Barras had been at Toulon and knew Napoleon's abilities. He now protected his own position and further improved Napoleon's by putting him in command of part of the troops maintaining order in Paris. It was a city still seething with political and economic dis-

---

[2] The year I, by decree of the National Convention, began on September 22nd, 1792. The months of the new calendar, which lasted until the end of 1805, were: Vendémiaire, Brumaire, Frimaire; Nivôse, Pluviôse, Ventôse; Germinal, Floréal, Prairial; Messidor, Thermidor, Fructidor.

content. The death of Robespierre had done nothing to curb inflation, and the British blockade was making it worse. Prices rose very sharply; a pair of shoes costing five livres in 1790 cost two hundred in 1795 and two thousand in 1797. Fortunes were made by speculators and black marketeers; and while property owners, including the peasants, were content, wage earners were hungry and desperate. Moreover, the new Constitution of the Year III (1795), while it was still republican, was calculatedly undemocratic; only property owners could vote. Extremists of both wings, royalists and left-wing mobs, threatened Barras and the Thermidorians. And when the Convention (regarded by many as the 'old gang' who had permitted the slaughter of 1792–94) passed the Law of Two Thirds, insisting, in the cause of continuity, on that fraction of its members sitting in the new assembly, it seemed that the royalists might ride in on the crest of popular discontents. Barras therefore called in the Left to help deal with the Right, releasing extreme republican prisoners and arming them. On October 5th (13th Vendémiaire) fighting once more broke out in the capital. Napoleon's share in the day's events was not quite so preponderant as Carlyle made it seem with his story of Napoleon scattering the mob with the "whiff of grape shot". He did, however, play his part in defeating the insurgents. The new Constitution was saved, with its five-man Directory in executive control. Barras and his friends had emerged on top; and among those friends one had now to count General Bonaparte.

It was at the house of Barras that Napoleon first met Josephine de Beauharnais. She was a widow of thirty-one, six years Napoleon's senior. Born in Martinique, she had married the aristocrat de Beauharnais and borne him two children, Eugene and Hortense, before separating from him and then returning to him in 1790. He was at one time President of the Assembly and later General in command of a section of the Rhine front; upon his defeat he was guillotined. Josephine was also sentenced to death, and but for the fall of Robespierre would have followed her husband to the scaffold. In the overcrowded Carmes Prison, in fact, awaiting execution together were Beauharnais, his current mistress Delphine de Custine, his wife Josephine, and her lover General Hoche—a somewhat macabre *ménage à quatre*. Josephine survived into the hectic, meretricious, post-guillotine world of Thermidor: mild, indolent, extravagant, superficial, wayward, tender. She was for a time Barras's mistress, as also was Tallien's wife, Thérèse, the most resplendent and scandalous of the era's salon hostesses. Josephine's beauty was less dazzling than Mme Tallien's, but her sparkle, elegance, and accessibility swept Napoleon off his feet. "His inexperience", writes J. M. Thompson, "was flattered and his sensuality indulged by the complacent art of a still seductive beauty. At one stroke he could secure a mistress and a partner; indulge a passion and forward a career." In judicious retrospect long afterwards Napoleon called Josephine "certainly the most charming person I ever met".

> I was certainly not insensible to feminine charms, but I had never till then been spoilt by women. My character made me naturally timid in their company. Madame de Beauharnais was the first woman who gave me any degree of confidence.

Coquetry came as naturally to Josephine as kindness and affection, and Napoleon's stormy love for her, the only genuine personal passion of his life, very soon after their marriage (which took place in March 1796) turned to gnawing frustration and well-founded jealousy. Quickly enough, he more than repaid her inconstancy; the succession of his mostly brusque amours defies cataloguing.

The Directory, threatened at home by conspiracy and discontent, determined to try that best of medicines for domestic troubles, a vigorous foreign war. Hoche was appointed to attack the British in Ireland, Moreau the Austrians north of the Alps, and Napoleon those to the south. For Napoleon this appointment, his supreme opportunity, came two days after his marriage to Josephine. He was a mere twenty-six; but the guillotine and the flight from it had thinned the ranks of his superiors, so that his youth did not seem astonishing then. He had, moreover, already proved his talent; and on taking up his command he immediately impressed his subordinate generals, Augereau, Masséna, Berthier, and Lannes. Masséna said:

> They imagined from the way he carried about his wife's portrait and showed it to everyone, and still more from his extreme youth, that he owed his appointment to yet another bit of intrigue. But in a minute or two he put on his General's hat and seemed two feet taller.

Success was sudden. Within three weeks he had defeated the Austrians at Montenotte, driven them across the Po at Piacenza, and forced the Piedmontese to sue for an armistice after their defeat at Mondovi. By mid-May 1796 he was in Milan. Pressing forward in a series of rapid outflanking movements down the Lombard plain, that dangerous mousetrap for invading armies, by May 26th he was at Pavia, by June 3rd at Verona. Soon he was besieging Mantua, the fortress at the heart of the Austrians' position in Italy. They did not let it go easily. Four times in the course of the next seven months they sent armies south to relieve it, and gave Napoleon moments of severe anxiety; but each time they were defeated, at Castiglione (August), at Bassano (September), at Arcola (October) and finally on the plateau of Rivoli, in January 1797. The following month Mantua capitulated, and by March the Austrians had been pursued to Leoben, a hundred miles from Vienna—a point at which each side found it prudent to call a halt and begin negotiations for peace.

Legend later lent some details to the campaign that do not belong to it: Napoleon, for instance, seizing the tricolour at Lodi and leading his troops in person over the bridge under a hail of bullets, and the famous words, first spoken in fact as he dictated his memoirs at St Helena: "Soldiers, you are destitute. I am leading you to the richest plains in the world." Romance attached itself readily to such formidable successes won by such a stripling general —and Napoleon himself never failed to add some artistic touches of his own. His troops, he reported to the Directors, "gamble with death with a smile on their lips".

> If we have won successes over forces very much superior to my own, and in spite of complete lack of resources, it is because, confident that you trusted me, my troops have moved as rapidly as my thoughts.

(How naturally he already slipped from "we" to "me"!) In his reports he repeatedly exaggerated enemy numbers and diminished his own. In proclamations to his army he never neglected the ringing phrase: "Soldiers, You have rushed like a torrent from the heights of the Apennines. . . ."

> You have in two weeks won six victories, taken twenty-one battle flags, fifty-five pieces of cannon and several strongpoints, conquered the richest part of Piedmont, made 15,000 prisoners, killed or wounded 10,000. . . . But, soldiers, you have done nothing, since there remains something for you to do!

Yet the truth needed little garnishing; it was rich enough. Within one year's campaigning the most powerful of France's continental enemies had been forced to sue for terms—and this despite the inability of Moreau's Army of the Rhine to gain its objectives north of the Alps. The dividends from these Napoleonic victories in Northern Italy were substantial even before the terms of peace were decided. Northern Italy was the key to the rest of the peninsula, and although Napoleon had resisted the temptation, almost irresistible to the Directors, to launch a full-scale southern offensive, he had spared a few divisions to threaten the invasion of Tuscany, the Papal States, and Naples; these states had been forced to buy terms from him in tribute. Loot of many kinds was taken: in hard money a million and a quarter sterling from the Pope, in paintings from the occupied areas of the north whatever the experts considered worth taking. "I will send you as soon as possible," wrote Napoleon to the Directors from newly conquered Piacenza, "Correggio's finest pictures, including a St Jerome which is said to be his *chef d'œuvre*." This sort of plundering later became systematic. While France imported gold and silver bullion, jewellery, Renaissance masterpieces, and military glory, she exported revolution and the ideas of the new age.

The central Europe of 1796 (roughly the territory covered by modern West Germany and Italy) still contained several hundreds of states—kingdoms, principalities, dukedoms, bishoprics, free cities, mercantile republics such at Genoa and Venice—a politically amorphous world, where such medieval vestiges as the Holy Roman Empire and the temporal empire of the Papacy still lingered. States were not national entities, but rather a kind of real estate, to be inherited by their rulers, enjoyed, enlarged, married into, bargained for, conquered. The smaller states were often pawns in the dynastic power game of the larger; nobody thought of paying attention to the wishes of the inhabitants. In such conditions wherever there were educated classes starved of any share in political power (as there notably had been in France itself before 1789) it was likely that the armies of the French Revolution, coming in the name of liberty and equality, would find sympathizers. The feudal dynastic world of the central European *ancien régime* waited, as it were a vacuum, for the wind of revolution to rush in upon it. *Peace to the peoples, war to the tyrants*, the propaganda of the Revolution had proclaimed since 1792.

When the French first entered Piedmont and Lombardy in the spring of 1796 they were on occasions greeted with encouraging enthusiasm by the educated Italians, most of whom regarded the Austrians as tyrants, and some at least of whom thought of Catholicism as a moribund superstition. "Milan", wrote Napoleon, "is strongly inclined for liberty: it has a club, 800 strong, all lawyers and merchants." The conquering French represented republicanism, liberty of thought, freedom from religious or feudal tyranny: *Vive la République*. Such honeymoon enthusiasm was hardly likely to last, and did not.

Napoleon reported that he found three parties among the Italians of the North—the pro-French republicans of aristocratic or moderate leanings; the democrats; and the pro-Austrian conservatives. "I support the first, restrain the second, and suppress the third." Certainly he did not propose to encourage an Italian Jacobinism. But he did move quickly (in October 1796) to set up a new 'Transpadane' republic of the lands to the south of the Po, and, since rhetoric cost no casualties, he was ready to speak fine words to his new creation:

> The time has come for Italy to take an honourable place among the Powers. . . . To arms! The free part of Italy is rich and populous. Put fear into the enemies of your rights and your freedom. I shall not forget you. . . .

But, as he once admitted, the language of such proclamations was "romantic fiction". He considered the Italian populace in general to be under the thumb of the priests and not worth the expense of French lives; he was not in Italy for the good of the Italians. Nevertheless, cynical as his views on Italy were to become, he found it delightful during 1797, between the truce of Leoben in April and the signing of the Peace of Campo Formio in October, to bask in the sunshine of his triumph. At the palace of Mombello, near Milan, briefly reunited with his errant Josephine, surrounded by his family, attended by a Polish bodyguard, lionized by Italian flatterers, he held court as though he were already a monarch. He gave audience, received addresses, talked of philosophy and politics, of science and of literature, with his senior officers; no-one knew better how to play at being Alexander, or Frederick the Great.

Meanwhile his hand in the peace negotiations was further strengthened by his intervention in Venetia—the considerable territories of the ancient and now decadent merchant republic stretching from the Lombard border to Albania and Corfu. When French troops were massacred in a Verona uprising he thankfully grasped the pretext, compelled the Doge of Venice to accept French protection and advice, opened the road to another great Paris-bound convoy of artistic treasures, and most valuable of all—used Venetia as a counter in his bargaining with Austria. If Austria could be brought to accept the consolation prize of Venice, France might gain from her all Belgium and Lombardy. This in effect was achieved at Campo Formio, Venetia being partitioned between Austria and France. (Austria, in possession of Venice, thus still maintained a foothold in Italy.) All the conquered and 'liberated' territory of the north—the Transpadane provinces, the Romagna, Lombardy, and western Venetia—were amalgamated into the new Cisalpine Republic, a daughter state of France, with a constitution modelled on that of the Directory. Genoa, the western republic matching Venice in the east, became the Ligurian Republic, another satellite state.

As Napoleon's Italian successes matured during 1796–97 the master–servant relationship between the French Government and himself began the process of reversal that was completed in 1799. More and more the Directory came to ratify, perforce, his *faits accomplis*. These, naturally, were more than favourable for France, and for the Directors there was always the reassurance of a constant inflow of loot. Napoleon himself was under no illusion: "Do you think I triumph in Italy for the benefit of the Messrs Carnot and Barras, et cetera?" he asked an interviewer in a revealing moment. He followed closely every move of the political game in Paris, where, after the execution of the communist Babeuf, the principal danger to the régime came from the royalist plots. Louis XVI's son had died in prison, and the title of Louis XVIII had been assumed by the boy's uncle, the Count of Provence. Expelled from Verona upon the demand of Napoleon, he was active now on the Rhine, and Barras had reason to be nervous. By agreement with Napoleon, General Augereau was sent back from Italy to take command of the army in Paris; and there in Fructidor (September) 1797 an army coup purged both Directory and Assemblies. Carnot fled, Barras remained; but it was the army that men looked to now. Who would be the revolution's Caesar, and would his complexion be republican or royalist? Barras, the dissolute cynic, did not look the part. Hoche, Moreau, or the swashbuckling Augereau perhaps did. General Bonaparte, however, in rehearsal at the Palace of Mombello, was beginning to feel capable of doubling the rôles of both Caesars, Julius and Augustus.

With Austria defeated, and only Britain remaining of the original First Coalition, how should the French follow up their Italian successes? A direct invasion of England presented vast difficulty, but there were other possibilities, the most exciting and rewarding of which appeared to be an attack on Egypt. This was not a new idea;[3] French strategists had been discussing its possibilities for a decade or two, ever since the growing weakness of the Ottoman Empire seemed to indicate that it would be powerless to defend such outlying parts of its territory. (In reality Egypt was no longer Turkish at all; it was governed by the Mamelukes, once the slaves and agents of the Turk, but now locally the masters.) There were thought to be great opportunities for French trade in the Levant; this was why Napoleon had pronounced the Ionian Islands of Corfu, Zante, and Cephalonia to be "more important for us than the whole of Italy". Talleyrand, the Directory's new Foreign Minister, was in favour of the project, which he thought need not mean war with Turkey; and in Italy, ten days after the coup of Fructidor, Napoleon was looking ahead, from the Ionian Islands to Malta, to Egypt, to the mastery of the entire Mediterranean. As for the British fleet, it had been forced out of the Mediterranean after Spain allied with France in 1795, and Napoleon judged, mistakenly, that Britain would not be able to risk sending a major fleet back to the area.

So the Egyptian campaign was decided upon. It was to be more than a campaign—a cultural exercise on the grand scale. When the expedition left Toulon in May 1798 it contained not only three hundred transports, with convoying warships, but also a travelling academy of 167 *savants*—writers and artists, historians and geographers, experts and scientists of every kind. Napoleon, himself

---

[3] The Comte de Volney, for instance, in a book published in 1788 on the war between Russia and Turkey, had written: "Only one thing can compensate France . . . the possession of Egypt. Through Egypt we shall reach India; we shall re-establish the old route through Suez and cause the Cape of Good Hope route to be abandoned." But Volney knew enough about Egypt to discount the tales of a land flowing with milk and honey that other writers had described. Berthier, Napoleon's chief of staff, said after all the sufferings of the Egyptian campaign that Volney was "the only guide who never let them down".

just made a member of the National Institute and proud of it, was to be no vulgar conqueror; he claimed to take with him the Enlightenment.

On the way the French took Malta without difficulty, expelling the island's sovereigns, the Knights of St John. One month after leaving Toulon the armada was off again. Its protecting convoy of warships included thirteen ships of the line, including the great *Orient* of 120 guns. Hunting for them was Nelson in *Vanguard*, also with thirteen battleships. Unfortunately for him, however, he had parted company with his frigates, the 'eyes' of his fleet, in the storm of May 20th–21st. Twice in the nine days that it took Napoleon to reach Alexandria, Nelson's ships came within a whisker of sighting his convoy; with frigates they must have done so. What might have happened to Napoleon and the course of European history if the British ships had been a few hours slower? However, his wonderful luck still held. Nelson, correctly guessing Napoleon's destination, arrived in Alexandria[4] too soon and left it two days before the French arrived. On capturing the place Napoleon put his Arabic Press to immediate use:

Have we not destroyed the Pope, who preached wars against the Muslims? Have we not destroyed the Knights of Malta, because those madmen believed it was God's will that they should make war on the Muslims? Glory to the Sultan! Glory to his ally, the French army! A curse on the Mamelukes! Happiness to the Peoples!

The French army advanced to Cairo under the harshest conditions; many died of hunger, of heat, or of thirst. Reaching Gizeh and the Pyramids, they confronted the Mameluke cavalry, armoured and heroic, but musket-fodder for the French, who lost only ten men killed. Entering Cairo, the army found it squalid and stinking.

During the next six months Napoleon worked hard to convince the Egyptians that the Koran and the Marseillaise could go hand in hand. He did not succeed (nearly a thousand were killed in a rising in 1798), and had inevitably to use repression. "Obedience means fear", he wrote; "here in Cairo I have heads cut off at the rate of about five or six a day." All the same, he went about reforming the government and administration like a true child of

[4] Or, more accurately, near the paltry mud village that still went by that ancient name.

the Revolution; he set up new central and local *divans* (governments) with French advisers, and an Assembly of Notables; he founded the *Institut d'Egypte* "for the progress and propagation of enlightenment". Enlightenment cannot be superimposed on a lethargic and suspicious people, and Napoleon failed. Nevertheless his expedition was Egypt's first important contact with Western civilization, and in a sense he must be counted among the pre-founders of modern Egypt.

In Cairo he soon had bad news. Nelson demolished the French fleet in Abukir Bay, leaving the expedition to live on its own dwindling fat. Even its bullion, which was aboard the *Orient*, had disappeared when the flagship blew up. Napoleon did his best to play down the effects of Nelson's victory both to the Directory and to his own troops, and he characteristically tried to make sure that the dead Admiral Brueys should carry the blame, for failing to shelter in Alexandria harbour. The size of the disaster could not, however, be hidden from the Turks, who proceeded to declare war on France. Another of its effects was to starve Napoleon himself of news; he heard nothing at all from France for five months, time enough for both political and personal worries to gather strength. He wondered if he ought to be back at the centre of affairs. Still assailed with rumours and torn with jealousy concerning Josephine, he meanwhile consoled himself with Mme Fourès, the wife of one of his officers.

When at last news came through he judged the situation in France not critical enough to cause the cancellation of his projected invasion of Syria. Quickly taking El-Arish, Gaza, and Jaffa, he next laid siege to Acre, where his forces suffered torments from heat, hunger, thirst, and flies. Even so, they decisively defeated at Mount Tabor a Turkish force advancing to attempt the town's relief. Acre continued to hold out, assisted by British naval and military forces under Sir Sidney Smith, and Napoleon was obliged to abandon the siege. On the return journey plague struck his already weakened army, and some men too ill to continue the retreat were given an overdose of opium on Napoleon's orders. (It had been on his orders, too, on the outward journey, after the taking of Jaffa, that 3000 prisoners he could not feed were butchered.)

When the Turks followed up by landing at Abukir, Napoleon and his troops showed their deadly quality. The battle of Abukir was in its way the equal on land to Nelson's victory in Abukir Bay. Barely a Turk escaped: of the force of 16,000, 4000 were killed in the battle, 2000 were taken prisoner, and the remaining 10,000 shot or drowned as they tried to swim to their ships.

The victory was classic but unavailing; already Napoleon had made up his mind to return to France. In truth, for all its thorough preparation, the whole Eastern project (especially its vaguer dreams of an advance to India or Constantinople) had had a quality of mirage about it. For the men the vision soon became bitter mockery. For Napoleon, despite his capacity for self-delusion, the insubstantial pageant must have begun to fade when he lost his fleet. To jog his sense of reality Sir Sidney Smith, cruising off Alexandria, had obliged him (still starved of news) by supplying copies of newspapers from London and Frankfurt. The facts told a harsh story. A Second Coalition had grown up, of Britain, Austria, Russia, and Turkey; Joubert's army had been defeated by the Russians in Italy, and Jourdan's on the Rhine. Smith was also kind enough to let it be known that Nelson had intercepted a letter from the Directory ordering Napoleon back to France. Since the larger game in the East appeared to be up, he was itching to go. Accordingly, in secrecy, accompanied by four hundred of his leading men, military and academic, he took two of his newly built fast frigates and slipped away. Leaving Kléber in command in Egypt, he instructed him, if deaths from plague should exceed 1500 or if no reinforcements should arrive, to sue the Turks for peace. The wretched, disillusioned troops, officers and men alike, many now crippled or blind, first learned of their leader's departure when he was already at sea. However, in France, a hero's welcome awaited him, for he arrived only a week after the news of Abukir.

Napoleon now began to plan a *coup d'état*. He could hardly put himself forward as the honest soldier who would save the fatherland, for the fatherland had just been saved once more, this time by the double victory of Masséna over the Russians at Zürich and of Brune over the Anglo-Russian force in Holland. The Directory, however, had little popular support. Its troubles were numerous— continuing inflation, a large deficit, Jacobin threats, royalist revolts. Nobody expected the régime to last much longer. Barras, the only one of the original Directors still in office, seemed too listless and too exhausted by his dissipations to make much of a fight. Fouché, the chief of police, was ready to jump on to any promising-looking bandwagon—and General Bonaparte's looked by far the most promising.

Fouché apart (his rôle was important but passive), Napoleon's principal fellow-conspirators were Talleyrand and Sieyès. Ex-noble, ex-bishop, ex-revolutionary, ex-émigré, Talleyrand, wary as a cat, had already lived a fair number of his nine lives. Denounced by the Pope for his part in the nationalization of Church property, a prudent absentee during the Terror, first in England, then in America, he had intrigued his way back under Barras, become Foreign Minister, and championed the Egyptian campaign. For thirty years of French history his voice is always to be heard in some corner of the stage or in the wings; to the drama of Napoleon he supplies the saturnine chorus. Unprincipled, moderate, pragmatical, he always had an eye to an accommodation with the *next* régime, and in 1799 that appeared to mean Bonaparte. It was thus Talleyrand who acted as intermediary between Napoleon and Sieyès, the Director who had long been regarded as the leading theorist of Revolution and now had come to regard himself as a practitioner too. Sieyès wished to replace the 1795 Constitution with one that would express his own accumulated political wisdom; what he required was a "sword". He had thought to employ Joubert, but Joubert had been killed in Switzerland. Now he considered he could use Napoleon; as for Napoleon, *he* was sure he could use, and soon dispense with, Sieyès.

The agreed plan was that the Assemblies should be persuaded by the scare of a Jacobin rising to abandon the capital and seek Napoleon's protection at Saint-Cloud. This first stage was successfully accomplished on 18th Brumaire (November 9th) 1799. Barras was persuaded to resign, and the other Directors were taken care of. The generals followed Napoleon's lead. The next day, however, there was some very un-Napoleonic fumbling. The Upper House listened with hostility to his confused and hectoring speech, but in the Lower House (the 'Five Hundred'), where the opposition had had a day to muster their forces, his blustering rhetoric, not at all what Sieyès had planned, was shouted down. To cries of "Down with the dictator!" the General fled the chamber. Both Sieyès and Lucien Bonaparte proved themselves that day better and cooler men than Napoleon. Lucien, temporarily worsted as President of the Five Hundred and unable to prevent Augereau from proposing a motion to outlaw Napoleon, slipped out from the Orangery, where the deputies were in session, to the park, rallied the hesitant guards, and mustered the grenadiers, who returned under Murat to expel the Five Hundred at the point of the bayonet.

The details of the new 1799 Constitution were not of great importance. The subtleties of Sieyès were largely discarded, and he himself was paid off with a large country estate. In effect, power lay in the hands of the First Consul, Napoleon. The two other Consuls, an ex-regicide (Cambacérès) and an ex-royalist (Lebrun), served principally to broaden the new régime's popular base. All things to all men, General Bonaparte was the universal toast. He reassured the rich by his relaxation of taxes, the Jacobins by his clemency, everybody by the vigour of his personality. Once more the Republic was saved, the Revolution over. A plebiscite in February 1800 gave him an overwhelming vote of confidence.

Everybody, except the war profiteers, wanted peace; but a favourable peace was not practicable while Masséna's army was hemmed in at Genoa in acute peril. To gain peace, therefore, France must once again make war. While Moreau led one army against the Austrians north of the Alps, Napoleon crossed the St Bernard pass to the relief of Masséna. Legend has built massively on the St Bernard crossing: the romantic painters displayed to a doting France its young hero at the head of his troops, ready above the fiery nostrils of his steed to defy the enemy, the elements, and the Fates themselves. The First Consul himself, conscious of Hannibal, neglected no opportunity to assist the projection of the myth.

We are struggling against ice, snow, whirlwinds, and avalanches. . . . The First Consul came down from the summit balancing on snow, bridging precipices, and sliding upon frozen torrents.

The truth is more prosaic: Napoleon on muleback followed three days behind the army. Fiction too has overlaid the accounts of the subsequent victory at Marengo (June 1800). This was hardly his victory at all; he was rescued from disaster by the dash and resource of Desaix (killed in the action) and Kellermann. Documents unflattering to Napoleon's tactics were destroyed, and his official account was largely propaganda. On the other hand, Moreau's great victory at Hohenlinden (December 1800) was as carefully soft-pedalled as Marengo was romanticized.

These victories enabled Napoleon to force upon the Austrian Habsburgs the Treaty of Lunéville—a repeat dose of the medicine of Campo Formio. Belgium, Savoy, Luxemburg, and the Rhineland remained French (and Piedmont and Parma were soon to become so); France's hold on her satellite republics—the Batavian (Dutch), the Helvetic (Swiss), the Ligurian and the Cisalpine (Italian)—was confirmed.

The only obstacle to general peace was now Britain, and Napoleon planned, reversing the game of coalitions, to build up against her a continental confederacy. To this the key was Russia: a friendly Russia could yet enable him to save Egypt, threaten India, and cripple England's Baltic trade. Together with Russia the northern neutrals (Denmark, Sweden, and Prussia) were already reforming their anti-British league first formed twenty years earlier. Spain was induced to sell Louisiana to the French and invade Portugal, thereby promising further injury to British trade. Naples too was forced to exclude British ships and accept a French army of occupation. However, suddenly, within the space of one month, March–April 1801, the promising edifice collapsed. The French remnants in Egypt were swept away by Abercromby, the mad Tsar of Russia was assassinated and his policies reversed, and the Danish fleet was destroyed off Copenhagen by Nelson. Napoleon now had no immediate prospect of victory over England; he therefore set in hand the negotiations that led in 1802 to the peace of Amiens, by which he was to evacuate Egypt, Naples, and Portugal, and Britain the Cape of Good Hope, Martinique, Minorca, and Malta. As they watched the development of Napoleon's dream of an American empire to console him for the pricking of the Eastern bubble, few Englishmen thought the peace likely to last long. They assumed that Napoleon was buying a breathing-space to build up his navy, and noted his obvious determination to exclude British trade from Europe.

The American dream was short-lived. In the West Indian islands, where the slaves had been in revolt, French authority had by this time been re-established everywhere but in Haiti (San Domingo), to which an army of 30,000 under Leclerc was now dispatched. Toussaint Louverture, the slave leader who had succeeded in setting up a largely self-governing authority, was seized and brought to die in a French prison. Slavery, abolished under the Revolution, was re-established and mixed marriages prohibited. Altogether,

Napoleon's colonial policy was as illiberal as it was unsuccessful. Disease and the persisting slave rebellion destroyed Leclerc and his army as they had earlier armies both of French and British. The lack of success in Haiti and pessimism concerning French prospects of holding New Orleans against the British led Napoleon soon to become disenchanted with the New World. In 1803, after holding it for only six months, he sold Louisiana, a rich territory five times the size of France, to the United States Government of Jefferson for a trifling four cents an acre.

During the five years of the Consulate, Napoleon seized upon every chance that might serve to tighten the hold of his dictatorship. After Marengo there was a conspiracy to assassinate him. Fouché showed that it was of royalist origin; but since Napoleon considered he had most to fear from the extreme Jacobins, it was they who were sent away to rot in Guiana or the Seychelles. After the Peace of Amiens the Senate proposed as a mark of national gratitude to extend the First Consul's term of office from ten to twenty years, but on the proposal of the Second Consul (Cambacérès) Napoleon obtained the consulate for life, with the right to nominate his successor. A plebiscite ratified this promotion by an enormous majority. If only Josephine had given him a son his almost monarchical status would have been securer still; but their marriage was barren.[5] However, Napoleon was edging steadily towards monarchy over these years 1799–1804; the Christian name was creeping regally into official pronouncements; dress swords, silk stockings, and ladies-in-waiting were proliferating at the Tuileries. If the Bourbons were to topple him they must strike soon.

A second royalist conspiracy was unearthed in 1804. Like the first, it was organized by the Vendéan, Cadoudal; it implicated General Pichegru certainly and General Moreau possibly; and both the Bourbon pretender, the Count of Artois, and various officials of the British Government were privy to it. Cadoudal and eleven others were now executed, Moreau exiled, Pichegru 'found strangled' in prison. Acting on the misapprehension that the conspira-

---

[5] The next best thing to a son might well be a nephew who was also a stepgrandson. Napoleon's brother Louis was therefore ordered to marry Josephine's daughter Hortense, and a potential heir (Napoleon-Charles) was duly born in October 1802. This child, made much of by Napoleon, died aged four; it was the second son, Louis-Napoleon, who was to be Napoleon's belated successor as Napoleon III.

tors had worked on behalf of the Bourbon Duke of Enghien, Napoleon had him kidnapped from his residence beyond the Rhine at Strasbourg and summarily shot in the prison of Vincennes. The crime was long held against Napoleon, who never ceased to protest the necessity of his ruthlessness. ("You wish me to be murdered," he had snapped at Josephine when she pleaded for the innocent Enghien.) The kind of shock and disgust produced on foreign opinion may be illustrated by its effect on Beethoven. The great Third Symphony, recently completed, had been dedicated to Napoleon; after Enghien's murder the name of that particular 'hero' was struck from the title-page and the masterpiece became, simply, the *Eroica*. Of this cold-blooded murder it was said that "it was worse than a crime, it was a blunder"; but this is debatable, for it did end the royalist plots, and it did establish a kind of blood brotherhood between Napoleon and the Jacobin regicides. It certainly hastened Napoleon's decision to assume the full hereditary title and dignity of Emperor.

The Empire was to provide the dizziest of military triumphs; but it was during the Consulate that Napoleon's most durable work was done. This concerned the administration of France, her laws, her commerce and finance, her educational system, and the place of religion in the state.

After the shifts and stresses of the Revolution Napoleon and his Council of State—the cornerstone of the new administrative structure—gave France a strong centralized government capable of transmitting the will of Paris to every corner of the Republic. In a sense it was a revival of the *ancien régime*: equally with Louis XIV, Napoleon could say *L'état, c'est moi*. France's 36,000 towns and communes, which before the Revolution muddled along under a confusion of authorities, were systematized now into *arrondissements*, under sub-prefects, and into *départements*, under prefects. ('Prefects' like 'Consuls' and the ladies' fashions, harked modishly back to the palmy days of Rome.) The Napoleonic prefect came to stay, a modernized version of the Bourbon intendant. His resplendent silver and tricoloured uniform, a Napoleonic innovation, somewhat symbolized his function. He guaranteed uniformity; he executed the majestic will of the central government. The people, while in theory after 1799 enjoying universal male suffrage, were effectively excluded from a share in government, even before the institution of the Empire, by a complicated system of indirect voting. Six million voters elected one tenth of their number to a *liste communale*; this 600,000 elected again a tenth to a *liste départementale*; the now select 60,000 finally chose the *liste nationale* of 6000 persons judged "fit for the public office"—a sovereign prescription for conformity and conservatism.

In jurisprudence the achievements of the Napoleonic age were great; Napoleon's own part in them may be exaggerated. The laws of France before 1789 had been a tangle of competing jurisdictions and practices—Roman law, customary law, ecclesiastical law, royal edicts. The Revolutionaries swept away the last relics of seigneurial privilege and had endeavoured to move forward to a general simplification and codification, an enterprise Colbert had begun over a century earlier; but their reform was submerged beneath the mass of new revolutionary edicts. It was Cambacérès who now presided over the work; what Napoleon did was to provide it with the momentum of his personality. He personally attended about half the committee's sittings, usually to listen, sometimes to inter-vene. Where his influence was brought to bear it was almost always in the more conservative and authoritarian interest. He helped to re-inforce parental authority, check divorce, which had become easy and fashionable, and limit women's rights. But the new Civil Code had shining merits, however little it deserved its 1807 title of *Code Napoléon*. It stated, or restated, the laws of France clearly in 120,000 words, a moderate-sized volume. It travelled in the wake of the armies of France through Europe and influenced eventually the laws of many lands, European, African, American, even Japanese. Like all legal codes, it enshrines principles; and among those of the Napoleonic Code are the equality of all Frenchmen before the law, the authority of the father in the family, of the husband in the marriage, of the property owner in society. "My true glory", said Napoleon on St Helena, "is not to have won sixty battles. What will live for ever is my Civil Code."

The Revolution had nationalized the Church's property and dug a deep pit between Catholicism and the Republic. However, the attempts of the extremists to enthrone Reason and destroy Christi-anity altogether had been but a brief charade; and Robespierre's attempt to make deism compulsory in the 'Worship of the Supreme Being' had proved a nine days' wonder. Now Napoleon proposed that the Republic should make its peace with the Church and heal the sores of a decade. A new Pope, Pius VII, came fortunately upon the scene; by courtesy of General Bonaparte (who after Marengo dominated the Italian peninsula) he was allowed to proceed to the Holy City in July 1800. The negotiations that began soon afterwards culminated a year later in the Concordat.

For many Frenchmen of the middle class, however, the Church was not to be lightly readmitted to influence. It was another nine months (April 1802) before Napoleon could translate his agreement into law and attend at Notre-Dame the Te Deum that was to signalize the reconciliation of Church and State; to some a grand and moving occasion, to others as nauseous and contemptible as to General Delmas: "A fine monkish show. It only lacked the presence of the hundred thousand men who gave their lives to end all that."

Under the Franco-Papal Concordat and the French 'Organic Articles' that accompanied it Catholicism became the established religion of France, and in return the Church recognized the legality of the Republic—another blow for the fading royalist cause. The nationalization of Church property and the legal rights of those by whom it had been purchased, whether as land or securities, remained undisturbed. Bishops and clergy were to be paid by the State. Clergy were to be appointed by bishops, bishops by the First Consul—who saw them, and attempted to use them, rather as ecclesiastical Prefects, and subjected Catholic observances to the most precise regulations and police supervision.

Even so, it was made to appear for a time in 1801–02, amid a great trumpeting of fanfares, that the new Charlemagne had healed the scars. The peasantry, the faithful, and the conservatives (and most Frenchmen were all three) were delighted. The "altars were restored"; but the reconciliation was fleeting and illusory. Within a few years Napoleon was treating Pius VII as a troublesome but tenth-rate princeling; Rome was incorporated in the French Empire and the aged and frail Pius, kidnapped in the middle of the night, bundled off to a military prison.

Central control, unity, and discipline: the same ideas lay behind Napoleon's educational reforms. He did not wish to see French schooling in the hands of the 'liberal' and irreligious, and he found little difficulty in preventing this; but neither did he wish to see the Church re-establish its ancient hold, and here he found much stronger obstacles. For most boys, in any case, and all girls, education mattered little, he considered, beyond providing a grounding in morals and patriotism, and for girls housekeeping.[6] As for primary education, he largely neglected it. But secondary education was important, since the efficiency of the State demanded that its servants be sufficiently numerous and well educated. Hence the *lycées*, state boarding schools, with a strong military and religious flavour and an 'academic' curriculum based on Latin, philosophy, rhetoric, mathematics, and science. But when the middle classes seemed to prefer the Church's private schools, despite the *lycées'* generous state scholarships, Napoleon attempted to impose total control of education by the State. His 'University of France' (1808) was in fact a Ministry of Education licensing *all* teachers and controlling provincial universities and colleges.

Napoleon's view of education was strictly utilitarian. He needed a 'meritocracy' and a docile people. He wanted, and he obtained, a high output of graduates and experts both civil and military. Like all dictators, he would not allow free discussion. Yet the centralization that he imposed on French educational institutions, though it was of lasting importance, remained incomplete. At his fall, although there were over a hundred *lycées* and many more *écoles secondaires*, there were still almost as many children attending the Church's secondary schools as those of the State.

The Consulate progressed steadily away from the stern principles of the Revolution. In 1802 Napoleon revived what the Revolution had abolished in 1793, a system of titles and dignities. The patronage that this put into his cynical hands became a strong weapon. His new Legion of Honour had sixteen 'cohorts', each with its hierarchy of grand-sounding titles. "You are pleased to call them baubles," he replied to Thibaudeau, who had criticized them; "well, it is with baubles that mankind is governed. The French are unable to desire anything seriously except perhaps equality. Even so, they would gladly renounce it if everyone could entertain the hope of rising to the top." The institution of the Empire in 1804 intensified the play of rank; soon all France and half Europe

---

[6] Napoleon's views on the education of girls could hardly have been more illiberal: "You must begin with religion in all its strictness. . . . It is the mother's surest safeguard and the husband's. What we ask of education is not that girls should think but what they should believe. . . . The main thing is to keep them occupied for three-quarters of the year with their hands. . . . With the exception of the Headmaster, all men must be excluded from the school. . . . I need hardly say that the only women employed in the school must be elderly spinsters or widows without children."

was peppered with titles great and small. Napoleon created 31 Dukes, 452 Counts, 1500 Barons, and 1474 Chevaliers; in all he admitted 48,000 to the membership of the Legion of Honour. It was a sizable number to attach to the régime by the little length of red ribbon.

As for liberty, Napoleon succinctly dismissed it; "it is necessary", he said, "to only a few endowed with faculties superior to the common man's; this is why it may safely be restricted." Napoleon's France became increasingly a police state. Arbitrary imprisonments were common and Fouché's spies were everywhere. Newspapers critical of authority were suppressed; the stage was closely supervised, and only those artists subservient to the régime enjoyed patronage. Eventually (1810) all publishers had to obtain the State's licence and a total censorship of books was imposed.

The ultimate 'bauble' was the imperial title, the 'crown of Charlemagne', and the last impetus in its direction had been given by the royalist plots. "We have done more than we hoped to do," was Cadoudal's wry comment as he awaited execution. "We meant to give France a King and we have given her an Emperor." In May 1804 the First Consul was installed with the utmost pomp as Emperor of the French, a notable and at the same time an ironical feature of the occasion being the presence of Pope Pius in Notre-Dame. Thus the Concordat was ceremonially underlined, and both the Revolution and the new dictatorship legitimized, to the horror of the true-blue old guard of Catholic royalists. Commanded, almost, by Napoleon, Pius made the journey in some trepidation; but he was surprised to note the affability of his reception by ex-Jacobin atheists and regicides (even by Dr Guillotin himself) and told a solicitous Fouché that he had found "a people on its knees". Josephine, still childless by Napoleon and now forty-one, seized her opportunity to bind him more closely to her by revealing to the papal legate that she was wife by civil marriage only; the Church insisted on a second wedding, which the Pope conducted in secret. There were limits, however, to Napoleon's ecclesiastical play-acting. He would not make confession; neither would he let the coronation be performed by the Pope. After himself placing the Imperial crown upon his own head he crowned Josephine Empress.

This Notre-Dame ceremony of December 1804 was swiftly followed by moves which showed that "the crown of Charlemagne" was more than a rhetorical phrase. Napoleon had already become President of the Italian (previously Cisalpine) Republic; now he grasped the Iron Crown of the Lombards and elevated himself in Milan to the kingship of Italy (May 1805); Genoa (the Ligurian Republic) was at the same time simply annexed to the French Empire. All this was in breach of the Treaty of Lunéville, and the Habsburgs could plainly not live at peace with an upstart of such limitless ambitions; Austria accordingly joined Britain and Russia in the Third Coalition. For two years Napoleon had already been in a renewed state of war with Britain, though British supremacy at sea and French supremacy on land had between them imposed a barrier to active fighting. To be master of Europe Napoleon must bring England to her knees. The problem was, how? There were two possible answers: indirectly, by crippling her trade, or directly, by invasion.

By denying them their European markets he might put British manufacturers and merchants in such straits that they would compel their government to make peace. Unable to balance imports with exports, Britain would be forced to pay gold—so the theory ran—and the threat of national bankruptcy would force a demand for peace. Economic arguments such as these had been behind French policy for years; unfortunately they suffered from many drawbacks. Economic attrition was at best a slow business; an effective embargo against British exports demanded a total control of the European coastline that even France's victorious arms could not command; and in any case France's own economic condition—her need for gold, her demand for ocean-borne goods such as sugar and coffee and for manufactures such as boots and greatcoats on a scale which only Britain could supply—required that she should trade, however indirectly, however contradictorily, with the enemy who controlled the seas.

The second answer was invasion. In 1798 Napoleon had turned it down; the naval problems posed insurmountable difficulties. After 1804, however, he gave concentrated attention to various schemes for launching his armies upon southern England. At first he talked himself into believing that the thing was possible by one swift rush in thousands of flat-bottomed boats, without prior naval supremacy; the Channel was "a ditch which it needs only a pinch of courage to cross". Later he developed a scheme both more cautious and more elaborate; this was for the French Toulon squadron to break out, to join forces with the Spanish from Cadiz,

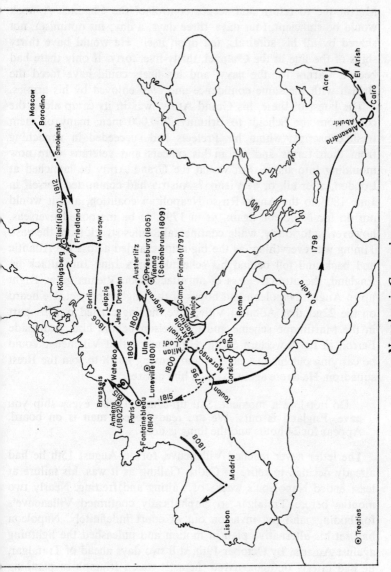

Napoleonic Campaigns

Moscow

Borodino

Smolensk

1812

Tilsit (1807)

Friedland

Königsberg

Warsaw

Berlin

1806

Leipzig

Jena Dresden

1809

Waterloo

1805

Ulm

Brussels

Amiens (1802)

Paris

Lunéville (1801)

Fontainebleau (1814)

1815

1796

Corsica Elba

Toulon

1793

1798

O Malta

Austerlitz

Pressburg (1805)

Vienna

(Schönbrunn 1809)

Wagram

Campo Formio (1797)

Venice

Rivoli

Lodi

Milan

Marengo

1800

Rome

1808

Madrid

Lisbon

Acre

El Arish

Abukir

Cairo

Alexandria

O Treaties

to decoy the British across the Atlantic, and after rendezvous at Martinique to return and secure control of the Channel. A week would be sufficient, four days, three days, a day; his optimism, not shared by all his admirals, fed upon itself. He would have thirty ships of the line in the Channel, thirty-five, forty. If only there had been a Carnot for the navy, and his fleets could have faced the British with the same confidence and *élan* enjoyed by his armies.

The latest of these, his Grand Army, was in its camp along the coast from the Scheldt to Brittany: 200,000 men, many of them fresh conscripts whom his Prefects had succeeded in wrenching from their farms and whom his officers and veterans were now moulding into shape. But would the Grand Army be launched at London, after all, or at Vienna? Austria had committed herself in June 1805 to the Anglo-Russo-Neapolitan coalition, and it would not do for Napoleon again, as in 1799, to be marooned overseas, however victoriously, while continental armies struck from the east. Timing was everything: as the big ships crawled across the Atlantic and back and fell behind his schedule for a June–July attack on England, the attractiveness of an attack upon Vienna grew. Right up to August Napoleon had hopes of the English project. He heard on the 22nd that Admiral Villeneuve, having carried out his part in the Martinique scheme and left Nelson behind him, had made Ferrol, in north-western Spain. He assumed that Villeneuve could be carrying out his instructions and moving north to join the Brest squadron. He wrote again to reach him at Brest:

> Do not lose a moment. Sail up-Channel with every ship you have. England is ours. We are ready: every man is on board. Appear for 24 hours and the thing is done.

The letter never reached Villeneuve, for on August 15th he had already decided to retire to Cadiz. Galling as it was, his failure at least ended Napoleon's weeks of waiting and fretting. Nearly two months before Trafalgar so emphatically confirmed Villeneuve's forebodings and put invasion out of court indefinitely, Napoleon had set his alternative plan in motion and unleashed the lightning against Austria. By October 19th, still two days ahead of Trafalgar, he had utterly outmanœuvred them. It was a triumph of planning and intelligence; seven closely co-ordinated columns, under Bernadotte, Marmont, Davout, Soult, Ney, Lannes, and Murat, moved swiftly round and beyond the Austrians as they advanced blindly through Bavaria. General Mack woke up too late to find himself outnumbered at Ulm.

The Napoleonic army, which was about to enter the period of its most resounding triumphs, was certainly a remarkable instrument. It was, of course, very large, the army of the greatest state in Europe, under the unified command of the man who was also the head of that state—whereas it fought against the armies of improvised and ill-co-ordinated coalitions. Napoleon's leadership—many of his troops believed him invincible—was itself an inestimable advantage. The morale of the officers was good; many of the generals and marshals were young, spirited, and athirst for glory—though they were not therefore averse to making the fortune that often went with it, and Napoleon deliberately encouraged his marshals to feather their nests. Promotion went, on the whole, by ability rather than birth, and conscription ensured the mixing of classes and the making of a true 'citizen army'. On the other hand, those conscripted were mainly those who had not been able to raise the cash necessary to buy exemption; only about one in three of those eligible actually served. Napoleon certainly promoted efficiency; but 'efficiency' is a relative term. Everything depended on mobility and the speedy knock-out. Muskets were of a pattern thirty years old; supply and equipment often broke down; pay was constantly in arrears; the hospital system was primitive. For food the Napoleonic soldier relied on pillaging the lands he conquered. He suffered, and grumbled, as much as the soldiers of other armies. For a long time the great victories brought sufficient glamour to outshine the miseries of war, and (in Napoleon's own words) everything was done "to excite enthusiasm and to give militarism fresh prestige".

After Ulm, Napoleon moved on to occupy Vienna, but there still remained against him another Austrian army and the Russians under the command of the young Tsar Alexander I. At Austerlitz, in Moravia, on December 2nd, 1805, the first anniversary of the coronation, about 70,000 French faced a combined Austro-Russian army of some 80,000. Correctly guessing the enemy's tactics, Napoleon issued a proclamation to his troops on the eve of battle: "While they march to turn my right, they present their flank." The counterstroke was to come from the French centre under Soult. It did, devastatingly; and the cavalry of Murat and Lannes completed the rout. Austerlitz, "the perfect victory", was a triumph on land as total and brilliant as the British naval victories of the Nile and

Trafalgar. The allied armies lost 27,000 killed, wounded, and prisoner.

A peace much more humiliating than Campo Formio or Lunéville was now imposed on "this hateful house of Austria". By the Treaty of Pressburg (December 1805) the Habsburgs, gaining only Salzburg, lost all their lands in Southern Germany, the Tyrol, Venice and the provinces of Istria and Dalmatia along the Adriatic coast. They were obliged to recognize the independence of the Kingdoms of Bavaria and Württemberg and of the Grand Duchy of Baden—the three South German states that had hopefully thrown in their lot with Napoleon. Talleyrand, who in fact dictated the Treaty's terms on behalf of his Emperor, himself disapproved of them just because they *were* so humiliating; like Bismarck later, Talleyrand saw the prudence of moderation in dealing with the Austrian Empire. But it was Napoleon who was the master, not Talleyrand; and where conquest and glory were concerned, Napoleon set no limits.

The echoes of Austerlitz continued to rumble round Europe in 1806. Masséna reoccupied Naples, whose Bourbon ruler retired to Sicily. The new King of Naples was at first Joseph Bonaparte, and then, when Joseph was transferred to the kingship of Spain, Murat, the husband of Napoleon's sister Caroline. The Batavian Republic became the Kingdom of Holland, with Louis Bonaparte as King. Soon a new Kingdom of Westphalia was to be created for Jerome,[7] Napoleon's youngest brother. The clan was well catered for. Then, in June 1806, Napoleon, the new Charlemagne, finally liquidated the Holy Roman Empire that had begun with Charlemagne himself a thousand years earlier. In the place of this venerable anomaly he created the sixteen-state Confederation of the Rhine, a French-dominated Germany to set beside the states of Austria and Prussia.

[7] Like Lucien, Jerome had contracted an 'unsuitable' marriage and so incurred the displeasure of Napoleon, who expected the hand of all his family to be at his disposal for deployment in the dynastic game. But Jerome's first marriage was annulled, and he was satisfactorily matched with a Württemberg princess. Similarly, the Emperor's stepson, Eugene, Viceroy of Italy, was married to a conveniently eligible daughter of the King of Bavaria. Lucien remained stubborn; seeking to emigrate to the U.S.A., he was captured by the British. Napoleon never ceased to grumble about his family's "disloyalty". Louis on different occasions declined the Kingship of Italy, refused to be 'transferred' from Holland to Spain, and was finally ejected from the Dutch throne in 1810. Murat and Caroline turned against Napoleon in 1814. Eugene, so he once said, was the only one who had never given him any trouble.

As for Prussia, she had failed to enter the Coalition when it was still promising, being beguiled by Napoleon's bribe of Hanover. She did somewhat equivocally enter after Ulm. Now, *after* Austerlitz, she chose to challenge Napoleon on her own. As a record of vacillation and double-dealing, the statecraft of Frederick William III was hardly unique; for folly and overconfidence it would be hard to match. With her armies living upon the reputation and yellowing drill book of Frederick the Great, Prussia marched them stiffly off to their ruin. Within a week of her ultimatum to the French it was all over. On the same day, October 14th, 1806, two Prussian armies were destroyed, one by Napoleon with a numerically superior French force at Jena, and one by a heavily outnumbered Davout at Auerstädt. Napoleon entered Berlin in triumph, riding behind the plumed and magnificent Murat in the dramatic simplicity of grey field uniform and black hat. To Paris, ever conscious of this need for drama and display, he sent back 340 battle flags and the sword of Frederick the Great. It was from Berlin that he issued the latest and stiffest of his decrees intensifying the trade war against the British.

Turning eastward again—for Alexander of Russia, recovering from Austerlitz and seeing Napoleon after the Treaty of Pressburg threaten Constantinople, was again in the field, in company with some Prussian contingents—Napoleon was in Warsaw by Christmas, being hopefully received by many Polish patriots[8] who saw him as the man who would deliver them from the Russians. Polish national aspiration, however, meant nothing to Napoleon. If the situation should arise where Russian friendship was vital, the Poles would be thrown to the wolves. If the situation required a war with Russia, as in 1807 or 1812, the Poles would fight for him, and fight well. (Eighty thousand of them were, in fact, among the fated army that went to Moscow in 1812.) All was grist to the mill of his ambition.

[8] One of these patriots was the septuagenarian Count Walewski, whose charming eighteen-year-old wife Maria, dazzled by Genius, became, in a romantic flurry of patriotic excitement, the Emperor's mistress. When Josephine asked to be allowed to come to Warsaw, Napoleon fobbed her off with "I love no woman except my little Josephine" and similar reassurances. While in Warsaw he heard that back in France he was at last the father of an illegitimate child—an event which confirmed that Josephine's childlessness in her second marriage was not (as had been suggested) due to Napoleon's own infertility. Thus he could begin to consider with more confidence plans for the divorce of his little Josephine, now aged forty-six, and for his remarriage.

The Polish winter of 1807 and the spring mud caused a breakdown in supplies and severe suffering among the French troops, whose greatest advantage had always been their mobility; and at Eylau in February Napoleon received his severest check yet, when in a bloody drawn battle he lost 25,000 men. He was glad enough, after another decisive victory at Friedland, in East Prussia (June 1807), to treat with the Russians for peace. Alexander too was anxious to come to terms; so at Tilsit with due ceremony and fraternization the two Emperors met on a pavilioned raft in the middle of the river Niemen, apportioned between them all of the Western world that they could reach, and planned the future partition of the Turkish Empire. Prussia was reduced to a third-rank Power. She was stripped of her western territories to provide Jerome's Kingdom of Westphalia, and of her eastern to set up the Grand Duchy of Warsaw, a sort of semi-Poland with another of Napoleon's upgraded allies, the King of Saxony, as Grand Duke. The Tsar, who anxiously protested to Napoleon how deeply he too hated the English, agreed to cease trading with them and bring pressure to bear on Sweden and Denmark to follow suit.

The Treaty of Tilsit, following the triumphs of Ulm, Austerlitz, Jena-Auerstädt, and Friedland, represents the high noontide of Napoleon's fortunes. He had mastered half Europe, broken the power of the Habsburgs, dominated Italy, humiliated Prussia, and defeated the Tsar, who now seemed to be under his spell. His relations and dependants sat on the thrones of a score of satellite states from the Scheldt to the Vistula, from the Elbe estuary to the farther shores of the Adriatic. He had reformed the laws of France, restored her religion, brought her domestic peace and foreign glory. Claiming to carry with them the ideas of the Enlightenment and the Revolution, his troops had been welcomed in many parts of Italy and Germany. They were still seen as the liberators of Poland.

If the embargo on British goods was to be successful it must be complete, and after Tilsit the need to make it so led Napoleon to overreach himself in attempting the impossible. In Italy, in the Iberian peninsula, and by 1812 in Russia, the consequences of the commercial war against Britain had enmeshed him.

To one who soared so high nothing now seemed impossible, and nothing must stand in the way of his imperious needs, of his megalomaniac ambition. If the Papal States with their seaports of Ancona, Civita Vecchia, and the rest, refused to break off trade with the

British, then the Papal States must be occupied by French troops. The 'Imperial Grand Customs Officer of Europe' could admit no exceptions. To Pius it was vain to point out that he was acting "as the protector of the Holy See"; the Pope well understood the contemptuous arrogance that underlay Napoleon's actions. "I expect the Pope", he wrote to his uncle Fesch, whom characteristically he had raised to the Archbishopric of Lyons, "to fit in with my requirements. . . . If he behaves I shall make no outward changes; if not, I shall reduce him to the status of bishop of Rome. . . . Make it clearly understood that I will not stand any more of this nonsense."

The aged Pius was frail but tough; when in 1807 Napoleon seized the whole Adriatic coastline Pius refused to negotiate further, whereupon Napoleon occupied Rome itself (1808–9). Pius had to be winkled out of the Quirinal by troops with scaling ladders. He was—though against Napoleon's orders—made to suffer poor food and physical hardship while being brought by carriage over the Alps to Savona. This last step of Napoleon's brought him excommunication; it aroused at best the suspicion, at worst the downright hostility, of devout Catholics throughout Europe. From France there was much grandiose airing of historical parallels: Napoleon the successor of the medieval Emperor was finally asserting the subordination of Papacy to Empire; Pius's very road to Savona passed through Avignon, home of the medieval Popes in their 'Babylonish captivity'. But Napoleon, who well appreciated the value to his régime of the Concordat, knew in his bones that he was making a mistake; typically he tried to shift the blame on to those who had mistaken his orders and maltreated the Pope.

Portugal, even more than the Papal States, offered to British exports an inlet that Napoleon could not tolerate. At the same time, an expedition to subdue Britain's Portuguese ally would have to traverse Spanish territory, and this necessity opened promising new vistas for Napoleon's ambitions. Spain, France's obedient ally until the time of Trafalgar, had begun to look for an opportunity to free herself from tutelage, but the victories of Austerlitz, Jena, and Friedland had confirmed her impotence. Napoleon now saw a chance of killing two birds with one stone. He would invade Portugal, necessarily through Spain. He would involve Spain as an accomplice in that invasion, and secure thereby the right to garrison French troops on Spanish soil. Once in position, they could turn on the corrupt and feeble Spanish Government and overthrow it. The whole Iberian coastline would be his. The effete Spanish Bourbons would go the way of the Bourbons of France and Naples.

General Junot took 25,000 French troops through Spain to Lisbon in October–November 1807, narrowly failing to capture the Portuguese royal family, who fled to Brazil. In February–March 1808 other French troops began seizing garrison towns in Northern Spain, while Murat's cavalry pressed on to Madrid. In panic, confusion and under duress both Charles IV and his son and rival Ferdinand were compelled to renounce the throne, and Joseph Bonaparte was installed upon it.

Napoleon was convinced that Spain, a country plagued by monks and Bourbons and ripe for French revolutionary enlightenment, would be easy to conquer:

> The Spaniards will quieten down when they see that I offer them the integrity of their kingdom's boundaries, a liberal constitution, and the preservation of their religion and national customs.

It was a miscalculation. Many Spaniards had certainly held in contempt their cuckold King and licentious Queen, and in hatred their Prime Minister Godoy, the Queen's paramour. But the members of the unloved triangle were at least Spanish; the new king was an alien and the brother of a trickster and tyrant, who, moreover, easily appeared to the Spaniards as a sort of anti-Christ. Napoleon had blithely chosen to invade the most Catholic lands in Europe at a time when his quarrel with the Pope was reaching its climax. The members of the Spanish and Portuguese bourgeoisie and intelligentsia who might have welcomed French enlightenment amounted to no more than a handful. Peasants and priests, high and low, united in an anti-foreign explosion. From the day in May 1808 that the Madrid mob rose up to slaughter some hundreds of the city's French garrison Napoleon was fighting simultaneously the Catholic faith and a national revolution. It was a new experience. "You cannot conceive", wrote Joseph to his brother, "how your name is hated here."

Still Napoleon underestimated his enemies. A little shooting down of rebels would surely suffice, as it had in Naples. It was not until these same rebels cornered General Dupont's army at Baylen in Andalusia, and forced its surrender, that the fat was seen to be in the fire (June 1808). An angry Emperor raged over this "disgrace".

Two months later the British defeated Junot at Vimieiro and forced him out of Portugal. The legend of French invincibility grew frailer. The "Spanish ulcer" which was to plague Napoleon for more than five years, was beginning to hurt.

At the Erfurt meetings that autumn he tried by diplomacy, charm, and display, but with no great success, to reassure his allies, impress potential enemies, and in particular to prevent the Tsar's retreat from the understanding reached at Tilsit. The following winter, in an attempt to settle the Spanish business once and for all, he himself took command of an army 200,000 strong, crossed the bitter snows of the Guadarramas, and began the pursuit of the largely demoralized British army of Sir John Moore. In mid-chase, however, at Valladolid, he received the news that caused him to hand over the command to Soult (who was to miss his prey at Corunna) and to return home at high speed. Once again Austria, buttressed by British money, was planning to strike, taking advantage of the tide of events in Spain and Portugal, and of the mounting reluctance of the Tsar Alexander to become a full partner of the French. There were, in addition, important and influential enemies nearer home. The loyalty of Fouché, Minister of the Interior, and of Marshal Bernadotte was suspect. Fouché had been seen ostentatiously in company with Talleyrand, whom he detested. In fact, Talleyrand, who understood and deplored Napoleon's megalomaniac ambitions and wished to set French conquests at the limit of her 'natural' geographical boundaries, had already at Erfurt had secret nocturnal meetings with the Tsar. "The French", Talleyrand had said, "are civilized, their sovereign is not. The sovereign of Russia is civilized, his people are not. Therefore the sovereign of Russia must be the ally of the people of France."[9] And the ordinary Frenchman, however hypnotized by the Emperor's victories, was harassed by the dislocations of war and weary of its endless demand for men and taxes.

The army that Napoleon left in Spain to his brother Joseph and

---

[9] Napoleon did not, of course, know of Talleyrand's dealings with the Tsar. His pent-up anger and baffled suspicion broke out, however, upon his return from Spain. Before a crowded court Napoleon exploded in uncontrollable rage against his Grand Chamberlain, that "piece of dung in silk stockings". Talleyrand was obliged to let the tirade break over his head. But when at last Napoleon had stormed out, Talleyrand's *grand seigneur* irony scored the last point: what a pity that so great a man should have such atrocious manners.

the marshals was always hampered by divided command; Napoleon never trusted anybody sufficiently to delegate full powers. The marshals, watchful of one another's 'empires', squabbled like rival mistresses jealous of their master's favour. The army in Spain was frustrated, too, by bad roads and by mountains and rivers that lay east–west across the main French communications. It was opposed by both the Spanish army and a skilfully led British force that extracted, from Marshal Masséna's forces especially, a terrible cost; and it was mercilessly harried by guerrillas of a sullen and outraged people. An army of 250,000–300,000 men had constantly to be spared for this bitter sideshow.

The main theatre was, of course, elsewhere, in the heart of Europe. Napoleon's task was to knock out the Austrians before the smouldering resistance of Russia, Prussia, and the smaller German states should break into flame. He himself considered this campaign of 1809 to be techincally as brilliant as any; yet, although it contained the customary crop of victories and culminated in yet another defeat for the Austrians at the large-scale pitched battle of Wagram, it also showed several straws in an inauspicious wind. Before Wagram, at the costly battle of Aspern-Essling, as earlier at Eylau and on a smaller scale at Baylen and Vimieiro, the French were given a taste of defeat. Even Wagram was very far from being another Austerlitz: Napoleon's losses were heavier than the Austrians', and not all his troops distinguished themselves. The *élan* of earlier days was not there; the military quality of the men, and perhaps now of their leader, was in decline. Revolts were beginning to break out elsewhere than in Spain and Portugal. There were three—small, ill co-ordinated, and soon crushed—in Northern Germany; and the Tyrolese went on fighting a mountain war long after the Habsburg Government had officially made peace on their behalf.

Just as the Tsar after the defeat of Friedland had arrived at a sort of alliance at Tilsit with his conqueror, so after Wagram the Habsburg Emperor, now under the shrewd guidance of Metternich, came to a somewhat similar arrangement with Napoleon. At the Treaty of Schönbrunn Austria paid heavily for the fourth time for her defeat —a painful indemnity, together with the loss of $3\frac{1}{2}$ million subjects and the remainder of her Adriatic coastline. In return, however, she had something to offer to a Napoleon who was being increasingly rebuffed by the Tsar. Alexander refused to permit his sister to marry

Napoleon. What then more natural, more inevitable—and yet more astonishing—than that he should marry a Habsburg princess, Marie-Louise? It was defeated Austria that had now become a sort of ally: it was the Tsar who was on the way to becoming a sort of enemy.

The divorce of Josephine had long been pondered by Napoleon. Amicable now as were his relations with her, he needed a son and heir. He needed too, upstart that he was, to be himself 'legitimized', to prove to himself and the world that a Bonaparte was now, in the charmed circles of Romanovs, Bourbons, and Habsburgs, *primus inter pares*. What prize could be more glittering than a Habsburg princess? What could be more symbolically satisfactory than the marriage of Marie Antoinette's great-niece with the erstwhile child of the Revolution, Napoleon? "I wished", said Napoleon to Metternich, "to unite the past and the present—gothic prejudices and the institutions of the century." He could even refer now to "my uncle Louis XVI".

So Josephine, despite her armoury of tenderness and tears, was finally discarded, and in her place came a healthy girl of eighteen, of no great intelligence or beauty. Marie-Louise was commonplace, but fulfilled at least part of her function with commendable punctuality: she bore a male child, grandly named King of Rome, within the year. With his young wife's physical qualities Napoleon was delighted: "Marry German girls," he advised his staff. "Nothing like them. Healthy, honest, wholesome, fresh as roses." Insensitive and egocentric as ever, he kept Josephine (whose devotion to the Emperor, despite everything, increased rather than diminished with the years) well in the picture with his new wife's pregnancy. A few months later he was writing to Josephine:

> L'impératrice . . . m'est fort attachée. Mons fils . . . a ma poitrine, ma bouche, et mes yeux. J'espère qu'il remplira sa destinée.

In the long run it turned out that Napoleon's Habsburg marriage could no more command the friendship of Austria than his demonstrations at Tilsit and Erfurt could that of the Tsar. And always in the background there was Britain, dangling subsidies, straining the European economy by her blockade, assisting the Peninsular rebels. In 1809, when Napoleon was involved in the Austrian campaign, she even attempted to capture Antwerp. As it happened, the affair was yet another disaster for the long-suffering British army, whose plans petered out in fever and frustration on the island of Walcheren. The considerable alarum that was occasioned in France, however, gave Fouché the excuse temporarily to take over full control. On his victorious return Napoleon, deeply suspicious of Fouché's presumption, nevertheless thought it prudent to praise him fulsomely for his resource and decision. But he well knew Fouché's strength and cunning, and Talleyrand's too, and the unreliability of Bernadotte; and when in 1810 he discovered that Fouché had been conducting his own secret peace negotiations with the British he dismissed him. Even so, though he temporarily shook Fouché's outrageous self-confidence and had him scurrying abroad in some panic, he did not judge it wise to proceed further against him. He even made him Duke of Otranto (as Talleyrand became Prince of Benevento). These dangerous, experienced, influential ministers remained to threaten the imperial fabric, quiet as woodworms.

Asked why he essayed to climb Everest, the mountaineer Mallory answered, "Because it is there." Napoleon's reasons for attacking Russia in 1812 were similar. The ostensible cause of the war was the Tsar's refusal to exclude from Russian ports the 'neutral' ships that were bringing British manufactures in and taking Russian grain and timber out; but more fundamental was the sheer challenge. Napoleon's compulsive ambition, growing hungry by what it fed on, became ever more swollen and insatiable. Master of most of Europe, he must be master too of the Ottoman and Russian Empires; and beyond, "we must throw ourselves like robbers upon robbers less daring than ourselves and become masters of India". The reaching of one horizon merely offered the prospect of a new and vaster one; there was no limit.

Complaints of Alexander's failure to observe the blockade led to Napoleon's seizure of Swedish Pomerania. For the Tsar, whose admiration for Napoleon had been cooling ever since the ink had dried on the Treaty of Tilsit, this was the last straw. (The Swedes, too, whose trade was being throttled by the Napoleonic blockade, and who had recently made Marshal Bernadotte their Crown Prince, now steered towards an anti-Napoleonic alliance with Russia.) When Alexander presented Napoleon with an ultimatum demanding withdrawal from both Pomerania and Prussia, Napoleon's answer was to raise the largest and most cosmopolitan of all his armies, totalling over 600,000 men, of whom about 250,000 only were French. The rest, under French officers, were conscripts from his conquered territories—Poles, Lithuanians, Italians, Germans, Croats, Dutchmen, Spaniards, Portuguese. The foreign element in this motley army (Poles and Lithuanians perhaps excepted) could hardly be expected to fight with enthusiasm, and there was a good deal of pillaging and desertion; but the disasters that were to overcome them all were not the result of inefficiency or indiscipline. They arose from Napoleon's failure to bring his enemy to the decision of a super-battle—another Austerlitz—and to his own reckless over-confidence. Underestimating the men opposed to him, Napoleon thought Alexander "false and feeble". He could not grasp that once he had launched his armies against Russia, against Moscow itself, the Tsar, unstable though he was, would fight it out to the end. Alexander had sufficiently warned Napoleon on this very point: "Once the war has begun, one of us . . . must lose his crown." Napoleon chose to go on thinking that, after a big defeat, the Tsar would negotiate.

It was not that Napoleon was without warning of the dangers, or that he did not, in a general sort of way, realize them. Indeed, the very hugeness of them presented a fascination and a challenge to his megalomania. He made unprecedented provision for food re-serves behind the front. He had an edict ready for promulgating the liberation of the serfs; but he was quite unprepared, as he had been in Spain, for the patriotic ferocity of the popular resistance. His swollen army found it ever harder to commandeer supplies, as village after village burned them on its approach. The starvation of his horses crippled his transport system and accelerated the starva-tion of his troops. They were hungry long before they reached Mos-cow. On the terrible march back they famished before they began to freeze.

The Russians themselves were confused and divided on the con-duct of the war. A year before the campaign began Alexander had said:

> The system which has made Wellington victorious in Spain, and exhausted the French armies, is what I intend to follow— avoid pitched battles and organize long lines of communication for retreat, leading to entrenched camps.

At other times Alexander envisaged grand encircling movements. It certainly gave no joy either to the Tsar or his generals (Barclay de Tolly and Bagration) to yield thousands of square miles of Russian soil and burn hundreds of Russian towns and villages in the path of the invader. The disparity of numbers, however—three to one—forbade set battles in the early stages. Vilna, Vitebsk, even (after some severe skirmishing and bombardment) historic Smolensk, were in turn abandoned. Napoleon's famous speed and mobility deserted him, and he bitterly reproached both Jerome and Junot for their failure to envelop the retiring army. As the advance continued, however, Napoleon's numbers dwindled until something approaching parity was reached. Further, the combined effect of the retreat upon public opinion and of the bickering of the Russian generals forced the Tsar to make a change of command. The aged but thoroughly competent and wholly Russian Kutusov replaced Barclay, who was of Scots origin. It would be politically impossible to yield Moscow now, like Smolensk, without a major stand. At Borodino, therefore, sixty miles from Moscow, Kutusov prepared his defences, stood, and fought.

It was the most terrible of all the many battles of the Napoleonic wars. Nearly 30,000 on the French side, over 50,000 on the Russian, were lost: half the Russian army, a quarter of the French. The dead, reaching the same end earlier, were more fortunate than the wounded and the prisoners in Borodino's bloody chaos and its aftermath. Afterwards both sides claimed a victory, but in fact both lost their power to strike again in a great battle. So much for Napoleon's hope of another Austerlitz. Yet, in the words of a French colonel present:

> When it was all over I saw Napoleon riding over the battlefield; I followed him everywhere; he was beaming and rubbing his hands: "There are five dead Russians"—he said it repeatedly with satisfaction—"to every Frenchman."

The mauled Grand Army staggered on to Moscow, which Kutusov, and with him most of the civilian population, did now abandon without further fight. Moscow, which was to have furnished winter quarters and provisions, proved to be a dead city. Within an hour or two of the arrival of the French it was alight, on the instructions of the fled governor of the city. The quarter of Moscow that survived would nevertheless have provided billets enough, and Napoleon could have risked staying on; but his position there was dangerously exposed, and plainly he could not venture farther eastward, or northward to St Petersburg. He was torn with indecision for weeks, waiting vainly for a peace move from the Tsar. None came. At last, on October 18th, he decided to try to extricate the 100,000 of his Grand Army that still remained. Uncharacteristically, and as it turned out unsuccessfully, he first ordered the demolition of the Kremlin.

The army fought its way back in good weather, harassed continually by Cossacks and irregulars, and by contingents of the regular Russian army. But Kutusov's main force shadowed the retreat on a parallel course at a respectful distance to the south. He would not risk another Borodino. It seemed that he would not need to: the Grand Army was disintegrating. Every hour more stragglers had to fall out; it was a case of which would destroy them first—hunger, the peasantry, or the Cossack cavalry.

For short periods Napoleon would march beside his haggard regiments, but for the most part he travelled in fair comfort in the imperial carriage, well provided. "My health is excellent," he wrote to Marie Louise; he appeared to worry more over the news of a Paris plot against his régime than over the nightmare sufferings of his men.

Smolensk had been picked clean; it offered neither food nor shelter to these now desperate remnants, who had no alternative to pressing on westward. Some were demoralized; but not Ney's rearguard or the magnificent Guard, which, enclosing their Emperor, "passed through our Cossacks like a hundred-gun ship through a fishing fleet". Narrowly, almost miraculously, the Grand Army avoided encirclement. When it appeared to be trapped at the river Beresina the sappers working in the icy water still managed to get two bridges built, over which 60,000 men crossed, including most even of the rearguard. The cavalry had swum across. The bridges were then fired and the stragglers, perhaps as many as 10,000 of them, left to their destruction.

The last horrors were added now, early in December, with the first severe frost. On the 5th Napoleon abandoned his command to Murat and his men to their fate. Accompanied by his valets, by Caulaincourt, lately his ambassador in Russia, to whom he reminisced spiritedly *en route*, and by an escort of Polish, Italian, and French cavalry, some of whom froze to death on the way, he made his way by carriage to Vilna; thence by covered sledge to Warsaw and Dresden; and so by carriage again to Mainz and Paris. He arrived at the Tuileries a week before Christmas, just four days after Ney, with the few hundred scarecrow heroes remaining to him, fought his last rearguard action on Russian soil. By then Murat too, pleading bad health, had abandoned his command. It was the faithful Eugene who brought the few thousand bewildered survivors of the Grand Army back over the Niemen. The disaster had been on the grand scale and almost total.

Napoleon, as usual, lied about his defeat, which he publicly attributed to "the premature rigour of the season". (Winter had in fact come late that year.) He maintained a great show of not being cast down; Caulaincourt had never known him more cheerful. There still remained honour to be won. The 1813 age group had already been called to the colours one year in advance, but now the 1814 age group, 150,000 of them, were conscripted, and conscripted more rigorously than before. *Remplacement* became harder; the price of buying exemption rose steeply. Horses, in fact, proved more difficult to conscript than men: 80,000 of them had been lost—killed, starved, or eaten—in Russia.

Of Napoleon's potential enemies in the field in 1813, the Tsar was now inexorable. He would have nothing of Kutusov's policy of breaking off pursuit at the frontier; Alexander aimed now to dictate peace in Paris. He had entered his religious phase: perhaps he had been chosen as the agent of God—the 'white angel' whose mission would be to destroy the Angel of Darkness. He made an alliance with the Swedes under Bernadotte, and with the Prussians, now resurgent under the influence of the banished Stein and the leadership of Scharnhorst, Gneisenau, and Hardenberg. "Germany," jointly proclaimed the Tsar and the King of Prussia, "rejuvenated, vigorous, united, will once again take its place with advantage among the nations of Europe." Germany a nation: these were exciting, even dangerous, words, not likely to win much enthusiasm in Vienna. Napoleon's two hard victories over the Russo-Prussian alliance, at Lützen and Bautzen in May 1813, were by no means wholly unwelcome to the Austrians, whose position at this stage was ambiguous and shifting. As Napoleon's father-in-law, Francis owed at least a measure of friendship; as Habsburg, he had no desire to see Prussia dominate Germany or Russia bestride all Europe.

Everything depended on what Napoleon was prepared to offer to maintain the shaky Austrian alliance. If he had been ready to suppress the Duchy of Warsaw and the Confederation of the Rhine, and if he had agreed to retire to the Rhine frontier, he might still have had Metternich's support; but he was not. The famous interview between the two men at Dresden in June brought no agreement: it needed only the news of Wellington's big victory at Vitoria finally to tip the scales. So once more an Austrian army took the field against the French, and in circumstances more propitious than before. Victory, said Napoleon, belongs to the big battalions; and massed against him now, with his fair-weather German friends, were three big armies—one under Bernadotte in the north, one under the Prussian Blücher in the centre, and another in the south under the Austrian Schwarzenberg. Moreover, the allies pursued the sensible policy advocated by their two eminent French renegades, Bernadotte and Moreau: defeat Napoleon's lieutenants first; then concentrate upon the outnumbered forces of the Emperor himself. These tactics worked well. Napoleon's victory at Dresden was more than counterbalanced by several defeats sustained by Oudinot, Ney, and Macdonald. When the big battle came, near Napoleon's headquarters at Leipzig, his army could muster only 160,000 to face allies totalling 300,000. In three days of heavy fighting during which each side inflicted 60,000 casualties, Napoleon was significantly defeated.

He had not shown during this German campaign of 1813 anything like his old flair. His tactics had been cautious and his movements, for him, slow-footed. The old self-confidence was not always with him now. He was, moreover, growing big-bellied, irritable, and moody. Middle age was bringing a need for comforts and for sleep, which he had previously been able to scorn or command at will. At the end of the second afternoon of the Leipzig fighting he sat exhausted on his stool by the camp-fire, realizing more certainly with every fading minute that the battle was lost. He gave orders for retirement (which were bungled) and then collapsed into sleep. He himself was swept up in the murderous confusion of the retreat.

Leipzig was a signal for the remaining waverers. Holland went over to the House of Orange. Brother-in-law Murat of Naples went over to the enemy. The Saxons and Württembergers deserted Napoleon actually in mid-battle. The Bavarians seized the same moment to enter the war against him—which caused him to rage that "Munich must burn"; and although his retreating army brushed the Bavarians aside, it lost many more men doing so. One state after another hastened to join the victorious allies as

Napoleonic Germany crumbled. By November its creator was back across the Rhine, having lost during 1813 almost as many men as in the disasters of 1812.

Napoleon could probably have still maintained his throne and made peace on the basis of the Rhine frontier, which (though it placed millions of Germans on its 'French' side) had come by Frenchmen to be described as 'natural'. At Frankfurt the advancing Powers (rather to the alarm of the British) declared that they were still "willing to recognize an extension of French territory which the country never knew under its kings". It is true that the Tsar was thirsting for a more crushing victory and that Prussia was hungry to revenge her many humiliations to the utmost; but Metternich was by now more alarmed by these Powers' ambitions than by Napoleon's, for, on any objective judgment, Napoleon must now lose the war. Russia and Prussia might win it all too thoroughly.

A few more French victories, Napoleon's obstinate faith in his star, and his belief that he could play off one hostile ally against the others, encouraged him to fight on. His long-suffering people, incredulous still of defeat and besotted by the optimism of Napoleon's propaganda, but weary of the war's burdens—its taxes, its shortages, its toll of ever younger young men—had, of course, no say in the decision to continue the fight.

Military men, from the Duke of Wellington onward, have made much of the technical brilliance of the Emperor's 1814 campaign, as from his interior lines he struck at the converging columns of his more numerous enemies. Napoleon was doing what he of all men knew best how to do—fight; but it was an exercise of futile brilliance, conducted by a man who had lost touch with reality. He talked of recrossing the Rhine and advancing again to the Vistula. He was furious to hear that his brother Joseph, back in Paris, was trying to negotiate peace: "Today", he told him, "as at Austerlitz I am the master." "Everyone has betrayed me," he moaned to Marie Louise—warning her at the same time not to trust Joseph: "He has an evil reputation with women and an ambition that grew upon him while he was in Spain." Even the marshals were now divided about continuing the war. Prussians, Russians, and Austrians were converging on Paris from north and east. Wellington was pressing up from the south against Soult. Holland and Belgium were already overrun, while Davout, with 100,000 men, was helplessly locked up in Hamburg.

The final battle was fought at Montmartre; the *ci-devant* Kings Joseph and Jerome watched it long enough to see the outcome, then mounted their horses and rode off. (Marie Louise had fled the preceding day.) Napoleon himself was still making optimistic plans for cutting the Allies' rear communications when Marmont back in Paris was signing the city's capitulation.

The Tsar, after all, was to have his way and dictate peace in Paris. Together with Frederick William of Prussia and the Austrian commander Schwarzenberg, he made his ceremonial entry on March 31st, 1814. That night, while Napoleon was at Fontainebleau, still feeding on phantasms and contemplating counter-offensives against the city, the Tsar lodged at the house of the man who for ten years, believing that treason was merely "a matter of dates", had been positioning himself for such a situation—the indestructible Talleyrand. By April 6th, the day when the Emperor was finally persuaded by his followers that abdication was his only course, the main action of the Napoleonic drama was over. Even then he could hardly credit the extinction of his star; after he had signed the Act of Abdication he suddenly flung himself on a sofa, slapped his thigh, and cried, "Nonsense, gentlemen; let us leave that and march tomorrow. We shall beat them!" Six days later he was signing the draft Treaty of Fontainebleau, and over dinner with Caulaincourt discussing his reign "as though he was talking of someone else". That same night a half-hearted attempt at taking poison misfired: the Emperor was merely sick.

The Allies treated Napoleon with leniency. He retained his title of Emperor. He was given the island of Elba, between Corsica and the Italian mainland, and an allowance from French funds of two million francs. All the Bonaparte clan received a pension, and Marie Louise, who wished to join her husband in Elba but was not allowed to, was awarded the Duchy of Parma—where her rule proved, for a time, surprisingly enlightened.

Napoleon paid an emotional farewell to the Old Guard and travelled south full of nervous apprehensions; perhaps reasonably so, for at Lyons and Aix the mob booed him, and at Avignon he narrowly escaped lynching. He spent ten months as Elba's sovereign, actively administering the affairs of the little state; improving his residences and estates; and receiving a constant flow of relations and visitors, among them his Polish mistress Marie Walewska and their child. A certain Captain Smith, busy with his notebook, describes him at this time as plump, sleek, quick-glancing, with more the appearance "of a clever, crafty, priest than of a hero".

To all Napoleon affirmed that his heroic days were over; he was a dead duck. But of course he did not believe it. Fortunately for him (or *was* it fortunately?) France was weary under her restored Bourbon king. Louis XVIII himself was moderate and sensible enough, but he was surrounded by returned émigrés who "had learned nothing and forgotten nothing". The symbolic tricolour was banished; "they imposed on us", wrote de Ségur, "the flag under which they had fought us." The peasants and middle classes were anxious for the security of their lands. The nobility had owned these once; would they now again? The army was out of love with the new régime; even more disgruntled were the demobilized veterans and officers retired on half-pay. In Vienna, meanwhile, the conferring Powers were, in the manner of conquering allies, falling out.

Napoleon laid his plans, therefore, for a last throw of the dice. He was nothing if not an adventurer. With his small Elban flotilla and rather over a thousand men, he slipped away under a winter moon northward past the loose British patrol. Landing undisturbed between Antibes and Fréjus on March 1st, he began the three weeks' march to Paris. News of the landing reaching the diplomats at Vienna in the midst of their junketings and squabbles had the sobering effect of a cold shower; the alliance was knit together in no time at all. As Napoleon moved on the capital, avoiding royalist Provence and being warmly greeted in revolutionary Lyons (where they cried *A bas les nobles! A bas les prêtres!*), the troops sent against him melted away like snow in summer; Ney's desertion of the Bourbon cause was decisive. But in Vienna the Powers, who had now declared Napoleon an outlaw, were concerting military measures which could hardly fail to blot him from the European scene.

A few Frenchmen greeted the returned Emperor with enthusiasm; many with apathy; some in Vendée and Provence with rebellion; most with a confusion of emotions. After Louis XVIII fled there was the customary rhetoric of professed loyalty to the Emperor. Following so unheroic a monarch as Louis, King by the grace of Talleyrand and the Allies, the return of Napoleon naturally carried a promise of excitement, even of glory. Most Frenchmen, however, would welcome him back only on conditions. Even Louis had granted a charter of liberties; Napoleon must do no less. Aware of these feelings, Napoleon posed strenuously as a liberal. Moreover (though, in view of what was happening in Vienna, fatuously), he promised peace and forswore any ambition to restore his 'Grand Empire'. Indeed, in these Hundred Days between Elba and Waterloo there was a strong element of make-believe. Napoleon himself pursued the same sort of chimerical ambitions as he did before his first overthrow. Many Frenchmen chose with him to shut their eyes to the military and political facts of life; but for most the glories of the great days could not reasonably be expected again. As Thibaudeau, who was very far from a royalist, wrote: Napoleon "had been struck by lightning and carried the scar".

All was soon over, at Waterloo; but if it had not been there it must have been at some other Waterloo, and soon. Wellington, it is true, considered that Napoleon could have fended off the final disaster for a longer period. He thought Napoleon should have played a defensive game and by some kind of repetition of his dazzling 1814 tactics put the allied armies into severe straits to find subsistence in war-torn France. Napoleon "was certainly wrong to attack at all. . . . But the fact is, he never had patience for a defensive war."

Napoleon, as in the old days, aimed by swift movement to get in his blow before all the forces of the Allies could be deployed. Advancing on Brussels with 125,000 men, and hoping first to separate Blücher's Prussians from Wellington's Anglo-Dutch-Belgian-German forces and then to defeat the two armies in turn, he did succeed at Ligny in forcing Blücher to retreat, and Ney at Quatre Bras did push Wellington back towards Brussels. Neither of these victories, however, was conclusive, and it was Napoleon who, on Wellington's chosen field of Waterloo, was caught with divided forces, having misjudged Blücher's movements. It was Blücher who succeeded, though belatedly, in reuniting his troops with Wellington's. Still Waterloo was, as Wellington remarked, "the nearest-run thing you ever saw in your life". His mixed forces—mixed in nationality, mixed in quality—hung doggedly on, the British squares holding off charge after charge, even at last of the Old Guard itself. As the afternoon progressed the desperation of their defence was matched by the increasing desperation of the attackers, until at 4.30 the full weight of Blücher's fresh troops, arriving to take the French flank, swelled their defeat into a rout.

The war was clearly over—clearly, that is, to all save Napoleon. Having fled ahead of the bad news to Paris, he began to concoct plans for "reassembling" his forces, raising further levies and "overwhelming the foe". But he was no longer master of the situation, even in Paris. This time it was not Talleyrand but Fouché who, with a foot in every camp, had worked himself into a position from which to determine events. Head of a Provisional Government, he demanded that Napoleon should again abdicate and leave Paris.

For a few nostalgic days Napoleon lingered at La Malmaison, the gracious house he always associated with the honeymoon days of the early Consulate—latterly Josephine's La Malmaison, where, just a twelvemonth before this last stay of Napoleon, she had lain, elegant and extravagant to the last in rose-coloured satins, upon her gilded-swan death-bed. Not until Fouché had pushed the ex-Emperor south to Rochefort did Blücher agree to spare Paris. The city surrendered on July 4th, two weeks after Waterloo.

Napoleon still existed in a world of self-deception. He might go to America, he thought, or, better still, settle in England (as his brother Lucien had done for a time) as a private citizen. Before going aboard the British warship *Bellerophon* at Rochefort he penned a florid letter to the Prince Regent, putting himself "under the protection of British law—a protection I claim from Your Royal Highness as the most powerful, most stubborn, and most generous of my enemies".

However, neither the British nor their European allies saw any need for generosity a second time. There was no particular vindictiveness in the British decision to send Napoleon to the isolation of St Helena; after his first escape it was simple prudence. The other allies concurred in the decision. If it had been left simply to the Prussians he might have fared much worse; if Blücher had captured him, which he nearly did, he might well have had him shot.

By fighting on in 1814 Napoleon lost the throne of France. By the 1815 escapade he exchanged the sovereignty of Mediterranean Elba for the Atlantic gloom of an island 600 miles from other human habitation (and that too was a British colony, Ascension Island). France paid for the Hundred Days by being forced back to the frontiers of 1790, by having to suffer a war indemnity and allied occupation, by the surrender of the art treasures looted from

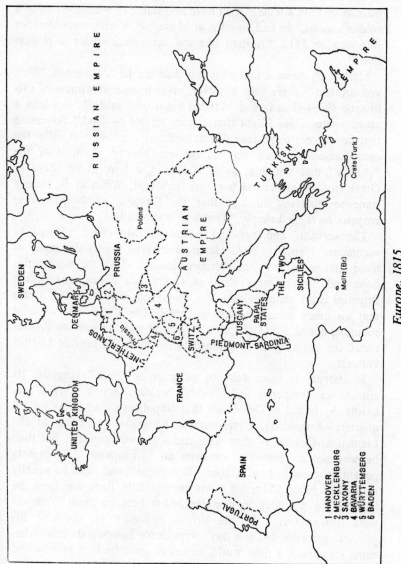

Europe, 1815

1 HANOVER
2 MECKLENBURG
3 SAXONY
4 BAVARIA
5 WÜRTTEMBERG
6 BADEN

abroad, and not least by the loss of a few more tens of thousands of her sons. This last consideration, by Napoleonic standards, was little more than a trifle. "You have no inkling of what goes on in a soldier's mind," he had shouted at Metternich during their Dresden interview in 1813. "A man like me cares nothing for a million lives."

Metternich claimed that after this outburst he commented, "Sire, you are lost"; there was, however, no independent witness of this historic tête-à-tête. It was Marshal Foch who said of Napoleon a century later, "He forgot that a man cannot be God." Assuming that he was not to be regarded as ordinary mortals who suffer the consequences of their actions, he was bitterly resentful of the "perfidy" that sent him to St Helena. For him, as for Zeus in Greek mythology, moral law was irrelevant. When at St Helena someone observed to him that the Chinese worshipped their emperor he replied simply "That is as it should be."

The servants and personal attendants who were allowed to accompany Napoleon to St Helena numbered twenty-six; many of these later published their reminiscences, of which the most ambitious and literary were those of Count Las Cases, one of the Imperial court chamberlains. For Napoleon, who was well aware that his every remark was being noted, Las Cases was a useful sounding-board. For Las Cases, Napoleon was the modern Prometheus, the suffering Titan chained to his rock, the prey of English vultures.

St Helena, in fact, was not as grim as "rock" suggests. Its climate was temperate and tolerably healthy; though rainy, it was hardly the Island of Desolation that Napoleon called it. As for his quarters—Longwood, a six-roomed bungalow belonging to the Lieutenant-Governor—they were mean for an Emperor; but then he was not an Emperor, or even an ex-Emperor. His captors pedantically insisted on "General Bonaparte"; and since he equally insisted on being addressed in his imperial title, there was from the beginning a deadlock in communication between them. Tempers were further frayed by the British insistence on checking his physical presence twice a day. Napoleon's Longwood 'court' became very much a little world turned in upon itself, a moody and quarrelsome band, united only in resentment against their captors. Still, etiquette was strict; nobody, for instance, sat down in the imperial presence except at his express invitation.

The British Governor of St Helena, Napoleon's jailer, was Sir Hudson Lowe, a small-minded, pettifogging fellow who took a sour satisfaction in obeying his Government's instructions to the letter. Wellington called him "a damned fool". After the St Helena courtiers had returned to France and published their memoirs the perfidious English were seen as the villains of the piece, with the petty tyrant Lowe, who had daily clipped their caged eagle's wings anew, the arch-villain. When Dumas staged *Napoléon Bonaparte* in Paris in 1831 the actor representing Lowe was judged to be in such danger from the people's wrath that it was thought prudent to give him police protection.

"What shall we do in this land of the lost?" asked Napoleon of Las Cases. "Sire," Las Cases replied (so he says), "we will live on the past." This they did, and in so doing helped to create the future, and to prepare the path for the return of another Napoleon to the imperial throne. An egoist by nature, a propagandist by long practice, Napoleon knew that he was talking to the world; and for its part the world was keenly curious to know what this great man thought of himself, of his campaigns, of his enemies, of the past and the future. As may be supposed, he took a lenient view of his own failings and a severe one of his enemies'—especially those of the malevolent English (now the *least* generous of his foes) who had thwarted all his peaceful designs. He claimed that he had never wished to make conquests beyond France's natural frontiers. Neither had despotism ever been his intention; if things had gone favourably in 1812 he would have introduced a liberal régime. Given more time, he would have brought to birth a united Germany and a united Italy, even a United States of Europe:

> I wished to found a European system, a European code of laws, a European judiciary; there would be but one people in Europe.

Thus the Napoleonic Legend was born. It turned most of the facts of recent history upside-down, but it had just sufficient of the truth in it to appeal to a France which saw in its political life after 1815 only a long littleness and hankered after the imperial eagles. With the aid of the Napoleonic Legend they could have the best of all worlds—glory, freedom, *and* peace.

Napoleon's health, already deteriorating before his fall, went downhill fast in St Helena. He soon became less active, and according to O'Meara, a doctor in his entourage, he suffered from "indigestion, catarrh, headache, rheumatism, swollen legs, inflamed gums, biliousness and constipation". It is extremely probable that he also had cancer, but it was not diagnosed. The controversy surrounding his death (which came in May 1821) still continues, many patriotic Frenchmen remaining convinced that the English slowly poisoned him with arsenic. Napoleon himself gave this theory a powerful send-off by adding an explosive codicil to his will: "I die prematurely," he wrote, "murdered by the English oligarchy and their hired assassin."

Thus to the myth of the epic hero, the liberal idealist, the apostle of peace, was added yet another facet—the suffering martyr. When in 1840 Napoleon's corpse was disinterred for solemn reburial in the Invalides, and carried thither in magnificent procession under the Arc de Triomphe whose building he had himself inaugurated, the apotheosis was reached, and France was well upon the road to accepting a second Napoleon as her Emperor.

Napoleon dominated the destinies of Europe in his day, as Hitler and Stalin between them did theirs. Like Hitler, Napoleon managed for a brief period to conquer most of the land area of the Continent, but was contained by the vastness of Russia on the one side and enemy naval superiority on the other. Like Stalin, Napoleon rose to power following a national revolution of international significance, and, like Stalin, he consolidated part of the revolution's achievements while destroying another part. Napoleon certainly possessed intellectual powers that the twentieth-century dictators lacked. Moreover, uniquely among modern European statesmen he was an outstanding leader on the field of battle. To find a soldier-statesman to set beside him one must look not forward to the twentieth century but back to Charlemagne, Julius Caesar, or Alexander the Great. Inside France the civil reforms of the Consulate period were of lasting importance, and the glamour of his victories will always thrill the French. To parts of Europe he brought too some positive benefits, such as equality before the law and the abolition of serfdom. He gave to much of Germany and Italy a significant foretaste of national unity—though it may well be thought, if this is to be counted to his credit, that he did more to whet the national spirit of Spain, Russia, and Prussia by defeat and humiliation than to promote European nationalism by any progressive intention. As Metternich said, he "confiscated" the Revolution for his own purposes. The liberator and modernizer proved also a trickster and tyrant. A cynic, he preached honour. In the last resort nothing mattered but the greatness of Napoleon. In the pursuit of that end he put a whole generation of Europe upon the rack.

Table of Events

1769.	Napoleon Bonaparte born in Corsica.
1779–85.	Military schooling at Brienne and Paris.
1792.	Revolutionary wars begin.
1793.	Bonaparte at capture of Toulon.
1794.	Fall of Robespierre; reaction of Thermidor.
1795–99.	France under the Directory.
1796.	Marriage to Josephine Beauharnais. First Italian campaign (1797: Treaty of Campo Formio).
1798–99.	Egyptian and Syrian campaigns. Abukir Bay and Abukir.
1799.	First Consul after *coup* of Brumaire. Second Coalition.
1799–1804.	Educational, legal, and administrative reforms.
1800.	Second Italian campaign. Marengo. Treaty of Lunéville.
1802.	Concordat with Pope. Peace of Amiens. Legion of Honour.
1804.	Royalist conspiracy; Enghien murdered. Napoleon Emperor. Plans invasion of England.
1805.	King of Italy. Third Coalition. Ulm. Trafalgar. Austerlitz. Treaty of Pressburg.
1806.	Confederation of the Rhine. Jena-Auerstädt. Berlin decrees.
1807.	'Code Napoléon'. Eylau. Friedland. Grand Duchy of Warsaw and Kingdom of Westphalia. Treaty of Tilsit. Junot in Lisbon.
1808.	University of France. Rome and Madrid occupied. Peninsular War begins.
1809.	Aspern-Essling. Wagram. Treaty of Schönbrunn. Marries Marie Louise.
1812.	Invades Russia. Borodino. Retreat from Moscow.
1813.	Fourth Coalition. Lützen, Bautzen, Dresden, Leipzig.
1814.	Retreat into France. First abdication. Elba.
1815.	Hundred Days. Waterloo. Second abdication.
1821.	Death in St Helena.

2
METTERNICH
(1773-1859)
And the Despotic Reaction

For four centuries and more the history of Central Europe was largely the history of the Habsburg family and their lands. An Austrian archduke of that name had slipped quietly into the position of Holy Roman Emperor in 1438, and for the next 368 years (excepting three years only) he and his descendants stayed there, hereditary German Emperors in all but name. When Napoleon abolished the Holy Roman Empire the reigning Habsburg simply sidestepped to become Emperor of Austria; and when in the nineteenth century the Hungarians' demand for parity with the Germans became irresistible, the last but one Habsburg was quietly metamorphosed into the Emperor of Austria-Hungary. By a series of fortunate marriages the Habsburg Empire reached massive size and importance very quickly: by 1526 Charles V and his brother Ferdinand were rulers of Austria, Bohemia, Hungary, the Netherlands, Spain, the New World, and much of Italy. Thenceforth the Habsburgs were always trying to achieve the impossible—to maintain the integrity of their empire. The Dutch soon set themselves free; Spain and its colonies were lost to the Bourbons in the days of Louis XIV; despite the 'Pragmatic Sanction' that was intended to preserve the remainder inviolate, Frederick of Prussia seized Silesia in 1740. Yet it was not till 1919 that the Habsburg Empire finally disappeared in the great shipwreck of empires that followed the First World War.

The Habsburgs were thus bound by the very nature of things to be conservators. Metternich once observed that it seemed that he had given all his life to shoring up a crumbling edifice. In a sense the Habsburgs, his masters, had been doing that for centuries. They were trying to prolong into the modern Europe of nation-states a shadowy version of the medieval universal-empire. By Metternich's day all the historical trends were setting in against this feudal and dynastic world of theirs; Jacobinism, liberalism, capitalism, nationalism, all sped their decline.

The Habsburg dominions were more a gigantic piece of real estate than an empire. As A. J. P. Taylor puts it, they were "landlords, not rulers. . . . They could compound with everything, except the demand to be free of landlords; this demand was their ruin. . . . They changed ideas, territories, methods, alliances, statesmen, whenever it suited dynastic interests to do so. Only 'the August House' was permanent", and its single aim was "to exist in greatness". To become a national state like France or England or Spain was beyond its powers and irrelevant to its ambitions; for within its territories, even after the loss of Spain, Holland, and the Indies, were Flemings, Walloons, Italians, Czechs, Slovaks, Serbs, Croats, Slovenes, Rumanians, Ruthenians, Poles, Hungarians— and, of course, Germans. The Habsburg Emperor had for centuries been popularly referred to as 'the German Emperor', or simply as 'the Emperor'. But he was both more and less than that: more, in that his subject-peoples were widespread and multitudinous in race, language, and nationality; less, in that the championship of specifically German solidarity was never a paramount interest of the Habsburgs. It is true that at various times they somewhat vaguely essayed the leadership of 'Germany'; but essentially they were European first and German second. Vienna, their capital, was a Europeon rather than a German city. "*C'est que l'Europe*", said Metternich once—speaking, it will be noticed, not German but French, the language of the European aristocracy—"*a pris pour moi la valeur d'une patrie.*" The very terms 'German' and 'Austrian' were both of them somewhat ambiguous and elastic. The 'Germans' of the Habsburg Empire were essentially the town dwellers, and more especially the middle classes—those engaged in trade, shopkeeping, manufacture, the crafts, the arts, and the learned professions. If an ambitious Slav peasant moved to Vienna or Prague and succeeded there he began to become a 'German', and he spoke German as naturally as in a later stage a first-generation Polish immigrant to the U.S.A. spoke English. The composer Haydn is a case in point: he was the son of a village wheelright of Croat stock. Vienna claimed him young, and his Croatian ancestry was swiftly forgotten.

The Habsburg dominions after the loss of the Netherlands

contained few towns of any size outside Italy—Vienna, Prague, Budapest, and a number of middle-sized provincial places such as Innsbruck, Linz, Brünn, Pressburg, Agram, Lemberg, Laibach, and Carlsbad. The very names of many of these places, *German* names, emphasizes the urban aspect of this term 'German' in older times. Agram and Laibach are respectively the modern Yugoslav Zagreb and Lyublyana; Lemberg is Ukrainian Lvov (though Poles and Jews, not Germans, predominated there); Brünn and Carlsbad are the Czech Brno and Karlovy Vary; Pressburg is the Slovakian frontier town of Bratislava. Prague (Praha), capital of Bohemia, was a city much less Czech than German, and to be heard speaking Czech in the street would convey a message of social inferiority. Even in Budapest Hungarian citizens were a minority until the second half of the nineteenth century. Thus the Germans were, on the whole, urban classes in a world of peasants and great rural landlords; 'German' signified class as much as language or nationality. The description 'Austrian' was even more non-national: an 'Austrian' might very well be one of the Hungarian nobility, such as Haydn's patron Prince Esterhazy, or a Czech aristocrat such as Metternich's great rival Kolowrat.

There were occasions, indeed, when the Habsburg Emperor talked vaguely of leading 'the German nation': in 1809, for instance, the year of Metternich's appointment as Foreign Minister, when ardent German minds dreamed hopefully of liberation and unity, it seemed politic for the Emperor Francis I to promise such leadership. But vagueness was of the essence; so cosmopolitan and universal an empire could not seriously propose to confine itself within the bounds of a German national state—even if such a thing were a possibility, which most doubted. To Metternich the idea was a chimera.

The Habsburgs had always had other missions. Chief among them was the preservation—from barbarians, infidels, and heretics—of Catholic Christendom, the heir and beneficiary of the Roman Empire. Thus the Habsburgs of Austria and Spain, with their allies the Jesuits, were the spearheads of the Counter-Reformation. It was the Habsburg Philip II who strove against the Calvinists in Holland and sent the Armada against Elizabeth of England; and it was imperial Austrian armies that attempted in the Thirty Years War to cleanse Germany from the stain of Lutheranism. On the one hand there was the Protestant danger, on the other the ever-present menace of the Turks. Twice Vienna was besieged by the Turks, and twice the Turks were turned back. Hungary, which they did conquer, was then reconquered by the Habsburgs. (Budapest was Turkish for 150 years.) Then there were the Russians, whom certainly no Catholic Austrian would consider either fully Christian or civilized; it was another of Austria's missions to keep them at arm's length in Eastern Europe and the Balkans. Here, amid the motley peasant populations of the Balkans, she saw herself as the civilizing agent, much as the late Victorian Englishman tended to regard it as his 'white man's burden' to spread civilization among the peoples of Africa and Asia. Metternich himself, no nationalist, described the German element in the Habsburg lands as "the civilizing principle", though he denied any desire to "Germanize". The difficulty was that not everybody could agree with these Austrian concepts of cultural penetration and a 'superior' civilization. The Hungarian nobility (the term was very inclusive and there were altogether half a million of them, one in twenty of the population of Hungary) also saw themselves as a cultural élite and did not rest until in 1867 they achieved political parity. Even within the subject Slav peoples (serfs until their late-eighteenth-century liberation by the Emperor Joseph II) there were strongly subjective cultural gradations: the Serbs, for instance, were convinced of their superiority to the rest of the southern Slavs.

During the eighteenth century there were sweeping reforms in the Habsburg lands, begun by Maria Theresa and prosecuted at breakneck speed by her son Joseph II, the most radical of the Enlightened Despots. Joseph died in 1790, in his own eyes a total failure and with revolutions breaking out in Belgium and Hungary. The events that followed turned Austria back from radicalism to her traditional rôle as the champion of conservative stability. The Queen of France, Marie Antoinette, was a Habsburg, Maria Theresa's daughter: the sister of Joseph and of his successor Leopold. By 1792 Austria was at war with the French people and their revolution, though she was unable to save the French King or his Austrian wife from the guillotine the following year. Thus the age of the French Revolution, of Napoleon, and in Austria of the Emperor Francis and of Metternich, provided the Habsburgs with still one more mission: to save European civilization from Jacobin revolution. Despite repeated defeats inflicted by Napoleon, whose forces twice occupied Vienna, and despite compromise and appeasement, including the sensational marriage of the Habsburg Marie Louise to the upstart Napoleon, the Habsburgs were by 1815 again at the centre of a Europe free of Napoleon. They were apparently stronger than ever, secure in their own lands and dominant in Germany and Italy.

By that year Metternich had been Austrian Foreign Minister for six years. For the next third of a century, till 1848, his tasks remained the same: to maintain the unity and integrity of the Empire, to preserve it from revolution within and without, and to provide Europe with an era of repose.

It need not surprise that the leading statesman of so cosmopolitan an empire was not himself by birth Austrian. He was born at Coblenz, in the Rhineland, in 1773; Count Franz Metternich, his father, a diplomatist who began by representing the Archbishop-Elector of Trier at the court of Vienna and transferred to the imperial service, was ultimately Austrian minister in the Netherlands. Young Clemens Metternich was brought up amid the graces of the last days of the *ancien régime*; the Archbishop of Trier was uncle of the King of France, and his court, like those of many of the German princelings, followed in miniature the fashions and manners of Versailles. Metternich's upbringing belonged, like his native Rhineland, partly to Germany and partly to France. He spoke both languages impartially (as well as English and Italian). Equally impartial seems to have been the parental choice of tutors: one was a Catholic priest and another a Protestant disciple of Rousseau. Before he was sixteen Metternich began to attend Strasbourg University, but his career there was interrupted by the French Revolution. The young aristocrat watched the mob running loose in the streets looking for its own Bastilles to wreck; his reactions of distaste and fear were to last him a lifetime. At the other extreme and vastly impressive to the seventeen-year-old Metternich was the high pageantry at Frankfurt of the new Emperor Leopold's coronation. He took some part in the ancient ritual himself, as Master of Ceremonies to the College of the Imperial Counts of Westphalia. From Frankfurt he proceeded again to the university at Mainz, whose lecture halls and ladies' boudoirs he frequented with varied profit and pleasure until once more the French Revolution caught up with him and with the aristocracy he moved among. His birthplace of Coblenz was for a time the headquarters of the émigrés, among them now the Metternichs: by 1795 the appointment and estates of Count Metternich were both lost to him, the armies of the Revolution having overrun the Netherlands and the Rhineland. He did the only thing possible—returned to Vienna, where he was fortunate to be awarded a pension.

That same year (1795) in the not yet famous little Moravian town of Austerlitz the younger Metternich married the first of his three wives—Eleonore von Kaunitz, the granddaughter of Maria Theresa's Foreign Minister. It was as much a marriage of convenience as any Habsburg dynastic match. Charm and beauty he could find where-ever else he wished: his first wife brought Metternich, the relatively obscure young Rhinelander, into the inner circles of Viennese political society. Yet his climb to the top was by no means swift. The first six years after his marriage, the dying years of the eighteenth century, he spent much as might be expected of a hand-some and cultured young aristocrat of the old régime. He dabbled in history and philosophy, in science and medicine; he moved easily in the salons and ballrooms of the fashionable world; he made love to rather numerous society beauties, being (as a cen-sorious Englishman observed) "intolerably loose and giddy with women": a rather sententious man of the world; a rational man of the Enlightenment, cool of judgment, at home in any company, but especially and by preference in that of his admirers; superficial— Talleyrand described him as "inconceivably" so; complacent; in-tellectually vain—he never in a long life ceased from emphasizing the justice and sagacity of his own views. "Error," he once told Guizot, "has never approached my mind." And he wrote:

> There is a wide sweep about my mind. I am always above and beyond the preoccupations of most public men; I cover a ground much vaster than they can see, or wish to see. I cannot stop my-self saying about twenty times a day, "How right I am, and how wrong they are."

In 1801 he was appointed Austrian minister at Dresden; in 1803 he became ambassador at the Prussian court; in 1806, between Austerlitz and Jena, he went as Austrian ambassador to Paris. The Napoleonic Empire was riding upon a plateau of triumph. The archaic pattern of Germany was being destroyed, the authority of the Holy Roman Empire, of the free cities, of the ecclesiastical princes, being swept away. Only the kings and secular princes re-mained, at the head of thirty states instead of the old three hundred. Prussia was stripped of territory and humiliated; her great minister Stein could be dismissed on a word from Napoleon in Madrid. Some of West Germany was put under the direct rule of Napoleon (Jerome's Kingdom of Westphalia); a great deal more (the Confederation of the Rhine) was under his indirect control. Austria, three times defeated, remained, certainly not intact, but a great Power still, and still capable of dexterously influencing the balance of power. The attempt to maintain this threatened balance was the key to all Metternich's diplomacy.

The Napoleonic Empire, Britain, Russia, Austria, and Turkey: these were the five principal weights in the scales. Turkey (the Ottoman Empire), a declining Power, had long seemed ripe for partition, as Poland had been earlier. "The great question," said Napoleon in 1808, "is always this—who shall have Constantinople?" France, Russia, and Austria were all, as potential beneficiaries, vitally interested in the answer. So too in another sense was Britain, who was determined Constantinople should remain Turkish. Britain herself, sustained by her financial, industrial, and commercial strength, appeared, after Trafalgar in 1805, to be invincible against direct methods of war. On a visit in 1794, Metternich had stood on a hill overlooking the Solent and recorded his impression of the "noble sight" of the East and West Indian fleets, 400 strong, preparing to sail under convoy—a memorable and majestic reminder of Britain's resources. Russia, Austria's principal rival in Eastern Europe, seemed for a time after the Treaty of Tilsit in 1807 to be in league with Napoleon to destroy Britain's trade, to partition the Turkish Empire, and to attack Austria. None of these projects, however, prospered quite as they once promised. The Tsar Alexander cooled towards Napoleon; Turkey remained unpartitioned; British commerce survived; and when the moment came for a further Napoleonic assault upon Austria she too, though again defeated, survived and took severe toll of Napoleon's forces. It was significant that the Tsar, although he formally took the side of the French, sent only small forces against Austria; he would rather see the Austrian Empire in Habsburg hands than in French. Three years later, during Napoleon's Moscow campaign, Austria was to return the compliment, taking small part in the attack on Russia. The fear of Napoleon common to these two Powers proved in the long run greater than their mutual rivalry and mistrust.

Paris under Napoleon provided Metternich with rich scope for both his diplomatic and his personal talents. Nothing stood still for long in those days; every new campaign brought new patterns to the

European scene, new dangers and opportunities. Metternich's task was to know everything before it happened, to inform and advise Vienna, to ride upon the whirlwind's back. He was in his element, moving shrewdly and knowledgeably in political matters, and easily in society. It was during these years that he and Talleyrand, now beginning to turn against Napoleon, first took one another's measure. As for Napoleon, Metternich began that close study of him at close quarters that culminated in the historic interview at Dresden in 1813. He genuinely admired "the force of his character, the activity and lucidity of his mind" and his military genius, while deploring his lack of moral sense and (like Talleyrand) despising his *parvenu* manners. Who but an upstart adventurer would have received the Austrian ambassador *with his hat on*? And even imperial conquerors, Metternich remembered, would die one day or be overthrown in the fullness of time. The task of Austria was, by opportunism and evasion, to win through to that time.

Metternich may well have earned, as he claims, Napoleon's respect; he certainly won something more intimate from Napoleon's youngest sister Caroline, Grand Duchess of Berg. She was the wife of the flamboyant cavalryman Joachim Murat, and was soon to accompany him to the throne of Naples—a woman whose ambition was as devouring as that of her husband or brother. While they were reaping glory on the fields of Jena and Friedland she became the mistress of the Austrian ambassador. She was, moreover, sufficiently jealous of his attentions and piqued by their subsequent diversion elsewhere to make public Metternich's later affair with the wife of another of Napoleon's generals—Junot, Duc d'Abrantès. (This vindictive disclosure from so high a source was vigorously acted upon by the virile and unpredictable Junot: he gave his wife the Duchess a summary thrashing.) This tangled skein of intrigue is given a further twist by the suggestion that Napoleon chose Junot to occupy Lisbon in 1808 partly at least to separate him from Caroline Murat. Tangles of various kinds attracted Metternich. "Spiders", he once said, "interest me . . . charming little creatures, always busy, and arranging their houses with the greatest neatness in the world"; and again, "I have the feeling that I am in the middle of a web which I am spinning after the manner of my friends the spiders." This, no doubt, was what Napoleon meant when he said that Metternich mistook intrigue for politics. The double sense of 'intrigue' in English translation is here peculiarly fitting: upon many the first impression of Metternich was of the intriguer, the ladies' man, the social butterfly, the "political harlequin" (Castlereagh's phrase). "A society hero, nothing more" was Wellington's verdict.

By 1808 Austria began rearming, encouraged by French set-backs in Portugal and Spain and by the Tsar's obvious cooling-off towards Napoleon. In Metternich's view she should not provoke war but must be ready for it; his master Francis I went further: "Even if war does not enter into Napoleon's calculations, it should enter into ours." The assumption of this aggressive-looking attitude fired some enthusiasm throughout Germany, where many romantics and nationalists looked to the Habsburg emperor to free them from French rule. In the Tyrol there was even a pro-Habsburg peasant rising against French influence. Francis I, the most conservative of autocrats, was perhaps alarmed at his own temerity; it was in any case soon punished on the bloodstained field of Wagram. For the fourth time Napoleon defeated Austria; at Schönbrunn he imposed on her a very severe peace. But it was significant that before he left Schönbrunn an attempt upon his life was made by a German who went to his death shouting "Long live Germany! Death to the tyrant!"

Two days after Wagram (July 1809) the Austrian Foreign Minis-ter, Stadion, resigned; Metternich, just back from Paris, was appointed by Francis in his place. Thus he reached the highest office at the nadir of Austria's fortunes; at Schönbrunn she lost $3\frac{1}{2}$ million subjects and the last of her coastline. Yet she was still a factor in the situation, still one of the major Powers. (When one of the members of Napoleon's Grand Council ventured the opinion that Austria was not, Napoleon slapped him down promptly with *On voit bien, monsieur, que vous n'étiez pas à Wagram*.) After 1809, however, and this fourth great Austrian defeat, it would take all Metternich's diplomatic skill to keep his country afloat. In a memorandum to his emperor he summed up the situation and his own answer to it:

> From the day that the peace of Schönbrunn is made, our policy in all matters must be to tack, to efface ourselves, to come to terms with the victor. Only thus shall we preserve our exis-tence, perhaps, until the day of general deliverance. . . .

At least for the time being it must be for others to make war. *Alii bellum gerant*, said the ancient Habsburg maxim: "Let others wage war." But it was the second part of the old tag that now acquired a sensational topicality. *Tu, felix Austria, nube:* "Thou, fortunate Austria, marry." The traditional Habsburg card had never been played in odder circumstances, and nobody afterwards seemed quite sure who originated the suggestion that Napoleon, having first divorced Josephine, should marry Francis's daughter Marie Louise; apparently nobody was anxious to claim the credit. French diplomatic records make the initiative come from Vienna; Metternich's memoirs tell of a masked ball in Paris where a disguised Napoleon tried to use Mme Metternich as a go-between to broach the proposal to the Austrian court. Whatever its origins, Metternich soon perceived the advantages of the match, and advised Francis and his daughter in favour of it. During these years the Habsburgs would need to be in all camps and in no camp. A Habsburg consort for Napoleon would give Austria a qualified alliance with the conqueror—rather like the Tsar's after the Treaty of Tilsit. At least it ought to preserve her from future attack. And when it became plain, as it soon did, that Napoleon's next assault would be upon Austria's rival, Russia, this gave grounds for wary approval. Moreover, if Poland were to be reconstituted by Napoleon— which would involve Austria in the loss of her Galician territories in Southern Poland—Metternich saw opportunities for regaining, by the way of compensation, her lost Illyrian lands on the Adriatic. If Napoleon played the lion Metternich could well play the fox, or if necessary the jackal. He did not wish, unless forced, to join actively in the attack on Russia. He wrote, with characteristic sententiousness, to Francis:

> All eyes are fixed on your Majesty, and there is in this rôle a grandeur that nothing can supplant. The day that Austrian troops march side by side with French . . . in a war of destruction, that day your Majesty will lay down this noble character.

Metternich's actions were not quite so high-principled as his sentiments. He did negotiate with Napoleon: in return for 50,000 troops, would the French be willing to make over to Austria Illyria, Serbia, or even Silesia? At the same time he was counselling the King of Prussia, who possessed Silesia, to join Russia *against* Napoleon. His diplomacy at this time lends colour to a remark Napoleon once made about him: "Everybody lies sometimes. But to lie all the time, *c'est trop.*"

If Napoleon understood Metternich, certainly Metternich had no illusions about Napoleon, whose aspirations were, as he said "in his very nature". Neither, however, was Metternich under any illusion about the dangers of an overwhelming Russian triumph. Best of all, he considered, would be a negotiated general settlement, with the European equilibrium held, France confined to her 'natural' frontiers, and a Bonaparte-Habsburg dynasty perpetuated in Paris. After the Moscow campaign Metternich was certainly, for a time, working to prevent the destruction of Napoleon. The British Prime Minister Liverpool found the Austrian attitude "abject", and Castlereagh, the British Foreign Minister, complained of Metternich's "spirit of submission to France" as throughout the spring and summer of 1813 Metternich strove to achieve a compromise continental peace, excluding the over-pugnacious British.

He walked the tight-rope for as long as he could, keeping a large Austrian army mobilized while proposing "armed mediation" to the belligerents. At Reichenbach he met Alexander of Russia, who accepted his terms of mediation; at Dresden, in June 1813, he met Napoleon. Nine hours' straight talking and (by Metternich's self-flattering account) of Napoleonic posturing led nowhere. It was plain that Napoleon was not going to accept any compromise. It became plain, too, to Metternich that if, as seemd likely, France was to be defeated by Russia, Prussia, and Britain, it had better be by Austria too. Accordingly, in August 1813, Francis I joined the European coalition against his son-in-law. By 1814 he had, in return for a million-pound subsidy, engaged to Castlereagh by the Treaty of Chaumont that Austria would never make a separate peace.

Despite the bickering and mutual distrust that is always present between great Powers in alliance, the four major states of the coalition managed to hold together through the campaigns of 1814 and the first abdication of Napoleon. As it turned out, the military events of March 1814, with both Castlereagh and Metternich embarrassingly pushed around by Napoleon's last brilliant thrusts, meant that it was the Tsar Alexander, at the head of a Russo-Prussian army, who entered Paris substantially ahead of his Allies and rivals, and who took the vital decision to send Napoleon to Elba and restore the Bourbon line. On this last point there had been a remarkable lack of prior agreement, both between the Allies themselves and the half-dozen contradictory persons who together constituted the Tsar. At different times he had envisaged upon the throne of France Napoleon's son (under the regency of Marie Louise), Napoleon's stepson Eugene, Bernadotte, and the Duke of Orleans, as well as that Louis le Désiré, Count of Provence, who now became Louis XVIII. As for Elba, it was a 'snap' decision, and both Castlereagh and Metternich had well-justified misgivings about it.

The ambitions and ideals of Alexander I, the weather-vane of Europe, played during the first quarter of the nineteenth century an extraordinary and capricious part in the affairs of the Continent. He was the son of the crazy tyrant Paul I, Catherine the Great's son whom she had wished to exclude from the throne and whose murder in the palace revolution of 1801, connived in by Alexander, long haunted the young Tsar's conscience and inflamed his neurotic instability. Intellectually he was, like his grandmother—and in some degree like Metternich himself—a product of the Enlightenment; his tutor and mentor was the Rousseauist La Harpe. Though he deeply mistrusted people, he hankered after being the friend of all mankind. A capricious autocrat, he nevertheless sincerely worshipped liberty. Always the slave of his latest enthusiasm, he seldom pursued a reform to its realization. In his relations with Napoleon he had seesawed from hostility in 1801 to admiration in 1803, then back again to hostility after Napoleon's murder of the Duke of Enghien. He had fought in 1805–7 for "the sacred right of humanity" and been routed at Austerlitz and Friedland. At Tilsit he had been bowled over by Napoleon's charm and captivated by the imperial prospects dangled before him. Then again had come disillusion and the costly triumph of 1812. Now in 1814 this "Agamemnon of kings", self-dramatizing and self-assertive, saw himself as the man to save Europe from atheism and misrule, the peacemaker with a divine mission. Always prone to obscure mysticism, he had since 1813 been 'changed' in an evangelical sense; he was soon to come under the dominating influence of the Baroness von Krüdener, who saw in him the elect of God. Yet this prayer-meeting Tsar, a multiple contradiction, retained his earlier habits of a man of pleasure; nobody was to enter more spiritedly into the forthcoming gaieties of the Congress of Vienna. Even while posing as the lamb of peace he could not fail to be the social lion.

Metternich saw in him more than this: a *political* lion, an international predator. In the spring of 1814 Alexander was certainly
the most powerful figure in Europe. Over the ensuing months, however, his over-confident vanity rather ran away with him. He
deeply offended Louis XVIII of France, and later Talleyrand too.
He came to be fêted in England, where he mistakenly tried to hob-
nob with the Whig Opposition, and succeeded in affronting (and
being affronted by) high society in general and the Prince Regent
in particular; even the Whig Lord Grey wrote him off as "a vain
silly fellow". Metternich—in London also for these junketings and
skirmishes—was delighted to profit from the Russian *faux pas*.
More important, however, than the merely social events were the
Tsar's political plans for Europe; and of these the most alarming[1]
was the scheme for a restored, liberal, largely self-governing Poland
within the Russian Empire. To the Poles this seemed, as, indeed,
it was, too good to be credible. To aristocratic opinion inside Russia
it appeared dangerously quixotic. To Metternich too it looked
highly dangerous, not least because it was bound to threaten
Austria's own recent acquisitions in Southern Poland.

The rulers and diplomats of Europe began assembling at Vienna
after the defeat of Napoleon, in the late summer of 1814. The Congress that occupied the succeeding months produced a confusion of
high principles, acrimonious political squabbles, and social gaiety
on the grand scale. Metternich was in his element. "He swam",
wrote Treitschke, "as happily as a fish in the shining whirlpool."
There had probably never before been such a festive concentration
of European princes and aristocrats, such a welter of receptions,
balls, banquets, concerts, theatrical performances of every kind.
All these revels at least afforded some compensation for the political cold shoulder shown to the representatives of the minor
Powers who found themselves excluded from the discussions. The
Austrian Government spent a great deal on staging this prestige
demonstration of the Viennese *douceur de vivre*, while the Prussians contributed characteristically some imposing military
parades. The serious business of the Congress was, by contrast,
performed by a mere handful of diplomats, headed by Hardenberg
for Prussia, Nesselrode for Russia, Metternich for Austria, Castlereagh for Britain, and, soon, Talleyrand for France. Progress to-

---

[1] To all but the Prussians, who expected, and eventually received, handsome compensation in Saxony and Western Germany.

wards political solutions was slow, and the Prince de Ligne, asked how the Congress was going (*marcher*), replied with the famous quip: *Le Congrès ne marche pas: il danse.* By the end of 1814 there was, in fact, a complete break between, on the one side, the Austrian and British delegations and, on the other, the Russian and Prussian. Relations between Metternich and the Tsar could hardly have been worse; this was the point where Talleyrand seized his chance to promote France into the company of the major negotiators and actually concluded with Austria and Britain a secret treaty intended to thwart Prussia's designs upon Saxony.

As for the lofty principles that were publicly proclaimed by these tough bargainers, they were not all hypocrisy. The Tsar, Castlereagh, Hardenberg, Metternich, Talleyrand—each in his way wished to shape an era of peace and order for Europe. Necessarily, however, each was determined also to obtain the best settlement for his own country, and expediency overrode principle. With Metternich, indeed, expediency *became* a sort of principle. Gentz, the conservative publicist who acted as confidential adviser to Metternich, put it brutally: "The real purpose of the Congress was to divide among the conquerors the spoils of the vanquished."

Eventually, even before Napoleon's escape to Elba, compromise agreements were reached and a balance of power maintained. With the territorial arrangements Metternich and the Habsburgs could be well satisfied. In return for the surrender of the Netherlands and Austria's Rhine lands they won back Salzburg, the Tyrol, Illyria, and Lombardy; they also retained Venetia. Thus in return for a scattered empire they gained one that was geographically compact and dominant over the Italian peninsula. In addition, Austria succeeded in keeping part of Poland (Galicia) and in preserving for its king the independence of part of Saxony (including Dresden and Leipzig). Prussia took the rest, together with lands of high potential importance in Western Germany, including the valleys of the Lower Moselle, Saar, and Ruhr. She surrendered some of her old Polish lands but retained Posen and Thurn. The Russian colossus, though it took Finland and most of Poland, was held back from bestriding Europe as it had threatened to do early in 1814.

Austria henceforth for nearly half a century could overawe Italy by her physical presence and if need be by main force; to preserve her power in Germany required subtler means. During the Napoleonic period there had grown up for the first time throughout the German States a strong all-German sense of national identity. The new schools; the Romantic poets; university professors, most famous among them Fichte; politicians of the stamp of Stein, Humboldt, and Hardenberg; a whole generation, stimulated by the changes Napoleon had enforced, excited by the revival of Prussia after Jena and the victories of the War of Liberation, had glimpsed a vision of a new, united, federated Germany; and altogether eight separate proposals for German union were put before the Vienna Congress. Neither Castlereagh nor the Tsar was unfriendly to the idea; but to Metternich, as to Talleyrand, it was anathema. National Germany could come about only at the expense of multinational Austria. Fortunately Metternich thought 'Germany' was also impracticable, a political chimera.

The shape of the post-1815 Germany, which was to outlive its chief architect Metternich and to be refashioned half a century later by Prussian Bismarck, was a loose Confederation (*Bund*) of thirty-nine virtually independent states. Within this organization, with its Federal Diet (Assembly) at Frankfurt, Metternich could always rely on a majority of the princes of the smaller states, jealous of Prussia, to outvote any scheme for strengthening the central executive council, which remained in fact little more than a committee of ambassadors; 'executive' it decidedly was not. Nine of the thirty-nine princes came from the small district of Thuringia alone (population only 750,000); each had his own postal system, customs, coinage, even army in some cases; each had full powers of veto over the decisions of the whole *Bund*. Thus the political functioning of 'Germany' could be paralysed by Austria; and since the King of Prussia, Austria's only major rival in the *Bund*, was a timid conservative, as fearful of German nationalism as Metternich himself, for the time being and on the surface the omens looked favourable for a further lease of Habsburg life.

The King of Prussia, however, would not live for ever; after 1850 a new Prussia would emerge from the fusion of her military traditions with her industrial strength; and the Prussians of this next, Bismarckian, generation would forgive Metternich for his delaying rôle as little as the liberal patriots of his own day. The pages of Treitschke, for instance, whose celebrated *History of Germany in the Nineteenth Century* appeared between 1879 and 1895, are full of spleen against Metternich, this "Adonis of the salons," than whom none knew better how to initiate a diplomatic intrigue between dinner and a masked ball, how to dash off a dispatch before leaving for a rendezvous, or with an expression of the warmest tenderness in his fine blue eyes tell thoroughgoing lies to an intimate friend. . . . How miraculously had this ancient Austria, after so many defeats and losses, once again risen to a fullness of power . . .; rarely had a state at the conclusion of a world-wide war found itself so completely in possession of all its objectives. Metternich could be proud of how much he personally had contributed to this brilliant achievement by prudent procrastination and opportune expoitation of the Empire's powers; and since, in his early years, he already claimed to have foreseen and foretold everything, his egotism rose up to an immeasurable arrogance. The whole new order of European affairs appeared to him to be his own personal creation, the maintenance of this order the sole mission of his life. . . .

This Metternich, who "betrayed the German national spirit", had other than merely 'Austrian' reasons for his attitude. They deserve consideration. He was a cosmopolitan aristocrat of the Age of Reason. (His Catholicism was of an extremely mild and nominal kind.) He deplored fanaticism. Nationalism was to him a new disease; it was closely related to the revolutionary temper that had in his time torn Europe apart. To him Stein and his like were Jacobins; their fervent appeals to the German people displayed the spirit of revolution "hiding under the veil of patriotism". He saw nothing hopeful in the jingoism prevalent in the German universities at this time; to him it was hysterical, potentially dangerous, and vulgar. German unity he saw, therefore, as "an infamous objective".

The students' societies (*Burschenschaften*) originating in Jena University in 1815 and spreading rapidly through sixteen German universities, had begun in the flush of German revival and victory. At their most idealistic, they took on some of the moral fervour of the *Tugendbund*, the 'Moral and Scientific Union' founded in Prussia in 1808—earnest, patriotic, and liberal. But, not surprisingly, there was a good deal of fanaticism and folly in the students' movement. Moreover, not all the 'liberal' leaders were very liberal. Arndt's hatred of foreigners was rather stronger than his love of free institutions. Jahn, the father of the gymnastics movement, was a narrow-minded and violent patriot who loathed Jews and Frenchmen in equal measure. He tried to purge the German language of its foreign elements; he encouraged his fellow-countrymen to dress, as he did, in the "true German costume" and to preserve their racial purity. And this 'liberal' who so often spoke like the Nazis of a century later was already proclaiming the ominous Teutonic doctrine:

Germany needs a war of her own to feel her power; she needs a quarrel with the French way of life to develop her own national way of life to the full.

Physical exercise, language purification, and the rest were side issues. The real issue was German unification, which would destroy the Habsburg Empire—and very likely Prussia as well, with its million Polish inhabitants. "The gymnastic institution is the real training ground for the university mischief," wrote Metternich of Jahn and his followers. "One has to grasp the evil by the roots." The opportunity to do so was soon to be handed to him.

In October 1817 the Wartburg Festival was held at Eisenach to commemorate two anniversaries—the three-hundredth of the Lutheran Reformation and the fourth of the victory over Napoleon at Leipzig. Professors made speeches; students sang songs; a great bonfire, reminiscent of Luther's, was fed with a miscellany of unpopular books, a copy of the (un-German) *Code Napoléon*, and various symbols of authority and reaction. Among the books was a *History of Germany* by Kotzebue, an unimportant but much-resented German dramatist, who had just returned home after long service in St Petersburg, and was now acting as an informer for the Tsar Alexander. Seventeen months after the Wartburg Festival Kotzebue was murdered at Mannheim by a member of the Erlangen Students' Society, an unbalanced young theology student who had conceived a religious mission to rid Germany of a traitor.

It was enough to provide Metternich with the pretext he needed. He may even have been as frightened of the growing spirit of nationalism and revolt as he claimed to be. Already at the Congress of Aix-la-Chapelle (Aachen),[2] to which once-imperial city the European sovereigns and ministers had repaired in 1818, admitting France back into full and equal membership of the "Concert of Europe", he had been preparing the ground. On his way to Aix he had visited Frankfurt, the seat of the Federal Diet; a letter sent from there to his wife illustrates well his serene confidence and egotism:

[2] "Never", said Metternich, "have I seen a prettier little Congress."

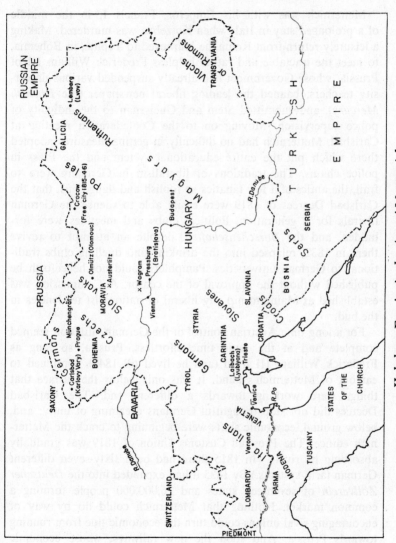

Habsburg Empire in the Age of Metternich

I came to Frankfurt like the Messiah to free sinners. The Diet took on a new appearance directly I busied myself with its affairs; the seemingly impossible was accomplished.

Metternich was with his Emperor, Francis I, in the middle of a prolonged stay in Italy when Kotzebue was murdered. Making a leisurely return from Rome, he journeyed to Teplitz, in Bohemia, to meet the tractable and rather helpless Frederick William III of Prussia, whose Government had already suspended various university teachers, banned the leading liberal newspaper (the *Rhenish Mercury*), and submitted Stein and Gneisenau to the indignity of police supervision. Moving on to the Confederation meeting at Carlsbad, Metternich had no difficulty in getting measures adopted there which put the entire educational system and the Press in police chains. The traditions of liberalism in Germany were so frail, the antics of a few fanatics so foolish and dangerous, that the Carlsbad Decrees of 1819 were easily able to silence the German liberals for a generation. Political clubs and meetings were forbidden, and the *Burschenschaften*, despite an attempt to revive them in 1832, relapsed into the drinking and duelling clubs traditional to German universities. Pamphlets could not henceforth be published without the approval of the censor. A Commission was established at Mainz to nip any liberal or nationalist tendencies in the bud.

For a long time Austrian control of the German situation seemed complete and at the same time effortless. Prussia, so long as Frederick William III lived (and he lived till 1840), continued to eat out of Metternich's hand. It was only below the surface that things were working towards a different end. The Carlsbad Decrees did not stop thoughtful Germans dreaming of unity; and, below ground, economic shifts were beginning to crack the Metternich edifice. The Prussian Customs Union of 1819 was gradually absorbing its rivals. (In 1815 there had been sixty-seven different German tariff systems.) By 1833 it had expanded into the *Deutscher Zollverein* of seventeen states and 26,000,000 people forming a common market. Nothing that Metternich could do by way of encouraging rival unions could turn the economic tide from running towards Prussia. And soon the new railways, whose economic and political importance Metternich was to understand very well, would prove far easier to build in flat Prussia than in mountainous Austria.

The King of Prussia had been drawn into Metternich's camp with the utmost ease; the Tsar Alexander presented a trickier proposition. His head swirled with contradictory theories. In Italy his agents encouraged anti-Austrian revolutionary agitation. In France his intrigues appeared to countenance the danger of another revolution. Those few German princes who wished to liberalize their states in 1815 looked to the Tsar for support. On the other hand, the obscurantist Kotzebue had been in Russian pay, and the ultra-reactionary Ferdinand VII of Spain, whose revival of the Inquisition shocked Gentz and Metternich, seemed to be hand-in-glove with the Tsar, who was even toying with the idea of assisting in the suppression of the South American revolutions. Everybody agreed with Talleyrand that Russia "meddled in every concern", though the phlegmatic Duke of Wellington did brush it all aside as "bustle and intrigue". Where, in any case, was the Tsar wishing to lead Europe? Simultaneously, it appeared, in contrary directions. The only fixed thing in the Tsar's opinions was that he was the instrument designed by heaven to save the world from the forces of moral evil and political disorder.

To preserve European peace the victorious Powers had in 1815 formed the Quadruple Alliance. Alexander, not content with so utilitarian a body, proposed to endow it with high morality and mystery by converting it into a Holy Alliance of Christian monarchs. From the beginning the down-to-earth Castlereagh considered this "a piece of sublime mysticism and nonsense", and Metternich wrote it down as "a loud-sounding nothing". Little that came out of Russia was good to Metternich[3]; as for the Tsar, the only fortunate thing about his character, he bitterly observed, was his lack of courage. However, as the frightened conservative inside the Tsar began to get the better of the starry-eyed liberal, Metternich saw in this preposterous Holy Alliance an instrument for his own purposes. The Tsar read with alarm the mounting story of insurrection and political murder during 1819–20: in Germany Kotzebue; in France the murder of the heir to the throne; in Spain an apparently successful liberal revolution; in Naples a military revolt that obliged the Bourbon king to grant a constitution.

At the next meeting of the European Congress, at Troppau, in Silesia, in October 1820, Metternich finally captured Alexander for

[3] Except possibly Princess Bagration and Countess Lieven, at various times his mistresses.

his European system, as he had already captured the King of Prussia. The fact that Britain and France, the constitutional Powers, held somewhat aloof from Troppau, certainly detracted from the unanimity of the European alliance; but it also meant that the three despotic Powers there—the Holy Alliance of Russia, Prussia, and Austria—were able to concert policies of stability and order entirely to Metternich's taste. The Tsar confessed privately the error of his earlier ways. He told Metternich:

> Today I deplore everything that I said or did between the years 1815 and 1818. I regret the time lost; we must study to retrieve it. . . . Tell me what you want me to do, and I will do it.

The three Powers proceeded to draw up the Troppau Protocol, setting out those celebrated 'principles' which express the essence of the Metternich system and finally antagonized British, and much French, opinion—even that of the firmly conservative Castlereagh, who shared many ideals in common with Metternich:

> States which have undergone a change of government due to revolution, the results of which threaten other States, *ipso facto* cease to be members of the European Alliance and remain excluded from it until the situation gives guarantees for legal order and stability. If, owing to such alterations, immediate dangers threaten other States, the Powers bind themselves, by peaceful means, or if need be by arms, to bring back the guilty State into the bosom of the Great Alliance.

The ferment in Germany had subsided; more dangerous unrest now lay in Italy, an area crucial to the Habsburgs after 1815. Italians under Napoleon had been exploited by high taxation, by military conscription, by the loss of their art treasurers; but at least Napoleon had taken pains, however cynically, to flatter the nascent Italian sense of nationhood. The Habsburgs who returned to Northern Italy in 1815 as 'legitimate' monarchs, appeared deliberately to flout the Italian spirit. The Civil Service was purged and henceforth dominated by Germans in faraway Vienna. The provinces were garrisoned by a Habsburg army that Italians saw as a symbol of Austrian arrogance. Yet by current Italian standards Austrian rule in Lombardy-Venetia *was* enlightened. It maintained Napoleon's Concordat and most of his Civil Code. The rights of the peasants were upheld against the landlord. Taxes were lower than under the French. Primary schooling was of a higher standard than in the great majority of European states.

Against this the rulers of the rest of Italy could set little besides petty tyranny and inefficiency, though in Tuscany and Marie-Louise's Parma the reaction was relatively mild. In Sardinia-Piedmont the restored House of Savoy in the person of Victor Emmanuel I had reintroduced most of the privileges and bigotry of the *ancien régime*. In the Papal States, despite the administrative reforms of the able Cardinal Consalvi, the powerful influence of clerical reactionaries and obscurantists militated (as Metternich himself noted) against every principle of good government or of enlightened Christianity. In the south the restored Bourbon Ferdinand II ruled Naples and Sicily,[4] possibly the most poverty-stricken state in Europe, in a notoriously autocratic and inefficient way. It was not surprising that discontent was rife throughout Italy; yet the diversity of the grievances, the difficulties of communication and above all the general political repression that forced every reformer to become a conspirator, denied all immediate prospects for an Italian national movement. Such revolutionary activity as there was—the most important was that of the secret *Carbonari*—was largely limited to local objectives. Metternich himself did not consider Italian unity an end any more worthy or practicable than German unity. "Italy" was but a "geographical expression". History was against its unification. The typical Italian, moreover, was not to be taken very seriously as a political animal. Schism and mutual dislike were too much a part of the Italian inheritance. "In Italy province hates province," he wrote, "town hates town, family hates family, individual hates individual. . . . *L'Italien crie beaucoup, mais il n'agit pas.*"

On his earlier 1817 visit Metternich had taken a rosy view both of the Italian situation itself and of his own powers of dealing with it. "My presence in Italy", he reported with customary self-satisfaction, "has an incalculable effect." In 1820–21, however, there was agitation in Italy that demanded to be taken seriously. Ferdinand of Naples had originally in 1815 accepted his country's wartime English-inspired constitution. Then on Metternich's insistence

---

[4] Metternich had at first favoured the retention of Joachim Murat as King of Naples—which many said was not unconnected with the continuing influence upon the Austrian minister of his old flame, Caroline, sister to Napoleon and wife to Murat. When, however, Murat declared for Napoleon during the Hundred Days he gave Metternich a probably welcome excuse to throw him over. Murat, rash to the last, landed on the Calabrian coast, was court-martialled, and shot.

he had promised in 1816 to annul it and never grant another. Now, however (July 1820), under the threat of a Carbonarist military revolt, he ceded a liberal constitution with what Metternich considered indecent haste. He then proceeded to use his Neapolitan troops to quell the separatist rebellion of his island subjects in Sicily. Summoned to the Congress at Laibach, whither it had adjourned from Troppau, the false and compliant Ferdinand found no difficulty in renouncing the oath he had so recently taken to maintain the constitution, and he was restored as absolute monarch by an Austrian army. The southern Carbonari were crushed; the Holy Alliance had scored an easy victory; and Naples and Sicily continued to be ruled by the unholy alliance of police espionage, clerical censorship, and firing squad.

The Carbonarist troubles spread that same year of 1821 to the north, in Piedmont. Victor Emmanuel abdicated, and, in the absence of the new king, the regent Prince Charles Albert granted a constitution. His liberalism was paper-thin; but at least he was at one with his people in hating Austrians. Once again Austrian and Russian armies took the field in a common cause, and the revolution was quickly extinguished.

Inside Austrian Italy itself there was trouble too that year. An anti-Austrian conspiracy was unearthed in Milan, and its authors served long prison terms in the fortress of Spielberg. Among them were patriots such as Count Confalonieri, whose death sentence was commuted to one of life imprisonment, and Silvio Pellico, the poet who published on his release in 1832 an eloquent account of prison brutality that shocked liberal and humane opinion throughout Europe. The reputations of the Habsburg Government, of the Emperor Francis and of Metternich himself, were certainly blackened by the affair and its publicity. But it must be remembered that to Metternich, and still more emphatically to his master the Emperor, these men were not romantic idealists. They were Jacobins whose activities could turn Europe back into chaos; they were therefore fortunate to have been spared execution.

Jacobinism had been quenched in Germany and Italy. Spain remained; and 'Congress Europe' met once again, in Verona in 1822, to consider how best to beat out in that country the flames of liberal revolt. By this time Castlereagh, who had himself mistrusted all such foreign intervention, was dead; his successor, Canning, was known to be even more strongly opposed to it.

Thus Britain was lost to the forces of the Congress. France, however, was firm: the French Government of Chateaubriand seemed as anxious as the Tsar himself to be awarded the privilege of suppressing the revolutionary régime in Madrid. Of the two governments, Metternich preferred Chateaubriand's, and was even ready to lend moral support to the French army that cake-walked across Spain and restored 'legitimate' Ferdinand for a last decade of misrule. Politics so often—indeed, almost always—involved a choice of evils. Ferdinand VII was an evil. Russian intervention would have been an evil. French intervention itself carried a risk of evil; it was, after all, only eight years after Waterloo. But over and above all these lay the ultimate evil of the Revolution. To keep it at bay Metternich had by now made his life's ambition.

As it turned out, the Spanish business was the last in which the Alliance could act successfully in concert. Britain under Canning's direction was soon giving military assistance to the Portuguese liberals and recognizing the independence of the revolutionary governments of South America. The Greek revolt against the Turks offered no such clear-cut solution on conservative 'principles' as the situations in Germany, Italy, and Spain seemed to present. No Christian 'Holy Alliance' could be expected to intervene on behalf of a Muslim Sultan. Indeed, Metternich would have welcomed a strong, Christian, monarchical, independent Greece. What he did not wish to see was a client state of either Russia or Britain.

It was not, however, Habsburg policy to see the Turkish Empire disintegrate, any more now than in 1809 when at Tilsit Napoleon and Alexander contemplated a partition. Gentz, Metternich's chief personal adviser, wrote in 1815 that the Austrian Empire would not survive long if the Turkish Empire disappeared, and Metternich's influence over the Tsar Alexander was never put to a tougher test than in 1822, when he managed to persuade him against unconditional support for the Greek cause, with a full-scale attack on Turkey. Francis I hailed this as his chief minister's greatest diplomatic triumph.

It was only temporary. Alexander died in 1825, and in 1828 his successor Nicholas I did launch Russian armies on the road to Constantinople. For a time it seemed that there might be an Anglo-Austrian alliance to stem the Russian tide. But not for the first or the last time there was a *volte-face* by the Russians. In 1829 Nicholas was persuaded, partly by his own advisers, partly by the toughness of the resistance, to conclude peace with the Turks (giving independence to the Greeks) at Adrianople. The following year came the second wave of European revolutions that gave the despotic monarchs plenty of common grounds for fright. In 1833 at Münchengrätz Nicholas came to Metternich, so he said, "as pupil to master". The Emperors of Russia and Austria and the King of Prussia—the core of the old Holy Alliance—met together once again to reaffirm the solidarity of their interests—suppression of "the Revolution" and no partition of Turkey. Metternich had perhaps been fortunate with Nicholas. Even so, A. J. P. Taylor considers that

> to keep the peace between Russia and Austria and yet to prevent any further Russian advance in the Near East was Metternich's greatest diplomatic achievement, all the greater for his rating it less highly than his struggle against "the revolution".

Nevertheless the couple of decades during which Metternich had (as he put it) "sometimes governed Europe", or at least given the illusion of doing so, were ending. The scenery of the European stage was being moved, and Metternich was in the position of being left speaking all the old lines of a play that the audience had ceased listening to. A good many of his old fellow-actors, too, had left or were leaving—Napoleon in 1821, Castlereagh and Hardenburg in 1822, the Tsar Alexander in 1825, Gentz (his intellectual prop and personal confidant) in 1832, the Emperor Francis his master in 1835. In retrospect they seemed giants: "all the world today is made by men of such pitiable stamp. It is hard indeed to play well with such poor actors."

To the world of his private affairs these years had also brought great changes and the realization that he was past the meridian. The self-portrait of Metternich presented to the world in his voluminous memoirs is of so self-justifying, stilted, and infallible a figure that the reader is liable to forget he was vulnerable flesh and blood at all. Sometimes the only facet of his character that seems quite human is his philandering; yet his very reputation as a "society hero" makes it harder to remember that he was, if not a faithful husband, at least a devoted father. The children of his first marriage all lived under the cloud of their mother's consumption, and in 1820 within a few months of each other both his beloved daughters died. The three remaining children were sent away from Austria for the good of their health; they were all destined to die

before their father. His wife, from whom, for all his numerous
affairs of the heart, he had never been estranged, herself died in
1825. He was sadly conscious of the stealthy advance of the decay
that attacks men as well as empires. He married again in 1827, but
his young wife died in childbirth. At the age of fifty-seven he took
a third wife, thirty years his junior; she bore him two sons.

It was the political world, doubtless, that he was referring to
when he made the frequently quoted remark:

> My life coincides with a detestable period. At present I am
> good for nothing. I spend my life underpinning buildings in decay

—but the sentiments were true of the often dispirited private man.
"My life is very like a clock; I move to mark the hours." And
when amid the revolutions of 1830 the signs were unmistakable that
the "Europe of Metternich" was in dissolution he wrote some celebrated lines to the Russian minister, Nesselrode:

> For the rest, my most secret thought is that the old Europe
> has come to the beginning of the end. Resolved to perish with it, I
> shall know how to do my duty. . . . From another point of view
> the new Europe is not yet begun; between the end and the be-
> ginning lies chaos.

For the fashionable progressive opinions around him he had
only contempt. Yet somehow, in some never specified way, there
would be progress. Perhaps he should have been born "in 1900
with the twentieth century before me" (alas, it would have brought
him little joy):

> It may be that someone in the year 2240 will discover my name,
> and tell the world that in the distant past there was at least one
> man less limited than the mass of his contemporaries. . . .

The Vienna settlement of Europe received a series of shocks in
1830–31. The Bourbons were expelled from France by the July
Revolution. The Belgians rose in revolt against the Dutch, and a
combination of French military intervention and Franco-British
diplomacy eventually secured their independence. There was a
Polish national revolt, and some rumblings of excitement and riot
even among the politically sleepy states of Germany. Throughout
Italy—most immediately alarming to the Habsburg position—
there was a fresh stirring of the troubles of ten years earlier. The
Pope's authority was overthrown in the Romagna and elsewhere;
Marie Louise fled from rebellious Parma to the shelter of the

Austrian garrison at Piacenza; Modena lay in the hands of the patriots—until once again, as in 1820–21, Austrian armies moved in to quell the revolts and re-establish the old order. By 1832, on the surface at least, Metternich and the Tsar had defeated "the Revolution" and reasserted conservative authority everywhere but in France and Belgium. Even Louis Philippe, the new French king, though contaminated by "the Revolution", proved the least Jacobinical and most conservative of liberals.

For Europe in general, and for the survival of the Habsburgs, Metternich aimed throughout to achieve a standstill; in Austrian internal affairs, however, he aspired to be something of a reformer. On various occasions he tried to persuade Francis I to set up an Imperial Council modelled on Napoleon's Council of State, whose functioning he had watched and admired at close quarters in his old ambassadorial days. (Napoleon, the old enemy, always remained for him the greatest of men.) A stern supporter of the monarchical principle, he had no wish to weaken the Emperor's power, but an Imperial Council (*Reichsrat*) would be a means of "restraining the ruler from momentary impulses" and of associating all the scattered peoples of the Empire with the formation of policy. Francis, "good Kaiser Franz", whose stiff-necked conservatism makes Metternich's seem by contrast supple, promised from time to time over eighteen years to consider these proposals. He died in 1835 with them still locked away in a drawer. "Peoples?" he once asked. "What does that mean? I only know subjects."

This problem of how, in an age of infectious national self-awareness, to contain the constituent provinces and cultures of the Empire was probably insoluble. Metternich laboured constantly at it. There did exist ancient Diets in Bohemia, Hungary, and Croatia, but there were none in the remaining provinces. What Metternich wanted the Emperor to accept was a rational extension of the system of Diets, so that there would be six, representing major cultural groupings: one for Austria proper and the predominantly German areas; one for Lombardy-Venetia; one for Hungary and Croatia; one for Transylvania in the east; one for the 'West Slavs', the Czechs, Slovaks, and Poles in Bohemia, Moravia, and Galicia; and one for the 'South Slavs' (Yugoslavs) in Illyria and Dalmatia. It was not that Metternich intended these nationalities to enjoy the substance of power, but he hoped that by patronizing their cultural revival he could draw the teeth of the extremer political nationalism.

His tidy scheme did not materialize. The national groups were not in the end to be denied their proud ambitions, their passionate patriotisms, their suicidal mutual hatreds.

Most passionate and articulate of all were the Magyars of Hungary. Still, even in the eighteen-forties, they constituted only a quarter of the peoples of the province of Hungary; non-Slav and non-German, they comprised in general the Hungarian aristocracy and gentry. They looked down on the Slavs; they resented the Germans; and they enjoyed a proud sense of their historical identity. Already in 1825 and 1830 they put forward demands for Magyar to be accepted as the official language in Hungary, in place of German or Latin. Meanwhile the aristocratic, 'Whiggish' nationalism of the older Hungarian leaders—Szechenyi chief among them—was ousted by the fiery fanaticism of Louis Kossuth, who preached that Hungary must become a fully independent national state, run by Magyars (the minority) for Magyars, to the greater glory of the Magyar soul. Metternich had countenanced Szechenyi's cultural nationalism; Kossuth's would mean ruin for the Habsburgs. As it turned out in 1849, it was to mean, after his brief stormy dictatorship, ruin for Kossuth too.

One of the factors in that ruin was to be the hostility of the Croat aristocracy and people. The Croats, South Slavs, possessed a Diet as ancient as the Hungarian. They had no wish to be a subject minority in a Magyar state. They long championed Latin against Magyar as the official tongue, but in the end the spirit of the age captured them too. Sauce for the goose was sauce for the gander, and in 1847 the last Latin decree of the Croat Diet fixed Croatian as the official *national* language. In Bohemia too over these years Czech cultural nationalism was growing, patronized by the members of the Bohemian Diet, all landowners and most of them not in the racial-linguistic sense Czechs at all. But the time was coming when the true Czechs would speak to some purpose. For Metternich as for Hamlet "the times were out of joint"; to set them right would be more than any statesman could hope for. The most that he could do was to apply his famous "principles"; hostility to liberalism, to democracy, to revolution, to separatist nationalism.

Since 1835, when Francis I died, Metternich's personal position in Vienna had deteriorated. The new Emperor Ferdinand was both epileptic and feeble-minded: "the next thing to an idiot," said Palmerston. Among the other leading members of the Habsburg family, who therefore acquired enhanced importance, there was no unanimity. Archduke Lewis generally supported and was supported by Metternich; but Archduke John, who had liberal sympathies, and other leading Habsburgs, who emphatically had not, possessed little love for him or his policies. Moreover, in domestic affairs Metternich was obliged to yield much of his authority to the Bohemian, Kolowrat, and between Kolowrat and Metternich there was strong mutual distrust and dislike. Already before the 1848 Revolutions Metternich's position was under all kinds of stress.

These uprisings, which embraced half Europe in 1848, had begun during the two preceding years. Long-standing dissensions between Catholics and Liberals in Switzerland had deteriorated by mid-1847 into revolution and civil war. In the previous year, 1846, there had been an insurrection of the Polish nobility against Habsburg authority in Galicia, and Metternich did not scruple, in quelling it, to foment a revolt of the peasantry against their landlords. In so doing he showed that as yet Polish nationalism was limited to the aristocracy; it was not yet a fully popular movement. Austria now annexed the free city of Cracow, the centre of the revolt, and Metternich appeared to have won a victory. But in Europe generally the leaky boat of the Vienna settlement was fast shipping water. There were presages of revolt in Paris; in Rome there had arrived in 1846 an apparently liberal Pope, an event of huge (though as it turned out false) encouragement to revolutionaries throughout Italy. By 1847 the cities of Lombardy were in such a state of tension that Austrian troops were confined to barracks for fear that their presence in the streets would provoke an explosion. The Magyars too, intoxicated by the threats and promises of Kossuth, were on the verge of revolution. In Bohemia the Czech 'nation' grew more conscious of itself every month. Throughout Germany, ever since the accession of Frederick William IV in 1840, the liberal-nationalist tide had run more strongly. In every great urban centre the economic depression of 1846–47 provided a catalyst for rebellion. The discontent of a peasantry still not free from feudal dues was general, however ill organized. In Vienna itself, and particularly in the University, the police could no longer hope to suppress the liberal clubs. When in February 1848 revolution came to Paris and Louis Philippe fled, Metternich's already waterlogged craft was ready to sink.

On March 10th a Vienna state official came to warn Princess

Metternich to put her jewellery in a safe place. Magyar student rebels were already in the streets of Budapest and Pressburg; the radicals in Prague were taking over the initiative from the Diet. On March 12th Metternich tried, and failed, to carry the Imperial government with him in a proposal to summon an Estates-General of the provincial Diets. The Court was no longer behind him. The popular liberal demand for his removal coincided with the desire of his influential enemies to be rid of him: Metternich the supreme conservative was being ditched by a Court essentially more conservative, more reactionary, less rational, than he—but readier to attempt a compromise with the growing hubbub.

Before the Imperial Council, on March 13th, he fruitlessly advocated toughness against the "rabble" in the streets below. The Archduchess Sophia saw her chance to oust the imbecile Ferdinand and place her own son Francis-Joseph on the throne. As for Ferdinand—"tell the people," he said, "that I agree to everything."

Metternich resigned. Five days later Lombardy broke into open revolt. All over the Habsburg dominions and the lands of Germany revolution blazed away. The seventy-five-year-old Chancellor slipped out of Vienna where he had been in power nearly forty years. After a month of hazardous and uncomfortable travel he reached at last the Brunswick Hotel in Hanover Square, London. In London, that haven for exiles of every hue, or in Brighton, he lived for eighteen months the life of an English gentleman, surrounded by Englishmen. The old confidence and equable temper, the old charm and diplomacy—and happily the aura of civilized living—had not deserted him. "The English people," he reported, "are prodigiously sensible." It was gratifying to be so constantly recognized and pointed out in the streets. "If I had passed my life in London, and if I were English, I could not see myself surrounded by a greater number of friends."

He still had a decade before him. Full of the conviction of his own essential rightness, he watched the revolutions of 1848 one by one collapse. He stayed for a time in Brussels; then at his Johannesthal estate in West Germany; at last in 1851 he was able to return to Vienna, where he took the "pretty villa" in which he lived out the rest of his days. Italy and Hungary had been reconquered; Habsburg absolutism was back in the saddle. Emperor, Army, and Church were again supreme. A new Concordat was soon made with the Pope (violently recovered from his 'liberalism'), by which the Catholic religion in Austria was given privileges and powers which it had long before lost (in the days of Joseph II) and never enjoyed under Metternich. The old man approved, however. He approved too of the arrangement by which Bach, the new Minister of the Interior, never became Prime Minister. The young Emperor Francis-Joseph was, and remained, his own Prime Minister.

Metternich lived long enough to hear of the Battle of Magenta, the beginning of the end of the Austrian Empire in Italy. He died in June 1859. One of the last contemporary pen-portraits of him was by Count Hübner, who visited him eleven days before his death:

> When I left [Hübner wrote] he said to me repeatedly and emphatically, "I was a rock of order." I closed the door but opened it quietly again to take one more look at the great states-man. There he sat at his desk, his pen in hand, looking up in contemplation, erect, cold, proud, distinguished, just as I had seen him many times before in the Chancellery in the full light of his power. ... After a time he noticed me at the door, fixed upon me a long look of profound benevolence, and said, half to me, half to himself, "A rock of order."

Table of Events

1773.	Metternich born at Coblenz.
1792.	Austria at war with revolutionary France. Francis I Emperor.
1796–1801.	Austria twice defeated by Bonaparte in Italy.
1805.	Third Coalition defeated at Ulm and Austerlitz.
1806.	Metternich Austrian ambassador in Paris.
1809.	Austria again defeated; Wagram. Metternich Foreign Minister, supports Napoleon-Marie-Louise marriage.
1813.	Dresden meeting; Metternich joins Fourth Coalition.
1814–15.	Napoleon defeated. Congress of Vienna.
1818.	Congress of Aix-la-Chapelle.
1819.	Carlsbad Decrees. Holy Alliance.
1820–21.	First wave of post-war revolutions (Spain, Portugal, Italy, Greece). Congresses of Troppau and Laibach. Austro-Russian intervention in Italy.
1822.	Congress of Verona sanctions French intervention in Spain.
1830–31.	Second wave of liberal and nationalist revolutions (France, Belgium, Italy, Germany, Poland).
1833.	Holy Alliance meeting at Münchengrätz. Near Eastern crisis.
1835.	Death of Francis I. Ferdinand I succeeds.
1840 onward	Revival of German liberalism.
1846.	Polish revolt in Galicia; Cracow annexed.
1848.	Revolution in Vienna and throughout Europe. Resignation and flight of Metternich. Abdication of Ferdinand I.
1848–49.	Liberal and nationalist revolutions universally crushed.
1851.	Metternich back in Vienna.
1859.	Death.

3

BOLÍVAR

(1783–1830)

And South American Independence

In 1780, when George III's British subjects in the Thirteen Colonies
of North America were in full revolt, the inclination of the states
of Western Europe to assist the rebels proved irresistible. In that
year Charles III of Spain joined France and Holland in making
war against Britain and helped to provide arms for the American
rebels. In retrospect it may be thought a dangerous encouragement
for him to have given the subjects of his own American dominions.
Until this time no one in South or Central America had contemplated the possibility of independence from Spain, and for some
years yet few did so. But for the educated Spaniards in Mexico
City or Caracas or Lima or Santiago or Buenos Aires, a number of
whom were already beginning somewhat academically to discuss
the writings of such French *philosophes* as Montesquieu, Voltaire,
Rousseau, or Raynal, events in the far north would certainly not go
unremarked.

These American provinces of the King of Spain were of prodigious extent. To the north lay Mexico or *New Spain*, a huge area
comprising not only modern Mexico and the states of Central
America but also Florida, Texas, New Mexico, Arizona, and
California. Along the north of the South American sub-continent
lay two more provinces: *Venezuela* with its chief city of Caracas,
Bolívar's birthplace, and inland the hot plains over which the cowboys called *llaneros* rode their herds; and *New Granada*, whose
port of Cartagena during the six weeks of its annual fair became
one of the great centres of world trade—three weeks away, by boat
and mule, from the capital city of Santa Fe de Bogotá, high in the
remote Andes. Southward again lay *Peru*, whose principal city of
Lima shared with Mexico City the dignity of housing a Viceroy and

a university. (At the close of the eighteenth century both Lima and Mexico City were more populous than New York.) Many hundreds of miles away to the south-east, 13,600 feet above sea-level in what is now Bolivia, was the chief source of Peru's legendary wealth, the silver mines of Potosí. *Chile* in the south-west lay narrowly for 3000 miles between the Andes and the Pacific—desert in the north, bleak and rain-soaked in the south towards Cape Horn, but in the centre, in the neighbourhood of the capital, Santiago, a land of such "paradise valleys" as that which gave its name to Valparaiso. Eastward round the Horn and lying between it and the Portuguese colony of Brazil were the widely scattered settlements centred upon the *River Plate*—Buenos Aires, Montevideo, and (nearly 1000 miles up-river) Asuncion, respectively today the capitals of the states of Argentina, Uruguay, and Paraguay.

It was an empire ruled, in theory at least, despotically. These enormous territories were simply the property of the Spanish Crown, governed under the direction of the Council of the Indies in Madrid. Despotism, however, did not necessarily imply tyranny, and the Spanish Crown had always considered that it had a special duty to protect the Indian from excessive exploitation by the settler. Indeed, one of the reasons why the Thirteen Colonies had enjoyed a much greater degree of self-government than the Spanish colonies was simply that the British Government had been infinitely more careless than the Spanish. A similar contrast in British and Spanish colonial philosophies is illustrated by their attitudes to the growth of towns and municipal life. In North America towns arose casually, pragmatically, to meet the varying challenges of the frontier. In Spanish America they were sited like Roman camps, with their rectangular street plans, their town centres (*plaza mayor*), cathedral, and law-courts (*audiencia*), their mayor, aldermen, and town council (*cabildo*). These *cabildos* easily declined into comfortable local oligarchies with only slight powers, but their part in the upheavals of the revolutionary era was to be important. Spain's empire in America diffused her culture over dominions at least as extensive as the Roman Empire, and, like Rome's, Spain's influence was long to outlive her political and military defeat.

Spanish America was royal; it was also, and essentially, Catholic. For centuries after Columbus took possession of the New World in the names of the King of Spain and the True Cross, Spanish civilization carried a missionary flavour. Fine Christian churches sprang up everywhere. The Inquisition came. The cults of the conquered Indian were assimilated or accommodated. The Catholic cathedral could easily become an extension of his temple; Catholic worship grafted readily on the stock of his pagan superstition. Spanish and Indian art and architecture became intimately mingled; the carved Christ was transmogrified into an Indian, the Indian goddess into the Blessed Virgin. Among 100,000 Indians of Paraguay the Jesuits even constructed their own version of a sort of paternal communism—until slave-raiders from neighbouring estates and finally a decree from the 'enlightened' Bourbon Charles III destroyed this impermissible "empire within an empire". On the other hand there was a record of cruelty and oppression, dark even by the rough standards of colonials, that no clerical or governmental good intentions had been able to prevent. It has been estimated, for instance, that in Mexico, in the first generation of Spanish conquest (1519–48), $18\frac{1}{2}$ millions of the original 25 millions of Indian inhabitants were exterminated. The early days brought undoubted disaster to the Indians. It may be argued, however, that in settler-dominated North America the British, unhampered by Church or Crown, managed to exterminate an even bigger proportion of *their* Indians; the Spanish authorities may perhaps be allowed a limited credit.

Church and monarchy together provided the elements of cohesion among a great confusion of races and social classes. There were two distinct white groups—the European or 'Peninsular' Spaniards, mainly holders of appointments in Army, Church, or Government, including the governmental regulation of trade, and the much more numerous American-born Spaniards or Creoles, the class from whom Bolívar sprang. Far more numerous again than these white colonials were the peoples of Indian, Negro, or (most frequently) mixed blood: mulatto, mixed white and Negro; *mestizo* or *pardo* ('brown'), mixed white and Indian; or *zambo*, mixed Indian and Negro. Mulattoes and *mestizos* would provide most of the craftsmen and small traders; the Negroes and *zambos*, who might be either slaves or freed men, were mainly the plantation workers, miners, or domestic servants; the Creoles formed an aristocracy of landowners, mine-owners, and cattle-breeders.

The conflict of interests between the European Spaniards and the Creoles lay at the heart of the movement for independence. This had been sharpened during the century or so before Bolívar's birth

by Spain's long and hopeless attempt to enforce her rigidly mercan-
tilist system of trade. In return for such American products as raw
cotton, cocoa, coffee, quinine, indigo, maize, hides, gold, silver—
above all the inexhaustible, indispensable, but ultimately fatal silver
—Spain exported to the New World her European manufactures:
woollens, silks, hardwares, and so forth. All this trade was funnelled,
both ways, through the narrow bottleneck of one or other of her
monopoly ports on the Caribbean or Gulf of Mexico—Vera Cruz,
Portobello, or Cartagena. At sea everything had to move under
naval convoy, and on land by pack-horse, mule-train, or ox-wagon
over immense distances at very great expense. To the Spanish
settlers anxious to buy and sell in the open market it seemed a
ludicrous and vexatious situation imposed by the European
Spaniards in their own supposed interests (though, truly, Spain was
cutting her own throat); and during the late seventeenth and
eighteenth centuries a large illegal trade had developed with French,
Dutch, Portuguese, and British merchants, 'smugglers' ready to
supply American needs. Most insatiable of all was the demand for
Negro slaves, which Spain could not satisfy but Britain could, and
did—even 'legally' after the monopoly granted to her by the Treaty
of Utrecht (1713).

The attempts of official Spanish policy to put down smuggling
widened the rift between the Creoles and European Spaniards, and
in the many colonial wars between Spain and Britain the settlers
were often in an impossible position, "never knowing when a strange
sail appeared whether it was to be welcomed officially as a Spaniard,
received discreetly as a foreign trader, or fired on as a raider". The
smugglers did a good deal to improve South American prosperity.
They brought much-wanted cheap manufactures from Europe. They
played some part too in introducing a vital cargo—ideas. No book
could be legally printed or sold in America without the licence of the
Council of the Indies in Madrid; but the combined surveillance of
government officials and officers of the Inquisition was unable to
prevent Spanish Americans from eating the forbidden fruit of the
Age of Reason.

It would, however, be wrong to suppose that enlightenment was
introduced into Spanish America wholly surreptitiously by a pack
of smugglers. Much of it originated from Spain itself. The rigidities
of her Habsburg era gave way in the mid-eighteenth century to the
relative progressiveness of the Bourbons. They divided their Ameri-

can territories into provinces, each under an intendant on the French pattern. They abandoned the system of monopoly ports and allowed Spanish merchant ships to proceed *via* Cape Horn to Chile and Peru. They set up a chartered trade company which did much to develop the economy of Venezuela and multiply the wealth of its leading citizens. In 1778 they set all trade free *within the Spanish Empire.*

Nevertheless, as commonly in the history of revolutions, improvement and increasing wealth did not bring with it an era of contentment, but rather an enhanced dissatisfaction with those grievances that remained and alarm at any sudden dip in the upward path. As for the intendants, enlightened or no, they were not received with enthusiasm. They were all European Spaniards giving the often resentful colonials what was judged good for them; and where they did well-meaningly revive the *cabildos* they merely succeeded in promoting an inadmissible desire for local self-government. Similarly, as many of the old trading restrictions were relaxed, the demand grew for their total removal. When Buenos Aires was at last (in 1776) detached from the rule of the Viceroy in far Peru her prosperity leaped ahead so fast that the shock was all the greater when the wars following the French Revolution disrupted her economy.

Buenos Aires was to be one of the principal starting-points of the movement for South American liberation. From here San Martín was to cross the Andes, defeat the power of Spain in Chile and (partially) in Peru. The other chief starting-point lay far to the north in Bolívar's own birthplace of Caracas, in Venezuela, a full 5000 miles distant by sea from Buenos Aires. From Venezuela the liberation movement led by Bolívar was also to cross the Andes, expel Spanish power from New Granada (modern Colombia) and Quito (modern Ecuador), and complete the liberation of Peru as far south as modern Bolivia.

Venezuela was a country in three distinct stages of civilization: deep inland, primitive Indian country of forest, and river; then a wide belt of *llanos*, a pastoral country of treeless plains; and the rich agricultural and commercial coastal territory containing the big majority of Venezuela's 200,000 or so Spaniards—well over 90 per cent of them Creoles. This last was a district of which Humboldt, the great Prussian naturalist and traveller, who was in Caracas when Bolívar was a boy of thirteen, wrote as follows:

The coasts of Venezuela, by their length, their developments towards the east, the multiplicity of their ports and the safety of the anchorages in all seasons, profit by all the advantages which the inner sea of the Antilles offers. Nowhere else has illicit commerce with foreigners been more difficult to check. No wonder that this facility of commercial relations with the inhabitants of free America and with the peoples of an agitated Europe should have increased on the one hand opulence and ideas and on the other that restless hankering towards home rule indistinguishable from love of liberty and republican institutions.

Amid this "restless hankering", but nevertheless in very considerable comfort and ease, Bolívar was brought up. His father, Don Juan Vicente de Bolívar—by all accounts a turbulent fellow and a Don Juan indeed—died when the boy was too young to be much influenced by him, but he may be taken to typify much in the mood of the Creole aristocracy of his day. He was, for instance, one of the signatories of a letter (addressed to Miranda, the "great precursor" of the liberation movement) that complained how the top men of Caracas were treated "like vile slaves" and were forced to swallow insults from the Intendant and "every good-for-nothing Goth"—*i.e.* European Spaniard. They were ready, so they vowed, to follow Miranda to the death. This was in 1782, the year before young Bolívar's birth. By 1786 Juan Vicente Bolívar was dead.

Simón recorded that "he knew no father" other than the black slave-woman at whose breast he was suckled. (Many years later at the height of his fame he abandoned his place in a triumphal procession when he caught sight of her.) His mother also died while he was still a child. His upbringing lay in the hands of a succession of tutors, far the most important of whom was a certain Simón Rodriguez, who had been born Carreño but changed his name because of his part in revolutionary activities. He also went under the name of Robinson—which would seem puzzling until we discover that *Robinson Crusoe* was the one book allowed by Rousseau to the hero of his novel *Emile*, and that Rodriguez had swallowed Rousseau whole. The questing intelligence of the boy Bolívar, like that of the young Emile, was allowed to search for its own food. Nothing must be forced. The mind must flower under the influences of Nature. So a great deal of Bolívar's schooling, like Emile's, took place under open skies. He became a strong and daring swimmer and a horseman with an *iron seat* (it became his nickname later with the *llaneros*); short in stature but lean and tough; an en-

BOLÍVAR [99]

thusiast for life. It is no doubt easy enough to encourage in a twelve-
year-old boy a passion for walking and climbing and swimming and
riding, but Carreño-Rodriguez-Robinson, surely an unusual man,
did more. He communicated his own passion for ideas and ideals,
for the dreams of the era of revolution. Under the infection of his
enthusiasm Bolívar learned to read the French philosophers of the
Enlightenment—Voltaire, Montesquieu, Rousseau, and the rest.
(Later he taught himself to speak fluent French.) He was a Spanish
colonial, the heir of conquerors and friars and slave-owners, Simón
José Antonio de la Santísima Trinidad Bolívar y Palacios; he could
ride a horse like a *llanero*; he could expect to own great estates and
live like a lord—but intellectually he had become a French radical.
His favourite author was already Voltaire, his pattern and hero
soon to be Napoleon Bonaparte. Many years later he was to write
to this tutor of his:

> You formed my heart for liberty, for justice, for the great, the
> beautiful. . . . You cannot imagine how deeply your lessons im-
> pressed themselves upon my heart.

Twice as a young man Bolívar journeyed to Europe. On his first
visit he fell in love with a girl from Bilbao and at the age of eighteen
married her. Returning to Venezuela with him, within a few months
his wife was dead of fever. Bolívar vowed never to marry again, and
he did not—though his passionate nature never allowed him to
keep away from women for very long. "See how odd things are,"
he said many years later.

> If I had not become a widower, my life would have been al-
> together different. I should never have become General Bolívar,
> or the Liberator. . . . I should never have made my second visit to
> Europe, and it is unlikely that at Caracas or San Mateo any of
> those ideas would have come to me which came to me on my
> travels.

In Paris during 1803–4 life was not all ideas. He put in some
fairly strenuous months enjoying the pleasures of the town. Yet the
fleshly passions by no means excluded the political. It was the year
of Napoleon's imperial coronation, and Bolívar was both fascinated
and horrified. There is no need to doubt the sincerity of his words,
as quoted by his aide-de-camp and biographer O'Leary, that he had
worshipped Napoleon "as the hero of the Republic, the bright star
of glory, the genius of liberty", but that now Napoleon had made

himself Emperor, "from that day I looked upon him as a tyrant and a hypocrite". That was true; but it was true too, as Bolívar later admitted to another of his followers and memorialists, Colonel Lacroix, that it was politically necessary for him to put abroad that he thought Napoleon was a tyrant "to prevent the view gaining ground that my policy is an imitation of Napoleon, that my ambitions and plans are similar to his". All this was a question that would assume significance later, when it seemed Bolívar might indeed be travelling an imperial road; but, though he became a dictator, he did in fact remain true to his republicanism: "The crown laid upon Napoleon's head I looked on as a miserable thing. What seemed to be great was the universal acclaim." At least there was nothing culpable in chasing glory.

From Paris Bolívar travelled south with Rodriguez, crossing the Alps and touring Italy. It was while he was in Rome, one evening at sunset on the Aventine Hill, the "Sacred Mountain", that he swore the solemn oath that he would "not rest nor his mind be at peace" until he had broken the chains that bound his country to Spain. Rodriguez (admittedly it was long afterwards) wrote that Bolívar turned excitedly to him "with shining eyes, heaving breast, flaming cheeks, and fevered animation" and swore "by God, by his ancestors, by his honour and his fatherland". Is it possible that already by 1805 Bolívar's dreams of emulating Napoleon were formed and distinct? At least one of his modern biographers, Salvador de Madariaga, thinks so:

> Twice Simón Bolívar had seen Napoleon crown himself, the first time with the imperial Crown, the second, with the iron Crown of the kings of Lombardy. On Monte Sacro, Bolívar crowned himself in the presence of an imaginary world he fancied at his feet: he crowned himself a martyr or a hero, as fate might decide.

In Venezuela itself matters had developed not quite so fast or so far as in the romantic soul of Simón Bolívar. The chief burden of the Creole complaints against the Madrid Government had recently been the age-old white-settler grumble about 'softness' towards the blacks. These were the days of the Negro revolts in Haiti and elsewhere. In the 1780's there had been confused and bloody Indian risings in Upper Peru (modern Bolivia). There had been more recent rumblings in Venezuela too. One *zambo* leader had been executed and his head exhibited in a cage on a pole, *pour en-*

courager les autres. The chief citizens of Caracas had petitioned
Madrid to beware of raising the legal status of

> low people who make up the greater part of our cities and are by
> their nature proud, ambitious of honours and seeking to be the
> equals of the whites despite the lower class in which they were
> placed by the author of nature.

As for home rule, despite all the talk among the Creoles they
gave little enough support to Miranda when in 1806 he made his
first attempt at liberation. Miranda, after visiting the U.S.A.,
London, and Paris and developing a grandiose scheme for setting
up an independent empire of 'Colombia' to stretch from the
Mississippi to Cape Horn, had succeeded in interesting the younger
Pitt in his schemes. (Pitt in fact secured him a pension.) Eventually
it was with unofficial British naval backing that he made his unsuccessful attempt of 1806. "The Spaniards would have nothing to
say to us," wrote an Englishman aboard H.M.S. *Leander*. "They
had no thoughts of accepting our proffer of liberty and we could
not oblige them to take it. Miranda, so long the idol of his foolish
followers, is not known to them." He might well have pointed out as
well that Britain was a Power hostile to the Spanish crown, from
whom it had only recently taken Venezuela's off-shore island of
Trinidad. The citizens of Caracas were understandably hesitant.

Another and much larger project in the south, also attributable
to Miranda's influence, failed in that same year, 1806. The British,
having taken Buenos Aires, were straightway evicted by the loyal
populace; and although the citizens of Montevideo waxed fat for a
time on trade with the British it did not seem that the Spanish
American colonists, grumble though they certainly did, were sufficiently disloyal at heart to the King of Spain to undertake insurrection, with or without the support of the King's enemies. As for the
blacks and *mestizos*, why should they feel disloyalty to the Crown,
their only safeguard against Creole landlords and exploiters?

It was Napoleon's overthrow of the Spanish monarchy in 1808
that revolutionized the South American situation. Both Charles IV
and his son Ferdinand VII were forced to abdicate; the new King
of Spain and of Spanish America was Joseph Bonaparte. In Caracas
there was a threefold division of opinion when the news arrived.
The authorities stood by Joseph Bonaparte; a popular majority
shouted for Ferdinand VII and the house of Bourbon; and a small

conspiratorial group of rich Creoles, among whom was the young
Bolívar, were for taking British help and plumping for independence.
(They were rich and in many ways privileged; their position as revolutionaries has been compared with that of the 'Etonian com-
munists' in England a century later.)

When in 1810 a new Captain General arrived in Caracas he tact-
fully suggested that Bolívar should get out of town for a space, and
Bolívar was prudent enough to take his advice. He was not therefore
involved in the first acts of hostility to the Captain General that
took place on Holy Thursday 1810. By that time French armies
had overrun southern Spain and the news had just arrived of the
crushing of the patriotic *junta* in Seville. Some of the chief citizens
of Caracas now formed their own *junta* loyal to the Bourbon
Ferdinand VII and deported their Captain General in a Spanish
warship. Where Caracas had led in April the other capitals—Buenos
Aires, Bogotá, Santiago—followed during the remainder of 1810.
When the Caracas *junta* sought to get help from London in return
for commercial concessions, among the emissaries they sent Simón
Bolívar, who proved able in London to make contacts not only with
the British Government but with Miranda. The position of the
British was tricky: Spain was now their ally in the war against
Napoleon, a war they must win; yet they were strongly attracted
to the prospects of trade with independent South American states
whose actions and representatives (especially the 'Jacobin' Miranda)
the Spanish Government must strongly disapprove. Bolívar, as the
emissary of a *junta* officially supporting Ferdinand VII, could be
allowed a British corvette, the *Sapphire*, to take him back to
Venezuela; Miranda, an overt rebel, though his luggage went with
Bolívar, was obliged to make his own way back by merchantman.

Both Bolívar and Miranda were back in Caracas before 1810 was
out. They and their supporters sufficiently worked upon the patriotic enthusiasm of the local citizens for the Venezuelan Declaration of Independence (July 1811) to be greeted with high excitement,
if not with unanimous joy. Bitter differences were present from the
start—well illustrated by a letter written from Caracas in August
and published by the London *Morning Chronicle*:

> Everything is in turmoil in South America: every day people are
> imprisoned on suspicion of plots against the Government, and
> visitors from outside the city dread to come together . . . the order
> of the day is: *Liberty and Equality*. . . . Traitors are beheaded

and their heads exhibited on poles, with a notice underneath which reads: This man was killed as a traitor to his fatherland. Two were hanged yesterday, sentenced by the Patriotic Society; but their crimes are not made public. The time for imprisoning is at midnight: a platoon enters the house, forces the man out of his bed, and the next day he loses his life. . . . We deem it dangerous to be seen talking together in the street; and more so to criticize the Government. Although we only meet privately we cannot tell whether our own servants are our spies.

Some were for a Venezuelan revolution on Jacobin lines. Some were ready to die for the Spanish Bourbons against the French. White Americans were divided among themselves; Indians and Negroes were often bewildered but in general saw little good likely to be coming from a rebellion led by their white masters. The deep Spanish instinct for separation came into full play in Venezuela as it would soon do in a broader way over the whole of South America to defeat the large federal visions of Bolívar. The Church too was divided: some priests supported independence, while the more conservative majority was loyal to Spain.

So the first Venezuelan Republic went down in bloodshed and chaos in 1812. Providence itself seemed to have given its verdict when on Holy Thursday, just two years after the creation of the original Venezuelan *junta*, Caracas and other towns in the hands of the republican forces were engulfed in a disastrous earthquake, while royalist-held towns escaped. Many thousands perished. Caracas became a heap of rubble, upon which some priests and monks lost no time in pointing out to a terrified and superstitious population their message of divine vengeance. One such, using a table as a pulpit, was clawed down by a furious Bolívar, active in his shirtsleeves among the ruins with a body of helpers and slaves. "If Nature is against us," he shouted, "we will war against that too, and subject it to our will"; grandiose, impious words, and an apt motto for Bolívar's Promethean career.

In the immediate future, however, there were only failures and desperate measures. Miranda set up a military dictatorship in Caracas; Bolívar, in command of Puerto Cabello, succumbed to defections in his own forces and the attacks of the royalist troops—a failure that in his own mind he took a long time to live down. Suddenly, in the middle of all this confusion, Miranda decided that he would throw in his hand: although numerically superior he authorized capitulation to the royalist commander Monteverde.

What went on in his mind is a mystery. Certainly there was disarray all around him, recruiting difficulties, financial troubles, political intrigues, threatened slave revolts; it is very probable that he had lost faith in the new Republic and its future. Wishing, he said, to reconcile all Spaniards to form "one community, one family, and one interest," he decided to leave Caracas before Monteverde's forces arrived. The *Sapphire*, that same corvette that had brought his luggage, though not his person, to Venezuela, was waiting at La Guaira to take him aboard on the evening of his arrival there: but he decided, being tired, to sleep that night ashore. At 3 A.M. he was roughly awakened by three men who ordered him to dress and marched him off to prison. There next day he was handed over to Monteverde, who shipped him away in irons to moulder away the few bitter years left to him in the dungeons of Puerto Rico and Cadiz. One of the three men in the night was Simón Bolívar, and some have never forgiven him for it. His enemies maintained that he betrayed Miranda in order to obtain a passport and thus get safely away. Monteverde himself said that Bolívar spontaneously delivered up Miranda and therefore "deserved a reward". He certainly did get away, to the British-held island of Curaçao; and during the following months, while hundreds of republicans less fortunate than Bolívar were being liquidated, the worst that befell him was the confiscation of his property. His supporters, and he himself, maintained that Miranda received the just deserts of a coward and a traitor.

> If Miranda believed that the Spaniards [*i.e.*, Monteverde's royalists] would observe the treaty he should have remained to keep them to their word; if he did not, he was a traitor to have sacrificed his army to it.

From Curaçao Bolívar returned in 1813 to the mainland at Cartagena, on the coast of Venezuela's neighbour, New Granada. There too there was a newly independent republic. He was in his thirtieth year, and, as his *Memoir addressed to the Citizens of New Granada* shows, he had been learning fast. "Well-meaning visionaries who imagine airy republics" are curtly dismissed. "We had philosophers instead of leaders, philanthropy instead of legislation, controversy instead of tactics, sophists instead of soldiers." Full democracy would prove a recipe for chaos; what was needed was patriotism, but also authority. He attacked the "criminal clemency" that had allowed enemies of the people to live. Things were moving in his mind towards that "war to the death" which he soon was to proclaim; the savagery of the revolutionaries was not merely a reply to the savagery of the royalists. Bolívar was not wantonly murderous, but there was a very Spanish lack of compromise about him; "he would have shed the blood of the whole world," said one of his followers, "if he thought it necessary for the independence of South America."

Within a few months the situation of 1812 had been reversed: it was the royalists now whose government in Caracas collapsed in face of republican troops advancing from New Granada. For Bolívar and his fellow-commanders the campaign was a series of brief, sharp raids, all over in three months. On August 6th, 1813, flower-decked and laurel-crowned, he entered in triumph the streets of the capital, still lying amid their earthquake ruins. It was his first taste of power and he enjoyed it fully: Dictator of the city, Captain General of the republican army, idol of many of the ladies (whom it was no part of his philosophy to resist), all vigour and drive and panache, officially styled now *Libertador*, the Liberator.

These rejoicings were premature. The complications and convolutions of the struggle now began to appear in earnest. The war had begun in a revolution of Creoles against Spaniards. A predominantly prosperous class of the community, many of them idealistically, some from motives of patriotism, others from envy, had taken the easy first step towards social and political breakdown. Now multiple perils presented themselves. There was the separatist danger: once the royal power was destroyed, any city, any dictator, could seek to set up its own authority: "remove or weaken that power", as the Duke of Wellington said of Spain itself, "and the provinces will fall asunder and set up for themselves". There was the racial danger: the black and brown majority, having faintly sniffed liberty afar off, might run berserk and overturn the rule of Creole and Spaniard alike. Nature itself had seemed to take sides in the struggle, with the earthquake of 1812; now in 1814 the geography of Venezuela began to assert its part in society and politics. Venezuela was more than Caracas, or the provincial centres, or the seaports—control of which had largely determined the contest to date. Venezuela was also the great plains of the interior, the *llanos*, where the wild cowboys, crouching half naked over their horses, drove their herds. A *llanero* was a kind of composite creature, half man, half horse. He had certainly not read Rousseau on the Noble Savage or the General Will, but he was second to none with a knife or a lance; and first under Boves[1] against the Republicans, and then under Paez on their side, he was to play a violent and gruesome part in the struggle.

Already before the irruption of the *llanero* cavalry, a proclamation of Bolívar shows how the mood had changed:

> The war is becoming more cruel and the hopes of a speedy victory I had aroused in you have disappeared. . . . We are living terrible days; blood flows in streams; three centuries of culture, enlightenment and industry have vanished.

Soon Boves had led 5000 of his cowboys, with 3000 infantry, to a crushing victory over "the so-called Generals Bolívar and Marino" at La Puerta. Half the republicans were left dead on the field; all the prisoners were speared or shot; and Bolívar himself was lucky to escape back to Caracas. Six weeks later it was the turn of Valencia; Boves ignored the terms of surrender and slaughtered 450 soldier and civilians. According to the contemporary historian Heredia,

> He gathered all the women into a dancing party, while he rounded up all the men and had them led out of the city where they were speared to death like bulls. . . . The ladies in the ballroom swallowed their tears and trembled hearing the hooves of Boves's horses, for they guessed what was actually happening; while Boves, whip in hand, made them dance the *piquirico* and other dances of the country, of which he was very fond.

Bolívar now abandoned Caracas to Boves' forces, and led a terrible flight of 10,000 of its inhabitants eastward. After three months of the grimmest suffering the survivors who reached Cumaná were evacuated, some to the British West Indies, some to the island of Margarita, which was soon the only Venezuelan territory left to the republicans. The sort of slaughter that had taken place in Caracas and Valencia was repeated by Boves (and after his death in battle by his successor, Morales) in Cumaná, Maturín, and each newly captured centre. This was "war to the death", *guerra a muerte*, in the most uncompromising Spanish manner. Bolívar accepted it fully,

---

[1] Boves was a white with a grievance, and led his *mestizo* and *zambo* forces on the simple bases of racial hatred and the promise of plunder and debauch.

publicly proclaimed it, and gave general orders for the killing of all royalist prisoners.

For the next year or so there was an extremely confused situation. Spain, freed now from Napoleon and restored to the crude reaction of Ferdinand VII, could afford to spare troops to subdue her unruly colonies. An expedition was fitted out, intended originally for Buenos Aires; it was diverted to pay attention to the even severer problems of Venezuela and secured control of much of the country. Bolívar was for a time an exile in Jamaica, sustaining the propaganda of the Republic with letters and pamphlets, and subsequently in the Negro republic of Haiti, where, the descendant of generations of wealthy slave-dealers and slave-owners, he first fully committed himself to a policy of slave liberation. From Haiti and with Haitian aid he returned to the mainland in April 1816 for another assault on the royalists.

All through 1816 there was chaotic and bloodthirsty fighting. South America abounded in would-be dictators, both royalist and republican, and in guerrilla chieftains of every hue. Bolívar, one among many, was unique only in his largeness of vision. Others were only too happy outdoing the enemy in the "war to the death"; Bolívar was anxious now to put to an end mere reprisal and butchery. He was seer as well as soldier; only he tried to focus South American issues in the wider perspectives afforded by history and philosophy—whether of the ancient world or of the America and Europe of his day. Not many men in that bloodthirsty time attempted to see, as he did, past their provincial horizons to the nation, the continent, the world beyond. It was Bolívar who proposed a great congress of newly emerged states (meeting, he suggested, at Panama) to discuss pressing questions of international relations.

By 1817 the republicans had recaptured Venezuelan Guiana, the town of Angostura, and all the lands bordering the lower Orinoco. A big factor in the improved situation was the change of sides by the *llanero* cavalry. Under the command now of the young *mestizo* Paez, one of the most brilliant of guerrilla leaders, they came over slowly, and it was their support, uncertain though it was at first, that helped Bolívar to conceive his boldest strategic stroke. With the men of the *llanos* on his side and Angostura as his base, why should he not bypass the strong royalist army in Venezuela, cross the difficult *llanos* and yet more difficult mountains beyond them, and strike at the Viceroy's army in New Granada? Napoleon had made the passage of the Alps; down in the South San Martín had recently led a brilliant expedition over the Andes to liberate Chile. Why should not Bolívar emulate or surpass these feats?

> From here [he wrote] we shall take the enemy in the rear all the way to Santa Fe [Bogotá]. We have an immense territory on both banks of the Orinoco and its tributaries the Apure, Meta, and Arauca; we have all the cattle and horses we want, and all we have to do is to hold our ground and prolong the campaign.

It was characteristic that Bolívar, before launching his perilous campaign, should call a parliament at Angostura and deliver before it an academic discourse on politics and government. The contrast between on the one side the high-flown theory and loftiness of phrase and on the other the savagery of the "war to the death" is at first glance grotesque. But Bolívar knew what he was doing. It was not merely that he was himself passionately aware of the lessons of history and principles of politics. He had already received both moral and practical support from abroad, from Britain and the U.S.A. in particular, and after his earlier failures he needed to rebuild abroad the reputation and dignity of his cause. In London his agent Mendez was busy seeking supplies and recruiting volunteers, not difficult in post-Waterloo Britain full of unemployed ex-soldiers and merchants with unmarketable stock. Already Englishmen and Irishmen formed a sizable proportion of Bolívar's troops; in all some 500 fought for him.

The Angostura address is a remarkable piece of South American self-analysis.[2] Ranging with penetration over the fields of history and philosophy both ancient and modern, it attempts to set reasonable goals and limits for the South American revolution. It weighs the virtues and drawbacks of democracy and dictatorship, republicanism and monarchy; it shows (following Montesquieu) how South America's geography and climate must determine her type of government. It points out the unwisdom of trying to follow the North American type of federalism, which in South America could

[2] O'Leary described how the Angostura address was composed. "Reclining in a canoe on the bosom of the Orinoco River, or lolling in a hammock under the shade of gigantic trees that fringed its banks, in the heat of the day, or in the cool hours of the night, as the mood seized him, with one hand on the lapel of his coat and a forefinger on his upper lip, Bolívar dictated the constitution . . . and the famous address . . . ."

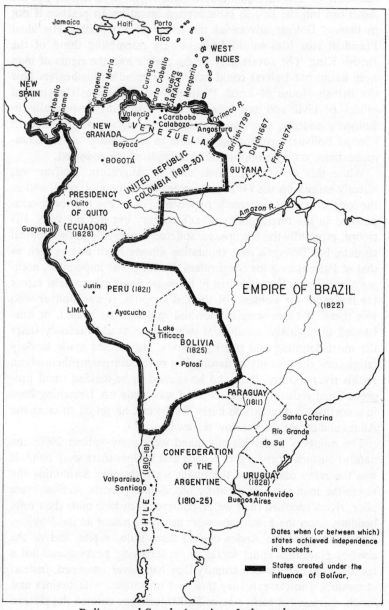

Bolivar and South American Independence

lead only to anarchy. Of modern patterns of government, not the American but the British most invited imitation, in practice if not in theory; Bolívar advocated the *forms* of a republic. His ideal President (for life) would have powers resembling those of the British King. The sovereignty of the people and the rights of man were basic; but Bolívar could not resist reminding his hearers how the British House of Lords "had proved themselves the stoutest pillars of civil and religious liberty". Listening respectfully to Bolívar's address, the representatives of Angostura (the modern Ciudad Bolívar) nevertheless felt free to reject most of its recommendations; only the opposition to federalism was endorsed.

While this debate was continuing in Angostura, Bolívar was already sailing up the Orinoco to meet Paez, his ally, rival, and in the long term most dangerous opponent. For a time they both campaigned in the torrid plains, Paez's country but not Bolívar's. His troops, especially the Europeans, suffered wretchedly in the tropical climate, but Bolívar's own reputation among them was as high as that of Paez among his roughriders. Nothing was impossible, nothing too difficult. If a river had to be swum five times to help across the last men—or women—or the last supplies, it was Bolívar who was there. If there were canoes and mules to be loaded, or husbanded through the pestilential swamps, he would tirelessly share the most daunting and menial labours. He seemed made to defy fatigue and the hostility of nature. But in the campaigns themselves, in this river country, Paez and he seemed to be making small progress. Then suddenly Bolívar's mind was made up. Detaching Paez in a northward direction to harry the enemy, he set off to cross the Andes and defeat the Viceroy in New Granada.

The numbers under his command were puny—about 2000; the natural obstacles prodigious. Roads and bridges there were none. It was the rainy season and the plains were swamps. Swimming the rivers the men were attacked by blood-thirsty fishes. Rations were poor; rivers supplied their water, hammocks or hide mats their only bedding. Soon the Europeans were nearly as naked as the *llaneros*. The foothills of the Andes offered them little respite, and as the cowboy plainsmen came nearer to the terrifying peaks ahead not a few deserted. This was a country they had never imagined. Instead of swamps and torrents they now had to contend with ravines and rough stairways of rock. Above 10,000 feet they entered the plateau of the *cordillera*, a region of foggy, boggy wilderness with ceaseless rains and searching winds. By now all the pack animals had died, and soon many men, including fifty-six Englishmen, had perished of exposure. Many more suffered nausea from the effects of altitude. A woman gave birth *en route*, and continued the march with the baby.

It was no expedition for any but the hardy—and the foolhardy, Bolívar must sometimes have thought. For the young too: at thirty-five Bolívar was a senior in age as well as rank: a slight, shortish, wiry figure wrapped in a scarlet cloak; strong of heart as well as body, pitting himself and his ferocious will against dire natural odds, knowing too that beyond the peaks lay hostile forces more numerous and better equipped than his.

The survivors recovered swiftly upon the farther slopes. Indeed, glancing back "at the white crests they had crossed, they swore they would die fighting rather than repass them". The few hundred *llaneros* still present were provided with horses, and soon, at Vargas in July 1819, both they (riding bareback and charging with their deadly lances) and the British infantry, steady under severe losses, were able to show their worth. A few weeks later they defeated the Viceroy's army at Boyacá, and on August 10th Bolívar was able to enter Santa Fe de Bogotá, the capital.

By December he was back in his headquarters at Angostura (for Caracas and the northern towns were still in royalist hands), and at Angostura, in holiday atmosphere, the Liberator proclaimed a new State: Greater Colombia (*Gran Colombia*), which was a union of Venezuela, New Granada, and the Presidency of Quito (what would now be called Ecuador). Doubts, intrigues, and disaffection were for a space no more. Everywhere, and among all classes and races, there was enthusiasm for the new Republic. Nothing succeeds like success, and suddenly all the luck seemed to be running Bolívar's way: the 1820 Revolution in Spain meant that even Ferdinand VII could not, for the time being at least, afford to be too unyielding. The troops that Ferdinand had assembled for a reconquest of his rebellious subjects were more than half sympathetic to them. Conciliation was in the air. General Morillo, Ferdinand's commander in Venezuela, showed himself anxious for it, and treated with Bolívar on a basis of equality, man to man, Spaniard to Spaniard. An armistice was signed, and Morillo's account of it shows how the warmth of Bolívar's impulsive personality had quite won him over:

We were all wildly happy; it seemed like a dream to be meeting there as Spaniards, brothers and friends. . . . We embraced
each other again and again.

Unfortunately Morillo carried no weight with Ferdinand, to whom
conciliation meant simply defeat. When therefore Bolívar's peace
emissaries in Madrid were given no status he decided to renew the
battle.

His forces had grown fourfold, to 6500 infantry and 1500 *llaneros*.
In June 1821, at Carabobo, commanding the entry to both Valencia
and Caracas, he fought one of the war's decisive battles. Paez and
his *llaneros*, in desperate trouble, were rescued by the steadfast discipline of the veteran British brigade, who lost 600 out of 900 men
but gave the cavalry time to reform and take the royalists in the
rear at the moment when Bolívar's main forces were making the
direct attack. Caracas opened its gates, and for several days there
was nothing to be seen or heard but dancing, feasting, and bull-
fighting.

In 1822 Bolívar and Sucre, after stubborn fighting in the high
Andes, succeeded in liberating—or subduing, for the predominantly
Indian population was in the main hostile—the Presidency of Quito.
Greater Colombia was thus an accomplished fact, but from the start
it was built on quicksand. Towering above his compatriots was
Bolívar, President. Of his three chief subordinates, only one, Sucre,
was entirely faithful to his ideals and person. The Vice-President,
General Santander, though ostensibly loyal (and, indeed, later was
to save Bolívar from assassination), did not rise above the ruck of
scheming politicians; and the horizons of General Paez were
bounded by the plains of his *llanos* and the reach of his own ambition. He was the boss of the plainsmen and the most powerful
man in Venezuela.

Already Bolívar feared peace more than war, and said as much.
Already he was being driven two ways—forward to glory, to the
domination of the whole of Spanish America and (as he sometimes
dreamed) the conquest of Brazil, towards the peaks of his Napoleonic destiny; and backwards to disengagement from the pettiness
and impossibilities that surrounded him, towards the troughs of his
private despair. In 1822 he wrote to Santander:

We have two and a half million inhabitants scattered over a
vast wilderness. Some of them are savage; some are slaves; most
are mutual enemies; and all are vitiated by superstition and

despotism. . . . Such is Colombia, and they will want to divide her.

He allowed himself to be elected President of his Greater Colombia; but to the same Congress that elected him he declared:

I vowed I would never be more than a soldier. . . . I am not the kind of ruler the Republic wants. . . . My destiny lies in camp or barracks. . . . For me an office desk is a place of punishment.

Conquering the Andes had been a simple matter compared with conquering the contradictions in his own nature and his own judgments. Increasingly after 1821 he was a split man: idealistic and visionary, but much given to sensual pleasure; contemptuous of fame but impelled by his private demon to pursue it; liberal and generous-hearted, but driven by habit or necessity to outbursts of rage and bloodthirstiness. "That rabble", he wrote of his countrymen, "can be kept at bay only by exemplary rigour"; and when, for instance, the district of Pasto in Ecuador twice rose against his rule his vengeance was terrible.[3] He was a man detached enough to stand aside from himself and quiz his own character; intelligent enough to see through himself; sufficiently human to delight in the idolatry that surrounded him while despising it in his heart. He loved finery, display, the outdoing of his rivals in the grand gesture or the ringing phrase, but the philosopher and realist in him taught him the vanity of human glory and the readiness of the brightest ideals to tarnish. He could leap on the table, dash off a toast, and crash his glass against the wall, all flamboyance and fire; but back in his quarters with his secret thoughts he could soon become Prince Hamlet, his will corroded by contemplation. He genuinely despised riches and was the least corrupt of conquerors; but still (seeing ahead to the days of his overthrow or retirement) he would take care to instruct his sister to invest their new wealth prudently in copper mines: "We have enough estates and houses, which any earthquake may bring down. If we have 100,000 sterling safe in a bank in England we can enjoy our 3 per cent." By 1822, moreover, Bolívar's health was beginning to decline: the rigours of

[3] The following instruction of Bolívar to a local governor may illustrate the harsh choice that 'liberation' afforded to some: "Every man between fifteen and thirty-five to present himself for taking up arms within three days. Those who fail to do so to be shot where they are and in whatever state they are. Those not caught to be outlawed, their goods confiscated, and their families arrested."

campaigning, and perhaps of his sexual indulgence too, started to take their toll. His hair went grey, and though he was only thirty-nine he began to complain of old age.

While Bolívar and his followers had been creating an independent Colombia in the north, there had been parallel events in the south. Caracas and Buenos Aires had proclaimed their independence in the same year, 1810, but while Caracas was suffering every imaginable disaster—earthquake, revolution, and reconquest, terror and counter-terror—Buenos Aires (Republic of the River Plate) had been able to maintain its independence. It could not, however, feel fully secure until the power of Spain was broken on the far side of the Andes, in Chile and Peru. Hence, gradually from 1814, an expedition was assembled on the eastern slopes of the Andes, and in 1817 under the leadership of José de San Martín—South American born, but an experienced professional soldier who had fought for Spain throughout the Napoleonic Wars—it advanced over the Andes into Chile. San Martín's was a much more carefully prepared crossing than Bolívar's dash of two and a half years later; nevertheless it defeated natural obstacles equally forbidding, suffered similarly severe losses, and stands as a major achievement of organization, daring, and courage. The Spanish armies were defeated, Santiago taken, and a new Chilean Republic established with, at its head, Bernardo O'Higgins, the son of an Irish-born South American who had risen to be Viceroy in Lima. O'Higgins proceeded to purchase, man, and equip a navy, one-third of whose crews was British or North American, and fit out an expeditionary force to sail the thousand miles up the Pacific coast to Peru. The naval side of the expedition was under the brilliant, but vain and quarrelsome, Englishman, Admiral Cochrane. He chafed with impatience when the methodical San Martín, having landed, failed to march at once upon Lima; but both the military and the political situation were more complicated than Cochrane allowed. San Martín's army was weakened by epidemics, and Creole opinion in Peru was much more conservative and royalist than in Venezuela, Buenos Aires, or Chile. There were hopes too that the Spanish Revolution of 1820 might bring about a negotiated settlement between San Martín and the Viceroy without bloodshed. These negotiations in fact broke down over the issue of independence, and San Martín's patience seemed justified when in July

1821 the Viceroy abandoned his capital city of Lima without a fight. True, most of Peru was still unconquered, and the Viceroy's army, though it suffered desertions, was largely intact; but San Martín was able to enter Lima, proclaim the independence of Peru, and assume the title of Protector. These events preceded by a few months the capture of Quito by Bolívar and Sucre, which completed the union of Greater Colombia.

Thus the two great movements from north and south had converged upon Peru, the heart of Spanish power in South America. What was to be their attitude to one another? They were comrades yet rivals; they represented similar ideals but different interests. In particular the two leaders eyed one another hard and shrewdly. They corresponded. Bolívar offered San Martín troops. San Martín expressed his conviction that they "should draw closer together to complete the expulsion of the Spaniard from the entire continent".

In July 1822 the two met. San Martín arrived by corvette, with the immediate short-term aim of securing for Peru Guayaquil, the Ecuadorian port of their meeting. Since Bolívar had already occupied it with Colombian troops, he had taken the first trick and put San Martín at an initial disadvantage. Though all the forms of accord and solidarity were observed, with troop-lined streets, gun salutes, toasts, balls, and celebrations (which Bolívar loved and San Martín hated), the most that was achieved in the two-day secret discussions of long-term aims and policies was an agreement to disagree. San Martín offered to serve under Bolívar, but Bolívar affected not to take this seriously; San Martín, for his part, found Bolívar "evasive" and "lacking in frankness". There was certainly a clash of personalities and ambitions, but the disagreements at Guayaquil arose too from fundamental differences of political outlook.

San Martín's answer to the problems of newly emancipated South America was monarchy—and European monarchy at that. His agents had already been dispatched to Europe to sound out the chances of importing a prince of the House of Brunswick as Emperor of Peru. He would not have ruled out a Spanish Bourbon. Of one thing he was certain: South Americans were not fitted to run republics. When as military dictator of Lima he had been approached by the local republicans he had declared to them his intention of avoiding "all inopportune meetings of congresses and committees which could do nothing but embarrass the management of public affairs with vain arguments". *In practice* this was not so far from Bolívar's own attitude, but Bolívar stood stubbornly by the *theory* of the republicanism that he had imbibed in his youth. He might himself be forced into dictatorship, but he would have no monarch, whether Spanish or foreign.

San Martín soon saw the brick wall ahead of him:

> On the night of 27th July a ball was given for San Martín. Bolívar as usual at affairs of this kind thoroughly enjoyed himself. San Martín remained cool and aloof and seemed depressed. At one o'clock in the morning he called his aides and told them he wanted to leave because he could not stand the noise. His luggage was already on board, and, unobserved, he left the ball, went to his ship, and set sail from the port.[4]

He knew that he lacked support from among his own officers, from the governments of both Chile and Buenos Aires (the latter had practically disowned him), and from many of Peru's leading citizens. He was ill and exasperated. In Peru he had reaped nothing but ingratitude and misunderstanding.

> Believe me, my friend [he wrote to O'Higgins, himself soon to be ousted], I am tired of being called tyrant and of having it said in all quarters I wish to become emperor. . . . . Further, the climate of this country is bringing me to my grave. Lastly, as my youth was sacrificed in the service of Spain and my middle age in the service of my native land, I believe that I have the right to dispose of my old age.

So San Martín sadly withdrew from the scene, departing towards Europe and a long exile, and "looking to history for a just verdict". History has in general agreed upon it: in the winning of South American independence his contribution was second only to that of Bolívar.

With San Martín out of the way, but a royalist army of 14,000 undefeated on the *sierra*, Bolívar was irresistibly drawn towards the conquest of Peru. For some time the Hamlet in him held back, but the Napoleon was stronger. Many times he denounced the "miserable mania of wanting power at any cost", but "no-one imagines that Peru can manage without me." Already, he wrote, America had had three Caesars—San Martín, O'Higgins, and Iturbide, the

---

[4] G. Masur, *Simon Bolivar*, p. 482.

Liberator of Mexico; these men had fallen "because they did not love liberty". Everybody, he complained—just like San Martín—now assumed that he, Bolívar, wished to be the fourth and greatest. "The desire to end war in America drives me on towards Peru, but I am held back by my love of my reputation." Held back, but of course not finally.

In August 1824, at Junin, high in the Peruvian Andes, Bolívar won the most fantastic of his victories:

> The combatants were chiefly hussars and lancers. No fire-arms were used by either side, and except for the sounds of hoofs on the plains and the hoarse shouts of the men engaged, the battle was fought in silence—in a landscape more like the mountains of the moon than an earthly battlefield.[5]

Four months later Sucre completed the work; at Ayacucho the troops of Spain in America lost their last battle. But for Bolívar the triumph and its celebrations—and he threw himself into these as passionately as ever—were tinged with apprehensions of ruin.

> The future [he wrote just before Ayacucho] is my torment, my torture.... In this unhappy revolution victory is as unfortunate as defeat; we shall always have tears to shed over our destiny. Like the wounded doe, we carry in our flank the arrow which cannot fail to cause our death.

This sombre letter was written by a conqueror whose sun was approaching its zenith. The men of Peru had accepted him as dictator, the ladies ("very agreeable and handsome", he judged) thought no honour higher than to be taken as his mistress. "The table is excellent," he wrote, "the theatre passable . . . carriages, horses, promenades, bullfights, *Te Deums*, nothing is missing." Nothing, that is, but the confidence of ultimate success.

Before long he was setting off upon a long triumphal tour of Southern Peru. Cuzco of the Incas, Lake Titicaca, La Paz, Chuquisaca (to be renamed Sucre), Potosí, the city of silver, which the inhabitants were restrained from renaming Bolívar—at one place after another he was offered golden keys, symbolic embraces, civic harangues; Emperor in all but name. Southern Peru became yet another new republic, with the enlightened Sucre as its first president. Bolívar framed its constitution, which abolished slavery and provided, in theory, for religious liberty. Suffrage was

[5] J. B. Trend, *Bolívar and the Independence of Spanish America*, pp. 183–184.

to be universal for literate males—which, of course, left the
Indians and *mestizos* without the vote; the system of indirect voting
harked back to that of Napoleonic France. The new state could,
naturally, have no name other than Bolívar, later Bolivia. Its
future, torn by the civil wars of petty dictators, was to be very
different from what its parent planned.

He had high if fragile hopes of a great congress of American
states that he planned to hold. His dream was to found a greater
Spanish-American federation with British support.

> If we tie ourselves to England we shall survive; if not we shall
> inevitably be lost. . . . Only England, mistress of the seas, can
> protect us from the united forces of European reaction.

But Canning and the British Government, though they were ready
to give diplomatic recognition to the new South American republics
and were most anxious to expand trade with them, were not prepared to do more than send an official to the Panama Congress to
guard British interests. In particular he was instructed to resist
"any project for putting the United States at the head of an
American Confederacy". Brazil and Buenos Aires declined Bolívar's invitation to attend; the U.S.A. sent delegates but they arrived
too late; Chile had already lapsed into anarchy and nobody knew
which was her true government. Eventually in 1826 after nearly
two years' delay the Congress met. It was attended only by Colombia, Peru, Guatemala, and Mexico, and it achieved nothing. As
Bolívar wrote to Paez, "the Congress of Panama amounts to no
more than the mad Greek who thought that from his rock he
could steer the passing ships".

Probably the vision of a federated Spanish America had been a
mirage in any case. After 1826 it looked ever more insubstantial.
The problem was rather to prevent the Union of Colombia itself
from breaking up. It suffered from every conceivable handicap, geographical, racial, political, economic. Its size was immense considered in relation to the formidable natural obstacles and lack of
communications. Its people and races were diverse and mutually
resentful. The Indian-Spaniard from the Peru highlands looked
down on the mulattoes of Venezuela and was very ready to wage
war on them. "The people of New Granada", reported the British
respresentative in Bogotá, "say they may as well be under the King
of Spain as be degraded and commanded by a Venezuelan faction."

On their side the Venezuelans were glad to rally to their own man Paez, who had never had any use for Bolívar's high-flying ideas.

> Of all countries [wrote Bolívar] South America is perhaps the least fitted for republican governments. What does its population consist of but Indians and Negroes who are more ignorant than the vile race of Spaniards we are just emancipated from? A country represented by such people must go to ruin. *We must look to England.* . . .[6]

Much of the country, moreover, was facing economic ruin. Bolívar and his followers had made a desert and called it liberation; some of the disillusioned conservatism of his later years sprang from this fact. It was bitter to consider that, by contrast, the days of servitude to Spain had been prosperous. The tobacco and coffee plantations were now in a ruinous condition. The wastage of cattle and horses had been immense. Imports, too, especially from Britain, had had a crippling effect on the domestic economy: "I must repeat," wrote Sucre, "that if the introduction of ordinary wool and cotton manufactured articles and even of wheat flour is not prohibited in the south, these provinces will be ruined." Sometimes it seemed that the chief beneficiaries of liberation were the moneylenders and the gangs of thieving cowboys. The slaves, officially freed, were still largely not so. "Citizens," proclaimed Bolívar towards the end, "I blush to say it; independence is the only benefit we have acquired, at the cost of all others."

The country abounded in would-be dictators and scheming politicians. Vice-President Santander in Bogotá soon became in effect intriguer-in-chief against Bolívar. Paez in Venezuela was alternately for Bolívar and against him—and always against Santander—calculating his chances and biding his time. Among the army leaders only Sucre could be fully relied on, but he was soon ousted by the Peruvians as a "foreigner". Bolívar had been right to fear peace more than war. There was no peace, only a babel of voices, a rabble of factions, a turbulence of petty wars, plots, and revenges.

Bolívar's own popularity had itself been created by war and sustained by the glamour of victory. The removal of Spanish power meant the removal of the only force that had made for a sort of unity. It meant too that Bolívar, a man in failing health but still

[6] He looked favourably on inviting British capitalists and engineers to construct a Panama Canal, but the ideal was lost amid the myriad difficulties of the times.

hungry for power—and many said for a throne—was obliged to re-consider all his political attitudes; and in the last four years of his life (1826–30) he became more and more authoritarian, so that the most vocal opposition, led discreetly by the ambiguous Santander, came from those calling themselves Liberals and Bolívar tyrant. Many tried to persuade him to become king—including at different times and in their own immediate interests both Paez and San-tander. Among his papers at the end was a scribbled margin note. "To accept a crown would stain my reputation. I prefer the glorious title of First Citizen of Colombia."

Like that other freethinker Napoleon, who was never far from his thoughts, Bolívar came increasingly to rely on the Catholic Church. When he assumed full dictatorial powers in Bogotá in 1828 he de-clared "the Roman Catholic Apostolic Religion" to be dominant in the state. So once more, in Napoleon's phrase, religion was to be "the cement of the social order". It was a surrender perhaps in-evitable in such a country with such a history, but for Bolívar a surrender all the same.[7] In much the same strain this apostle of liberty censored books, specially banning the works of the radical Bentham. He built up the army too to the unprecedented and ruinous figure of 40,000, and leaned heavily on the apparatus of adu-lation and public ballyhoo that has sustained military dictators in all ages. A critical English observer commented in 1829:

> Ambition absorbs every other feeling in him; he wants to command, to govern without fetters, constraint, or law; he wants Colombia to be fully his, to be indispensable. . . . He wants but one big figure to be seen in America. . . . Immense Colombia is too small for him.

But none of his critics was more perceptive or destructive than himself; always he could observe, as it were from the outside, his own scepticism and ambition. He writes to Santander:

> Do not forget to declare a crusade against the heretical and atheistic French, destroyers of priests, temples, and images— everything sacred. The Bishop of Merida will come in handy for this, as well as the fanatics available in churches, pulpits, or streets.

[7] Bolívar's fundamental materialism is well illustrated by some comments that he made to Colonel Lacroix, one of the Frenchmen of his 'foreign legion': "Man has a material body and an intellect also material, represented by the brain, and according to present-day science the intellect is just a secretion of the brain; for me the brain dies with the body, and once the brain is dead, there is no more secretion of intellect."

An acute Frenchman observed of him: "He seeks power, accepts it, yet wants to come out at the head of those who protest. . . . Everything in him is uncertainty and contradiction."

In September 1828 there was an attempted *coup* in Bogotá from which Bolívar never fully recovered. The aim was to kidnap him and his ministers and put Santander at the head of a new government. An earlier attempted assassination on September 21st[8] had been foiled by Santander himself, who shrank from such an extreme course; on September 25th Bolívar was saved by the resource of his mistress, Manuela Saenz—the last of his 'official' mistresses—who first got him out through a window and then held the conspirators talking and gained time for him to escape. Several of his entourage were killed or wounded, among them the Scot, Colonel Fergusson, shot dead. Bolívar himself, his lungs already affected by the tuberculosis that was soon to kill him, spent three shivering hours hiding under a bridge as troops above, of whose loyalty he was unsure, rounded up the plotters. Fourteen of them were shot for their part in the affair and Santander sentenced to death as an accessory. The sentence was, however, reduced to banishment; he was yet to become President.

This was not the first or the last time on which Manuela Saenz showed her spirit. Spear in hand, she once repelled an attack during political riots in her native Quito. Her greatest days had been in Lima as *maîtresse en titre* to the Liberator at the peak of his glory. She rode about the city in a scarlet and gold hussar's tunic, with white breeches; accompanying her an escort of lancers. She smoked and in various ways offended polite opinion. She dabbled in politics, and once at a party staged a shooting of Santander in effigy, to Bolívar's embarrassment and the general scandal. The day came in 1830 (by which time Bolívar was down and almost out) when, galloping through the streets of Bogotá with two attendant Negresses dressed as hussars, she with her sword and they with their lances scattered the crowd which had gathered in the town square to enjoy a fireworks display whose set pieces were meant to guy Bolívar and herself.

In 1828 Bolívar was forced to abandon Venezuela to Paez. In

---

[8] This was not the first attempt to assassinate Bolívar. In 1815 a Negro servant killed with a dagger the man sleeping in the hammock usually occupied by Bolívar, who happened to be away that night on amatory pleasures.

May 1830, after he had made futile attempts to reconquer and pacify Quito, Guayaquil, and Peru, the Congress in Bogotá deprived him of his dictatorial powers, granted him an annual pension, and dispensed with his services. He knew better than to stay. The long daydream of relinquishing authority had now become an unwelcome necessity. A few months earlier he had written:

> There is no good faith in America. . . . Treaties are scraps of paper, constitutions so much printed matter; elections are battles; freedom is anarchy; and life is a torment.

A sick and defeated man, yet even so not totally surrendering hope of a return to power (for his successors soon began to lose popularity), he proceeded slowly to Cartagena. He was wasted, and coughing continually. The grievous news came of the murder of Sucre, his most reliable and able lieutenant. He came at last in total despair to Santa Marta. *I have no hope of salvation for the fatherland*, he wrote. He sent his last letter, which was in the nature of a testament. South America was "ungovernable. . . . He who serves a revolution ploughs the sea." He had been reading *Don Quixote* a few weeks before his death. "The three greatest *idiots* in history," he said with the despairing egoism of the true romantic, "have been Jesus Christ, Don Quixote, and myself."

When Bolívar entered Guayaquil in 1822 the triumphal arches had hailed him as *The Lightning of War, the Rainbow of Peace.* Destruction, however, had proved easier than building. His lightnings had brilliantly flashed and struck and sundered, but his rainbows of peace and unity were as elusive then as they have proved since.

Table of Events

1783.	Bolívar born at Caracas. Britain recognizes independent United States.
1789.	Fall of the Bastille.
1803–5.	Bolívar's second journey to Europe.
1806.	Miranda's first rising collapses.
1808.	Napoleon overthrows Spanish monarchy.
1810.	Revolutions in Caracas, Buenos Aires, Bogotá, Santiago.
1811–12.	First Venezuelan republic collapses.
1813–16.	*Guerra a muerte.*
1817.	San Martín crosses Andes; Chilean republic.
1819.	Angostura address; Boyacá, 'Greater Colombia'.
1821.	Bolívar defeats Spaniards at Carabobo.

1822.	Bolívar and Sucre 'liberate' Quito (Ecuador).
	Bolívar and San Martín meet at Guayaquil.
1823.	Monroe Doctrine.
1824.	Junin and Ayacucho. Republic of Southern Peru (Bolivia).
	Britain recognizes South American republics.
1826.	Resumption of civil wars.
1830.	Bolívar stripped of powers; death.

4

ANDREW JACKSON

(1767–1845)

And the Expanding Democracy of America

Sometimes a statesman presents in his character and personality a picture of his countrymen's idealization of themselves. Such among Englishmen were Palmerston and Churchill in their heyday; such was Andrew Jackson, "Old Hickory", the champion of the new American democracy of the eighteen-twenties and -thirties, the nucleus round which the Democratic Party was built, the tough, lean warrior from the Old West, with his "hawk-like frontier face" and unpretentious dignity. Jackson, write Professors Morison and Commager,

> had all the virtues and many of the faults of the American back-woodsman; but none of the vices. Loyal, pugnacious, and honest, he was also credulous, intolerant, and unlearned, with slight conception of the complex forces that were moulding themselves under the shadow of his personality. . . . Jackson's frontier simplicity made him over-trusting of friends and too suspicious of opponents. An intellectual check on his emotions was wholly wanting. Yet Jackson's simplicity was his strength, for the American people looked through his eyes, and thought with his brain.[1]

This hundred-per-cent American was also an Irishman—the child of very new Irish immigrants. In 1765 the Andrew Jacksons senior, with their two sons, Robert, five months, and Hugh, two years, had taken ship from County Antrim, in Northern Ireland, for the American colonies, and after a daunting passage of the North Atlantic had settled on "200 acres being in the county of Mecklen-burgh, Province of North Carolina". Within two years, however, Andrew Jackson senior was dead. His wife bore him a third, post-

[1] *Growth of the American Republic*, vol. i, pp. 471–472.

humous son and named the baby Andrew in his honour. A sharp
lad, quick at 'book-learning', young Andrew was at the age of nine
doing trojan work as a public reader for the small community, and
his most dramatic opportunity came when in August 1776 to an
audience of "thirty or forty" he read aloud from the just-delivered
newspaper: "In Congress, July 4, 1776. The Unanimous Declaration of the Thirteen states of America. 'When, in the course of
human events it becomes necessary for one people to dissolve the
political faults . . .'" These were certainly momentous times for a
boy to be growing up in. Apart from his commendable prowess as a
reader, Andrew Jackson's scholastic attainments never reached a
very high standard. Yet in the frontier environment where he grew
up and first made his mark, common sense, straight-forwardness,
leadership, and manliness meant more than mere book-learning,
and these were qualities that Jackson proved early that he possessed
abundantly. However, his mother's dreams for him to be a minister
in the Church seemed unlikely to be realized; his own ambitions
were rather to excel in the footrace, jumping match, and musket-
shot. Though lightly built, he was tall and a tenacious wrestler: "I
could throw him three times out of four, but he never would *stay
throwed*," said a classmate. He would fight whenever his honour
was challenged. An excellent judge of chances in a cock-fight and a
sage assessor of horse-flesh, he could swear to damnation as well as
some and better than most.

For Elizabeth Jackson the War of Independence put an end to
many hopes, and a religious or academic career for Andrew was
perhaps the least of them. In 1775 the fighting began, but the royal
forces were repulsed at Charleston in 1776 and the rebellious
Carolinas were not deeply involved again until 1780, when the
British under Clinton made a last effort to retake the South. Andrew's eldest brother, Hugh, had died at the Battle of Stone Ferry;
against Clinton now, Robert (aged fifteen) and Andrew (only thirteen) joined the company commanded by their uncle Major Robert
Crawford. Both boys were engaged in fighting on more than one
occasion; in April 1781 both were captured by a company of
dragoons. At this point Andrew, cocksure and fully committed to
the cause of independence, nearly succeeded in getting himself
killed. When he was commanded, "in a very imperious tone", to
clean the boots of the officer of the dragoons, "he promptly and
positively refused, alleging that he expected such treatment as a

prisoner of war had a right to look for". From the ensuing sabre slash Andrew Jackson's left hand, thrown up in defence, was cut to the bone and his head gashed and scarred for the rest of his life. Released from prison on the plea of their mother, both boys were sick with smallpox; after a terrible journey home Robert died, and Andrew was kept alive only by the dedicated nursing of Elizabeth. With her last remaining child recovered, Mrs Jackson now prepared to go to the prison hulks in Charleston to nurse her nephews held there. "Kissing at meetings and partings was not so common as now," reflected Jackson on that farewell. "Wiping her eyes with her apron", his mother gave him her worldly advice to make friends by honest conduct and to keep them by loyalty. "Andy . . . never tell a lie, nor take what is not your own, nor sue . . . for slander. . . . Settle them cases yourself." She was dead from plague by the November.

So at the age of fourteen Andrew Jackson was an orphan, albeit a most self-reliant one. Living in his uncle's house, he tried to pick up old threads. He started back at school, but gave it up; he was apprenticed to a saddler, but again the life was too staid and he could not take to that either. Coming into a few hundred pounds on the death of his grandfather in Ireland, he showed that his love of excitement had not changed by gambling away all his little legacy in the Charleston horse-racing season.

Returned home, Jackson tried school once again—he even tried teaching—but nothing satisfied him, and in December 1784, a year after Great Britain had recognized the American colonies as a single independent nation, he packed his saddle-bags and left for Salisbury, in North Carolina, intent on becoming a lawyer. As a pupil in a law office he was, reports one witness, "the most roaring, rollicking, game-cocking, horse-racing, card-playing, michievous fellow that ever lived in Salisbury . . . head of the rowdies . . . more in the stable than in the office. . . . His ways and manners [to the girls] were most captivating. He would talk fast with a very marked North-Irish brogue. . . . Either calm or animated, there was something about him I cannot describe except to say it was a *presence*." He was now "full six feet tall and very slender, but . . . graceful. . . . His eyes were handsome . . . a kind of steel blue." In 1787, after nearly three years of legal apprenticeship, Andrew Jackson, at the ripe age of twenty, qualified as an attorney.

Working his way round the circuit with the itinerant court, he learned much, but with hardly a penny to his name he decided to try his luck out West. North Carolina then extended right to the Mississippi, and out of the forested wilderness west of the Alleghenies rugged pioneers had cut two areas of rough settlement 150 miles apart; the whole was in 1796 to become the new state of Tennessee (the name, tradition claims, being then suggested by Jackson). Into this territory, where savage death from the angered Cherokees was commonplace, rode Judge John McNairy, aged twenty-six, and his law-school friend and new public prosecutor, Andrew Jackson, aged twenty-one. The raw frontier town of Nashville, capital of the district, lacked reliable law enforcement and was controlled by debtors, but within a month seventy writs of execution for debt were forced home by the young Jackson, and business confidence returned. The prosecutor flourished too in his private legal practice. With money scarce and land a convenient substitute, he became, moreover, a substantial landowner in a very short time.

It was now that he met his Rachel, the love of his life. In 1788, already unhappily married to Lewis Robards, she was "irresistible to men" (and Jackson was undoubtedly a man), with her "beautifully moulded form, firm red lips", and "a glowing, oval face . . . rippling with smiles and dimples". Constant quarrels caused the Robards to separate, and Jackson was impatient to marry Rachel. Away in Virginia, Robards did obtain permission to sue for divorce, but the report of this to reach Nashville made the lovers believe that a divorce had actually been obtained. Certainly Jackson as a lawyer was remiss in failing to check the report and obtain documentary proof; nevertheless in August 1791 he married Rachel Robards. In his defence it may be admitted that communications were poor and that he was extremely busy in his legal and business ventures, but nevertheless by his carelessness he had given sizable hostages to fortune. For two years the Jacksons lived their passionate idyll, but then came the the thunderclap: Robards had gone ahead with the divorce that everyone thought was over and done with. Rachel was guilty, the court said, of desertion and adultery, and found for Robards, who therefore got his divorce, with the maximum of damage done. Undoubtedly Jackson's intentions in the unfortunate affair were honest; he was culpable only in his professional capacity of lawyer. Yet the sneering gossip, real and at times imaginary, remained a permanent cloud which Jackson on numerous occasions in the long future tried angrily and unsuccessfully to dispel. Even after a second marriage ceremony Rachel's peace of mind was never to be quite restored.

In 1790 the part of North Carolina west of the mountains took the first step to statehood by being organized as a separate territory. By 1793 it had established its own legislature, and two years later, with the required population, it had the right to prepare a frame of government. In 1796 this was done, with Jackson one of the three delegates from his county, and in the same year the new State of Tennessee came into existence. By now he was a good deal more than private lawyer and public prosecutor (or attorney-general to give it its grander name); he was also a military man, "judge advocate for the Davidson Regiment" of the newly formed militia; and as a capital recognition of public esteem he was elected as the new state's member in the national House of Representatives.

In Congress at Philadelphia Jackson found himself a small fish in a big pond. He was seen there as a "tall, lanky, uncouth-looking personage" with his "queue down his back tied with an eel-skin"; his dress was "singular", his manners "those of a rough backwoodsman". Jefferson himself noted his lack of self-control; he "choked with rage" during one speech and could not finish. For the rest he proved himself a foe to pretension when he voted against a sugary motion in praise of President Washington on his retirement, and he succeeded in securing federal finance to help Tennessee veterans of the Cherokee War of 1793. Returning to Nashville locally popular, he was further honoured by being returned in the same year (1797) as senator. The House of Representatives had been difficult enough; the Senate, a much more dignified body, suited him even less, and early in the following year, his finances being troubled, he resigned.

Six months after his return home he accepted a judgeship on the bench of The Tennessee Supreme Court, where his decisions were "short, untechnical, unlearned, sometimes ungrammatical, and generally right". At Jonesborough a miscreant named Bean resisted arrest and held off the sheriff and a posse of ten. Jackson ordered the sheriff in a sharp rebuke to conscript as many men as were necessary. Stung by the lecture, the sheriff, waiting for the bench to adjourn for lunch, summoned all three judges to join the posse. Jackson's associates haughtily refused; he accepted immediately. With drawn pistols he faced Bean and threatened to shoot him down if he did not surrender; and the sheriff was handed his man. But although Jackson was respected for his vigour and the forthright way he did business and carried out his public duties, there is no doubt that his too quick resort to violence to settle personal quarrels lost him many friends in the state. Yet it was this very impulsiveness which pushed him to the front at time of general crisis and gave him command over men and events. It is true too that on some occasions when he resorted to violence he had good reason. For example, he challenged the Governor of Tennessee, earlier a famous Indian fighter, one Nolichucky Jack Sevier, when in a heated public argument the man roared, "I know of no great service you have rendered the country except taking a trip to Natchez with another man's wife." "Great God!" cried Jackson, "do you mention *her* sacred name?" But, rightly or no, Sevier was a popular man, and in local politics it was the judge rather than the Governor who lost favour.

In 1804 Jackson left the bench. But he was not heartbroken at leaving civil public life, for he was now a major-general of militia and his military rôle was the most important to him. Again at this period he was in financial straits. Already, in 1795, involved in the general crash of that year, he had had to sell his fine estate of Hunter's Hill and had moved to a smaller place, The Hermitage, eight miles from Nashville, and having to sell many of his slaves to pay his debts, he had had to struggle to keep afloat. Again now by careful handling of his estate and some knowledgeable racing of his horses on the local courses he succeeded in restoring his affairs. A much grander Hermitage eventually emerged, with a mansion to match Washington's Mount Vernon or Jefferson's Monticello; and Jackson lived and entertained there in style. (When, much later while he was President, the place was burned down he had it rebuilt according to the old plans; it stands today, one of America's historic houses.)

Jackson was a typical frontiersman in his careless consideration of Indian property and rights. He was typical too in his desire to expel Spain from the northern shores of the Gulf of Mexico, and especially from the Floridas, and it was his eagerness to accomplish this that led him now in the dangers of the Burr Conspiracy. Aaron Burr, Vice-President of the United States under Jefferson (1801–5) and the man who had killed the statesman Alexander Hamilton in a duel in 1804, was a smooth but dangerous schemer who had been devising various plans by which Louisiana (newly purchased by Jefferson from France) might be detached from the Union. In 1805 Jackson, assuming that a Vice-President's word could be believed, and understanding that *Spanish* territory was Burr's target, offered his assistance. But as soon as he glimpsed the truth he was all action, sending letters of warning up and down the Mississippi and to the Government in Washington offering his soldiers against "aggression . . . FROM ANY QUARTER". He needed to protest loudly, however, as a letter from the Secretary of War showed that rumour in Washington put Jackson and his militia fully behind Burr in his proposed treason. Fortunately Jackson was quickly able to prove to the Secretary the loyalty of his intentions, but it appeared to him that there had been collusion between Burr and the commander of the New Orleans garrison, and that Jefferson's Government was shielding traitors. Previously Jackson had been a strong Jefferson man; he had "loved Jefferson as a man and adored him as a President". No longer; by 1808 Jackson was supporting Monroe in Tennessee against Jefferson's protégé Madison and moving into the camp of those who opposed the old Virginian influence in national politics. This was eventually to have important results for the nation. As for Aaron Burr, he was tried for treason, but escaped on a technical point of law; Jackson was furious.

American events over these years were, of course, closely linked with those of Europe, where the Powers were now grappled together in the long series of wars arising out of the French Revolution; the Louisiana Purchase itself was made possible only by Napoleon's recognition of his helplessness to maintain a transatlantic French empire. In the Anglo-French struggle there was no doubt in which direction Jackson's sympathies lay. When in 1797 France, triumphant in the Netherlands and Italy, turned her attentions towards an invasion of England, Jackson wrote hopefully— perhaps his left hand was rubbing the scar on his forehead as he wrote—of British tyranny being humbled, her throne crushed, and a "republic springing from the wreck". That was Senator Jackson in 1797. General Jackson in 1805 was, as we have seen, itching to lead his men forward against 'aggression' from any quarter—and "any quarter" could mean indifferently Spaniards or Englishmen or Indians. However, the military adventurer in him had to wait a few more years yet.

Although he was denied the chance of going to war in 1805, it was not long before the bellicose Jackson had the chance to lead his men "on to victory and conquest". War with Great Britain came in 1812. The apparent causes arose from the struggle between Napoleonic France and Britain: the Royal Navy's impressment of American seamen, its stopping and searching of U.S. ships on the high seas, and its insults to the American flag. But the principal motives behind the American declaration were the hope of conquering Canada and the prospect of ending the Indian menace on the Western frontier, with all the valuable lands which might be acquired if these aims succeeded. In 1811 the Twelfth Congress met in Washington; prominent in it were new, young men, many of them from the bellicose West. These were the 'War Hawks'—among them Henry Clay from Kentucky, Felix Grundy from Tennessee, and John C. Calhoun from South Carolina. As soon as the news of war reached Jackson he offered the President his militia of 2500 men; and when no orders came he raged with impatience. But he was made Major-General of Volunteers—at least this was an improvement in status—and soon he was gathering men for operations in Florida. With extraordinary speed and control he got his men to Natchez only to hear that the nervous Government had called the campaign off. He now had to get his soldiers back home, and, with what he could beg or buy in the way of supplies, he set off again, for Nashville. It was exhausting and dispiriting going, but Jackson was everywhere encouraging the weary, supervising ration distribution, always on foot until his men offered their horses. Because of his stamina and endurance on this march his men began to call him "Old Hickory"—hickory, one of the toughest of woods—and the nickname was to stay with him for the rest of his life. This annoying false call to the colours was not altogether without value; it allowed Jackson to weld officers and men into a useful campaigning force and sharpened everybody's desire to be involved in more serious service.

Evidence already abounded that the Creek Indians were preparing for war when, to remove all doubts, they massacred 250 settlers at Fort Mims in Mississippi Territory. Jackson was confined to bed when the call came in September 1813, but he immediately issued orders to recall the regiments. "The health of your general is restored. He will command in person." His plan was to take the army straight to the heart of the Creek strength, and again he pushed his force speedily through the wilderness. "We shot them down like dogs," said Davy Crockett; and at Talladega, against guns, arrows, and tomahawks, the Tennesseans slew three hundred Indians for the loss of fifteen whites. Having moved with such celerity, the army had outstripped its supply arrangements, and when Jackson, with the rest of the campaign in mind, refused to move back to civilization he faced mutiny. After holding out as long as he could he eventually had to agree to retire. Twelve miles out from their fort the starving soldiers met the drove of cattle that Jackson had long awaited; fires were lit on the spot and the men feasted. When the General then ordered a return to the fort to carry on the fight the men refused. Most of them were without proper footwear and clothing for a winter campaign; they had left their homes in haste and expected to return as soon as the frontier was safe—which most of them considered that it now was. Virtually alone, "Old Hickory" sat his horse in front of the mutineers, levelled his musket, and threatened to shoot; slowly, the men obeyed. Morale, however, did not improve. Later he had to parade a whole brigade and have cannon at the ready, with matches lit, before discipline was a second time restored. Eventually the disaffected troops were replaced, and as soon as the new force arrived he moved them against the Indians; once more the whites gained quick success and the patriotic American newspapers had something to sing hurrah for. The main war against Canada had been going badly, and the news from Jackson's army brought cheer and consolation to the people. It also brought to the notice of ordinary folk the name of the army's courageous and successful hero.

At first light on March 27th, 1814, all his efforts came to the test. His army of 2000, on the Horseshoe Bend of the Tallapoosa river, faced 8000 warriors, the Indian main force. The river was swum by Jackson's scouts and the canoes carried off; then, after he had allowed the Indian women and children to escape, the fighting began in earnest. Among those present was Ensign Sam Houston, the future Texan leader, who long after recalled the "arrows and spears and balls flying", and the bands of braves always fighting to the last man. At the end Indian losses were seven hundred and fifty dead; Jackson's were forty-nine killed and a hundred wounded. "The *carnage* was *dreadful*", he wrote to his wife. He had won the Creek War and returned to Tennessee to a great reception from the populace. It was the state's first major achievement, and Andrew

Jackson was the architect of it all; a great hero. In addition to the tumultuous acclaim, Jackson received something that pleased him even more: promotion into the United States Regular Army as Major-General over Tennessee, Louisiana, and Mississippi Territory. His military successes against the Indians in the south were rounded off by a treaty which they were forced to accept. He took from them twenty-three million acres of land, or what is now a fifth of the State of Georgia and three-fifths of Alabama. The chastened chiefs named him Sharp Knife, as well they might.

Worried about possible British attacks in the Gulf of Mexico, Jackson now moved to make safe the town of Mobile and if possible to take a cut at Spanish Florida. The British had had things very much their own way in attacks down the American coast from New England to Washington, where they had even burnt down the Presidential mansion and sent President Madison in ignominious flight from the capital. Now it seemed that the South was to have its turn: British troops and warships were already at Pensacola, in Spanish Florida, and the plan was to take Mobile, and New Orleans, and then to detach from the Union anything that would come. Without orders, Jackson in a well-planned lightning stroke, crossed the border, took Pensacola, and only just missed the British, who blew up their fort and sailed off to join the much larger force now preparing to take New Orleans.

New Orleans was of supreme importance to the United States in the War of 1812; not only was it the mouth of the whole river communications system of the West, but its loss would mean the turning of the American flank with all the dangers which that entailed. The city stands 105 miles from the mouth of the Mississippi, and because of its watery approaches and the surrounding swamps a small force could, in defence, hold up a much superior one. Fear of a British attack had already produced some preparations for self-defence, but there was still much to be done, and as Jackson rode there from Mobile in late November 1814 he calculated the opportunities that the terrain offered, for defence or attack.

The lakes to the east he patrolled by a small fleet, and the other routes he blocked and earthed; the great river itself was controlled by his fort below the city. He told his cavalry commander at Baton Rouge to be ready for "a fandango . . . in the Christmas holidays". Out in the Gulf lay a large British fleet and 9000 men, many of them veterans of the Peninsular War. They were to be led by

Lieutenant-General Pakenham, Wellington's brother-in-law and an experienced commander. The coming fight was likely to be rather rougher than a fandango, but "Old Hickory" remained confident that he could deal the British a blow they would not forget. Suddenly, however, by a brilliant move, the British got to within a mere four miles of the city, taking, instead of the easiest route across the Plain of Gentilly, a reed road built with great stealth along a swamp edge, from where they swept out, 2000 strong, on to firm ground within sight of the rich prize. It seemed that New Orleans must fall quickly. But the British decided to wait until their main force arrived before continuing the assault. Their sudden caution proved mistaken; as an accomplished Indian fighter and dueller Jackson was the last man to give a second chance to. "I will smash them, so help me God!" he said. By hand-to-hand fighting in the pitch black of that first night he achieved a counter-surprise, and by building a solid breastwork in frantic haste he gave himself an excellent line of defence. Now he was ready for what was to come.

The final battle for New Orleans began at first light on January 8th, 1815. The ground between the two armies was flat and without cover, and right across from river to impassable swamp stretched Jackson's high breastwork punctuated by cannon and served along its whole length by rank upon rank of probably the best marksmen in the world at that time. The British, in their regiments as on parade, presented a beautiful sight with their scarlet tunics and immaculately white cross-straps under a forest of bayonets. Then came the 'Advance' and the redcoat army moved forward. Immediately death was everywhere; Pakenham was soon down and dying, and his men caught in a murderous fire. Many fell; some stumbled back; only two score redcoats actually reached the rampart; only one scaled it, a Major Wilkinson, and he fell mortally wounded as he did so.

British losses in this battle were over 2000 killed, missing or wounded; the Americans lost 13 killed and 58 wounded; Pakenham's body was carried away in a casket of rum by the retreating army to preserve it on the long journey home to England. Yet in one sense Jackson's victory was ironic and futile. The treaty ending the war had already been signed at Ghent on Christmas Eve, 1814, but the news did not come through until March.

Until Jackson could be certain that peace was proclaimed he kept New Orleans under martial law, which brought him into conflict both with the citizens chafing under his rule and with the district federal judge, whom he dared to banish from the city. (When civil authority was restored Jackson was fined a thousand dollars for contempt of court; and in his old age Congress voted to refund him the sum, with twenty-nine years' interest.) But with the nation at large Jackson was a hero. Soon he was put in control of all military forces south of the Ohio.

By 1818 the Creek Indians were showing by their attacks on frontiersmen and their families that they did not accept the vast cessions of the Jackson treaty of 1814. Old Hickory was more convinced than ever that Spanish Florida, the seat of most of the anti-American trouble, should be occupied, and on his way south to subdue the Indians once more he wrote to President Monroe that this could be done "without implicating the government. Let it be signified to me [as] desirable . . . and in sixty days it will be accomplished." He claimed later that Monroe in fact sent him the asked-for nod; Monroe in his turn denied this. But Monroe knew well Jackson's character and should have been more explicit if it was intended to limit his activity. The upshot was that the General did all he had said he would, although he did take a little longer than he had estimated. In one non-stop sweep he proceeded to put down the Creek and Seminole Indians, execute two British adventurers, and take Florida from the irate but helpless Spanish Governor.

In Washington the news of Jackson's triumph threw the Administration into panic. Negotiations with Spain for the purchase of Florida had been taking place over a long period, and to save these from disaster most of the Cabinet, including Calhoun, Secretary of War and Jackson's political superior, argued that his activities be repudiated. But John Quincy Adams, the Secretary of State, defended Jackson strongly. And Adams not only converted his colleagues, but convinced an angry Spain that this might not be the last time that the terrible General was loosed on Florida, and that it would be best to "cede to the U.S. a province of which she retains nothing but the nominal possession". By the Adams-Onis Treaty of February 1819. Spain sold Florida to the U.S. for five million dollars.

Against his inclinations and better judgment, Jackson was persuaded to be Florida's first Governor. "The General, I believe, wants to get home again as much as I do. . . . He wishes he had taken my advice. . . . Amen." So wrote his wife during their journey to the new post in 1821. After a short but very stormy term of five months he resigned, and at long last returned with Rachel to The Hermitage, intending, as he put it, to live by the ".... cheirful fire for the ballance of our lives." This could hardly be; he was already a national figure, and, though there were some who thought him uncouth and dangerous, there were many more who spoke his name with pride. And close about him even now was a group of men who saw him as their candidate for the Presidency.

America in the early nineteenth century was already undergoing rapid transformation. When Jackson had crossed the Blue Ridge into Tennessee in 1788 Jefferson's dream of a nation of farmers free of the corrupting influences of industrialism seemed possible; by 1820 the dream was fading fast. The area of the U.S. had doubled in that time; the population had risen from about 4 million to over 9 million; and while the rural population still outnumbered the town-dwellers by thirteen to one, in 1790 it had been nineteen to one. The two largest cities focused this change: in 1790 New York had 33,131 citizens, in 1820, 130,881. Philadelphia had increased from 44,092 to 108,809 in the same period. The West too was growing at a furious rate, while the steamboat and the post-roads were tying the new United States to the old ever more closely. In 1790 it had taken five weeks to reach the Mississippi river boundary of Tennessee; in 1820 it took only two. Along the east coast industry had begun to expand, spurred on by American demand during the long period of the European wars, and especially after the War of 1812. Even Jefferson himself said as early as 1816, "We must now place the maufacturer by the side of the agriculturist", and by the same year once stern supporters of the old Republican Party were acclaiming dressed-up Federalist Party aims as vital to the progress of America. Calhoun was now for the Bank of the U.S., for a tariff, and for internal improvements to be paid for from the federal revenue; and Clay was making all these ideas into his "American system". Times were on the move, and the old Virginian dynasty was on the wane. It was to be Jackson's rôle to complete the change, to challenge the old 'establishment', and to personify the new democracy that indeed came to be called 'Jacksonian'.

By 1824 Jackson was a Presidential candidate, his opponents being John Quincy Adams, Calhoun, Clay, and Crawford. Jackson himself spoke little, considering his military record sufficient recommendation, but the campaign was by no means velvet-gloved; the affair of the marriage, for instance, was too good for the opposition to miss. However, with support for Jackson growing, Calhoun understood by 1824 that he stood no chance of the Presidency, so accepted the nomination for the Vice-Presidency; and when the election took place in the electoral college Jackson seemed to be the people's choice with 99 votes; Adams had 84, Crawford 41, and Clay 37; and thus under the Constitution it was now for the House of Representatives to decide the issue, balloting by States. At this juncture, however, Clay's votes were thrown behind Adams's, and it may be that there was a shadowy understanding between the two that Adams should appoint Clay as his Secretary of State. When Adams was elected there was an immediate cry of "treachery", though Jackson himself was silent until Clay was in fact offered the Secretaryship. Then he exploded: Jackson and the people had both been swindled by the "corrupt bargain". With such tempestuous spirits aroused, Adams and Clay were not to have a quiet term; in fact, the next four years were one election campaign, and few doubted who was to be President in 1828.

All America's Presidents down to and including John Quincy Adams had come from the old States of the north and east, but now the centre of gravity of American life was beginning to shift, and this was inevitably reflected politically as the frontiersmen who had built the state west of the Alleghenies became increasingly vocal and influential. Moreover, their democratic influence had ensured by 1828 that all men had the vote, not only in the new western States but in the old States too; the people, who in the 1824 election had to some extent been thwarted by the politicians, were about to have their say. Democracy was on the move, and Jackson, the personification of the frontier, seemed certain to be its man.

In 1824 all the Presidential candidates had been from the Republican party; it was the clash of personality rather than of party principle that dominated that contest, as it continued to dominate the political manoeuvring of 1824–28. Gradually, however, out of these internecine Republican battles, which continued into the 1830's, it was clear that two new parties were emerging—those for Jackson, to be known as Democrats, and those against him, to be known as Whigs. Each of these groups vilified the other as the term progressed; the "corrupt bargain", and even more virulent charges, were laid against Clay; Jackson was attacked as a man unfit to be

President, with every disreputable anecdote from his impulsive and wilful life catalogued to cast doubts on his dignity and judgment. Again the details of his marriage proved grist to the mill of his enemies. But as long as he heeded good advice and let others do his work his success seemed assured. In 1826 Jackson supporters carried both Houses and the bandwagon continued to roll. The virtual certainty of the prize made others' hopes loom larger; who was to be heir presumptive? Calhoun, already Vice-President and leader of a major wing of the new party, was a powerful candidate; but Van Buren, the "red fox", the businessman and political organizer from New York who "rowed with muffled oars", was certainly a man to watch. In 1828 the more brilliant and flamboyant Calhoun still seemed the stronger contender and was adopted to run as Vice-President on the ticket with Jackson.

Election day came, and the feeling of foregone conclusion was borne out by the result—Jackson 173 electoral votes, Adams 83. Calhoun was again made Vice-President. Old Hickory, now sixty-one years of age, was "filled with gratitude"; but within a month tragedy had marred everything. Tradition claims that Mrs Jackson inadvertently discovered what had long been kept from her—the slanders on her character used in the election struggle; in a state of deep shock she took to her bed and died. Jackson loved her beyond all else and was grief-stricken by her death.

Mid-February 1829 saw a haggard President-elect in Washington, preparing his new Cabinet. Van Buren was made Secretary of State, Senator Eaton of Tennessee, Jackson's chosen confidant, War Secretary; as a whole the Cabinet has been charged with mediocrity. By Inauguration Day, March 4th, 1829, Washington was packed with people. The tall, straight Jackson, like Jefferson before him, insisted on walking to the Capitol; many had feared he would exploit his military reputation and lay on a pageant. Standing in the roped-off portico, he spoke his inaugural address quietly, and was sworn in by Chief Justice Marshall. Then, pushing through the crowd, he mounted his horse and rode to the White House, followed by a multitude of "countrymen, farmers, gentlemen mounted and dismounted, boys, women and children, black and white". Unable to stem this tide of humanity, the few officials at the gates of the Presidential mansion were swept aside and the mob flowed in to crush round the President, eat the refreshments laid out for invited guests, break expensive china and glass, to stand on damask-covered chairs, and ruin beautiful carpets with the mud from unpaved Pennsylvania Avenue. "It would have done Mr Wilberforce's eyes good [wrote one who was there] to have seen a stout black wench eating . . . a jelly with a gold spoon at the President's House." Jackson was rescued and hustled away, and the rabble were at last enticed out only when tubs of punch were placed on the lawns. Polite Washington society grimaced expressively and reckoned it had been right all along. In a way they *were* right; Jackson's election was the culmination of a long process of decay in the power of the old ruling élite and their combination of property and education—a decline begun with the end of the War of 1812 and hastened by the popular upsurge that had now made Jackson President. The slogan was 'Reform'. A new era had begun. A new class was taking over, vigorous and self-assertive, typified in some degree by Jackson himself, the self-made aristocrat of Tennessee.

To tie the new classes to the new party, to clinch the only half-understood revolution, and to satisfy reform by removing the corruption of the old order, it was necessary to make a redistribution of federal offices. It has been wrongly charged that Jackson invented the 'spoils system', the practice by which men are appointed to administrative posts purely on the grounds of party loyalty—'jobs for the boys'. But it was already occurring widely in state governments, and at federal level Jefferson had made political support a condition of appointment. Jackson dismissed something between a tenth and a fifth of all federal office-holders during his eight years as President; Jefferson had done about the same. The difference is that after Jackson the practice became regular in national government. He believed that such jobs were so straightforward that anyone with intelligence could soon learn and carry out the duties satisfactorily and that it was good to rotate offices; government was not to be

an engine for the support of the few at the expense of the many. . . . I cannot but believe that more is lost by the long continuation of men in office than is generally to be gained by their experience. . . . He who is removed has the same means of obtaining a living that are enjoyed by the millions who never held office.

Unfortunately these honest intentions became somewhat tarnished; there proved to be as much corruption and inefficiency among his own appointees as among the people they replaced, and as the century wore on succeeding Presidents used the system more extensively.

Jackson being Jackson, he not surprisingly chose to surround himself with kindred spirits, often not acceptable to the old 'establishment'. The official Cabinet, chosen largely to placate party factions or sustain sectional influences, were not always the men with whom Old Hickory could argue out policy with no holds barred. From the first there existed a group completely in his confidence which, though it included members of the regular Cabinet like Van Buren and Eaton, brought to a position of influence others like Major William Lewis, who lived at the White House, Amos Kendall, later appointed to the Cabinet proper, and Francis P. Blair—these last two both newspaper-men, a hitherto despised class. The group came to be called the "Kitchen Cabinet"; its members had much ability, and gave both good advice and moral support to the politically inexperienced Jackson. It was Jackson who was in control— he used his "Kitchen Cabinet" only as occasion suited—but by its very obscurity it drew upon itself highly critical attention. The very able Calhoun from South Carolina was not in the "Kitchen Cabinet"; this was his second term as Vice-President and, with his strong following in the Party, he was aiming for the Presidency in 1832. But signs were already appearing of rivalry between him and Van Buren and of a cooling of relations with Jackson himself; and during the following years each of the troubles that the Government ran into only widened the breach between President and Vice-President.

Jackson's first Cabinet then was a Cabinet of factions, taking issues on causes both serious and trivial. Chief among the trivial was the affair of Peggy Eaton. Major Eaton, Jackson's Secretary of War and intimate friend, had married his mistress, a Washington tavern-owner's flirtatious daughter, whose previous husband (conveniently, it was murmured) committed suicide at sea. Eaton was not a Calhoun man, and Peggy became the lever by which her husband could be removed from office. At official functions the wives of the rest of the Cabinet (led by Mrs Vice-President Calhoun) cold-shouldered the alleged "hussy" Mrs Eaton; at balls and dinners they would not speak to her until, worn down by it all, she stopped attending such occasions altogether. Jackson, remembering bitterly the slanders on his beloved Rachel, took Eaton's side; he berated the Cabinet and, with the widower Van Buren, paid studied attention to Mrs Eaton (whom he declared "as chaste as a virgin"). Soon the President was forced to recognize that he was fighting an organized attempt to drive Eaton from the Cabinet, and, reasonably, he put the blame on "the great intriguer Mr Calhoun". Loyal to Eaton, Jackson retained him in the Cabinet until 1831. Mistrusting Calhoun more and more, he threw his influence—and nobody was allowed to doubt who was master—increasingly towards Van Buren as his principal adviser and likely successor.

Relations cooled even further as Calhoun became the champion of the theory of extreme states' rights and more specifically of the thesis of 'nullification', by which a state in convention might declare a federal law null and inoperative within its boundaries if it believed the law to be beyond the powers of the Constitution. The point at issue really was the tariff, and the state foremost in the controversy was South Carolina, Calhoun's own state.

In the U.S.A. tariffs were an issue as explosive as the Corn Laws in Britain. In general, the North-east, needing protection for its manufactured goods—against British imports in particular—was in favour of high duties. The West, and above all the exporting South, both overwhelmingly agrarian regions, wanted to keep their imports cheap and therefore bitterly opposed a tariff which could benefit the industrial North-east. Federal laws of 1816 and 1824 had both raised import duties to the increasing resentment of the South, especially of South Carolina, a state from which, since it was not sharing in the cotton boom, prosperity was relatively receding. In 1828 one of the last acts of Adams's term raised the tariff still further—upon which feelings in Charleston ran so high that there were threats of a boycott on northern industries and of South Carolina leaving the Union. This was the "Tariff of Abominations", which Calhoun declared to be "unconstitutional, oppressive and unjust". In Charleston they flew flags at half-mast.

Jackson, a Westerner and not much in love with protection, had nevertheless spoken in favour of a moderate tariff as an aid to national defence. With his eye on the Presidency at that time, he had attempted to steer a prudent, moderate course between Southerners and New Englanders, but the "Tariff of Abominations" remained to plague his first term of office and to engender a dispute which, like the issue of slavery later, threatened the very integrity of the American Union.

By 1829, when he became President, the original thirteen ex-colonies had expanded to twenty-four states enjoying self-government and independent rights. The question was, how far ought these rights to extend? It was an old quarrel, which the tariff was to waken anew, and soon slavery was to embitter intolerably. How much authority had the states surrendered under the Constitution to the federal government? Calhoun argued that any individual state—in the tariff argument South Carolina—had the right to decide whether a law was or was not unconstitutional. The Supreme Court could not, according to Calhoun—since it was itself committed as an organ of federal authority. If South Carolina declared the tariff null and void, then within the borders of South Carolina the tariff was null and void.

Jackson was himself a states' rights man, but he recognized limits and would not countenance disobedience to the laws of Union and the threat to its continued existence. The argument had raged inside Congress and out, but the Calhoun faction now decided to involve Jackson himself. It was intended to entrap him into support for the extreme views at a Jefferson birthday banquet on April 13th, 1830. The speeches and toasts were plainly in favour of nullification, and Old Hickory, outwardly calm but inwardly fuming, bided his time. Finally he seized the opportunity of a volunteer toast to make his position unmistakably clear; he stood grey-haired and straight-backed, and called: "Our Federal Union —it must be preserved", which, says one onlooker, hit the assembled company "with blinding, staggering force". Calhoun, visibly shaken, rose slowly to reply to the challenge: "The Union—next to our liberty, most dear." In the eyes of the nation, with the exception of the State of South Carolina, Jackson had won the skirmish.

The chilled relationship finally froze when Jackson eventually learned the full truth of Calhoun's stand against him in the Cabinet of 1818 at the end of the Florida campaign; Calhoun had been for repudiation of Jackson's actions. Knowing the sort of man he was dealing with, Calhoun might have done better to make a clean breast of his earlier hostility; he must be considered foolish for keeping silent on the matter so long. Jackson now denounced fiercely what he saw as Calhoun's duplicity and insincerity; he lacked, said Jackson, "those high, dignified, and honourable feelings which I once thought he possessed". The breach was complete. Van Buren, on the other hand, had continued to rise in the

President's estimation. They rode daily together discussing current problems and issues, and Jackson listened carefully to his astute young Secretary of State. By 1831, pretending ignorance of the motivation of the various squabbles and recognizing that a complete reorganization of the Cabinet was necessary to remove Calhoun's friends, Van Buren suggested his own resignation as a way out. Jackson, no intriguer and supremely honest, took a long time to be convinced, but at last agreed, and in one great reshuffle in 1831 Calhoun's men, Eaton, and Van Buren were all relieved of their offices. Jackson proposed to send Van Buren to London as ambassador, but the Senate (on Calhoun's casting vote) refused to confirm the appointment. "It will kill him, sir, kill him dead," said a triumphant Calhoun. "He will never kick, sir, never kick." But Calhoun had seriously misjudged. His own vindictiveness had been laid bare. Van Buren, with Jackson's strong support, was made to appear, like Jackson himself, as the champion of democratic interests against the malicious opposition of the old conservatives. He was clearly now Jackson's heir apparent, though since Jackson himself was to stand again in 1832, he would have to bide his time.

Old Hickory's hold on the nation, pugnacious personality, and sound understanding of the democratic forces which supported him are all to be seen both in his handling of the continuing issue of 'nullification' and in his stubborn struggle with the Bank of the United States. In 1830 he had made his position clear on nullification, but when a new tariff was passed in 1832 South Carolina exploded with indignation and determined to put into effect Calhoun's doctrine. A Convention met, declared null and void the tariffs of 1828 and 1832, and forbade the collection of revenue in the state by federal officers after February 1st 1833. Should coercion be attempted South Carolina would defend itself and secede from the Union. In Jackson's mind there could be only one answer to such a threat; the Union was in danger and he knew his duty. He issued a "Proclamation to the People of South Carolina", in which he warned the 'nullifiers', appealed to the nation, and stated plainly the constitutional rights of the Union. Calhoun's claim to annul a law of the United States was

> incompatible with the existence of the Union, contradicted expressly by the letter of the Constitution, unauthorized by its spirit, inconsistent with every principle on which it was founded,

and destructive of the great object for which it was formed. . . .
The Constitution of the United States, then, forms a *government*,
not a league. . . . To say that any state may at pleasure secede
from the Union is to say that the United States are not a nation.
. . . Disunion by armed force is *treason*. Are you really ready to
incur its guilt?

The nation was on his side; the other states sent him assurances of
support and tenders of volunteers to the extent that he could have
thrown 200,000 men into the field in forty days. To Congress he
sent a request for additional powers which became the so-called
Force Bill, or Bloody Bill, according to which side a man supported.

None of this was bluff, and nobody doubted that Jackson was
prepared to use military force if necessary; but the Administration
was also ready to listen to compromise, and two tariff proposals
were soon before Congress. That of Henry Clay, "the great com-
promiser", proved the more acceptable—a gradual reduction in
duties until by 1842 there would be a top level of duty of 20 per
cent only. When the Force Bill and the new tariff passed Congress
together and were signed by the President in March 1833, South
Carolina rescinded the Ordinance nullifying the tariff, but as a
last act of defiance passed a new one nullifying the Force Bill.
Jackson's initiative, decisiveness, and statesmanship had averted a
mortal danger to the Union. For the time being at least, except for
a few diehards, it was the end of talk about secession. However,
Jackson saw well enough that there would one day be other issues.
The "next pretext", he predicted, "will be the . . . slavery question."

The second Bank of the United States had been given a twenty-
year charter in 1816. The first Bank had been a child of the Federalist Party and opposed in its time by the Republicans, who had let
it die in 1811; the second Bank had been in fact enthusiastically
proposed by Republicans like Calhoun and Clay during the
nationalist fervour which had gripped the country after the War
of 1812. Second thoughts about much that was then done were
now full in fashion. Because of its size and connection with the
Government, which had subscribed a fifth of its capital and used
it for the deposit of all its funds, the Bank had tremendous power,
and was thus heartily hated both by other banks and by their
champions, the state politicians. In addition it drew upon itself
the anger of thousands of ordinary folk when in times of depression

and financial stringency it took over huge amounts of real estate, especially in the West. States had tried to check the 'Monster' by local laws, but these in their turn were frustrated by the protective decisions of the Supreme Court. At the Bank's head Nicholas Biddle, whose financial record was second to none, had come to look upon the institution almost as his own and believed that the Bank's importance and influence were so great that, if attacked, its position was unassailable. Perhaps he cannot be blamed for not understanding the will and temper of the man already deciding to oppose him. Banks and paper-money were not much to Jackson's liking; he was a 'hard money' man, having seen (and, indeed, himself experienced) the hardships arising from too deep a trust in banks and their notes; and he felt himself the spokesman and defender of the class which seemed to him always to suffer from such dependence, the "shirt-sleeves democracy", the hard-working ordinary folk. Deep down in Jackson there was the same country-man's mistrust of "city slickers" that one finds, say, in his English contemporary Cobbett, the same disapproval of a system under which honest farmers and "the great body of the working people" who created the nation's 'true' wealth were at the mercy of mani-pulators who merely exploited it and them.[2] Old Hickory detested privilege, and the Bank seemed to him to be built upon it. It alone handled federal government business, which made it monopolistic. A quarter of its wealth was in foreign hands, which made it un-American; the remaining three-quarters belonged to "a few hundred of our own citizens, chiefly of the richest class, especially of the East"—which made it anti-democratic.

He had opened fire in 1829 in his first message to Congress and returned to the battle again in 1830. Biddle, confident of victory, wanted to avoid publicity and 'politics'; he tried at first to concili-ate Jackson. And there is no doubt that the Bank had benefited the economy of the U.S. and facilitated the operations of the Govern-ment's finances. In Congress there was no lack of prominent men on the Bank's side, headed by Adams, Clay, and Webster. Biddle, moreover, as the contest progressed, used the Bank and its money power to buy support in Congress and in the Press; he still felt

[2] Cobbett, himself inspired by Jackson's fight against the Bank, wrote that he was the "greatest soldier and greatest statesman whose name has ever yet appeared upon the records of valour and of wisdom". On their side many Jacksonians read and applauded Cobbett's robust swipes against paper-money, speculators, and the financial aristocracy on his side of the Atlantic.

that the new charter would go through. But, for Jackson, democracy and the power of the Bank were incompatible.

Anti-Jackson men, who had now coalesced into the Whig party, saw in all this a contest they could win, and Clay and Webster made the rechartering of the Bank a principal issue in the election of 1832. They were successful, up to a point. The Bill was brought in, and within three weeks of being accepted by the Senate it passed safely through the House of Representatives on July 3rd, 1832. Biddle and his henchmen were cock-a-hoop. For Jackson, ill and confined to bed, the issue had become more than a matter of political principle; it was a personal contest. "The Bank, Mr Van Buren," he said, "is trying to kill me, *but I will kill it!*" and on July 10th he delivered his counter-stroke, a presidential veto on the Recharter Bill.

The election followed, with Clay basing his case on sound finance and the Bank, and attacking Jackson's attempt to "stir up the poor against the rich". However, the poor had one advantage against the rich—there were so many more of them; and the election results soon showed Old Hickory's popularity: 530,000 votes for Clay, 687,000 for Jackson, giving a handsome electoral college majority of 219 to 49. It was an election both glorious for Jackson and important in the history of American politics. Jackson stood as a 'Democrat', abbreviating the old label of 'Democratic Republican' of Jefferson's day. Clay, representing another wing of the old Republicans, stood under the description of 'Whig'. Thus Jackson was the first Democrat President; and it was under the leadership of Jackson and Van Buren that the Democrat Party was forged.

With the election over and the veto sustained it was hoped by many that the Bank would be allowed to die quietly, but Jackson was afraid that the subtlety of the "Monster" would undermine the good sense of his beloved democracy. He decided, therefore, to remove the government deposits from the Bank and so cripple it before any new intention to recharter could be formed. There was a last frantic rearguard fight by the Bank and its friends in Congress; by refusing to grant credit, calling in its loans, and thus inducing financial distress, Biddle attempted to show the stupidity of Jackson. "Rely upon that," he said. "This worthy President thinks that because he has scalped Indians and imprisoned judges he is to have his way with the Bank. He is mistaken." But he was not; when two Secretaries of the Treasury refused to sanction the withdrawal of Government deposits from the Bank the Secretaries were removed first and the deposits afterwards. Jackson had got his way; the Bank was beaten.

Candour and straight dealing, dominant qualities in Andrew Jackson, were strongly displayed in his conduct of foreign affairs. The three main areas of difficulty were with Great Britain over the West Indies; with France; and with Mexico over Texas. Trade with the West Indies, closed by Britain at the end of the American War of Independence, had remained so despite protracted negotiations. Jackson, finding this situation on entering office, decided on the use of shock tactics. He requested Congress, in 1830, to pass a non-intercourse law against trade with "Canady", as he called it, with the coastguard strength necessary to back it up; Congress complied. Britain, seeing that the withdrawal of the American law depended on her agreement to reopen the West Indies trade, removed the restrictions and so within five months of signing the non-intercourse bill, Jackson was issuing a proclamation declaring his object achieved and the trade resumed.

Relations with France were complicated by unmet American demands for compensation arising out of the destruction and seizure of property under Napoleon. (European countries had had similar claims, but these had all been paid as early as 1815.) After a wearying history of patient and unprofitable politeness, and feeling that the French were showing contempt for America, Jackson decided that there was "nothing now left for me but a recommendation for strong measures". In 1834, therefore, he ordered the navy to be ready for service and suggested to Congress the seizure of French property, public or private, to satisfy the claim—belligerent moves which were received with popular enthusiasm throughout the Union. The French, having first made a conventional show of 'firmness', proceeded, with one or two face-saving gestures, to climb down and pay up.

Texas belonged to Mexico, and the U.S. in her treaty with Spain for the purchase of Florida in 1819 recognized as much. But by the 1830's 30,000 American settlers, drawn by its fertile cotton and grazing lands, had moved into Texas, and a movement for separation from Mexico was already strong. These Texans wanted to join the United States, and Jackson tried to buy the province. God, he claimed, "had intended this great valley [the Mississippi and its tributaries] to belong to one nation"; but the Mexicans would not sell. Reports kept coming in of Texan intentions to break from Mexico; the leading spirit was Sam Houston, Jackson's old comrade-in-arms. In 1835 the revolution came. In effect self-governing now, the Texans repeatedly asked the United States to recognize their independence; Jackson would not. Americans everywhere were watching the drama; in the Northern states anti-slavery sentiment was strong and the number of abolitionists was growing. The following year (1836) was again to be election year, and Jackson knew that any move that looked like a step towards the annexation of Texas, because it would extend the area of slavery, would bring Texas and slavery into the election as a sectional issue, split the Democratic vote, and lose Van Buren any chance of success. Only after the victory of his favourite, and on his last full day as President, did Jackson send a *chargé d'affaires* to the "Republic of Texas", thus officially recognizing it. But neither Jackson nor his successor Van Buren would go further. Texas as a potential extension of 'cotton culture' and the slave system made it too hot a proposition for them to hold. It was another nine years before the Republic of Texas, by the narrowest of Congressional majorities, was admitted to the Union.

Jackson was a true Westerner; nothing underlines the fact so emphatically—and perhaps to the modern conscience so saddeningly—as his attitude to the Indians. It had long been argued that the Indians remaining in the areas fast becoming populated by white men should be removed across the Mississippi to new territory, leaving their tribal lands for more civilized development. Those in favour of removal claimed that the Indians—"noble savages"—would thus be saved from the sophistication and corruption of the worst elements of frontier society; that they would thus assimilate the new civilization more slowly and painlessly; that the "Almighty's command" was "to till the earth", and that, since Indians were blocking progress, God would have been for their removal. In fact the main motive for transplanting the Indians was straightforward greed for their land. In Jackson's two terms ninety-four Indian treaties were made and several million acres taken from them. Bribery, intimidation, and alcohol were all used to induce the Indians to sign away their lands, and the majority, though cheated at every turn on matters such as removal expenses and compensation for improvements, left without resistance. In the North-west the Sauk and Fox tribes did try, in 1832, to fight for their rights, but a force of regular and militia soldiers from Illinois massacred them during their attempted escape across the Mississippi. (The twenty-three-year-old Abraham Lincoln was a volunteer on this expedition, though he saw no fighting.) In the South the Cherokees tried to win by legal means, and though they were given good professional advice and aid by their numerous white friends, and though the Supreme Court decisions favoured them, all this availed them nothing. The local state officials refused to be bound by the decisions and the Administration refused to interfere. In 1835 the Cherokees gave in and signed. In Florida the Seminoles had in 1832 agreed to removal, but then decided that they did not like the terms and in 1835 began hostilities. The war lasted until 1842 and cost the United States 1500 men and over 50 million dollars before full military operations were suspended and most of the tribe sent off to what is now Oklahoma. For most of the Indians transferred under Jackson's policy the journey was a "trail of tears"; many thousands died on the way. At the time things looked differently. To Van Buren, for instance: "That great work", he said, referring to Jackson's part in removal, "was emphatically the fruit of his own exertions. It was his judgment, his experience . . . vigour and . . . activity that secured success." Of course Jackson did what he did in the name of progress. He regretted the hardship and suffering that went with his policy, but these he regarded as prices which had to be paid. De Tocqueville, the contemporary commentator on the American scene, prophetically saw that the Indians would be safe beyond the Mississippi only until some new wave of settlers reached them. Eventually they would face extinction. He seems to have been right.

By 1834, the Administration was in the enviable position of having paid off the national debt and accumulated a surplus from the revenue, from the tariff, and from the sale of public lands. A long and surely unique debate then took place on what to do with the surplus, which in the end was deposited with the states, to be used by them without interest and to be repaid to the federal government on demand. Very many local improvement schemes were thus financed by this federal money, and the middle thirties became a boom period of rapid expansion. In 1834 four million acres of public lands were sold, in 1836 twenty million. Speculators throve; money-raising was easy. With the big Banks out of the way, hundreds of newly chartered little banks lent freely and pushed up the circulation of paper currency.

To Jackson all this was highly dangerous and improper; his faith rested firmly on silver and gold. In future, therefore, said his 1836 Circular, buyers of public lands must pay in specie (gold or silver). This decision, an attempt to prevent inflation from getting disastrously out of hand, itself certainly helped to spark off a severe deflation—the 'panic of 1837'. Banks failed by the score; paper-money was utterly in discredit; everywhere assets were sold for hard cash, prices driven down, and thousands were ruined, many of them speculators—and this last at least had been Jackson's intention.

By the time the worst of the depression struck, Jackson's Presidential term was over. His high standing with the people and his dominance within the Democratic Party had by then enabled him to choose his own successor. There could be little doubt who it was to be. Ever since Calhoun had attempted, and failed, to break Van Buren following the Peggy Eaton affair, the future of the suave little New York political boss had been assured. Like Jackson a champion of popular democracy, he had throughout remained the President's confidant and right-hand man; and in 1836 he inherited Old Hickory's popularity with an absolute majority of electoral votes over all his opponents. Unfortunately for him and the Democratic Party that Jackson and he had built up, Van Buren was also to inherit the legacy of the 'panic of 1837'.

Jackson's last annual message to Congress, in December 1836, was still able to be made in the sunshine of prosperity. He could look back over his eight years with quiet pride. He had kept the Democracy safe. He could claim to have triumphed over all the issues that faced the nation in 1829. "All that has occurred during my administration," he wrote, "is calculated to inspire me with increased confidence in the stability of our institutions." But he had long felt the need to warn them of the dangers of division that could arise from sectional jealousies which would "shake our happy confederacy"; he did this in a formal 'Farewell Address' after the manner of President Washington, which his enemies called gross conceit and his friends copied on to white satin to bequeath as a rich legacy to their issue.

On March 4th, 1837, eleven days from his seventieth birthday, President Jackson accompanied Van Buren to the Inauguration.

Again, as eight years before, the route and all about was crowded with people, though now quiet and hatless; "for once", it was said, "the rising was eclipsed by the setting sun". With the ceremony over, a great shout of farewell rose from the vast concourse. He was soon on his way back to Tennessee and The Hermitage, beset by hosts of well-wishers at every stop; the only President, it has been said, more popular at the end of his term than at the beginning. For the eight more years that he had to live he kept his keen old eyes constantly on national affairs. He poured out letters to all and sundry, advising, arguing, criticizing, praising, and the burden of them all was that the ground that had been won for the people and the party should be held, and advance be made along the same path.

Who were these people who had looked so steadily to him, and what was the path? Jackson's support, and therefore the support for the Democratic Party, came from many classes and occupations. It included the poor and the new immigrants; most small farmers and the fishermen of the North-east; many of the city working-men, artisans, and labourers; from a richer class the small and middling planters in the South as well as the farmers in the expanding grain areas of the North-west; and among men of wealth the bankers who opposed the overmighty United States Bank. From his own section, the West, he gained emphatic approval from the men of the frontier who had long hated the idea that the East controlled them. But from all over the U.S.A. he attracted support too because people admired him as the Old Hero, the victor of New Orleans, the successful military chief. The path that has been named Jacksonian democracy was that of republican virtue, of equality and justice for *all* the people. And central to it was the party's recognition of and dependence upon the political power of the great body of the people themselves. Jackson once spoke of the "absurd doctrine that the Legislature is the people". His own calls to the common folk in ringing phrases over the heads of the politicians, and their supporting response, were enough to prove him right.

In his personal affairs Jackson did not have an easy life. He loved children dearly yet had none of his own, and although he and Rachel adopted a son, he turned out, with his constant debts and other inadequacies, to be a sad disappointment. In later years, and especially through his terms as President, Jackson suffered constantly from illness and the pain from old wounds; yet though irascible at times he never lost his sense of humour, was never dull company. Gradually the old man weakened, until on Sunday June 8th, 1845, aged seventy-eight, he breathed his last. His nicknames are redolent of the kind of esteem in which his contemporaries held him—the Old Chief, the Old Hero, Old Hickory. His surname was to remain immortalized in the description of his times—the Age of Jackson.

Table of Events

1767.	Andrew Jackson born to Irish immigrants.
1775–83.	War of the American Revolution.
1791.	Marriage (re-marriage 1793).
1796.	State of Tennessee instituted.
1797.	Jackson in Senate.
1803.	Louisiana Purchase.
1804.	Major-General of Militia.
1805.	Aaron Burr affair.
1812.	War with Britain.
1813.	Campaign against Creek Indians.
1815.	Jackson's victory at New Orleans.
1824.	J. Q. Adams defeats Jackson in Presidential election.
1828.	"Tariff of Abominations". Jackson elected President.
1829–32.	Jackson *versus* the Bank of the United States.
1829.	Peggy Eaton affair.
1830–32.	Jackson *versus* Calhoun.
1832.	Jackson defeats 'Nullification' and the Bank. Re-elected.
1833.	Tariff Compromise.
1835.	Revolt by Americans in Texas. Cherokees submit; war against Seminoles.
1836.	Boom expansion. Specie circular. Von Buren elected President.
1837.	"Panic of '37".
1845.	Death of Jackson.

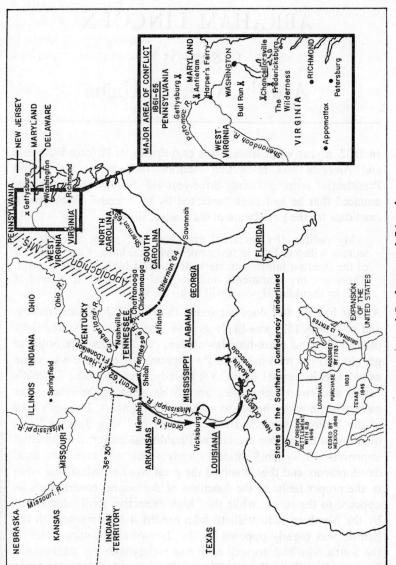

Age of Jackson and Lincoln

5

ABRAHAM LINCOLN

(1809-65)

And the American Union

In 1832, a year when Britain was engulfed in its Reform Bill crisis and America was re-electing Andrew Jackson for his second Presidential term, a twenty-three-year-old Abraham Lincoln announced that he had been "solicited by his friends" to become a candidate for the Legislature of the State of Illinois.

> My politics [he declared] are short and sweet, like the old woman's dance. I am in favour of a national bank. I am in favour of the internal improvements system and a high protective tariff. These are my sentiments and political principles. If elected, I shall be thankful. If not, it will be all the same.

At first hearing this does not sound the stuff of drama or tragedy, and no-one in 1832 was likely to have seen in the raw young jack-of-all-trades and spare-time law-student (who incidentally failed to get elected) the man in whom the supreme national crisis to come would find its central figure. Yet already, even in young Lincoln's "short and sweet" principles, are visible some of the cracks that were to open wide enough to split the nation apart. Jackson's veto of the National Bank had raised the cry of "King Jackson" and question of the proper exercise of Presidential power; the "internal improvements system" meant spending national taxes on local developments and thus involved the great issue of federalism—that is, the proper limits to the functions of the central governments as opposed to the states; while the "high protective tariff" demanded by the Northern industrialists, who needed it to compete with the British, was bitterly opposed by the slave-owning cotton states of the South, who had no such need and preferred to buy their manufactures cheap from Britain. This tariff issue underlined once again what a challenge the founding fathers had laid down in 1787 when they proclaimed their new republic to be a United States. Men

might continue to reverence the Union in theory, but every new
political quarrel seemed to show how ill-tempered was the marriage
of North and South, with separation, whether as a fear or a hope,
more and more in the partners' minds.

It was the confluence of two basic historical facts that brought the
great crisis of the Union in Lincoln's day. One of these was the
institution of slavery in the Southern states, and the other, the insatiable drive westwards of the east-coast settlers of America. From
the earliest days slavery had become one of the facts of existence
for the colonial South; yet it was not until the development of the
cotton industry in Lancashire after 1780 and the consequent demand for vast quantities of raw cotton that slaves really began to
pay off economically. The rising demands of Lancashire's mills and
the revolutionary invention of the cotton gin combined to mean
that cotton-growing was suddenly big business; and slavery, which
many Southerners of the later eighteenth century had been inclined
to condemn, or at least prepared to write off (slaves were so lazy),
became within a few decades vital to the planters of Georgia and
South Carolina. From these states cotton, and with it slavery, spread
rapidly westward to Mississippi, Alabama, and Arkansas, all of
which were admitted to the Union between 1817 and 1836. Although
only about a quarter of the Southern white population owned
slaves (the commonest type of white Southerner being the non-slave-
owning independent farmer), that quarter included the richest and
most influential citizens; and many of the remaining three-quarters
who owned no slaves were nevertheless strongly hostile to the Negro,
seeing in him a possible economic competitor and in slavery the
only sure means of holding him down. Thus cotton interests could
generally call the tune.

In a strictly material sense most slaves were not worse off, probably, than hired labourers or Northern factory workers. Most of
them were tolerably well fed and looked after—house servants
better usually than field hands. Undoubtedly many masters were
fond of their slaves, and slaves too of their masters—always within
the conventions of a father-and-child relationship, which included
the giving and taking of punishment for misdemeanours. White
children often had black mammies to nurse them, and might well
grow up with slave children as playmates. Less prosperous owners
frequently worked side by side with their Negroes in the fields. All
over the South slavery was so old and accepted an institution that,

until the North's attacks forced self-justification, there was little self-consciousness about it, and little theorizing. It was simply that a Negro was regarded as a lower form of life—and one drop of 'black' blood in a white man's veins turned him into a Negro. Moreover, a slave was not legally a 'person', and the law would not accept a Negro's evidence against a white.

The North from the early decades of the nineteenth century made much of the slave-owners' brutalities, and, of course, there were brutalities. There were even slave revolts. But most masters respected their Negroes at least as they would respect any other items of valuable property; and only a fool would want so to punish his slaves that they would run away.

The westward expansion of the slave states was matched—and even outmatched—by that of the free North. Already by 1820 Ohio, Indiana, and Illinois had been attached to the Union, and a full quarter of United States citizens lived west of the Appalachians. First had come adventurers, hunters, and trappers living off the wonderful abundance of wild life. Following the hunters came the pioneer farmers, either squatters with their rough cabins and their clearings among the rich wilderness, ready to move on at the earliest sign of failing fertility or the first sound of another's axe, or else settlers who had legal title to their wonderfully cheap land, who built permanent homesteads and founded the first frontier settlements at such places as Cleveland, Cincinnati, Indianapolis, Detroit, or Chicago. Some, selling their property at a good profit, advanced with the tide many times; Lincoln's father used to tell about a "family that moved so often that the chicken were trained to walk to the wagon, lie down, and put their feet up to be tied for the trip". By now New England was by comparison a long-settled place with its own hierarchies; the South was increasingly dominated by its planter aristocrats; but the conditions of the new North-west invited equality, democracy, and individualism in the highest degree. "The fittest survived," as one old settler put it, "and the rest the Lord seen fittin' to take away." Physical stamina, resource in an emergency, ruggedness in the teeth of nature, were endowments more to be prized than any advantage of class or birth. Here one had to earn the right to be called 'sir'. It was an expression, so a visitor noted, that even servants rarely employed.

Of the original thirteen ex-colonies, six became slave states and seven free. By 1819 four more free and five more slave states had been admitted to the Union—giving a delicate and exact balance in the Senate, dividing along the line of the Ohio river. But the east–west Ohio terminated at the north–south Mississippi; what was to happen as the tide of settlement swept westward beyond that great river over the lands of the Louisiana Purchase? This immense tract of territory stretching from the modern state of Louisiana in the south to the old Mexican and (undefined) Canadian borders, over a quarter of the modern United States, had been bought in 1803 by Jefferson from Bonaparte for a knock-down price, and now it lay wide open to exploitation and settlement. It was under federal sovereignty and not yet organized into states, but as its various 'territories' became sufficiently populated they would be likely to apply to the American Government for admission to the Union as states. When in 1819 Missouri did so it became very clear that the slavery question would not go quietly to sleep, as many had hoped.

Nothing had been done, when newly purchased Missouri was first settled by United States pioneers, to interfere with the institution of slavery which already existed there by virtue of earlier French and Spanish laws. On the other hand, most of Missouri lay to the north of the extended line of the Ohio river, and a good deal of it to the north of the old Mason and Dixon line demarcating free Pennsylvania from slave Maryland and Delaware. A long and bitter controversy, which many thought must split the Union, was ended in 1820 by the 'Missouri Compromise', which accepted Missouri as a new slave state (balanced by Maine, a new free one) but forbade slavery in future north of latitude 36° 30'—that is to say, in the whole 'unorganized territory' of those vast plains and as-yet-undreamed-of horizons that are now Kansas, Nebraska, Colorado, Wyoming, the two Dakotas, and Montana. There for the time being the explosive matter rested.

The statesman who did the most to secure the Missouri Compromise was Henry Clay, and it was Clay who was to become young Lincoln's pattern and ideal. But in 1820 Lincoln was still the Indiana backwoodsman's son, a lad of eleven concerned more about his skill with the axe—which was already considerable—than with politics, though surprisingly enough for one in his station he was already beginning, in his father's phrase, "to fool hisself with eddication".

Lincoln's is a classic instance of the tough frontier upbringing.

He had been born in 1809 in a cabin in Kentucky, the only son of Tom Lincoln, carpenter and farmer, and his wife, Nancy. Tom Lincoln never settled anywhere long; something in his temperament, combined with bad farming luck and, once, a dispute over title deeds, caused him to move several times while Abraham was still of tender years. Not that children stayed of tender years long in these pioneer circumstances; they either toughened or died. Two of Nancy Lincoln's three children survived infancy, Abraham and Sarah (and Sarah was to die young, in childbirth). Abraham's constitution was strong—it always remained so—and he soon became handy with odd jobs about the farm. When he was nine he had the sad task of making the dowel pins for his mother's home-made coffin. Together with an uncle and aunt who had joined the Lincolns in their latest venture, she succumbed to an epidemic that carried off men and cattle alike; it was known as the " milk-sick ".

By that time the family had moved the two hundred miles from Knob Creek in Kentucky to Spencer County in Indiana, where father and son between them felled, cleared, and planted some seventeen of the eighty acres that Tom Lincoln bought at two dollars an acre. The young boy did have some very scanty schooling, and was soon to be encouraged in his desire to read books by his new and excellent stepmother, a young widow with three children of her own already; but the chief occupation of those early years—indeed, right up to the time he was twenty-two—was the felling and trimming of timber and clearing away of surplus wood. The boy lent a hand also, of course, with ploughing and harvesting, and men remembered his habit, eccentric indeed for one in his circumstances, culpable even, of taking a book with him to fill his days' crevices of leisure. Among the volumes he got hold of were Aesop's *Fables*, *Pilgrim's Progress*, *Robinson Crusoe*, Parson Weems's *Life of Washington*, and Grimshaw's *History of the United States*. Doubtless he read the Bible too, but although his father and stepmother were members of the local Baptist church, and despite the strength of the religious organizations on the frontier—often of the hot-and-strong variety—he never became much of a church- or chapel-goer, an omission for which later as an aspiring vote-winner he had to find the best explanation he could.[1] Hungry as he was to pick up

[1] In the *Illinois Gazette* in August 1846 he wrote: "A charge having got into circulation in some of the neighbourhoods of this District, in substance that I am an open scoffer at Christianity, I have by the advice of some

such morsels of book-learning as presented themselves, the young Lincoln, a raw, muscular, and very tall boy, all arms and legs and ill-fitting clothes, was far from being a bookworm. His local reputation was chiefly as a wrestler, where he gave considerably better than he got among the lads of the village, and as a crazy humorist, a 'character', slow and laconic of speech, but an excellent story-teller and mimic. Politics was as yet an unopened book.

By the time he was twenty-one he had done a spell of work at the local ferry, and once taken a cargo in his own home-made 'flat-boat' down the Mississippi to distant eye-catching New Orleans. Then in 1830 Tom Lincoln sold up again, hitched his horses and oxen to the wagons, and moved away another two hundred miles to the Sangamon river in Illinois, where all the clearing and cabin-building and pioneering began again. Abraham also hired out his skill with the axe, splitting rails for fencing, and again he and some others took a flat-boat cargo down the Mississippi to New Orleans. Then yet once more Tom Lincoln shifted quarters, and when Abraham returned from his second Louisiana journey he did not return home. Settling instead on his own at New Salem in Illinois—settling rather as driftwood settles against a snag in the stream—he took a job as a clerk in the village store; again made his local reputation as a wrestler; studied mathematics and grammar with the help of a local schoolmaster; joined the New Salem Debating Society; and eventually dipped his toes into politics with the "short and sweet" principles of his candidature already quoted. Unsuccessful, and soon after unemployed as well, he enlisted to fight the Indians who under their chief Black Hawk were still menacing paleface settlers among the forests of northern Illinois and southern Wisconsin. This campaigning, which gave him his first taste of authority, was short and hardly hazardous. A speech he made about it long afterwards in Congress, pouring scorn on the Democrats' attempt to build up the heroism of their man Cass in fighting the Indians, affords incidentally an excellent example of the mature Lincoln's style of public debating, intimate, humorous, and telling—as Carl Sandburg wrote, "as if he and another man were driving in a buggy across the prairie exchanging their thoughts":

friends concluded to notice the subject in this form. That I am not a member of any Christian Church is true; but I have never denied the truth of the Scriptures; and I have never spoken with intentional disrespect of religion in general, or of any denomination of Christians. . . ."

By the way, Mr Speaker, did you know I am a military hero? Yes sir: in the days of the Black Hawk War, I fought, bled, and came away. Speaking of Gen. Cass's career, reminds me of my own. . . . It is quite certain I did not break my sword, for I had none to break; but I bent a musket pretty badly on one occasion. If Cass broke his sword, the idea is, he broke it in desperation; I bent the musket by accident. If Gen. Cass went in advance of me in picking huckleberries, I guess I surpassed him in charges upon the wild onions. If he saw any live, fighting Indians, it was more than I did; but I had a good many bloody struggles with the mosquitoes; and, although I never fainted from loss of blood, I can truly say I was often very hungry. . . . I protest they shall not make fun of me, as they have of Gen. Cass, by attempting to write me into a military hero.

Home from the Indians and the mosquitoes, Lincoln kept a shop for a time. Then for three years (1833–36) he was postmaster for the New Salem district; continued to pick up a little extra by rail-splitting and other occupations; succeeded at the second attempt in getting himself elected to the Illinois state legislature; acted meanwhile as assistant to the local county surveyor; and in his twenty-sixth year set himself in his spare time seriously to study law.

In all Lincoln sat four terms for the Illinois legislature. Seven months after he had begun practising as an attorney he found it convenient to leave New Salem (which was soon to become a ghost town) and move to the state capital of Springfield, where one day in April 1837 he rode in, carrying all his worldly possessions in his two saddle-bags. The little town, then of 1500 inhabitants, was to be his home for the coming quarter-century, ceasing to be so only when he moved to the White House. But though he became a successful and quite prosperous lawyer and a prominent and popular local politician—a loyal Whig subscribing to the 'American system' of Clay and Webster, fighting strongly for his own and his party's advancement, working hard through stormy, financial crises for Illinois' 'internal improvements', canals, railroads, and so forth— yet nothing he performed at Springfield for the first eighteen years or so seemed to be marking him out for any peculiar distinction. Even when in 1846 he was elected to go to Washington as one of the Illinois Congressmen, little about Abraham Lincoln seemed out of the ordinary, except his appearance.

Many thought this ungainly to the point of uncouthness. He was very tall, six feet four, rather stooped and gangling; a sinewy, leather-skinned man, with a jutting chin and a prominent mole on his right cheek, his black hair "coarse and rebellious", his swallow-tail coat loose and ill-fitting, his trousers some inches too short for his long legs, his hat "old and rusty", his boots unblacked. Yet if his manner and style seemed lacking in polish one could not deny that his was a striking face: lined early in life, and rugged; with deep-set eloquent eyes that changed expression rapidly from the animation of argument or anecdote to an intense abstracted melancholy. When his humour flowed it was boisterous or pungent—hostile newspapers wrote him down as a bit of a clown—but he was a man too of cavernous silences.

He approached matrimony in the manner of a nervous non-swimmer advancing into a rough sea—glad, having wetted the ankles, to regain contact with the bachelor shore. With confused emotions, but principally relief, he escaped from his engagement to a Miss Mary Owens, who found him lacking both in social refinement and in gallantry, so that in his turn he was happy to discover and report, that she was too fat, wanted teeth, and was generally "weather-beaten". Years later, when Lincoln had already become a prominent citizen of Springfield, he courted Mary Todd, the daughter of another leading Springfield politician, a well-connected and genteelly educated girl nine years Lincoln's junior and in almost every respect his opposite—short, plump, volatile, sociable, sharp-tongued, highly-strung. "One 'd' is enough for God," he once said, "but the Todds need two"; and though such typical banter need not be made too much of, Lincoln could hardly be unconscious of the disparity between their social origins. A second time Lincoln's engagement was broken off, though by whom is not clear. What is plain is that he was in a turmoil of self-doubt, indecision, and foreboding, "the most miserable man living". But to the surprise of many of their friends and to Lincoln's own "profound wonder" the two came together again and were married in November 1842. It is related that on the morning of the wedding a boy in the house where Lincoln lodged, seeing him unwontedly dressed for an occasion, asked him where he was going, and Lincoln answered, "To hell, I suppose."

Marriage, which he had approached with such apprehension, did indeed provide choppy waters and squally patches. Both partners possessed the defects of their qualities. Mary's vivacity could easily turn to shrewishness, her eagerness in her husband's cause to acerbity when they differed. She was quarrelsome and censorious,

not only with Lincoln but also with tradesmen, servants, and neigh-
bours; she exploded and raged a good deal; and with her violent
headaches was perhaps, more frequently than was at that time apparent, on the verge of mental illness—but then Lincoln, for any
woman who was neither a pudding nor a doormat, must have been
at times a most difficult husband. "In eating, sleeping, reading, conversation, study", reported his friend Speed, "he was regularly
irregular, with no stated time for eating, no fixed time for going to
bed, none for getting up." His abstractedness too must often have
turned to taciturnity, his melancholy to moodiness. His sartorial
failings and contempt for social niceties must have exasperated his
more conventionally minded wife. Yet though they fell into quarrels,
they fell out of them; respected and were loyal one to the other,
both in public and in the intimacy of the family circle (four sons
were born to them). She believed in him and his 'star', and learned
to live with his shortcomings; so too he with hers. And

> when her upbraidings became unbearable he would not talk back
> or censure her, but simply slip off quietly to the office. . . . Over
> the slow fires of misery that he learned to keep banked and under
> heavy pressure deep within him, his innate qualities of patience,
> tolerance, forbearance and forgiveness were tempered and re-
> fined.[2]

Although he took his law seriously as a good attorney should,
and with his friend and junior partner William Herndon built up
a thriving practice, the legal profession for Lincoln was primarily a
way into politics. Four years after his marriage he was elected to
the federal House of Representatives, and in 1847 set off for
Washington for the first time. It was a Washington heavily concerned with those two dominating and inescapable problems: first,
the expansion of the United States, how far, how fast, how ruthlessly? and second, the associated issue of slavery: was the newly
conquered territory to be slave or free? These were the days of
"manifest destiny"; rampant nationalism, especially in the frontier
states of the South-west and North-west, demanded that the
American borders should be extended to the utmost limits, northward over the whole vastness of 'Oregon', westward to California,
southward to the Rio Grande, which was deep inside territory that
the Mexicans, at least, were sure was Mexico. The quarrel with
Britain over the Oregon (Americo-Canadian) border was settled

2 B. P. Thomas, *Abraham Lincoln*, p. 60.

peacefully by the Ashburton Treaty along the 49th parallel of latitude, but this let-down for the all-out expansionists only whetted
their appetite for dynamic policies to the south and west, where no
great Power such as Britain stood in the path. First Texas was
formally annexed in 1845.[3] Then, the next year, President Polk's
government seized the pretext of the border dispute with Mexico
to start a war which exposed to America's grasp vast new prizes—
the territory comprising California, Nevada, New Mexico, Utah,
Arizona, and parts of Colorado and Wyoming.

The Mexican War provided the only issue before his Presidency
on which Lincoln stood firmly against conventional and popular
policies. He agreed with Clay—"this is no war of defence, but of
unnecessary and offensive aggression"—and also, though he did
not yet know it and had never heard of him, with a certain hard-
drinking young officer called Ulysses Grant, General and President
to be, who fought against Mexico and thought there was never "a
more wicked war". In 1848 Lincoln voted for a Whig resolution
condemning Polk's actions that had precipitated the conflict. Even
Lincoln and his friends did not wish to go so far as to renounce
the fruits of the war—merely to criticize its origins and immorality—
but his 'anti-patriotic' line was too much for the newspapers and
voters of Illinois. After his two years as Whig Congressman he was
not re-nominated, and much against his will he was forced into retirement from national politics. He continued active in the affairs
of Illinois, but his relative lack of influence depressed him.
"Melancholy dripped from him as he walked", said his legal
partner Herndon, and, indeed, his dejection was often intense and
prolonged. For the next five years he busied himself again in his
practice, travelling the circuit by buggy, or for long ruminating
hours in the saddle; much respected in court, a byword for straight-
forwardness and lack of affectation.

Lincoln was still in his last term in Congress when the slavery
issue, always smouldering, burst forth again following the rapid
acquisition of new territories in the West and South-west. Was
slavery to be permitted in all of these, or none, or some? And if
some, which? On each side there was an extreme view. In the
South there had grown up since 1825 or thereabouts a new aggressive theory in favour of slavery. Before King Cotton took over
(and 60 per cent of the Southern slaves were eventually employed on

[3] See pp. 147–148.

cotton plantations), in so far as any theory existed at all it was that slavery would in the course of time wither away. But now Calhoun of South Carolina and his supporters—Southern aristocrats, small planters, in fact a weighty majority of all Southern whites, high-minded Christian clergy among them—were claiming that slavery was not just an evil to be excused as necessary, but a positive good, since it simultaneously raised the Negro out of African savagery and afforded the white man leisure to lead a civilized and cultured existence. And if the North proposed to abolish slavery, then the South, in order to protect its states' rights and the very fabric of its civilization, had the right and indeed the duty to secede from the Union. Against all this the North had its own extremists, abolitionists of the school of William Lloyd Garrison, passionate humanitarians, intellectuals and moralists, among them those practical idealists who organized the very successful[4] 'underground railroad' to assist runaway slaves to escape to the North. Whatever the social and economic consequences, the evil of slavery being morally intolerable and an affront to the brotherhood and dignity of man, must be outlawed throughout the Union, and either the recalcitrant Southern states must be forced to come into line, or, if that proved impossible, the free Northern states must themselves secede from so contaminated a Union.

Between these passionately opposed views lay two more moderate. One envisaged a division, temporary or permanent, of a still *United* States of America into a Northern non-slave group of states and a Southern slave group, simply by extending the line of the old Missouri Compromise (36° 30′) to the Pacific coast. The other, whose most powerful spokesman was to be Lincoln's great rival Douglas, propounded the policy of the popular vote: irrespective of latitude, each new territory on becoming a constituent state of the Union should have the right by simple majority to determine its own status in the matter of slavery.

By 1850 there was once more in America a danger of the Union's break-up. The Southern secessionists were not in the mood to compromise, and if the Northern 'free soilers' had their way Southerners saw their 'superior' civilization excluded for ever from every new American state. On the other hand, if the South did

---

[4] Successful, but, of course, small-scale against the general background. It has been estimated that 0·006 per cent of slaves made this hazardous escape to freedom.

secede the North would certainly go to war. Middle Westerners in particular, the men of the upper Mississippi basin, would never quietly allow the mouth of their great river highway to be under the control of an independent foreign Power. In 1850 the immediate battleground lay in California. Gold had just been discovered there; the great rush was on; and California, unlike arid Utah and New Mexico, had conditions that might well attract a slave-owning society. Once more, however, a bargain was struck between North and South that postponed the great showdown, and again—as in 1820 with the Missouri Compromise and in 1833 with the Tariff Compromise—it was Henry Clay, Lincoln's beau-ideal of a statesman, who, with Webster's eloquent support, succeeded in fending off the disaster of civil war. The Compromise of 1850 that these men persuaded Congress to accept made California 'free soil'; left slavery in New Mexico and Utah to the decision of their inhabitants, though in any case their climate was unsuitable for plantation agriculture; abolished the Washington slave trade (which had so offended the sight of Lincoln on his first arrival in the capital, with its Negroes being herded south from the slave market "precisely like droves of horses"); and finally, a counterweight for the South, made much stricter the law against runaway slaves.

This give-and-take was not to last long. In the Presidential election of 1852 both Democrats and Whigs (though Southern Whigs were slipping away and the party was disintegrating) were still standing officially for peace and moderation, and extremists did badly at the polls. However, the Democrat who was elected, Franklin Pierce, lacked all qualities of leadership, and during his term the activists on both sides began to make the running; Clay and Webster both died in 1852, and the spirit of compromise gave way before the excitements of challenge. Indignant Northern editorials and sermons fulminated against the working of the new fugitive slave law, and some Northern states, stealing Southerners' political clothes, even passed acts to 'nullify' it. The 'underground railroad' grew, to infuriate the South. The sentimental best-selling novel *Uncle Tom's Cabin*, Harriet Beecher Stowe's tract for the times (1852) depicting Negroes as fully-qualifying human beings, while it powerfully stirred the sympathies of the North, appeared to the South as dangerous "nigger-lover's" cant. Everywhere by 1853 the political temperature had risen, but the man whose challenge to the North raised it above fever level was not as it happened a Southerner at all, but one of the Senators from Lincoln's own Illinois, Stephen A. Douglas, the "Little Giant" (so-called from his massive head and mane of hair on a very short frame); able and ambitious, belligerent and energetic; a fluent orator and most persuasive reasoner; and by a coincidence the suitor whom Mary Todd had rejected before she accepted Lincoln.

It was in opposing Douglas and his policies that Lincoln emerged from his lawyer's office in 1854 and made his first mark on the American national scene. Douglas was the champion of a trans-continental railway project, with the new line to run westward from Chicago rather than from its southern rivals, and in order to further this interest the area to the west and north of Missouri (vaguely known still as 'Nebraska') needed to be administratively organized into 'territories'. In 1854, therefore, Douglas, with the blessing of President Pierce and his largely Southerner Cabinet, managed to secure Congress approval of a bill setting up two new territories, to be known as Kansas and Nebraska, "with all questions pertaining to slavery left to the decision of the people residing therein". This was Douglas's bait to catch Southerners' votes for his project, but to the free soilers of the North it represented a criminal betrayal of the Missouri Compromise; to the abolitionist zealots it was a blasphemy actually to *extend* the potential area of slavery. Even to Northern moderates this was the last straw, and Douglas cheerfully admitted that the road from Chicago to the Pacific could be lit by the effigies of him made for burning. Douglas, himself no partisan of slavery,[5] was unalarmed by the hornets' nest he had roused. For him the question was not moral but practical: where the geographical conditions suited slavery it seemed sensible to permit it, and where they did not, no question arose. "Popular sovereignty"; let the people decide. Negroes did not count as people.

This was the vital issue between Lincoln and Douglas. Each of them disliked the extremists, on both sides of the fence. But Lincoln saw a moral issue where Douglas did not. For Lincoln the Negro was a man. "Popular sovereignty" sounded all very fine if he was not.

> But if a Negro is a man, is it not to that extent a total destruction of self-government to say that he too shall not govern himself? When the white man governs himself, that is self-

[5] But no lover of Negroes either. He preferred the white man to the black, he said, just as he preferred the Negro to the crocodile.

government; but when he governs himself and also governs another man, that is more than self-government, that is despotism.
. . . No man is good enough to govern another without that man's
consent. . . .

Douglas's Kansas-Nebraska Act had first brought Lincoln out to
speak on behalf of one of its opponents in the local elections. Soon
he too was a candidate and wholly involved. Gathering conviction
and power as he proceeded, he announced that he would reply to
Douglas the day after the "Little Giant" was due to speak at
Springfield. The three-hour reply, made with Douglas listening in
the front row, was repeated at Peoria twelve days later and published; it is among the four or five most celebrated speeches that
Lincoln made. It is not entirely free of inconsistency. At one point
(quoted above) he strongly implies the right of Negroes to govern
themselves; at another he concedes that his "own feelings will not
admit" giving Negroes political and social equality, "with equal
votes, equal rights of intermarriage and so on". Certainly his attitude was measured, cautious, uncensorious. He did not "undertake to judge our brethren in the South", still less to propose the
abolition of slavery there. Slavery *existed* as a 250-year-old historical
fact; you could neither hold contemporary Southerners responsible
for it nor get rid of it quickly; but what you could do was to ack-
nowledge that it was an evil, to work towards its gradual abolition,
and above all to prevent it spreading to Kansas or Nebraska or anywhere else.

> [You will argue that] inasmuch as you do not object to my
> taking my hog to Nebraska, therefore I must not object to your
> taking your slave. Now, I admit that this is perfectly logical, *if
> there is no difference between hogs and slaves.*

It came back to the basic fact: a Negro slave was not a hog.
Morality was part of human nature, and not to be swept into a
corner.

> Repeal the Missouri Compromise—repeal all compromises—
> repeal the Declaration of Independence—repeal all past history,
> you still cannot repeal human nature. . . . The great mass of
> mankind . . . consider slavery a great moral wrong; and their
> feeling against it is not evanescent, but eternal. . . . It cannot be
> trifled with.

Some of Lincoln's supporters in Illinois, anti-slavery radicals,
called themselves Republicans from the Peoria speech onward.

Lincoln himself, still shunning radicals, was more cautious, but he was sleeping, as Herndon said, "like Napoleon, with one eye open. . . . His ambition was a little engine that knew no rest." He first stood for the Senate in 1855, but was defeated. The following year, at the first National Convention of the new Republican Party, he succeeded as Illinois' 'favourite son' in winning the second-highest vote for the Vice-Presidential nomination, but he was not yet sufficiently known beyond his own state borders. He still had to earn his living from the law, and continued to until 1860; a good living too—the coming of the railways, particularly, earned him much good business.

In Kansas and Nebraska, meanwhile, a situation had developed which was near to civil war. When Douglas's bill went through, pro-slavery men from Missouri rushed their forces into Kansas to ensure a popular majority for the Southern cause. Abolitionists from New England, not to be outdone, set up societies to finance 'free soil' emigration. The outcome was "bleeding Kansas", each side considering no tactics too extreme to use against the other: fraudulent ballots, rival constitutions, sacking the enemy's settlements, arson, outrage, murder. When the pro-slavery men were undeniably outnumbered they considered that they had been swindled and refused to accept the majority verdict. Then in 1857 the federal Supreme Court, the highest court of appeal, gave a verdict that was a shattering rebuff to the anti-slavery party. Dred Scott, twenty years earlier a slave in Missouri, had first been taken by his owner to live in free Northern territory and subsequently been taken back to Missouri. There he sued to be set free on the grounds that his residence on free soil had cancelled his slave status. By five to four the Supreme Court found that Scott, being a slave, was not a citizen of any state; could therefore not be considered a citizen of the United States; and accordingly could not sue in a United States federal court. Further, only fully fledged *states* could prohibit slavery within their confines; and since the Constitution guaranteed the rights of property and slaves were property, the American Congress had no constitutional right to ban slavery in the *territories*. In short, the Missouri Compromise had all along been invalid.

The Dred Scott decision, with the plain prospect it afforded of slavery spreading far and wide over the West, seemed such a disaster to many Northerners that they were for refusing to accept it; some, like William Lloyd Garrison, were for seceding from the Union straightway. Not Lincoln, however. He deplored the judgment, of course; it was "erroneous", and Americans must hope to get better judges who would reverse it. But there must be no illegality, and above all no break-up of the Union. In some degree the Supreme Court's ruling even paved his way forward. His party, the Republican, was united in opposition to it, whereas the Democrats were divided. They were split too over Kansas, where Douglas, anxious to see fair play for his policy of popular sovereignty, quarrelled with President Buchanan, who tried to force through a fraudulent pro-slavery constitution for the new state.

Douglas, the "Little Giant", courageous, magnanimous, and fair-minded, enjoyed an immense reputation in his home state of Illinois. Because of his hostility to Buchanan's Democrat administration there was even talk of his standing in the 1858 Senate elections as a Republican. In the event he did not, and Lincoln did. So the Senatorial contest lay between Douglas the Democrat and the Republican Lincoln, a historic confrontation of worthy antagonists. "I shall have my hands full," Douglas admitted. "Lincoln is the strong man of his party—full of wit, facts, dates—and the best stump speaker with his droll ways and dry jokes, in the West."

Accepting his party's nomination, Lincoln made one of the best-remembered of his speeches, attacking, not slavery, but the failure to prevent the spread of pro-slavery agitation.

> That agitation has not only not ceased but has constantly augmented. In my opinion it will not cease until a crisis shall have been reached and passed. *A house divided against itself cannot stand.*

By the standards of their day both Lincoln and Douglas were moderates. Neither liked slavery; neither contemplated its rapid abolition. And both men were what in modern parlance would be termed 'white supremacists' or 'racialists'—as, of course, were the vast majority of their fellow-Americans. "The American government", said Douglas, "was made by the white man, for the white man, to be administered by the white man." And Lincoln considered that

> there is a physical difference between the white and black races which will ever forbid the two races living together on terms of social and political equality. . . . There must be the position of superior and inferior, and I as much as any other man am in favour of having the superior position assigned to the white man.

Through the summer and autmn of 1858 these two men toured the prairies of Illinois, arguing in each provincial town the issues before the electors and all America. Widely reported, it developed into the most celebrated debate in the nation's history, and although it was conducted from both sides with high seriousness, and usually with good temper, it also became something of a gladiatorial contest. Something too of a travelling carnival: the "Little Giant", with his immaculate suit and his wide-brimmed white hat, would be delivered to the day's meeting-place in the personal Douglas train, which signalled its arrival by firing a timely salute from its own twelve-pounder. Brass bands played the hero to the speaking-platform; banners proclaimed slogans; flags and bunting festooned the streets; and the open-air crowds were there in their thousands, having driven in in their buggies or come by special train. Lincoln's processions arrived accompanied by fireworks, singers, cavalcades of horsemen, bevies of pretty girls. The leonine Douglas strode purposefully to the platform, spoke masterfully, gestured powerfully; Lincoln by contrast would unwind his long limbs from the special wagon, shamble on to the stand, and take time to warm up his tones and his melancholy features. He spoke more shrilly as his theme began to excite him, his movements vigorous but awkward; he would bend at the knees a good deal as he spoke, and then shoot up on his toes to bring a point home. And the central point, the issue on which the argument hinged, was essentially a moral one: was slavery *wrong*? If it was, as Lincoln held, then America must at least forbid its extension.

Douglas defeated Lincoln in the election; but by admitting that slavery could legitimately be excluded from a territory (despite the Dred Scott judgment) he split with the Southern Democrats and thereby opened wide the gap that would lose him the Presidency in 1860. Lincoln, on the other hand, was seen for the first time as a potential President, a moderate behind whom the Republicans could unite for victory. He was sufficiently against slavery to satisfy all New Englanders except the extreme abolitionists; sufficiently conservative for the 'middle states' of Pennsylvania, New Jersey and New York; and he was the only Republican candidate who could hope to win in Illinois and Indiana, and even perhaps in Maryland and Delaware, the northernmost of the slave states. When in October 1859 the extremist anti-slavery veteran John Brown made his famous raid on the federal arsenal at Harper's Ferry in

Virginia (for which he was duly hanged) it was notable how Lincoln balanced his comments. John Brown had intended to arm a slave revolt, and Lincoln condemned such treasonable violence outright; but John Brown was also, for many in the North, a hero who had "made the gallows glorious like the Cross", and Lincoln did not fail to remind the South that treason—an attack on the Union—from that direction would be equally intolerable. "It will be our duty to deal with you as old John Brown has been dealt with."

Thus it was the man who a year before would have been thought an outsider who managed at the 1860 Chicago Convention to secure the party nomination, rather than the stern abolitionist Chase of Ohio, or the earlier favourite and party leader, Seward of New York (who was outraged at the choice of Lincoln). The Republican campaigners proceeded to make great play with Lincoln's humble pioneer origins, his rail-splitting, his virtuous rise, true-American fashion, from the log-cabin to the gates of the White House; and their "Honest Abe" duly triumphed with 173 electoral votes. Of his opponents, the pro-slavery Breckinridge carried all the Southern states except Delaware and Maryland, with 73 electoral votes; Bell of Tennessee and Douglas, though together they outscored Lincoln in the popular vote, gained in the electoral college only 39 and 12 votes respectively.[6] It was a handsome but not overwhelming victory—and it was fraught with terrible dangers.

The South, despite Lincoln's disclaimers and attempts at reassurance, insisted on regarding him as an abolitionist; and throughout the election campaign Southern leaders had threatened that a Republican victory must mean secession; the South would fight for its rights—"liberty, property, home, country—everything that makes life worth living". Now the South wasted no time; by February 1861 the states of South Carolina, Georgia, Florida, Mississippi, Alabama, and Texas had taken the plunge, announced their secession, established a Southern Confederacy, and elected Jefferson Davis as provisional President. (At his oath-taking an actress had danced on the Stars and Stripes.) They were soon to be joined by North Carolina, Arkansas, Tennessee, and—most crucial of all

---

[6] In American Presidential elections the voters choose electors to represent their state in the electoral college, where voting is weighted broadly in proportion to population. Thus a candidate who narrowly wins in the populous states, as Lincoln did, will always defeat one who sweeps the board in the more sparsely populated ones.

—Virginia, making ten states in all, the ten who had voted for Breckinridge and slavery, with a total of 5½ million free citizens (and 3½ million slaves) to set against the North's 22 millions. They proceeded to occupy all but two of the federal forts and navy yards in the South; of the two outstanding, Fort Sumter in Charleston harbour was closely invested by the forces of South Carolina, while in the White House the spent and helpless outgoing President Buchanan waited, talked of compromise, and did nothing decisive; in any case his Cabinet had Southern sympathies.

Lincoln was not to be inaugurated until March, four months after his election. In the uneasy interim he could do little but stiffen ranks within his own party and counsel them to stand firm against secession or any compromise that would end in the extension of slavery. Many Northerners would have settled for allowing the two incompatibles of North and South to go their separate ways in peace; but Lincoln for his part gave that policy short shrift. The idea of an America united by her history and her sacred Constitution was deeply embedded in him. "The Constitution will not be preserved and defended," he said, "unless it is enforced and obeyed in every part of every one of the United States." If you bent the Constitution you broke it. And there was another reason why the Union must be preserved. Without it there could be no democracy, and ballots were "the rightful, and peaceful, successors of bullets". If every time that a minority was defeated on an issue they could hive off, the future of America could be nothing but dissension and fragmentation:

> The central idea pervading this struggle is the necessity that is upon us of proving that popular government is not an absurdity. We must settle this thing now, whether in a free government the minority have the right to break up the government whenever they choose.

The American Civil War was a fight to the finish between two civilizations separated by as wide a gap in culture and attitudes as in climate and distance. Slavery, of course, helped to widen the gulf; it was the irritant that brought the conflict to a head, but the war was not fought, either ostensibly or principally, to abolish or to maintain slavery. Southern secession had been in the air long before the slavery issue became acute. In the North only a minority were antislavery crusaders, and Lincoln was emphatically not one of them.

There was no neat division on the subject. Robert E. Lee of Virginia, for instance, the South's most distinguished general, was personally opposed to slavery, while the North's General Ulysses Grant had no strong views against it; Grant's wife owned slave property, while Lee set *his* slaves free. (Lee, in fact, though he was the highest trump in the Southern pack, was not himself even in favour of secession; he refused to fight for the North because he could not support the North's intended invasion of Southern territory—which meant of his Virginia first and foremost.) There were many difficulties and contradictions, and often much anguish, over taking sides in this, as it proved, terrible and prolonged war. Many individuals, and many families, especially in the border states, were bisected by their loyalties—Lincoln's own wife affords as sad an instance as any: a husband, one brother, and a half-sister on one side; another brother and six more half-brothers and half-sisters on the other. Polite Washington society looked askance at a President's wife who was "two-thirds slavery and the other third secesh", and the nastiest rumours circulated. On one occasion Lincoln had to testify before a Congressional committee to his own wife's loyalty. He himself preserved a flinty resolution on the central issue, but he was very far from being a man of stone and could not fail to be saddened by the tide of events and aged by the constant pressure of bitter decisions.

For a month after assuming the Presidency he debated with himself before sending an expedition to attempt the relief of Fort Sumter, and when he did act it was against the advice of five out of seven of his Cabinet. Even then Seward, his Secretary of State, took it upon himself to divert the most powerful vessel to the relief of another fort, with the result that the expedition watched impotently as South Carolina guns pounded Fort Sumter and obliged its occupying forces to surrender. It was the decisive moment; the years of blood had begun. Lincoln, at that point assured of the loyalty of an overwhelming majority of Northerners (Douglas in the last months of his life was one of those who hastened to his old rival's support), issued a proclamation calling for 75,000 men to fight for the maintenance of the Union, and many more than that were soon in training. The Southern Confederacy had set up its capital at Richmond, Virginia, facing Washington a hundred miles to the north; the immediate task of the Union forces therefore was to strike south and capture Richmond. Most hoped, and some even expected, that the rebellion would then collapse. "On to Richmond!" shouted the Northern newspapers.

It soon became plain that there was going to be no easy victory, and that some important advantages lay with the Confederacy. For one thing, in the South they had seen the war coming and made preparation for it. Many, too, of the ruling classes in the South had military traditions, so that, especially at the beginning, the Confederacy was much superior in officer material, and even among the lower ranks there were relatively few who were not used to handling firearms. Moreover, Southerners enjoyed the moral advantage that comes to those who fight for their independence, to defend their lands and heritage against the invader. To win they had only to survive; the North must conquer. The Confederacy also enjoyed a good deal of support abroad, notably among the English governing classes and those liberals who "took naturally to rebellion—if foreign". In 1861, after the *Trent*[7] incident, there was real danger of war breaking out between Britain and the North, and as long as Lancashire needed the South's cotton and the Northern navy stopped her getting it there was bound to be the constant possibility of trouble.[8] Neutrality—but by no means at *any* price—was the policy of Palmerston and Russell, and had they gone even as far as diplomatic recognition of the Confederacy—and they came very near to that—the weakening effect upon the North's naval blockade must have been tremendous.

Naval power was probably the North's most important weapon, and though the South could procure blockade runners and armed merchantman, she could never fully overcome the relentless pressure of the Northern blockade. Of course the North could also command greater manpower and infinitely richer manufacturing resources. And although Lincoln had more than enough disunity and backbiting and intrigue to contend with, on their side Jefferson Davis and the Southern leaders had even shakier ground to tread on. The Confederacy was always a very loose affair, with each

---

[7] *Trent*, British mail steamer, boarded by U.S.S. *Jacinto*, whose captain forcibly removed from on board the Confederate commissioner to Britain, Mason, and to France, Slidell, causing jubilation in the North and belligerent indignation throughout Britain. See also pp. 255–256.

[8] *Punch*, 1861:

> Though with the North we must sympathize
> It must not be forgotten,
> That with the South we've stronger ties,
> Which are composed of cotton.

state determined doubtless to fight the North, but strictly after its own fashion and in its own time, *lending* its troops merely to the Confederate authority at Richmond.

Partly for this very reason it is highly improbable that the South would have collapsed, as Lincoln briefly hoped, even if the Northern volunteers had swept "on to Richmond". In any case, what happened was very different. At Bull Run, watched by a throng of sightseers and newspaper-men who had driven out from the capital, the quarter-trained Northern volunteers ran into disaster at the hands of the half-trained Southerners and streamed back demoralized into a Washington uncomfortably near the scene of the defeat. This was the battle where General "Stonewall" Jackson and his brigade determined the issue—and afterwards Jackson declared that if he had had 10,000 fresh troops he could have captured the capital. The Southern victors, however, fortunately for Lincoln, were almost as exhausted as the Northern vanquished.

Lincoln had the chastening experience of watching from the White House the returning stream of mud-soaked, rain-drenched fugitives, some dropping with fatigue in the streets. The following day he appointed General George McClellan to the command of the Army of the Potomac. Young, magnetic, and self-assured, McClellan was capable enough of carrying the North through to victory (he had visions of the Presidency for himself afterwards), but he was going to have no more Bull Runs. The enemy must first be pinched and constricted; preparation must be thorough and complete. Consequently Lincoln's new commander was soon being harshly criticized for inaction. Lincoln, who was prepared to take his full share of responsibility for rushing novices too soon into battle, understood McClellan's difficulties and intentions and defended him before angrily impatient anti-slavery men. Politically, however, this hanging fire was severely embarrassing and irked Lincoln more than McClellan's tendency to behave towards him as a West Point graduate towards an Illinois rail-splitter. Lincoln was never one to stand on dignity; his reaction was that McClellan was the best general he could get, and he would "hold his horse for him" if only he would begin to win victories. But Lincoln's wry patience was heavily tried. "If something is not done soon," he said, "the bottom will be out of the whole affair. If General McClellan does not want to use the army I would like to borrow it."

A President of the United States need never expect a quiet life, but the troubles that beset Lincoln were something more than ordinary. The war was not going well—indeed, for the North for half a year after Bull Run it was hardly going at all. The newspapers were largely hostile to him and continued so until his assassination, after which they canonized him as the greatest of men. In his own Republican Party the abolitionist radicals mistrusted him as a conservative and constantly complained in Congress—yet as party leader somehow he had to carry these men along with him. Of the Democrats, those supporting the war were highly critical of his leadership, and the "peace Democrats" were bitterly opposed to him. In his own Cabinet, which he had picked with shrewd calculation largely from his principal rivals, there were several men who thought they should themselves have been President and, at least to begin with, looked down on Lincoln. Seward in particular began by being convinced that his own superior judgment and experience would enable him to dominate this small-town lawyer. At the Treasury, however, the unbending abolitionist Chase, another disappointed Presidential candidate who was inclined to patronize the "honest but ineffective" Lincoln, to some extent cancelled out Seward, and Lincoln was ably deftly to balance one against the other. Then there was the disastrous Cameron as Secretary of War, who had been 'wished' on Lincoln because of vote-bargaining promises made by his party manager at the Chicago Convention, and, being revealed as scandalously corrupt, had to be removed from his office. His successor Stanton, villainous-looking and domineering, but also relentlessly energetic, had before his appointment spoken contemptuously of the "painful imbecility" of Lincoln, the "Illinois ape", expressions which Lincoln chose not to know about if Stanton could help him win the war. And, indeed, Stanton was to prove among the staunchest in the struggle. One of the few Cabinet members who were from the earliest days convinced of the President's stature was Gideon Welles, Navy Secretary in charge of the vital blockade—who, however, himself regarded Seward with "icy revulsion". There was no question of this Cabinet being a band of brothers.

Lincoln, however, was not by any means "an innocent among thieves", and his handling of these men, and of the American political situation that they mirrored, was wonderfully adroit. The fact that he was a vivid and vulnerable human being should not obscure his political opportunism and cunning. He had chosen after all to be a professional politician, and he played politics as hard and as realistically as the next man. He used his immense power as the fount of patronage to bargain very successfully for electoral support and was not above attempting a little tactful bribing of hostile newspapers and buttering-up of editors (of the New York *Herald*, for instance) in a good party cause. If men wanted jobs and honours they must be prepared to pay up a substantial commission to the Republican organization. When he wished, he was adept at keeping all men guessing, at having "a policy of no policy at all", as he himself once said. There was "no virtue in irritably seeking to perform the impossible". Like Bismarck, but with infinitely greater respect for the collective intentions of the common people, Lincoln knew that the best a statesman could do, being borne forward on the currents of history, was "to steer". He used something very like Bismarck's expression himself: he noted that the old hands among the Mississippi pilots never set a course more ambitious than from the point of departure to the next favourable visible point; no aiming beyond the horizon.

Nobody was ever *entirely* in Lincoln's confidence. He mystified many who had over-simplified his character. They were surprised, and many of them shocked, at finding a President who by rights should have been profoundly disturbed by the enormous crisis surrounding him, or at least *concentrating* upon it, swapping some pretty raw and pungent stories with his Secretary of State or whatever other visitor was ready to match his mood. Once when a Congressman called Ashley was seeing him about McClellan's conduct of the war, and Lincoln, as so often, had arrived at "That reminds me of a story", the Congressman protested that he had not come to hear stories. Then, as he recorded, Lincoln, "with such a sad face", turned to him and said, "Ashley, I know how sincere you are. But if I couldn't tell these stories I should die. Now you sit down." With the passage of time his detractors did not become less numerous, and despite his narrow re-election in 1864, he never became a really popular President in his lifetime; but those working closely with him soon learned respect. His Cabinet certainly never became a team, but individually with its members, particularly with Seward and Stanton, and also with such Senatorial heavyweights as the radical Charles Sumner, he developed a close understanding. He encouraged both the formidable and irascible Stanton and the passionately anti-slavery Sumner to think that on occasions it was *they* who were directing affairs. "Don't I get along well with Sumner?" he remarked once; "he thinks he manages me." There was no doubt of the President's decisiveness when rapid decision was vital. When Frémont, the explorer, in charge of Union forces in Missouri, of his own initiative under martial law proclaimed the emancipation of all the Missouri slaves, Lincoln promptly dismissed him, despite his high popularity in the North. The risk of losing Northern support was great, but Lincoln reckoned that if Frémont's edict was allowed to stand the risk of losing the loyalty of the border states was greater.

Over these years Lincoln had personal as well as national disasters to cope with. His wife's health did not stand up well to the strain of being an unpopular—even despised—First Lady. She did not help matters by taking no trouble to conceal the fact that she loathed Stanton, and she once called Seward a "dirty abolitionist sneak". Only Mrs Welles of the Cabinet wives remained friendly with her. Mrs Lincoln oscillated alarmingly between parsimony and overspending; the severance from her Southern relations in the war, and the death of two brothers and a brother-in-law, grieved her and aggravated her own erratic behaviour. But the cruellest blow, to her and to Lincoln himself, that most proud and indulgent father, was the death of their beloved second son Willie early in 1862 at the age of eleven. (Another of Lincoln's sons had died back in the Springfield days.) The shock following the long nights of worry drove poor Mrs Lincoln to hysteria, from which she was slow to recover. At one period she sought her dead son through spiritualism. Her irrational rages grew worse, and were no respecters of persons —which sometimes made the President's position socially almost impossible. Her widowed sister, however,

noticed that she always brightened when she heard his footsteps in the hall. But one time after he left she held out her arms and cried: "Kiss me, Emilie, and tell me that you love me: I seem to be the scapegoat for both North and South."[9]

There were two distinct theatres of land warfare: the area west of the Appalachians, where control of the Mississippi basin was vital, and that between the Appalachians and the Atlantic—Maryland, Virginia, the Carolinas, and Georgia. The Northern strategy, as it eventually worked out, was first to conquer the west, squeezing the

[9] B. P. Thomas, *op. cit.*, p. 34.

Confederacy into its eastern territories, and then to chop these into two by driving eastward to the sea. Constricted and divided thus on land, blockaded from the sea, lacking industry and resources, the Confederacy, from a century's distance, appears to have been doomed; but for Lincoln and the North, riding one crisis after another between 1860 and 1864, things often looked very differently.

Only in the West was much progress made before September 1862. Here General Ulysses Grant, who eight years earlier on a lonely California border post had "drunk himself out of the army", and since then had failed in various occupations, drove the Confederates from Fort Henry in Tennessee, captured 12,000 more at Fort Donelson, and pushed on in April 1862 to win one of the bloodiest battles of a generally very bloody war, at Shiloh (or Pittsburg Landing). Between them the Federals and Confederates suffered nearly 24,000 casualties, and the attacks on the allegedly ruthless drunkard Grant, in Press and Congress, were so virulent that Lincoln was under heavy pressure to remove him—and Grant himself was despondent enough to consider resigning from the army. But Lincoln refused to get rid of him. When the Governor of Pennsylvania came to the White House as spokesman for a shocked public to plead for Grant's dismissal, he found Lincoln troubled but decisive:

When I had said everything that could be said from my standpoint, we lapsed into silence. Lincoln remained silent for what seemed a very long time. He then gathered himself up in a chair and said in a tone of earnestness that I shall never forget: "*I can't spare this man; he fights.*"

In the early stages of the war, with "only a few months' comic-opera experience as a militia captain" in the Black Hawk war, Lincoln was inclined to defer, perhaps overmuch, to the military men, McClellan, Halleck, Buell, Pope; they in turn "all wanted me to be the General", as he said to Grant later. Conscientious always, he began reading military textbooks, applied his very considerable fund of good sense, and as the war progressed became much more authoritative in directing military affairs. McClellan was a good general (as Lee was a supremely good one) on the old textbook lines; these opposing leaders had been military cadets together at West Point and spoke the same military language. But the American Civil War was a new sort of war that the military textbooks had not caught up with yet. Muskets, for instance, were old-fashioned now, and the new rifles, with an effective range of nearly half a mile, were making for more murderous casualties wherever troops were not in trenches, while the new railways and the industrial output behind them were revolutionizing ideas of military supply and largely nullifying the South's theoretical advantage of 'interior lines'. Lincoln's mind was receptive and adaptable; he eventually secured a team—Generals Grant and Sherman, and himself—which understood and mastered the innovations demanded of this first large-scale war of the industrial age. They learned, as Jefferson Davis and Robert E. Lee had neither the temperament nor the means to learn, how to prosecute such a war, with very large-scale armies and massive movements of men and supplies.

Lincoln freely admitted the extent to which he was governed by events. His attitude to Negro emancipation, the act with which more than anything else his name was to be remembered throughout the world, shifted significantly as the war proceeded. In essential principle he was firm and consistent:

> If I could save the Union without freeing any slave, I would do it; and if I could save it by freeing all slaves I would do it; and if I could save it by freeing some and leaving others alone I would also do that.

But in the working out of the principle he was forced to tack and veer in the winds of war. If, for example, he rushed strongly towards emancipation he would please his critics among the Northern radicals, but would lose the support of the border slave states. Striking the strictly military balance between "God and Kentucky" was desperately difficult. During 1862, however, as Lee and Jackson, having won a second big victory at Bull Run, looked like taking Maryland, and again threatened Washington, European opinion inclined more and more towards recognizing the Confederacy. To Napoleon III, busy in Mexico and anxious to co-operate with the Confederacy, and to Palmerston, Russell, and Gladstone in the British Cabinet, the South looked like a perfectly respectable 'nationalist' movement—and if Lincoln's government, in addition to imposing a blockade that cut off European supplies of raw cotton, was not even capable of proclaiming an unequivocal condemnation of slavery, there seemed little to choose on moral grounds between North and South. By September 1862 Napoleon III was waiting only for English approval before recognizing the Confederacy, and English approval was waiting only for one more big Confederate victory.

Antietam Creek was where this did not happen. It was more a drawn battle than the "complete" Northern victory that McClellan claimed, but after it he was able to clear Maryland of Lee's forces and end the immediate crisis. Antietam (also known as Sharpsburg) was a critical engagement for Lincoln in more ways than one. McClellan had been constantly under political attack for his excessive caution and obsessive conviction that his army was undermanned, and Lincoln was under parallel fire for continuing to bank on McClellan, despite his inadequacies (of which Lincoln himself was only too well aware). Antietam temporarily saved the bacon of both President and General. "If the battle had gone against us," said Lincoln, "poor McClellan and I too would be in a bad row of stumps."

If the President had plumped for emancipation after a defeat it would have looked very much like a weak attempt to buy sorely needed moral support; after Antietam it could be done more credibly. The world could now begin to see the North's war as a crusade. Only Gladstone (strangely at first sight) among Palmerston's Cabinet remained in favour of diplomatic recognition of the Confederacy. The exigencies of war and diplomacy had squeezed the promise out of Lincoln, but the promise remained: that from January 1st, 1863, all slaves in any state or district that was in rebellion against the Union should be regarded as "then, thenceforward, and forever free". To begin with the Proclamation had more effect outside America than in. Everybody there knew that any validity it might come to have depended on a Northern victory in the war. As for the noisily predicted slave revolt, in which white Southerners would be murdered in their beds, there was not a whisper of it.

In the west Grant, confirmed in his command after the slaughter at Shiloh, succeeded during 1863 in pressing southward down the Mississippi valley until he was held up by the natural fortress of Vicksburg. After many disappointments his tactics here were eventually unconventional and daring. Cutting loose from his base of supplies and travelling light (his own baggage consisted of a toothbrush), he marauded deep into enemy-held territory. In one period of eighteen days his troops covered 200 miles and fought five major battles to defeat forces more numerous than their own, and in July took Vicksburg, with 38,000 prisoners. New Orleans having already fallen to a combined naval and military assault, the Confederacy was now cut in two, and "the Father of Rivers", as Lincoln said, went "unvexed to the sea".

In the east McClellan did not long outlive his Antietam reprieve. It was not simply that he was tardy and over-cautious; Lincoln had begun to suspect that McClellan's own Presidential ambitions were being allowed to govern his strategy. Perhaps he did not even wish to defeat Lee outright, but to bring about instead a compromise peace ensuring the continuance of slavery. Lincoln therefore removed McClellan from his command and put in his place General Burnside, who unfortunately ran straight into a heavy disaster; unsuccessfully attacking Lee's strong defensive position on the hills above Fredericksburg, he lost 10,000 men to the enemy's 2000. Lincoln replaced him first by General Hooker, whom Lee and Jackson proceeded to defeat at Chancellorsville.[10] ("My God, what will the country say," groaned Lincoln.) Hooker then falling out with Halleck, the Chief of Staff, he in turn was replaced by General George Meade, a solid, dogged, hard-slogging veteran, and the fifth commander that the Army of the Potomac had fought under in one year.

While Lee penetrated beyond Maryland into Pennsylvania some of his far-ranging cavalry had produced near panic in parts of the North. His main force of about 70,000 and Meade's of 93,000 "fumbling towards each other like a pair of sidling crabs", converged in the summer of 1863 upon the small town and road junction of Gettysburg. Here, over the very same July days when far away to the west Grant was busy taking Vicksburg, was fought the greatest and bloodiest battle of the war. This time it was Lee who threw his whole weight against a defensive position bristling with Northern guns, but his losses were only slightly more terrible than those of the Union, 30,000 to 23,000—a grim testimonial to the killing power of the new rifle. To Lincoln's unconcealed chagrin the remains of Lee's army managed to retreat in good order; and Meade, instead of having his first victory hailed as a triumph, found himself blamed for failing to follow up with a second to finish the enemy off. In a letter he wrote to Meade—but later thought better of dispatching—Lincoln complained that Lee

10 Where Jackson, out reconnoitring, was shot and killed by his own men.

was within your easy grasp and to have closed upon him would
. . . have ended the war. . . . Your golden opportunity is gone, and
I am distressed immeasurably because of it.

Thus although it was true that after Vicksburg and Gettysburg
the chances of the Southerners actually winning the war looked
slim, they could prolong it, and Lincoln's cross was still heavy to
bear. War weariness was affecting both sides, and both governments
found it difficult to hold their bruised teams together. Both armies'
hungry appetite demanded men, and more men, and both sides had
recourse to conscription limited by exemptions. In the North a payment of 300 dollars would exempt—a class-weighted provision
which Lincoln disliked but Congress refused to remove. The system
worked very oddly. Since each district had a quota, and an un-
filled quota meant a compulsory draft, districts offered bounties
for volunteers—so the conscription law had the paradoxical effect of
producing few conscripts but over a million volunteers, some from
abroad. It also produced widespread riots, and in New York during
four days of arson, lynching, and looting not fewer than 500 were
killed and a million dollars' worth of property destroyed. The
North had long been a good deal less than unanimous about the
war, and now, with the fearsome casualty lists and the draft, and
doubts whether the conflict could be won outright, opposition grew
stronger. The Peace Democrats, or Copperheads, so called because
they cut the image of the Goddess of Liberty from copper pennies
to wear in their coat-lapels, were vociferous not only against the
war itself, but against the "tyranny" of the President, who had suspended *habeas corpus* and taken stern—and strictly unconstitutional
—special powers. Lincoln, that passionate friend of democracy,
argued patiently for what he had done—in particular for banishing
a Democrat ex-Congressman whose anti-war agitation had encouraged desertions.

> Must I shoot a simple-minded soldier boy who deserts [he
> asked] while I must not touch a hair of the wily agitator who
> induces him to desert? . . . I think that . . . to silence the agitator,
> and save the boy, is not only constitutional but, withal, a great
> mercy.

In November 1863, with his youngest boy Tad seriously ill and
Mrs Lincoln sick with worry, the President, a little reluctantly but
feeling it his duty, left Washington to attend the ceremony of

dedicating a cemetery in which were to be reburied the dead of Gettysburg. After the principal two-hour oration Lincoln rose, as seemed fitting, to say a few words, and he had finished almost before those present realized he had begun. The correspondent of the *Chicago Times* found the few words "silly, flat, and dishwatery". With this judgment, however, posterity has on the whole begged to differ:

> Fourscore and seven years ago our fathers brought forth on this continent a new nation, conceived in Liberty, and dedicated to the proposition that all men are created equal.
>
> Now we are engaged in a great civil war, testing whether that nation or any nation so conceived and so dedicated can long endure. We are met on a great battlefield of that war. We have come to dedicate a portion of that field as a final resting place for those who here gave their lives that that nation might live. It is altogether fitting and proper that we should do this.
>
> But in a larger sense we cannot dedicate—we cannot consecrate—we cannot hallow—this ground. The brave men, living and dead, who struggled here, have consecrated it, far above our poor power to add or to detract. The world will little note nor long remember what we say here, but it can never forget what they did here. It is for us the living, rather, to be dedicated here to the unfinished work which they who fought here have thus far so nobly advanced. It is rather for us to be here dedicated to the great task remaining before us—that from these honoured dead we take increased devotion to that cause for which they gave the last full measure of devotion—that we here highly resolve that these dead shall not have died in vain—that this nation, under God, shall have a new birth of freedom—and that government of the people, by the people, for the people, shall not perish from the earth.

Of all Lincoln's speeches this is the one that the world remembers best. Indeed, for its appropriateness to the occasion, its earnest sincerity, the chime of its cadences, and the austere simplicity of its rhetoric it would be hard to surpass. In substance it repeats what had come to be the core of Lincoln's political creed. The war began as a struggle to maintain the Union; but this had become merely a means to an end, and the end was democracy:

> a government whose leading object is to elevate the condition of men—to lift artificial weights from all shoulders . . . to afford all an unfettered start, and a fair chance in the race of life. . . .

The dead of Gettysburg were to be joined by many tens of thousands more before the war ended. Altogether 618,000 Americans would die before the South finally surrendered. But a few days after the Gettysburg speech, laid up with a virus infection (at last, he said, something he had to offer everybody), Lincoln received another, and overdue, instalment of good news, and again it was Grant that brought it; "such a quiet little fellow," Lincoln once said of him, "the only way I know he's around is by the way he makes things *git*." The Union strategy after clearing the Mississippi was to strike eastwards through southern Tennessee and Georgia and cut the remains of the Confederacy into two. But after capturing Chattanooga, the key to an advance into Georgia, the Union army under General Rosecrans had run into terrible trouble at Chickamauga, where they were rescued from total disaster only by the heroic resistance of the men under General George Thomas, the "rock of Chickamauga"—another of the great Northern heroes of the war. To hold Chattanooga Grant flung in all the troops he had ("We will hold Chattanooga till we starve," Thomas had assured him), and by November 1863 Grant was able to report another big victory to Lincoln, who now proceeded to put him in command of all the Union armies in the field.

The spring and summer campaigns of 1864, however, were to be the goriest of all. Lee, outnumbered now by two to one, chose to fight in the Virginian countryside known as the Wilderness— tangled woodland and thickets and marshy streams. He could not now honestly hope to defeat the North, but by tenacity and fighting skill he could take such a toll that they might despair of victory. He calculated well. In battle after battle the Union casualties piled up —Grant's dead and wounded eventually exceeded the total of Lee's forces—but "I propose to fight it out on this line," wired Grant to Lincoln, "if it takes all summer." Lincoln and Grant were agreed on this strategy—to hit and go on hitting all along the line—but day and night as the corpses and stretcher cases were taken off the mournful Sixth Street wharf at Washington the cost of the struggle was rammed home. Lincoln, a humane and merciful man, was widely attacked for maintaining a butcher in command. Chilled and sickened by the slaughter, and sustained only by the imperative necessity of Union victory, he stood by Grant and hoped for better days.

The grim war news might well have cost him the Presidency in 1864, when he stood for re-election. Earlier Chase, Lincoln's Attorney-General and a powerful wielder of patronage, had been a strong contender against him, laying his eggs, as Lincoln put it, like the bluebottle "in every rotten spot he can find". Then dissident Republicans under Frémont ran a rival convention of their own; Frémont eventually withdrew from the Presidential race only when Lincoln agreed to dismiss from his Cabinet the much-hated Montgomery Blair. At the official Baltimore convention Lincoln was safely re-adopted, and, just afterwards, Chase offered to resign once too often: to his astonishment and chagrin his offer was this time accepted.

As autumn approached there was gloom in the Lincoln camp. McClellan was standing as the Democrat candidate, and with the war news as bad as it could be stood a good chance of catching the votes of all malcontents, regardless of party. Grant, frustrated by the fighting spirit of Lee and his Confederates, had decided to starve them out. Under his orders General Sheridan scorched the earth of the beautiful and fertile valley of the Shenandoah that had for long sustained Lee's men. Every mill and barn, every stack of wheat and straw, was destroyed; the livestock were driven away.

It was a rancorous Presidential campaign, with the bitterness heightened by the war. There were even more smears than usual. On one occasion, Lincoln having been accused of taking his salary in gold while the troops had to accept pay in depreciated 'greenbacks', he got together all his personal moneys and securities (worth then $55,000) and walked into Chase's room at the Treasury with instructions to turn them all over to government bonds. Luckily for Lincoln's electoral prospects, the first big victory for a long time came in September. Sherman, striking out 120 miles from Chattanooga, along dangerously extended lines of communication, succeeded in capturing Atlanta, and to some extent this important centre's fall, as Seward said, "knocked the planks out of the Democratic platform". When the results were published early in November, McClellan had 1,800,000 votes to Lincoln's 2,200,000. "The election, along with its incidental and undesirable strife, has done us good too," said Lincoln from a window of the White House to a cheering crowd below. "It has demonstrated that a people's government can sustain a national election in the midst of a great civil war."

A week after election day Sherman and his army set out from Atlanta on what was certainly the most dramatic and audacious, and perhaps also the most disgraceful, adventure of the war. Tired of having his railway communications constantly cut by the Confederates and refusing to accept the proffered bait of a chase northward after the fast-moving enemy, he asked permission of Grant and Lincoln to send his wounded back to Chattanooga, burn Atlanta, blow up the railway, sever the telegraph, cut loose with his army, and blast his way through to sea. On the way he proposed to "make Georgia howl". Sherman persuaded Grant and Grant persuaded Lincoln to approve this dangerous plan, and a supply fleet was dispatched to wait off Savannah. For a month no-one in Washington had any hard news of Sherman's army. But in Richmond one by one the southbound telegraph wires went dead, the trains from the deep South failed to arrive, as Sherman went roaring towards the sea, ripping out his supplies and leaving a belt of smoking ruin as he went. Not a pig or mule or cow, not a barn or farmhouse or store of cotton, was left behind; "the destruction could hardly have been worse if Atlanta had been a volcano in eruption, and the molten lava had flowed in a stream sixty miles wide and five times as long"—and the anger and resentment were strong enough to smoulder for generations to come. Sherman's big army —60,000 men, including Negroes—met nothing strong enough to hurt them, and "marching through Georgia" turned out to be a common soldier's picnic and a looter's beanfeast; "broiled turkey for breakfast, roast lamb for dinner, and fried chicken for supper"; a wonderful "day of Jubilo" for the troops:

> How the darkies shouted when they heard the joyful sound!
> How the turkeys gobbled which our commissary found!
> How the sweet potatoes even started from the ground!
> While we were marching through Georgia!

Before 1864 was out Sherman had reached the coast, the Confederacy had been again chopped in two, the deep South isolated, and Lee's army, entrenched against Grant for the winter, menaced anew from the rear by 60,000 fresh troops advancing through the Carolinas with the scent of victory in their nostrils. Furthermore, the last Confederate army in the West had been annihilated by General Thomas near Nashville, in Tennessee.

In March 1865, Lee made a last effort to break out of Grant's stranglehold and join forces with the Confederates farther south, in order to make a combined attack on Sherman. When the scheme failed Grant ordered a general offensive. On April 3rd Union forces, bands playing, entered Richmond; and six days later Lee, recognizing that the odds against him were astronomical, asked Grant to meet him at Appomattox Courthouse, where he requested honourable surrender to prevent further bloodshed. For the occasion Lee, the dignified Southern gentleman to the last, wore a new gold-braided full-dress uniform, with jewel-studded sword. Grant by contrast, that "ordinary scrubby-looking man", with his "slightly seedy look", came in his Union-blue private's blouse with the five-starred shoulder-straps, the stump of a cigar as usual between his lips, glad to talk soldier's 'shop' to avoid having to come to the unpleasant business of the meeting, until Lee reminded him of it. By the terms of surrender officers were allowed to keep their side-arms; all those who owned horses or mules were to keep them for going back home to work their farms. "The war is over," said Grant; "the rebels are our countrymen again."

Lincoln had long given thought to this moment, particularly to the problem of how to reincorporate the seceded states into the Union. He had already come under criticism for his proclamation of 1863 promising recognition to any previously rebellious state that set up a loyal government by the votes of at least ten per cent of the registered voters. He was proud of what he had done in following out this idea in Louisiana, and was anxious to extend the franchise as far as possible—perhaps even among Negroes to the "very intelligent" and those who had served in the army. He was against all vengeful settling of old scores. In the famous closing passage of his second Inaugural Address, a month before the end of the war, he harped on the same theme:

> With malice towards none, with charity for all, with firmness in the right as God gives us to see the right, let us strive on to finish the work we are in, to bind up the nation's wounds, to care for him who shall have borne the battle and for his widow and orphan, to do all which may achieve and cherish a just and lasting peace among ourselves and with all nations.

And now in a victory speech he eschewed any songs of triumph (characteristically the previous day he had asked the band to play *Dixie*, a tune to make Southern hearts beat faster, and one of the best tunes, he said, he had ever heard); the crowd, ready for jubilation, received from Lincoln a long and thoughtful lecture on how best to heal the scars of war. At his last Cabinet, a few hours before his death, he commented how fortunate it was that Congress would not be meeting for over seven months. By that time perhaps the Southern states might have been "re-animated" into the Union without Congress interference and demands for retribution:

> I hope there will be no persecution, no bloody work after the war is over. [The Confederate army in the south still had to surrender to Sherman.] No-one need expect me to take any part in hanging or killing these men, even the worst of them.

About ten o'clock that evening a young actor named John Wilkes Booth, a fanatical pro-Southerner, managed to gain admittance to the President's box at Ford's Theatre in Washington, as he sat with his wife and two guests enjoying a satirical comedy about English life. He shot Lincoln through the head, leaped on to the stage amid the general hubbub and panic, brandished a knife, and shouted what sounded like the Virginian motto "*Sic Semper Tyrannis*" ("Thus ever to tyrants"). Lincoln was carried over the road to the back room of a poor lodging-house where, without recovering consciousness, he died the following morning. It was the end of any hope of a speedy statesmanlike reconciliation of North and South.

Men wrote what they made of the event, and of the man extinguished by it, before the shape already mistily forming round that splendid head had had time to crystallize into a halo. Some, of course, were in no danger of seeing haloes at all; the *Tri-Weekly Telegraph* of Houston, Texas, for instance:

> From now until God's judgment day, the minds of men will not cease to thrill at the killing of Abraham Lincoln. . . . Some will regard it with all the horror of a wicked assassination, others will feel it to be that righteous retribution which descends direct from the hand of God upon the destroyer of human liberty, and the oppressor of a free people. . . . *Sic Semper Tyrannis*, so say we, a thousand and a thousand times. . . . God's will be done.

Horace Greeley's New York *Tribune* had often criticized Lincoln. It had considered him too soft as a war-time President, though ideally suited to the future tasks of peace.

> War sometimes requires sternness; and he was at heart tender and merciful as a woman.

But it now wrote justly of him

> We have had Presidents before him sprung from the loins of poverty and obscurity, but never one who remained to the last so simply, absolutely, alike in heart and manner, one of the People.

And the New York *Herald*, after reckoning that stuffy future historians would have difficulty in formalizing "the kindly but powerful face of Mr Lincoln, seamed in circles by humorous thoughts and furrowed crosswise by mighty anxieties", saw him as

> essentially a mixed product of the agricultural, forensic and frontier life of this continent—as indigenous to our soil as the cranberry crop, and as American in his fibre as the granite foundations of the Appalachian range. He may not have been, and perhaps was not, our most perfect product in any one branch of mental or moral education; but, taking him for all in all, the very noblest impulses, peculiarities and aspirations of our whole people—what may be called our continental idiosyncrasies— were more collectively and vividly reproduced in his genial and yet unswerving nature than in that of any other public man of whom our chronicles bear record. . . .

A legendary and idealized Lincoln quickly took the place of the real man, and he was soon part not only of American history but of the national folklore. He so aptly and triumphantly epitomized the great American myth of the common man in the land of opportunity. He himself had been strongly aware of this; as he once said, "I happen temporarily to occupy the White House. I am living witness that one of your children may come here as my father's child has." However complex as a politician, he was always in his personal behaviour a simple man, who to the last received important guests in his shirt-sleeves and called his wife "mother" like a prairie farmer. Uncorrupted by eminence, he was the hundred-per-cent man of the people; yet, besides, he was the great and good leader who had preserved the United States of America and freed the slaves into the bargain. Only George Washington could hold a candle to him, and Washington had not been martyred in the hour of his triumph.

"A great man shoulders the torment and moral burdens of a blundering and sinful people, suffers for them, and redeems them with hallowed Christian virtues—'malice towards none and charity for all'—and is destroyed at the pitch of his success."[11] It did not then seem either ludicrous or blasphemous for his biographer and erstwhile secretary, John Hay, to describe such a man as "the greatest character since Christ".

[11] R. Hofstadter, *The American Political Tradition*, p. 93.

Table of Events

1809.	Lincoln born in Kentucky (moves to Indiana 1816).
1820.	Missouri Compromise.
1829–37.	Presidency of Jackson.
1830.	The Lincolns move to Illinois (at New Salem 1831–37).
1834.	Elected to Illinois legislature.
1837–60.	Practises law at Springfield.
1845.	Annexation of Texas.
1846.	Oregon border settlement (Ashburton Treaty).
1846–48.	Mexican War.
1847–49.	Lincoln in Congress.
1850.	"Compromise of 1850".
1854.	Douglas's Kansas-Nebraska Act.
1856.	First Republican Convention.
1857.	Dred Scott decision.
1858.	Douglas-Lincoln debates.
1859.	John Brown's raid at Harper's Ferry.
1860.	Lincoln elected President.
1861.	Secession and Civil War. Bull Run (1). *Trent* incident.
1862.	Shiloh; Bull Run (2); Antietam; Fredericksburg.
1863.	Emancipation proclamation. Chancellorsville; Vicksburg; Gettysburg; Chickamauga; Chattanooga.
1864.	Grant *versus* Lee in The Wilderness; Sherman in Georgia. Lincoln re-elected.
1865.	Second Inaugural. Defeat of Confederacy. Appomatox. Assassination.

6

GARIBALDI

(1807–82)

And the Unification of Italy

To the twentieth century its predecessor's enthusiasm for national freedom movements cannot help seeming naïve and over-optimistic. Viewed across the ruined landscape of two world wars caused largely by national vainglory, such heroic figures of resurgent nationalism as Kossuth or Mazzini or Garibaldi seem antediluvian; the passionate sentiments that to contemporary liberals sounded so noble and true ring less convincingly at this distance. When just before the First World War G. M. Trevelyan produced his three stirring volumes on Italy's 'resurrection' (or Risorgimento) he could still, in those days before the Flood, write as though the triumphs of Cavour and Garibaldi had enthroned liberty and order in Italy for ever. Like the Victorian generation that preceded his, Trevelyan saw Garibaldi not only as a crusader in a cause wholly righteous—the emancipation of Italy from foreign enslavement—but also as the hero of a story that had already had a happy ending. Great deeds had been done and *finis* written. But nationalism and liberalism do not necessarily go hand in hand, and historians of a generation later than Trevelyan cannot escape reminders of a less admirable *Duce* than Garibaldi, the man who was both his heir and caricature—the Fascist dictator Mussolini, *reductio ad absurdum* of Garibaldian nationalism.

Garibaldi was the most spectacular popular hero of the whole nineteenth century (Napoleon perhaps excepted), and if he seems to inhabit a world in some respects as remote as that of Hector and Achilles, he too possessed something of the epic quality of those warriors, something of the same uncomplicated valour. Yet he was a good deal more than merely a patriot hero. He fought passionately for freedom, even though by temperament and conviction he inclined towards dictatorship. He "believed in Italy as the saints believe in God", yet he despised the narrowness of those who could think only as Italians, and in his later life he became the champion of the then utopian notions of a League of Nations and a United States of Europe, just as he also came to call himself a socialist and follow the dream of working-class emancipation. He loathed ignorance, selfishness, and superstition, and since he found the Church guilty on those counts his hatred of popery and priesthood was intense; but it was the Church he hated rather than religion itself. He was never an intellectual heavyweight, but he was a good deal more than just the glamorous red-shirt and guerrilla chief, the hero with the heart of a lion (as Mazzini used to say) and the brains of an ox. In his day he was possibly the most widely known personage in the world, and very probably the most admired. If we consider his honesty and idealism, his simplicity and passionate conviction, his courage and imagination, as well as the more startling nature of his military feats, we may find the age's judgment, if on occasions hysterically expressed, by no means absurd.

After the peaks of the Renaissance era in Italy there had followed the long ages of submission to foreign power. From 1559 to 1713 the Italian peninsula was dominated politically by Spain and culturally by the Papacy, the Inquisition and the Jesuits. At a time when other Western Powers had established and strengthened their national unity Italy like Germany remained not one country but many, a disparate collection of kingdoms, dukedoms, and fiefs, politically pawns in the great chess game between Bourbon and Habsburg, weakened and impoverished by war, by the general absence of education and liberty, by the Church's inordinate wealth and worldliness, and in the poverty-stricken south by a medieval social system of feudal privilege. In 1713 by the Treaty of Utrecht Austrian Habsburgs supplanted Spanish as the preponderant power in the Italian peninsula, and in the following decades its states were shuffled and redealt according to the shifting necessities of the political balance of power.

In the later eighteenth century reforms by the enlightened despots (Habsburgs in the north, Bourbons in the south) made some attempt to limit the power and wealth of the clergy and to attack the feudal privilege of the nobility; and then came the French Revolution and Napoleon, hailed as liberators by the bourgeoisie, the only class in Italy politically conscious enough to wish to break the ancient domination of despot, Church, and baron. The promised blessing of *Liberté* turned out to be a great sham, as Napoleon ransacked Italy for its treasures, took its young men for his armies, and taxed it unmercifully; yet despite the resentment and disillusion something emerged. *Egalité* proved rather more real than *Liberté*: the *Code Napoléon* simplified the law and made all citizens equal before it. Most significant of all, there was under Napoleon for the first time a Kingdom of Italy, puppet of Paris though it was. It was one of the three parts into which Napoleon divided Italy as Caesar divided Gaul—the other two being the north-west (from the Papal States to the Riviera) which came under the direct rule of France, and the southern mainland (the Kingdom of Naples).

The town of Nice, in Liguria, part of the Kingdom of Sardinia, was contained in the north-western area, and thus it was as a French citizen that Giuseppe Garibaldi was born there in July 1807—a French citizen of Italian extraction speaking the Ligurian dialect. Italian therefore as well as French was to some extent a foreign language, and his speech was always to reveal his frontier origins. He was of poor parents, but nevertheless received a fair education from those clerics whom his pious mother revered and whom he was to spend his whole life hating. His chief tutors, however, were the mountains and the sea. He could swim from earliest infancy, and at the age of eight began what was to become a lifetime's habit of saving people from drowning. Heroism, as he himself observed, always came naturally to him. Running off to sea in oyster-trawling expeditions was another childhood habit; the adventurous and ungovernable boy at last so angered his parents that they allowed him at the early age of fifteen to go off on a voyage to Odessa as cabin-boy. Two years later he was finally off to sea, presumably for good.

When he was a boy of seven the politicians began dismantling Napoleon's Europe and piecing together again the old Italy. The King of Sardinia was restored to Piedmont, the Bourbons to Naples, the Austrians directly to the whole of Lombardy and Venetia; almost everywhere the dispossessed 'legitimate' Powers received back their possessions. The Church was confirmed in its position; the Pope himself regained those extensive states of his that ran from sea to sea and northward to the borders of Venetia. The clock was back to the eighteenth century, and most of the old evils were back with it—the tyrannies of secret police, the dominance of privi-

leged clergy, the heavy hands of political censors; corruption and
inefficiency in administration, brigandage in the countryside, torpor
in the towns. These evils were to some extent universal, but they
were least in the Austrian-dominated north, and worst in the Papal
States, Naples and Sicily. In Rome, where lay participation in
government was forbidden and priesthood was supreme, the
Napoleonic code went the way of such impious French innovations
as street lighting, vaccination, and the public drainage system, in a
general bonfire of progress.

Any opposition, even in such relatively enlightened states as
Modena, was perforce underground, and all over Italy there grew
up secret societies pledged to remove the worst evils of their particular locality. Some of these societies had originated in Napoleonic
times as a protest against foreign occupation. Most of them took
over the mumbo-jumbo as well as the idealism of freemasonry—
desperate oaths taken on a naked dagger, theatrical ceremonies of
initiation, threats of fearful penalties for backsliders. It would be
an over-simplification to see these secret organizations as consciously working for a united Italy; Italians were too divided by
geography, by historical tradition, by poor communications, even
by language—since the speech of the northerners and southerners
was often mutually incomprehensible. And although there was already a minority dreaming of an "Italy of all the Italians", the
idea would have seemed ludicrous to most thinking men; and the
very possibility never crossed the minds of the inert majority. The
many revolts of 1819-20 and of 1830-31 were the more easily
suppressed by Metternich and the Tsar just because they were so
unco-ordinated and ill organized. It was not till after the failure of
these revolts that an effective all-Italian organization was established
dedicated to the achievement of unity. That movement was "Young
Italy"; its founder was Giuseppe Mazzini, and in 1833 it acquired a
new member in Giuseppe Garibaldi.

Mazzini, a Genoese doctor's son, was two years older than Garibaldi. Sensitive, passionately idealistic, vital, eloquent, he was the
driving force and inspiration of the nationalist movement of the
thirties and forties. He was an intellectual and a visionary; from
the age of sixteen he had worn black for the woes of Italy, and as
things were to turn out he never had occasion to change his colour.
Fiercely anti-monarchical and anti-clerical, he was not a man to
compromise his principles. He had two religions—one the freedom

of all mankind, the other the unity and independence of his beloved Italy.

In his first eight years at sea Garibaldi had knocked about the world; sailed to Constantinople, Greece, North Africa, South America; had his first taste of battle in fighting off piratical attacks; seen the Greeks at war for their independence; and come into contact (in Constantinople, of all places) with the followers of Saint-Simon, who preached a revolutionary gospel which strongly affected Garibaldi—universal brotherhood, a classless society, sexual equality and freedom. When he met Mazzini in 1833, in Marseilles where Mazzini was already an exile, he was emotionally and intellectually ripe for high-principled adventure. The patriotic and religious ideals of "Young Italy", religious but anti-clerical, chimed exactly with his own aspirations. He took a solemn oath "in the name of God and the martyrs of Italy" and was "initiated into the sublime mysteries of the fatherland". Being at this time conscripted into the Piedmontese navy, he was soon involved in artless attempts to seduce his fellow-sailors from their loyal oaths in order to participate in a Mazzinian revolt being planned in Genoa early in 1834; but like so many previous nationalist attempts it disastrously misfired. Garibaldi, condemned to death in his absence, managed to get away over the mountains, first to Nice (calling on his shocked parents) and then to Marseilles. It seemed likely that he would never again be able to return home, and, indeed, he was not to see Italy again for thirteen years. But neither could he easily go back to what he now called "the dreary life of a trading sailor". For eighteen months he lived under a false name, doing odd jobs on land or sea; but such a life could be neither lasting nor satisfying, and in 1835 he became one of the many thousands of Italians emigrating at this time to Brazil. Garibaldi, however, was no ordinary emigrant; he was the sort of man who must have a star to hitch his wagon to, and although he could not yet do battle for Italy, at least he could fight for liberty somewhere else—and at the same time live the roving adventurous life, full of the danger that was the vital oxygen of his existence. Abandoning therefore his attempt to make a living out of the Brazilian coastal trade, in 1837 he offered his services and those of his little boat *Mazzini* to the breakaway rebel leader of the southernmost province of Brazil, the Rio Grande do Sul. So began his buccaneering career. At first he operated mainly at sea, preying on Brazilian shipping first from the *Mazzini* and then from a bigger boat which he had captured and which came to constitute 50 per cent of the Rio Grande navy. Gradually his force of a few hundred men became amphibious, fighting over all the plateau and forest country that lies between Brazil and Uruguay or between the River Parana and the Atlantic. Ashore, he and his men (South Americans, Italians, freed Negro slaves, half-breeds, and some Europeans—"brave sons of Columbus", as he called them) pursued their rough, tough warfare of swift pounces and vanishings, of "nameless scuffles in the wilderness". With these men, he wrote many years later, he first learned to despise danger and fight for "the sacred cause of nationality. . . . The wilder the country, the more beautiful I thought it"; all his life he looked back with nostalgia to the great plains with their teeming cattle herds, to the forests of pine, the punishing swamps and jungles, the great sierras at night under the stars, the cowboy world of lassos and galloping horses, the wild stallions of the Pampas, their glossy backs shining in the sun, their uncombed manes floating over their flanks.

Today, December 20, 1871 [he wrote], bending with stiffened limbs over the fire, I recall with emotion those scenes of the past, when life seemed to smile on me, in the presence of the most magnificent spectacle I ever beheld. I for my part am old and worn. Where are those splendid horses? Where are the bulls, the antelopes, the ostriches . . .?

Usually the guerrillas would feed handsomely from great carcasses of beef roasted in the open. For five years, said Garibaldi, he lived on flesh and water. In harder times, hunted and in hiding, they might have to exist off the roots of plants. It meant exhilaration, hardship, adventure, idealism, and sometimes too, for Garibaldi, disgust, as once when they sacked a village and the men got loose among the liquor and the women, murdering and raping and behaving "like wild beasts unchained".

Naturally robust, Garibaldi in these South American days became physically hard as nails. He had need to be, for at various times he was wounded in the neck, shipwrecked, captured, strung up by the wrists and flogged for attempting escape. Tough as he was, he almost certainly sowed the seeds at this time of the severe rheumatism that was soon to dog and sometimes prostrate him.

Strength, endurance, luck, and swimming prowess kept Garibaldi alive while around him his Italian companions succumbed. In 1839 he alone of the Italians managed to swim from a shipwreck to the shore of Santa Caterina, and although he was greeted as a hero by the local rebels and was soon afloat again in command of more captured ships, he was assailed by feelings of isolation and loneliness. A wife, perhaps, might help to assuage them. By his own account, he was casually viewing the shore one day from his schooner 'flagship' when he

> espied a young woman, and forthwith gave orders for the boat to be got out, as I wished to go ashore.

The result proved more fortunate than the method of choice perhaps deserved. The young woman was Anita Ribeiro, a black-haired half-bred Portuguese-Indian of eighteen, who in the years to come was to show a courage, toughness, and faithfulness to match Garibaldi's own. At this first meeting he swept her off her feet with what he himself called "magnetic insolence". He was already a legend locally; strikingly handsome, with his broad shoulders and chestnut-gold locks, his vivid (though narrowly set) eyes and his air of calm command. She did not apparently need telling twice that they were made for each other. The inconvenient circumstance that she was already married worried him less at the time than it did later. He simply abducted her, and they were unable to legalize their union until two years later, when her husband was presumed dead. Garibaldi was always at pains to conceal the full facts of their elopement, though he hinted myseriously at "the evil I had wrought". Especially after the horror of their last days together on the run, his conscience somewhat gnawed at him. But theirs was a stirring and romantic story. Garibaldi was a man capable of passionate and powerful feeling who adored his Amazon and was heartbroken at her death. Like him, she had qualities both tigerish and tender.

Their very first days together were spent in amphibious warfare among the lagoons of the Santa Caterina coast. Anita, "my treasure, was no less zealous than myself for the sacred cause of nationality". She had need to be: in her first severe action she was knocked down by a cannon-ball and fell among the dead men on the deck. A little later she was captured in a land battle; thinking her husband dead, she rummaged among the corpses for him and, not finding him, slipped away while her guards were drinking. Then she plunged into the tropical forest on a high-spirited horse which she had obtained from a peasant, crossed sixty miles of the most dangerous deserts in America, alone, without food, swimming great rivers in flood by holding on to her horse, riding through hostile pickets at the passes of the hills and the fords of the streams. . . . After four days she reached Lages, where her husband was soon to join her.

Their first child was born amid this kind of life and named Menotti, after the executed leader of the Italian risings of 1831. When he was twelve days old they had to flee again for their lives and nearly starved.

Anita was in constant terror of losing our Menotti and indeed it was a miracle that we saved him. In the steepest parts of the track and when crossing the torrents, I carried him, then three months old, slung from my neck by a handkerchief, trying to keep him warm against my breast and with my breath.

At the beginning of 1842, after six years as buccaneer and guerrilla, Garibaldi tried a quieter settled life in Montevideo. It was to last no more than a year or so; he was soon involved more deeply than ever in revolutionary struggles. The Republic of Uruguay at this time was fighting for its independence from Argentina. Who better than Garibaldi to help them found and train a navy, or raise an Italian Legion to fight in land? The Legionaries' flag was a volcano (for the fire within them) on a black ground (for the sorrows of Italy). Their uniform was the red shirt that was soon to be world-famous—but they wore it simply because a large consignment lay ready and available in a Montevideo warehouse. It had been intended for export to the Argentina slaughter-houses; the colour red concealed the stains of blood and had no special significance.

Twice between 1843 and 1848 the Italian Legion save Montevideo. They were heroes in Uruguay and heroes at home in Italy, where the Garibaldi legend was already born. Yet he and Anita and their growing family lived in the strictest poverty; Garibaldi, the most quixotic and unmercenary of men, ostentatiously rejected the rewards that could have been his, to the point of exhausting the patience of his wife, who could not so easily see the sense in bringing up four children in self-imposed penury, however virtuous. Anita's loyalty was taxed in other ways too: it was not only the *men* of Montevideo who idolized this dazzling husband (who as he claimed could easily, had he wished, have made himself dictator); he was the object also of a great deal of feminine adoration. One day he came home with his long locks shorn off as a sort of voluntary disfigurement which he hoped would quieten his wife's jealousy.

During all these years Italy was never long out of his thoughts, and as during 1846–47 he came increasingly to dislike Uruguayan politics and politicians, he began to contemplate the possibilities of return. Throughout Italy the liberal-nationalist tide seemed to be flowing, and the Mazzinians were confident that an anti-Austrian crusade would soon be starting. And then, wonder of wonders, there had arrived on the throne in 1846 a new Pope, Pius IX, who by his actions and pronouncements seemed to show himself a liberal. A political amnesty; laymen in the administration; gaslight in the public streets; a commission on railway building; promise of penal reform—these proposals and others all seemed to herald an era of reform in Rome. A liberal Pope—the one contingency, Metternich said, they had not prepared for! The air of expectancy was general. The Abbé Gioberti propagated the idea of a united federal Italy under the leadership of the Pope. Mazzini himself called on Pius to fulfil his God-given mission of uniting the fatherland. The cult of Pio Nono was for some months the religion of Italy. Away in Montevideo Garibaldi even envisaged fighting in the papal army to expel the Austrians from Italy—a daydream unreal in the light of future events, but far from unreal to him in December 1847. Accordingly he sent Anita and the three surviving children home to Nice, and in 1848 followed them, bearing with him an unrivalled experience of guerrilla warfare, a legendary reputation for heroism and daring, his own high hopes for the future of his country, and the secretly exhumed coffin of his beloved child Rosita, dead at the age of four. Her bones must lie, as his must one day lie, in sacred Italian earth.

During his two-month crossing of the Atlantic, Italy, like most of the rest of Europe, was in process of igniting. There was great joy aboard when, calling at a Spanish port, Garibaldi and the sixty members of the Italian Legion who accompanied him, learned that

Palermo, Milan, Venice and a hundred sister cities had brought about the momentous revolution. The Piedmontese army was pursuing the scattered remnants of the Austrian; and all Italy . . . was sending her contingents of brave men to the holy war.

The truth, as he was to discover, was not quite so rosy. It was a fact that Charles Albert of Piedmont had abandoned his earlier anti-liberal policy and put himself at the head of the forces fighting Austria. It was not, however, true that all over Italy men were "replying as one man to the call of arms", as Garibaldi exultantly declared. Neither was it true that the rulers of Naples or Tuscany or the Papal States were proposing to involve themselves in a pan-Italian war of liberation. Pius IX, who had complained "They want to make a Napoleon of me, who am only a poor country priest", was obliged to disappoint all the liberal and nationalist hopes that had fastened upon him. At the moment when 12,000 of his subjects were setting off to fight the Austrian (and while Garibaldi was still in mid-Atlantic) the Pope announced "clearly and openly" that war with Austria was "far from his thoughts". In the summer Charles Albert lost the battle of Custozza, surrendered Milan, and signed an armistice with the Austrians.

By that time Garibaldi and his men, having been refused admission to the Royal Piedmontese Army and waged on their own account some characteristically desperate guerrilla warfare along the Lombard hills near Bergamo, found themselves in severe straits, "more like a caravan of bedouins than a body of men ready to fight for their country". However, their poor condition did not prevent them from offering their services to the Tuscan government for a war of liberation against the Neapolitan Bourbons. "Yes or no; Garibaldi", demanded the brusque telegram. When, hardly surprisingly, no answer was returned, this rather ragged Italian Legion prepared to sail from Ravenna to the aid of the rebels in Venice (where under Manin they were holding out against great odds). At that moment the event happened that cut right through all the frustration and disappointments they had suffered since landing in Italy. On November 15th, 1848, Rome itself exploded into revolution.

In the Papal States violence was no novelty. Political assassination, whether of pro-government gangs and police spies by 'liberals', freemasons, and Carbonari, or *vice versa*, was almost a way of life in the ill-governed dominions. But Pius IX had raised immense hopes for improvement, mitigated some of the harshness of the clerical tyranny, and introduced reforming laymen as his chief ministers. One of these was Rossi, a moderate, attempting on the one hand to reform the abominable administration and on the other to suppress the democratic and nationalist violence rampant in many of the towns. (Bologna was the worst.) In mid-November 1848 he was stabbed to death by nationalist conspirators.

This murder of Rossi made certain of two things: it provided the signal for a revolution in Rome, and it gave the impetus necessary to turn Pius finally back from the road of liberalism that he had trodden—at first so hopefully, later with such misgiving. Within a week of the murder he had appointed as Rossi's successor Cardinal Antonelli, the most unscrupulous and obscurantist of reactionaries, and fled disguised as a parish priest to seek at Gaeta the protection of Ferdinand ("Bomba") of Naples. From 1848 onward the Papacy under Pius came to stand obdurately against all national idealism, all political reform, all liberal theology, and a majority of the great new discoveries of the age. Soon the very idea of 'progress' was to be specifically condemned as heresy.

From Gaeta the Pope refused to negotiate. Instead he demanded submission. The provincial government in Rome, therefore, had little alternative to proclaiming a republic, which they did in February 1849, and the following month the unchallenged leader of the Italian patriots, Mazzini, was welcomed to Rome; and soon, though officially only one of the three 'triumvirs', he assumed the leadership of the revolution. The Holy City, according to the Pope, had become "a forest of roaring beasts"—heretics, atheists, socialists—and the destruction of Mazzini's republic became the most urgent duty of every Catholic state in Europe. But in fact the Pope's words, even allowing for some natural exaggeration, were not true. Mazzini was at least as high-principled a man as Pius, and much less ready than the papal party to compromise with the powers of evil. He was neither a socialist nor communist, nor were most of his adherents, and his régime was remarkably—it might even be said unwisely—tolerant. He refused to permit the persecution of priests and condemned both the class war and the unjust violation of the rights of property. The swollen properties of the Church, however, he did propose to confiscate for distribution among "the classes least favoured by fortune". Certainly, like Garibaldi, he was passionately anti-clerical; but unlike Garibaldi (whose religious philosophy was inconsistent and confused and who sometimes did like to call himself an atheist), Mazzini was a "man of God". Like Garibaldi, he was as much a religious as a national leader. He lived simply and austerely in a single room of the Quirinal Palace, giving away his small salary, dining in cheap restaurants or supping at home off bread and raisins. *God and the People* was his watchword, and his whole life was a plea for spirituality, a denial of materialism. If there is to be criticism of Mazzini it is not that he was a "roaring beast"; it is that he was to prove as inelastic as the Papacy itself. As had already been written of him,

> he is pontiff, apostle, priest. . . . He wants to tether the world to his own immutable idea.

Le mieux est l'ennemi du bien; and when Italy would not follow Mazzini towards the "best" that was always before his eyes he spat out in sorrow and contempt the compromise that events were to force, refusing to see in it any good at all.

By the time that Mazzini had taken power in Rome the Italian national movement had in effect been already defeated for the time being. Charles Albert of Piedmont, after having denounced the 1848 armistice, had made one last effort to defeat the Austrians, but within a week the fighting was all over, and disastrously for Italy. Charles Albert, after the final catastrophe at Novara, abdicated in favour of his son Victor Emmanuel, passed into exile, and died four months later. By April 1849, the month when Garibaldi was at last able to come to Rome (he had been kicking his heels impatiently up in the Romagna), only Venice, Tuscany, and Rome itself were still in the fight, and very soon Tuscany too went back under the rule of its Grand Duke. As for the Venetian republic, its days were plainly numbered, and around Rome the forces of European Catholicism were gathering for the kill. It was a lost cause that Garibaldi arrived to espouse—but the heroism of desperation was by now his speciality, impossibilities his *métier*.

His men numbered about a thousand now, and they were soon to reach 2500, a strange-looking medley of students, adventurers, foreigners, youths, guerrilla veterans, criminals, idealists, and desperadoes—in a striking variety of apparel; some in the red shirts of the Legion, some in blue tunics; bearded mostly, and many with the tall 'Calabrian' hat, picturesquely plumed like seventeenth-century Cavaliers. Upon their arrival they provoked much excited applause among the citizens. Garibaldi himself, with his striking looks, his golden-brown beard and flowing hair; the mixture of dignity and melancholy, of nobility and flamboyance in his mien; his ostrich plumes, the fine white horse that he rode, the giant South American Negro who accompanied him as bodyguard—cut an unforgettable figure.

I had no idea of enlisting [said one who joined him]; I only went out of curiosity. He reminded us of nothing so much as of our Saviour's head in the galleries. I could not resist him. He had only to show himself. We all worshipped him, we could not help it.

But, in the words of another arrival, Emilio Dandolo, who came with a regiment of *bersaglieri* at the same time as Garibaldi, to another enthusiastic welcome:

All this array of warriors in glittering helmets with double-barrelled guns and belts full of daggers reconciled us but little to the scanty numbers of proper, well-drilled soldiers.

The enemy was approaching the gates: General Oudinot, with two French divisions, had landed at Civitavecchia; a Neapolitan force was mustering in the south. Deciding to fight it out, Mazzini still hoped that even now the Roman resistance would provide vital inspiration for a spontaneous national uprising. "We must act like men who have the enemy at their gates," he said, "and at the same time like men who are working for eternity." When the French attacked on April 30th, they were met by ferocious resistance from Garibaldi's forces. Though suffering heavy casualties— Garibaldi was himself wounded painfully in the side—the Italians forced Oudinot to retire and await reinforcements. Garibaldi was all for following up and driving the enemy into the sea; but Mazzini still hoped that the French (who after all had a republican government) would now desist, and he ordered, therefore, that pursuit should cease. This was the first of many differences that were to cloud relations between the two leaders. Soon Mazzini was accusing Garibaldi of insubordination, 'temperament', and peevishness. While acknowledging Garibaldi's courage, Mazzini thought him both weak and foolish. "You know the face of a lion?" Mazzini once asked. "Is it not a foolish face? Is it not the face of Garibaldi?" On his side Garibaldi found Mazzini bookish and unpractical; he blamed him for not following expert military advice— especially Garibaldi's own; for failure to follow up victories; and for jibbing at the necessity of taking dictatorial powers.

The recriminations were in any case irrelevant. Rome *could* not

have won in 1849, even if her whole population had stood steadfast for Italy and run to join the national colours—which they did
not. The young republic's forces were ill trained and ill armed.
Courage and willingness to die for Italy were not enough; the odds
were impossible. But the heroism of Rome's defenders and the brilliant dash of Garibaldi's leadership left behind a legend that was
to be a factor in the years to come. He did twice defeat the Neapolitans and was hungry to pursue them over the border, but Mazzini
recalled him to Rome, in imminent danger from Austrians and
French; Garibaldi obeyed but with a bad grace, and wrote to
Mazzini:

> You ask me to choose what I want. I tell you that I can exist
> for the good of the Republic only in one of two ways—as a dic-
> tator with full powers or as a simple soldier. Choose!

But of course neither alternative was acceptable, and when the
French began their final assault on June 3rd, 1849, Garibaldi was
back at the head of his troops as they launched a series of counter-
attacks attempting the recapture of the Villa Corsini. Not once but
many times that day he escaped death by inches; both his hat and
his white *poncho* (or cloak) were ripped open by gunfire. Time and
again his volunteers were mown down by the French, and devotedly
attacked yet again upon Garibaldi's orders. It was magnificent, but
it was not war: in this kind of fighting, where trained troops did not
flee (as the Neapolitans had) at the first Garibaldian bayonet charge,
the consummate guerrilla leader was at a disadvantage. And by
this time numbers too were against him: there were 20,000 French
now that they had been reinforced.

For the patriot volunteers there was an intoxication in it all, even
though the population of Rome, on the whole, stayed non-commit-
tally at home:

> This is a day of heroes [pronounced Mazzini], a page of
> history. Yesterday we said to you, be great; today we say to you,
> you are great. . . . Rome is inviolable. Watch over her walls this
> night; within those walls is the future of the nation.

And Garibaldi wrote to his wife (who, being unwell and pregnant,
had been persuaded by him to stay out of Rome, but was soon to
disregard his advice and arrive there):

> We are fighting on the Janiculum and these people are worthy
> of their past greatness. Here they live, die, and suffer amputation,

all to the cry of "*Viva la Repubblica!*" One hour of our life in Rome is worth a century of ordinary existence.

Anita disregarded his advice and came to Rome on June 26th, leaving her children with her parents-in-law. A week later the city's resistance was over, and the French marched in, bringing the Pope in their wake. Mazzini had already resigned in protest against surrender (he would have preferred a sort of civic martyrdom), and escaped first to Civitavecchia, and afterwards to live out his days in exile and indignation. Garibaldi too was against surrender, but only because he favoured continuing the fight in the hills, where—he persuaded himself—guerrillas could keep resistance going until the flames of popular revolt could ignite again, and perhaps ignite all Italy. For a month he led his band of diehards northwards through the valleys and over the mountains of Umbria and Tuscany, brilliantly eluding the baffled Austrians. But it was a constantly dwindling band; and the Italian peasant, patriotically idealized from the distance of Montevideo, turned out in reality to be no hero. Some towns and villages gave cheers and speeches of welcome; many more saw the Garibaldians as bandits and cattle-thieves. (The guerrillas lived off roasted oxen, South American style.) In fact Garibaldi condemned casual theft and thought nothing of ordering looters to be summarily shot; he favoured instead stiff levies on monasteries and nunneries, and paying the farmers with the proceeds. But the fact remained, his little army was melting away. He thought perhaps he could hold it together and run the gauntlet to Venice, where Manin's republic still held out, but the prospects became plainly impossible. Instead, taking sanctuary in the tiny republic of San Marino, he released his men from their obligation to follow him, and at the same time declared dramatically as he rode through the town gate northward:

> Whoever wishes to follow me, I offer him fresh battles, suffering, and exile.

Guides helped him and the little band of 250 or so who accompanied him through the Austrian lines and over the mountains to the Romagna plain. Anita was still with him, in the uniform of an officer, her long black tresses cut short. She was nearly six months pregnant, and in much pain now. They reached the coast not far from Rimini, under the noses of the Austrian and papal troops, and there in the middle of the night they hi-jacked the local fishing fleet and forced the fishermen to take them to sea, hoping to evade the Austrian patrols and reach the shelter of the lagoons. The following night, however, the bright moon betrayed them, and all but three of the boats were captured with their occupants. From one of the three boats that made land a frantic Garibaldi stepped ashore carrying his wife in his arms; she was by now acutely ill. Rescued and given shelter by a local patriot, hidden in lonely huts on the sand-dunes, taken hither and thither by farm-cart and fishing-boat, they refused to be parted—first she from him, then he from her, delirious as she now became from pain and fever. He held her in his arms, wiping the froth from her lips. At last they got her into a farmhouse, and a doctor was sent from the nearest village; as they were carrying her up to the bedroom she died.[1]

The urgency of prompt flight, the repeated imminence of capture as he and a single companion moved back towards Tuscany, drove some of the grief from his mind, though it lingered and grew remorseful as the years went by. Assisted by the patriot 'underground' and various disguises (merchants travelling by carriage, sportsmen out with their dogs), the two men managed to reach the coast opposite Elba, and from there were taken by friendly boat to Piedmont. This caused excitement among the populace, who voted him a hero, and embarrassment for the Turin government, who declared his civic rights forfeited; but a vote in the assembly went overwhelmingly against allowing his arrest. "Imitate his greatness if you can," said one member; "if you cannot, respect it." He was allowed to visit his relatives (he saw his mother in Nice for the last time) and was able to make arrangements for friends to care for his children. Then his wanderings in exile began. Tunis, Gibraltar, and Spain would not have him, and he did not wish to settle in England. For a time he kicked his heels in Tangier. In July 1850 he set out once again for the New World; worked for a time in a New York candle factory; travelled to Peru; and from there took on the mastership of a sailing-ship in which for the next two years he sailed round the world. But increasingly (he was arthritic and approaching fifty) he longed to put down roots in Italy.

[1] There is a macabre postscript. The body was hastily and secretly buried in too shallow a grave. When it was discovered the brothers who ran the farm were charged with murder, but acquitted when evidence was given of the "malignant fever" from which Anita Garibaldi had been suffering. Because the windpipe was severed, Garibaldi's enemies tried later to spread the story that he had strangled her to get her out of the way and be free to escape.

Equally, and perhaps contradictorily, he hungered to do something spectacular for his beloved fatherland. Not, however, with such optimism now. Italians, he complained, cared for their bellies more than their souls; as for Mazzini's perennial faith in the spontaneous patriotic revolution, Garibaldi could not share it. "I want to send him to Sicily, where they are ripe for insurrection," wrote Mazzini, but Garibaldi was content for a time to be accepted back as a Piedmontese citizen. Twice about this time he visited England, and for two years was formally engaged to marry a rich English widow, Emma Roberts, who travelled back with him to Nice. Garibaldi's romantic appearance and heroic reputation, to which he added a rugged honesty, simple outspokenness, and a contempt for the sophistication and pretence of polite society (Emma Roberts's footmen simultaneously depressed and alarmed him) were enough to turn any number of feminine and fashionable heads. One of the more serious of these admirers was a young Anglo-German novelist, Baroness von Schwartz ("Speranza"), who had buried one husband and divorced another, and who accompanied Garibaldi when at last he found a home that satisfied his longing to have some retreat near to the sea and far from the madding crowd. He eventually discovered it off the lonely coast of Sardinia, on the small island of Caprera, which measured four windswept miles by three. He bought half of it. Here among the junipers and myrtles, the eagles and wild goats, this "simple courteous gentleman, of few words", milked his cows and planted his churlish land with vines and figs, olives and vegetables, corn and sugar-cane: here he supervised the building of his eyrie, the white stone house into which he moved in 1857 with his daughter and the servant-girl Francesca from Nice who kept house for him and bore his fourth child, named after Anita. This notwithstanding, he proposed marriage to Baroness von Schwartz in 1858—and was refused by her;[2] their intimate companionship persisted, however, and in 1859, for all his desire to settle, they were planning to visit South America together when in Italy sensational news broke that pushed all such ideas out of his head.

[2] In 1860 this unaccountable man suddenly married the eighteen-year-old Marchesina Raimondi, with whom he had become infatuated. When his defeated rival revenged himself on Garibaldi by informing him of his bride's pre-marital behaviour this short-lived and disastrous episode ended. Garibaldi considered himself humiliated. The lady had in any case been pushed unwillingly into the marriage by her father; and in due course, after many years, it was annulled.

After its defeat at the hands of the Austrians in 1848–49 the land of Piedmont saw many changes. More rapidly than any other part of the peninsula it was transforming itself into a modern state. Charles Albert's constitution had survived his defeat and abdication; parliamentary rule was established; the privileges of the Church were curtailed, its special courts abolished, civil marriage permitted. The army was reorganized and strengthened. Economic prosperity grew; railways were constructed and tariffs reduced. As Piedmont moved forward into an era of liberal capitalism and industrial expansion it was inevitable that the eyes of Italian patriots should turn hopefully to Turin. There they saw a monarch, Victor Emmanuel II, undoubtedly vulgar and licentious (Bismarck called him "the bandit chief"), but also energetic and patriotic; and under him a chief minister, Count Camillo di Cavour, who had in earlier days edited a paper (*Il Risorgimento*) dedicated to Italian unification, and who now consciously pursued the sort of aristocratic-liberal policies that Peel had followed in Britain.

Italia fara da se, Charles Albert had said: Italy will get there under her own steam. This too was the faith of Mazzini, and of Garibaldi in the early days. But the all-conquering spontaneous popular revolution had looked unpromising ever since 1848, and Cavour was convinced that French help (and British too if he could get it) was vital for ridding Italy of the Austrians and thus enlarging the extent and influence of the Piedmontese state. Beyond that he could at first see only dimly. To set out to unify all Italy as a matter of immediate policy would have seemed to Cavour in the 1850's to be unpractical. Cavour was essentially a diplomat, scheming away in the subterranean manner of his kind. He was essentially too an aristocrat, a 'gentleman'—he liked the English word. But he knew very well the value of a popular symbol, and he knew that Garibaldi, an outstanding hero among the people, would be a powerful man to have on his side. Twice, therefore—in 1856 and again in 1858—Garibaldi had been summoned from Caprera, donned the rare garb for him of a conventional frock-coat, and gone to Turin to see Cavour and be briefed on the progress of his scheme to provoke a war with Austria, having first gained the assurance of French help. The second time he saw the King too and thought him a fine fellow; they should have him as *Duce*, supreme royal dictator—Garibaldi had little use for parliaments or politicians.

Cavour's plan for involving France in an Austrian war made only slow progress to begin with. He had assisted Britain and France in the Crimean War, spent freely on Italian propaganda in French newspapers, and even sent his beautiful young cousin the Countess of Castiglione to 'influence' the notoriously susceptible Napoleon III—the sort of conduct that shocked Mazzini, who thought that kings and emperors should be deposed, or even on occasions honestly assassinated, but not cajoled by bribes or seduced by patriotic countesses. In this case the lady made rather too much of a public meal of her Emperor, and Mazzinian conspirators attacked his coach as he was leaving her house. In January 1858 another Mazzinian named Orsini threw a bomb at the royal carriage as it left the Opera, killing ten and wounding 140.

As it turned out, Orsini had considerably more influence upon Napoleon III and the march of events than the Countess of Castiglione, now discarded. The Emperor's genuine desire to promote Italian nationhood was stirred. He allowed Orsini to make propaganda from the dock; he even tried to secure a reprieve. However, from this he was dissuaded, and the passionately patriotic Orsini, shouting to the crowd "Long live Italy! Long live France!" went bravely to the guillotine. The attempted assassination acted as a catalyst, wonderfully speeding the ends of Cavour's devious and long-laid plans. That same year (1858) Napoleon secretly promised the Piedmontese Government that he would send 200,000 French troops to help them free North Italy "from the Alps to the Adriatic".

Events moved fast now. While Garibaldi was allowed to lead a minor expedition of volunteers against the Austrians in the Lake Como area, the French and Piedmontese won (not without heavy losses) the battles of Magenta and Solferino. Then suddenly Napoleon, nervous of a threatening Prussia in his rear, under criticism from French Catholics and conservatives for the dangerous implications of his Italian policy, horrified by Solferino's slaughter and worried by the tough military commitments ahead of any future advance, withdrew from the struggle, by the Treaty of Villa-franca, and left Cavour in a frenzy of frustration. Lombardy had been liberated, but not Venetia; Cavour went into five months' retirement, and Garibaldi raged against "that fox of a Bonaparte".

Meanwhile there had been sympathetic rebellions in Tuscany, Modena, and the Bologna district of the Romagna, and by the close of 1859 all north-central Italy adhered to Piedmont. The great question then was, what would happen in the Papal States? Garibaldi, sent southwards by Victor Emmanuel to be a focus for popular support, made triumphal progress through Florence, Modena, Ravenna, and Bologna. He favoured a southward dash from Rimini to rouse general rebellion in the Pope's territories, and initially the King did not dissuade him. If Garibaldi succeeded merely in raising chaos Piedmontese troops could go to consolidate the gains. But caution prevailed, and the "foxiness" of the politicians and generals that Garibaldi railed against. Recalled to Turin soon after Cavour returned to office, he was offered (but refused) a generalship in the Piedmontese army. "Foxiness" was almost too mild a word in March 1860, when the news became public of the price Cavour had been willing to pay for Napoleon's help. He had given away to France the substantial prizes of Nice and Savoy. Cavour had thus made Garibaldi a foreigner in his own birthplace of Nice—the town too that he represented in the Piedmontese parliament. In bitterness he resigned his seat, and began to contemplate the great adventure that suited his patriotic ardour so much better than parliamentary debates and diplomatic calculations.

Mazzini, at this time hiding from Cavour's police in Genoa and lying under double sentence of death, had stirred up yet another rebellion in Sicily. Why should not Garibaldi, the supreme guerrilla leader, go there and use his immense reputation and popularity to rouse the island in the cause of a united Italy? The idea had much to appeal to Victor Emmanuel; it frightened Cavour; and it came to dominate Garibaldi, despite the prompt failure of the Sicilian rebellion, the unco-operativeness of the Piedmontese Government, and the difficulty of procuring adequate weapons. Volunteers began to assemble at Genoa. There were eventually 1089 of them, a wonderfully mixed band: patriotic idealists, students skipping their examinations, professional men of all sorts (a quarter of the 'Thousand' were lawyers or doctors), businessmen, artists, five army officers, a few criminals, some boys, and one peasant woman who was Crispi's[3] mistress. They managed to accumulate some Colt revolvers, a thousand antiquated muskets, a smaller number of rifles from England, a good deal of money from sources both Italian and foreign, and a mountain of goodwill. "It would be

[3] Francesco Crispi, Sicilian and radical, representative of Palermo in first Italian Parliament (1861), Prime Minister of Italy 1887–91, 1893–96.

madness to go," said Garibaldi; men even fiercer than he, however —Crispi, for instance, and Nino Bixio—prevailed, and in May 1860 they sailed. Twice *en route* they landed, once to steal coal and once to beg munitions.

Cavour now had a problem. He had not himself been ready to push the problem of Southern Italy to the point of crisis. He would have been quite content for the time being to come to an understanding with the King of Naples, and to evict the Austrians from Venetia, thus creating a united North Italy under the domination of Piedmont. As Crispi's paper put it: "The Piedmontese have never wanted Piedmont for Italy, but always Italy for Piedmont." Cavour had done everything in his power (short of arrest, which would have been too unpopular) to prevent Garibaldi from recruiting his force. When against Cavour's advice it sailed, he first ordered his navy to arrest it if it landed; a later message ordered arrest *at all costs*, with the last three words peremptorily underlined. Thus the old story, later put about by Cavour and his supporters, that all this was a blind, and that secretly Cavour backed Garibaldi, will not stand up. His situation was made worse by the knowledge that King Victor Emmanuel did secretly sympathize with Garibaldi; that the public quite openly did; and that he could not really afford to allow his navy to carry out the arrest.

In any case Garibaldi's two steamers slipped into Marsala undetected. To begin with, most of the local inhabitants greeted the Garibaldians with the utmost suspicion, though there were a few patriots who joined them. Within a few days, however, there was remarkable news: the Thousand, outnumbered and outclassed in everything but determination, had defeated the Neapolitan army at Calatafimi, a ferocious little battle which at one stage it seemed the Garibaldians must lose. Even the impetuous Bixio thought they must retreat. "What shall we do, General?" asked the sorely harassed, and in the main quite inexperienced, volunteers. "Italians," came the reply from Garibaldi, "here we must die!" They charged with the bayonet for the last time; the enemy fell back; and the Garibaldians fell to the ground exhausted but victorious. A fortnight later, ragged, many of them barefooted, all of them weary, the remaining 750 of the 1089, together with two or three thousand Sicilian civilians (who shot wildly in all directions, including upwards), astonished themselves and the world by scrambling into Palermo, the Sicilian capital, having forced out the incompetently commanded Neapolitan army. The rebellion was triumphant. There was consternation in Naples, delirium in Palermo; even the Archbishop was smiling and the nuns seemed "piously enamoured" of Garibaldi—who a few days earlier, 'atheist' though he was, had attended Mass and received a crusader's cross at the altar:

"How beautiful," exclaimed one. "He is the image of *Nostro Signore*," whispered another, while, a third, in the heat of her enthusiasm, seized his hand and kissed it; he withdrew it, and she, springing on his neck, impressed a fervent kiss upon his lips. Her audacity proved contagious; it spread to her young companions, then to the middle-aged, the venerables, and finally to the abbess, who at first seemed scandalized. We stood by, spectators.[4]

According to Odo Russell, the British minister in Rome and nephew of the British Foreign Secretary,[5] King Francis II of Naples was "seized with such a panic that he telegraphed five times in twenty-four hours for the Pope's blessing." He appealed also to Napoleon III for more material assistance, but the Emperor, like Cavour, urged him to seek protection from Piedmont.

While Garibaldi's volunteers went from strength to strength, winning the Battle of Milazzo—a costly one in casualties—and completing the conquest of Sicily, Cavour's anxieties grew. As an Italian patriot he dared not openly disavow Garibaldi, though he did in diplomatic dispatches to the Powers. When he sent a political commissioner to Palermo, hoping as he said to "put a brake upon democracy" and turn events to Piedmont's advantage, Garibaldi ordered the man to be arrested. Though Cavour did everything in his power to prevent Garibaldi crossing the Straits of Messina to the mainland, even persuading a rather reluctant Victor Emmanuel to send a letter expressly forbidding it, he was unable to prevent a further force of volunteers sailing from Genoa to reinforce the 'Thousand'. On the night of August 18th, having first paid a brief visit to Caprera to see his cows and his crops and the little son that his housekeeper had just borne him there, Garibaldi crossed the Straits without incident, immediately assaulted Reggio, and proceeded with remarkable speed to overrun the toe of Italy, Calabria. Within a fortnight 10,000 Neapolitan troops had surrendered to an army of half that strength. (They were given the option of fighting with the patriots, but most of them were glad to get back

[4] Albert Mario, quoted in C. Hibbert, *Garibaldi and his Enemies*, p. 238.
[5] See pp. 252–53.

to their farms.) Garibaldi trusted to speed, the poor morale of the enemy, the magic of his name—"our second Jesus Christ"—and not a little to bluff. False messages were telegraphed to confuse the Neapolitan command and spread wild exaggerations of the Garibaldian numbers. Some Neapolitan officers were shot by their own troops. Back in Naples itself the Bourbons' many enemies began to prepare for the great day when the idol of the hour should arrive; and the novelist Alexandre Dumas, Garibaldi's self-appointed unofficial ambassador, arrived in the Bay in his private schooner ready to celebrate the triumph of this perfect real-life hero. The King and Queen steamed quietly away to Gaeta. The chief of police, as prudent as he was effusive, hailed by telegram the advent of the "new redeemer of Italy"; and a few hours later, leaving his army far in the rear, Garibaldi arrived by the brand-new railway at Naples station to an overwhelming popular welcome. In his red shirt, flowing silk handkerchief, and black wideawake hat he drove, the calmest man that day in all Naples, through the streets to the Palace, where he made a short speech from the balcony to the briefly silenced crowds:

> You have a right to exult in this day. It is the beginning of a new era not only for you but for the whole of Italy, of which Naples forms the fairest part. It is indeed a glorious and a holy day—on which a people passes from the yoke of slavery to the status of a free nation.

What would Cavour and the King do now? Victor Emmanuel was secretly delighted and began straightway to establish his own private contact with Garibaldi in Naples, as earlier he had in Sicily. Only Cavour's threat to resign a second time brought him up sharply. And then Cavour proceeded very neatly to trump Garibaldi's ace.

The conquest of the South had been astonishingly swift. Garibaldi had achieved what had earlier seemed impossible, but now he was faced by what perhaps really was impossible. Without artillery he could *promise* the conquest of Rome—always his dearest dream—but surely he could not achieve it; and, indeed, he was soon held up along the River Volturno before the fortress of Capua. He fought there the biggest battle of his career—his only large-scale pitched battle—and after severe losses won it: but it was significant that it was a defensive engagement, to prevent the *re*-capture of Naples. There were to be no more swift and sensational

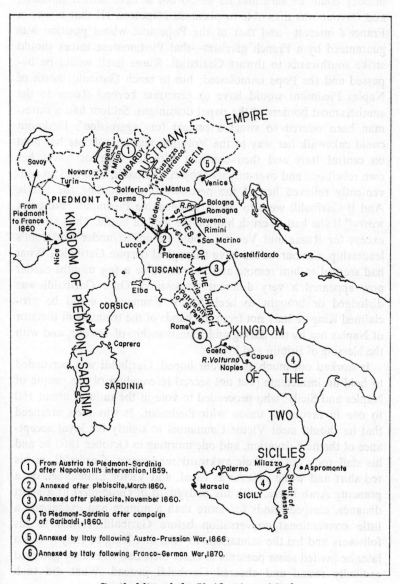

1. From Austria to Piedmont-Sardinia after Napoleon III's intervention, 1859.

2. Annexed after plebiscite, March 1860.

3. Annexed after plebiscite, November 1860.

4. To Piedmont-Sardinia after campaign of Garibaldi, 1860.

5. Annexed by Italy following Austro-Prussian War, 1866.

6. Annexed by Italy following Franco-German War, 1870.

Garibaldi and the Unification of Italy

advances. His star, however, had recently shone so brightly that nobody could be sure that he would not achieve further miracles, and Cavour was thus able to persuade Napoleon III that it was in France's interest—and that of the Pope too, whose position was guaranteed by a French garrison—that Piedmontese forces should strike southwards to thwart Garibaldi. Rome itself would be by-passed and the Pope unmolested; but to reach Garibaldi north of Naples Piedmont would have to penetrate beyond Rome to the southernmost borders of the papal dominions. Seldom had a states-man been offered so sweet a pretext for 'aggression'. Piedmont could cakewalk her way to the Volturno and consolidate her hold on central Italy and then confront with far superior forces her own rebellious and over-mighty subject Garibaldi, who had so conveniently relieved her of the necessity of conquering the South. And if Garibaldi were to prove unamenable Piedmont "must not worry" if she had to crush him on the field of battle. Thus all Italy except for Rome and Venetia would be united under Piedmont's leadership. Cavour would have triumphed despite Garibaldi. What had seemed to him remote and impracticable a few months earlier now appeared a very different proposition. Once Garibaldi was dislodged or brought to heel, Victor Emmanuel could be pro-claimed King of Italy not from the hands of the triumphant dictator of Naples but by the daring and statesmanship of Cavour, and with the blessing of Britain and France.

It worked out much as Cavour hoped. Garibaldi was persuaded to hold an immediate (but not secret) referendum of the people of Naples and Sicily, who proceeded to vote in the ratio of about 160 to one in favour of union with Piedmont. It was then arranged that he should meet Victor Emmanuel to signify his loyal accept-ance of the new situation, and one morning in October 1860 he and his staff rode out to their awkward rendezvous. Garibaldi, in his red shirt and white *poncho* as usual, and Victor Emmanuel, on a prancing Arab horse, with his bodyguard of *carabinieri* at a short distance, clasped hands for more than a minute and exchanged a little conventional conversation before Garibaldi turned to his followers and led the salutations to "the first King of Italy". When later he invited some peasants to cheer their new ruler they gathered excitedly round and cheered Garibaldi instead. What did such poverty-stricken illiterates know of "Italy"?

The King did not fail to put over the main point: Garibaldi's volunteers must be subject to royal command. One of them, Mario (who married an Englishwoman, Jessie White, a Hampshire ship-builder's daughter and a fellow-campaigner), saw his revered leader immediately after the interview, his expression "full of a gentle sadness. Never did I feel drawn towards him with such tenderness." "Jessie," said Garibaldi to Mario's wife, "they have sent us to the rear."

Every attempt was made by Victor Emmanuel and Cavour to deal well by Garibaldi. He was a hero far beyond the shores of Italy, as Cavour was well aware. Europe would condemn them, he wrote, if they slighted the great man. He was accordingly treated with honour, promoted to be a full general, and invited to ride cere-monially with the King in the royal coach through the streets of Naples; unhappily, however, it rained incessantly, and the King made a tactless speech. But it was the treatment of his men, the Garibaldini, by the commander of the regular Piedmontese army, General Fanti, that was to infuriate and embitter Garibaldi. The volunteers were indeed ragged and plebeian, many of them. Some were mere boys; some doubtless were criminals. The poorer-spirited of them had deserted before this, tired, hungry, or disappointed with the delays on the River Volturno. The best of them were men who had risked everything, suffered hardships almost intolerable, and uncorked the bottle from which Cavour was now pouring the wine of victory. To Garibaldi, who had led them to such a famous triumph, they seemed noble fellows all, and he was perhaps un-reasonable in expecting every one of his 'officers' automatically to achieve parallel rank in the regular army. He expressed the utmost disgust with what now happened; even the men of the defeated Neapolitan army were treated better, he complained (a few days had seen the capitulation of Capua, and Gaeta finally fell after a long siege in February 1861); yet many of his followers did remain and gain promotion in the royal service.

He was also angry at the decision to leave Rome and Venice for the time being in hands hostile to the new Italy. Everything, he urged, should be staked on attack. When the risks were pointed out —the hostility of the Pope, of the French Emperor, or the Austrian Empire—he brushed them aside. Had they not faced worse risks than that in Sicily and the South? As for Cavour, who acquiesced in French domination of Rome and Austrian rule in Venice, he had accepted "the degradation of his country". Cavour's Italy was no place for Garibaldi. Having resigned his dictatorship of Naples and accepted Victor Emmanuel as "King of Italy and Naples", and having bidden all Italians to be ready to follow the King "next spring" to the liberation of Rome and Venice, he decided to go, "his whole manner that of a man who was suffering a poignant grief". There was always Caprera, which he persuaded himself was more precious to him than wealth and the titles now dangled before him, which he spurned. So, taking with him two horses named after his greatest victories, one sack of dried fish and another of seed corn, a case of macaroni, sundry other provisions, and the bathtub that always accompanied him on his campaigns, he journeyed back by steamer to his island. Soon he was reported to be looking as happy as a schoolboy home for the holidays.

Describing himself now simply as "farmer", he gave his general's uniform to the man who dug his potatoes. Visitors (and some came every Friday with the packet-boat, politicians, admirers, autograph-hunters, literary big-game hunters) would discover him hoeing his shallow soil, breaking up granite for sale, constructing drystone walls against the wild goats, or returning perhaps from one of his regular fish-spearing or fowling expeditions. It was a strange existence that was led by this solitary individual who was yet "in and of himself one of the great Powers of the world", his name a legend throughout Europe and America. He was besieged by every kind of idealist and not a few cranks. The romantically inclined, especially females of the English aristocracy, would beg locks of his hair—in which he was quite content for there to be a brisk business —and might be discovered groping upon his bedroom floor to retrieve such holy relics as his nail-parings. In a sense he had retired; in another he could never retire, for he could never resist the call of further campaigns to capture Rome and Venice, and no Italian government could afford to ignore this Titan on his sea-girt rock. Furthermore the Titan himself had no intention of being ignored: nursing his grievances and his arthritis, clad again in his red shirt and *poncho* (his "prophet's mantle", as the sarcastic Cavour described it), he appeared at the debates of the Turin parliament in April 1861 to castigate Cavour and the army command in the bitterest terms, in particular over their treatment of his followers. Only after the sudden death of Cavour in June 1861 did he return disgruntled to Caprera once more, the campaigns for the completion of Italian unity being out of the question for the time being,

But the following year he was back again in Northern Italy, involved in the first of the disastrous sorties that marred the last decades of his active life.

Cavour's rôle in the unification of Italy had, of course, been central. His character, his methods, his ideals, were all miles apart from Garibaldi's. Machiavellian where Garibaldi was straightforward, conservative where Garibaldi was radical, shrewd and devious where Garibaldi was transparent and unsubtle, he moved in a different world, the politician's world of intrigue and calculation, where clever manœuvres counted for more than fine gestures and romantic revolutionary heroes were regarded as nuisances at best, at worst wreckers. On his side Garibaldi never understood Cavour's intricate and unmoral world of international diplomacy; finesse and deception were not for him. No-one better than Cavour illustrates the point about politics being "the art of the possible". No man had been less inclined to aim for the moon; yet Garibaldi had come along and suddenly enlarged the horizons of the possible, and brought the moon within Cavour's reach. It is fruitless to debate who played the greater part in the *Risorgimento*: the work of each of them would have remained stunted without the other's.

The most important of the Prime Ministers in this immediate post-Cavour era was Rattazzi, a politician who had all Cavour's taste for intrigue without his flair for it. His master Victor Emmanuel, now King of Italy, certainly continued to give secret encouragement to the adventures of Garibaldi, while drawing back from full public commitment. As for Rattazzi, he was willing to toy with the idea of further Garibaldian exploits, but unscrupulous in throwing over their leader when it became diplomatically inconvenient to be exposed as his backer. So to Garibaldi's intense indignation the nucleus of the volunteer army that was to have marched on Venice was arrested at Sarnico, and the patriotic anti-Austrian fever he had roused in the north was allowed to cool again. Undaunted he went to Sicily and was again urged forward to action by the yet greater enthusiasm, hysteria even, that his name still evoked in the south. The cry grew, "Rome or death!" and volunteers began to come forward in thousands. Again he persuaded himself, not entirely without justification, that the King and Government supported him. (Victor Emmanuel did admit privately that Garibaldi was acting on royal orders "to a certain extent"). The nettle was Rome; would the Kingdom of Italy dare to grasp it? How would Napoleon III, the man in possession—half-reluctant possession—react? Garibaldi gambled on favourable answers to these questions; they were not forthcoming.

The Italian Government and army took fright. They were already in trouble in the south, where smouldering discontent with the new north-dominated Kingdom of Italy had broken into revolt and banditry widespread enough to occupy the attention of 90,000 troops. If this lawlessness were now to be focused and intensified by the greatest guerrilla chieftain of his day the results might get out of hand. The army chiefs were spoiling for a showdown with this rogue elephant of a Garibaldi; the faithful were alarmed at his blatant anti-papalism (the Pope by now was "anti-Christ"; the priests would be "better engaged in draining the Pontine Marshes"). The French too were afraid of a Garibaldi-inspired revolution in Rome, and it had been part of Rattazzi's game to fan this fear in order to lever Napoleon out of the city. But his double game ended in August 1862, when Italian regulars confronted the ragged Garibaldians at Aspromonte, in Calabria. Not expecting to be fired on, and themselves with orders not to fire, the volunteers were nevertheless attacked, and the adventure collapsed. Menotti Garibaldi, the leader's eldest son, was wounded and Garibaldi himself was twice hit, once by a bullet in the ankle, where it remained long and painfully enough to cause him severe subsequent trouble. Twenty-three surgeons from various parts of Europe were to visit him before one of them extracted the bullet at last; English admirers subscribed large sums for expert advice; and Lady Palmerston, the Prime Minister's wife, sent him an invalid bed—so great was the concern.

Twice more in the 1860's Garibaldi did battle for the cause of united Italy. When Italy fought as Bismarck's ally in the war with Austria—and fought very unsuccessfully both on sea and land, though the Prussian victory at Sadowa indirectly won Venice for Italy—he again commanded red-shirt volunteers, up in the Tyrol this time. In the following year (1867) there was another episode in many respects similar to the Aspromonte affair. Again Rattazzi and the King played their devious game, using the credulous Garibaldi to stimulate the outbreak of a 'spontaneous' revolution in Rome, which would give the Italian Government an excuse to intervene officially. Once more Garibaldi was allowed to go just so far, raising volunteers, proclaiming that Italy expected every man to do his duty —and then once again the more cautious and conservative elements within the government and army were shown to be the more power-ful. In Rome the much-heralded revolution proved a damp squib, the Romans showing a disappointing half-heartedness in their de-sire to join Italy; and the combined forces of the French and the Pope were too strong for Garibaldi's invading army. At Mentana it was rather ignominiously defeated; returning by train, Garibaldi was indignant to find himself arrested by the Italian police and cast into prison. He cried treachery. His gamble had failed—it was to be his last—and the government had "sold him to the French". Rome had to wait, not for Garibaldi, but for the Prussian victory over France in 1870, which denuded the city of its French troops and laid it open at last to Italian annexation.

In the intervals between these abortive campaigns and for the three years following the final fiasco of Mentana (when he was in effect exiled) Garibaldi lived on Caprera in the full limelight of seclusion. A simple man and a modest one despite the hysteria and hero-worship, he yet accepted his status as "one of the great world Powers". He developed strong views on all prominent questions of the day, political, social, religious, moral, and from time to time he would issue communiqués. Incapable of mentally discarding his red shirt and *poncho*, he actively pursued on sundry occasions the possibility of leading volunteers to fight for the Polish rebels, for the North in the American Civil War, and for the Danes in their struggle against Prussian militarism. Like Don Quixote, he was all courage, restlessness, idealism, humourlessness, and melancholy. Wherever there was tyranny he was ready to ride out to do battle against it. In 1870 he did in fact raise a force of international volunteers to fight for the Third French Republic—that "sister nation" which had now cast off its "execrable tyrant" Napoleon III —against the just as execrable Prussians; a characteristically im-petuous action (he was by then a rheumatic whitebeard of sixty-three), but one in which he by no means disgraced himself.

A host of generous causes enlisted the support of this radical 'man of the people': free and universal education; the reform of taxation in the interest of the poor; the abolition of slavery and of the death penalty; the emancipation of the working class (he de-scribed himself as a socialist, though the term's meaning was im-precise to him); what he called the "religion of humanity", which would come when the mischiefs of popery and priesthood had been swept away; the brotherhood of man and abolition of national frontiers—for this most passionate of Italian patriots was also strongly devoted to the theory of internationalism. He despised parliaments and all their works. Indeed, not a few have seen him in a sinister light as being the spiritual father of fascism. He did use the very word *fasces* with approval, and had been hailed as *duce* by his fervent followers. The nation, he considered, needed a dynamic national leader (for a time he had hoped it might be Victor Emmanuel); and he lived to express his disillusionment and contempt for " the miserable, poverty-stricken, humiliated Italy that we now see, governed by the dregs of the nation". All the same, Garibaldi's love of liberty was fervent and sincere, and it is a long downhill way from the spirit of Garibaldi to the spirit of Mussolini.

In 1864, after a year spent largely in a bath-chair waiting for his ankle-wound to mend, Garibaldi came to England for the fourth time, and enjoyed (or suffered) the kind of reception that probably only he, of all men living, could have commanded. True, Queen Victoria disapproved, for he stood for everything that she did not, and she expressed herself ashamed to head "a nation capable of such follies". And Palmerston's government were not sorry in the end to see him go, for he not only made broad comments of a radical nature which might be forgiven in a foreign revolutionary, but, far worse, was embarrassingly indiscreet on international affairs, Denmark in particular. But the public in general, from Tennyson in the Isle of Wight (who noted his "divine simplicity") to the Working Men's Garibaldi Demonstration Committee, from the young gentlemen of Eton College to the workmen at Barclay and Perkins' Brewery, from the Duke of Sutherland, who was his host, to the Duke's servants, who made a little on the side by selling his dirty washing-water in bottles—high and low the British public voted him the greatest of men. Protestants loved him, for (as Earl Granville explained to Queen Victoria) "he has no religion, but he hates the Pope". The ladies from the Duchess of Sutherland downwards fell in love with him: Tennyson's aristocratic neighbour in the Isle of Wight, for instance, Mrs Seely, who could not let out of her sight the "grey kerchief" that "you wore round your neck at Brook House and with which I covered your dear head when it was windy." The radicals and trade unionists delighted to hear him proclaim his pride in being of the working class, "my brothers all over the world", and he went out of his way to pay generous public tribute to the "guide and counsellor" of his youth, his exiled "friend and teacher" Mazzini. (Hearing the words Mazzini grasped his hand; "too much, too much," he protested.) He was fêted, toasted, photographed, painted, sculpted. Garibaldi biscuits were named after him and Garibaldi blouses created for the ladies. There had never before been anything like it.

The latter years of this colourful man were darkened by his political and military failures; by his sense that the heroic noontide of the *Risorgimento* had been dulled and corrupted by the northern politicians who now controlled Italy; and by his old enemy arthritis which now increasingly crippled him. Frustration and disillusionment made him—at least in his public rôle—crotchety and difficult. And it is not surprising to find the man who had inspired such awe and reverence coming to regard himself as in some sense above the law of ordinary mortals. (This was quite compatible with his being, in his private life, modest, gentle, and courteous.) He lacked the taste and self-criticism to see that baptizing children in a new Garibaldian 'religion' was no less blasphemous in a non-Christian than a Christian, and he was overprone to accept without revulsion or ridicule the often preposterous hero-worship that surrounded him.[6] He thought that either the King or Parliament should intervene specially on his behalf to annul his disastrous second marriage so that he could wed his Francesca, the peasant woman who lived with him and bore him three further children in his seventh decade. (At the very end of his life he was at last able to marry her and legitimize her children.) When earlier a child of theirs had died they insisted on burying the body on their own estate, and an official who had come to claim it for legal interment was shown off at gun-point.

Garibaldi's last years on Caprera saw him in patriarchal sim-

---

[6] During the sixties, in the superstitious south, there were even Garibaldian 'catechisms'. D. Mack Smith, in his *Garibaldi* (p. 175), quotes the following:

Q. How does Garibaldi reward those who love Italy?
A. With victory.
Q. What does one gain by victory?
A. The sight of Garibaldi himself and every kind of pleasure without pain.
Q. What are the three distinct persons in Garibaldi?
A. The father of his nation, the son of the people, and the spirit of liberty.
Q. How did he make himself a man?
A. He took on a body and soul like ourselves, in the blessed womb of a woman of the people.
Q. Why did he make himself a man?
A. To save Italy.

plicity, tending his starved acres despite his stiffened joints, pruning his trees, doing his own rough carpentry, patching his own clothes and sewing on his own buttons as an old sailor should, washing his latest children under the spartan pump, feeding the birds that came to his window-ledge, smoking cigars many and strong, writing a good deal, eating raw shrimps (as his daughter, born when he was sixty, remembered) with a newspaper serving for tablecloth, sweetening his coffee with honey to save the cost of sugar. He owned two shirts, one off and one on; if he found he had a third he gave it away.

When he died his orders that his red-shirted remains should, without contamination of clergy, be burned under the open sky in a fire made from myrtle and aloe-wood, and that his ashes should be buried under his best-loved juniper-tree, were brushed aside as pagan eccentricity. The great Garibaldi belonged to Italy, the Italy he had helped to create, and Italy was a Catholic country. It did not signify that he had called the priesthood "humanity's atrocious foe"; Church combined with State to bury him with the utmost honour and sanctity, and with all the pomp and ceremony that he had despised. But then, as he had said—and in this at least Mazzini and he were one—"it was a different Italy that I dreamed of".

Table of Events

1807.	Garibaldi born at Nice.
1815.	'Legitimate' monarchies restored throughout Italy.
1820–21 and	
1831.	Carbonarist revolts.
1831.	Mazzini forms 'Young Italy'.
1834.	Garibaldi involved in Mazzini's revolt in Piedmont. Condemned to death. Flight.
1835–48.	Guerrilla freedom-fighting in South America.
1846.	Accession of Pope Pius IX.
1848.	Garibaldi returns to Italy. Revolutions in Rome, Lombardy, Venetia, etc. Charles Albert defeated at Custozza.
1849.	Novara; abdication of Charles Albert. Victor Emmanuel II accedes. Roman Republic overthrown by French. Fighting retreat and escape of Garibaldi; death of Anita.
1852.	Cavour Prime Minister of Piedmont.
1858.	Orsini's attempt on life of Napoleon III.
1859.	Plombières meeting; Magenta, Solferino. Lombardy freed. Peace of Villafranca.
1860.	Garibaldi and the 'Thousand'. Sicily and Naples freed. Piedmont invades Central Italy. Garibaldi retires to Caprera.

Napoleon Bonaparte
Engraving by J. Fiesinger after
Guérin (1799)

Napoleon aboard the *Bellerophon*
Sketch by Sir Henry Bunbury

224

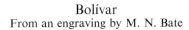

Bolívar
From an engraving by M. N. Bate

Metternich
By Anton Graff. Boze Collection

Andrew Jackson

Abraham Lincoln

Palmerston
Engraved by D. J. Pound from a
photograph by Mayall

Thiers, 1870

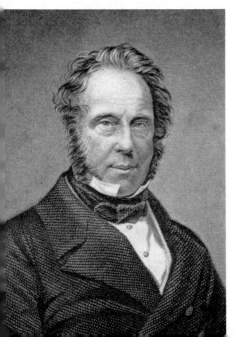

GARIBALDI [225]

1861. Victor Emmanuel King of Italy. Death of Cavour.
1862, 1867. Further attempts by Garibaldi to take Rome.
1866. Prussian victory over Austria gives Italy Venetia.
1870. German victory over France gives Italy Rome.
1882. Garibaldi dies in Caprera.

7
PALMERSTON
(1784–1865)
And the Supremacy of Britain

"For Europe I shall be desirous now and then to read England."
The words are those of the master, Canning, British Foreign Minister
in the 1820's; but the sentiment wholly expresses the attitude of
the pupil, Palmerston, who once proclaimed in a Commons speech
that "the sun never sets upon the interests of this country". In many
respects he was fortunate. Ruling the waves, Palmerston's Britannia
could impose her Pax Britannica upon all the world's oceans and
on many of their shores. Where such a government as the Chinese
attempted to defy her trading interests, she could brusquely force
entry; but more frequently the mere threat sufficed. Diplomats were
all very well, said Palmerston, but there were "no better peace-
keepers than three-deckers". In Continental Europe Britain's power
was less, but there was no major problem there in which she did not
claim an influential voice. By 1815 France had at last been forced
to yield primacy to her island neighbour; by the time Palmerston
died in 1865 Bismarck's Prussia was beginning to dominate Central
Europe and would soon be challenging British naval and industrial
supremacy. But in the intervening half-century Britain's world
dominance in manufactures, in commerce, and in maritime power
was beyond dispute. During this period she fought only one war of
any magnitude—the Crimean, of 1854–56; but in every diplomatic
tussle British diplomacy, and Palmerston's in particular, enjoyed
the reassuring consciousness of power. As he cheerfully wrote in
1840, "If France begins a war she will to a certainty lose her ships,
colonies, and commerce before she sees the end of it." Since most
sober opinion in France reluctantly shared the same view, peace was
preserved even though good temper was not. A German rhyme of
the mid-century ran:

> *Hat der Teufel einen Sohn*
> *So ist er sicher Palmerston;*

and not a few Europeans came to see the British Foreign Secretary as *ce terrible Palmerston.*

Not, however, European liberals. Palmerston's Britain not only enjoyed the consciousness of strength. Equally she was aware that the British were the freest people on earth. British parliamentary and legal institutions were, it seemed to them, incontestably the best in the world. To Palmerston, therefore, and to most of his fellow-countrymen it seemed proper and reasonable that their régime of freedom should serve as a model for all other Europeans:

> Our duty—our vocation—is not to enslave but to set free; and I may say without vainglorious boast, or without great offence to anyone, that we stand at the head of moral, social, and political civilization. Our task is to lead the way and direct the march of other nations.

Those governments that stood in the way of this march might indeed have to be tolerated as a necessary evil (the Russian, for example), or (like the Austrian) even supported as a necessary weight in the balance of power; but there was always a primary case to be presumed in favour of those movements rebelling against them in the name of constitutional government. "We shall drink to the cause of liberalism all over the world", he wrote in 1830 on the fall of the French Bourbons. And if tyrannical governments could not always be defeated or outmanœuvred, at least nobody would ever stop Palmerston from publicly criticizing them. One of the traits that most endeared him to his fellow-Englishmen was his readiness to dispense with diplomatic niceties and pitch into foreign tyrants in the plainest terms. It alarmed his colleagues; it exasperated Queen Victoria; it infuriated the objects of his criticism; but it delighted the English man in the street—"the man on the Clapham omnibus"—and helped the aristocratic Palmerston to transcend class differences and be widely regarded as the "minister for England"—"the most English minister that England ever had", as the *Daily Telegraph* said at his death.

Sometimes his patriotic drum-banging was crude, but he did not lack principles. His love of liberty was genuine, and one of his chief ambitions was to see the work of abolishing the slave trade completed by co-operation between nations. He was, indeed, notoriously high-handed in his dealings with foreign states, but with none more so than the Spaniards, Brazilians, and Portuguese, who lagged behind in this humanitarian work. In 1859 as Prime

Minister he was championing expensive coastal defences against the opposition of the economy-minded Gladstone, his Chancellor of the Exchequer. Only two public causes, he told Gladstone, were any longer of importance to him—the country's defences and the extinction of the Negro slave trade.

Henry Temple (Viscount Palmerston from his father's death in 1802) had been born under a fortunate star. His family was rich, though not in the first flight of the nobility; their various properties might in sum be considered adequate: an extensive country estate at Broadlands in Hampshire, where Palmerston was born in 1784; a suburban retreat in Surrey; a town house in Hanover Square; and 10,000 Irish acres in Sligo County. The youthful Palmerston was blessed with robust health, a handsome appearance, a lively but not too precocious intelligence, and an uncomplicated disposition. His childhood was spent on the parental estates and in Italy, his youth at Harrow School, Edinburgh University, and St John's College Cambridge, where he wore the nobleman's tassel and gold-laced gown and dined as of right among the dons at high table. As an Irish peer Palmerston had no seat in the House of Lords, but one in the Commons was procured without difficulty for a young man so amiable and promising—the rotten borough of Newport, in the Isle of Wight; and the new member was soon making his maiden speech in support of Canning's timely if high-handed seizure of the Danish Fleet at Copenhagen (1807). He could hardly have entered on a more fitting cue.

Not for such a one was there long to wait, in this age when the combination of 'connection' and ability was a sufficient entitlement to office. He achieved a junior appointment immediately and *refused* the Chancellorship of the Exchequer at twenty-five, preferring to accept instead in 1809 the post of Secretary of War, a purely administrative and financial office. Even so he could have a seat in the Cabinet, but turned it down, writing disarmingly: "Considering how young I am in office, people would perhaps only wonder how I got there." For the remaining six years of the Napoleonic Wars, and for thirteen more after their close, he laboured at his often humdrum War Office business, learning how to run a department efficiently, but never showing promise of eminence.

There was much to occupy him apart from politics: the shooting in his Broadlands coverts; his horses and the delights of country race-meetings; the London theatres and salons (that, for instance, of Princess Lieven, who was enchanted with him); Almack's Club, where he danced indefatigably and conquered many hearts, among them that of Lady Cowper. Some at least of her children were almost certainly Palmerston's, and after his own fashion he proved constant to her, being destined eventually to marry her in 1839 after Lord Cowper's death, when bride and groom were both past fifty. That was long after his War Office days. In those more youthful times he was still earning his nickname of "Cupid"; and he was always to carry with him, far into the more earnest era of the Victorians, a certain airy gaiety, a whiff of the Regency, one of whose 'bucks' he had once been. Queen Victoria always remained as unamused at the accounts that reached her of her minister's persisting amours as she was indignant at the "irresponsibility" of his political actions. And what was one to say in the eighteen-sixties of a Prime Minister who combined a notably happy marriage with the ambiguous distinction of being cited at the age of seventy-seven as co-respondent in a divorce case?[1]

Nominally a Tory till he was past forty, he had many of his friends among the "grand Whiggery". He shared their patrician manners and comfortably pagan morals, their easy-going tolerance and liberal broad-mindedness, their confident assumption that the nation—and, indeed, much of the world beyond—was theirs to command, and that presumptuous foreigners and domestic democrats were alike to be held firmly in their place.

It was not exactly for choice that Palmerston laboured so long at his humble War Office tasks. Twice during these years he accepted the Chancellorship of the Exchequer (which he had earlier refused), but each time the offer was withdrawn before he could take it up, the second time through the personal opposition of George IV. Three times he turned down the Governor-Generalship of India. He might generally appear to be merely "Lord Cupid", a man of the world already greying above the ears; but he never abandoned his intention of becoming a politician to be reckoned with. Still at the War Office, he achieved Cabinet rank at last under Canning in 1827.

Foreign affairs absorbed him more and more; he became a Canningite, and when after their leader's death the Canningites

---

[1] Withdrawn when the husband found he would have difficulty in proving his marriage and when Palmerston successfully showed that the case was brought to extort £20,000.

broke with Wellington and the Tories, Palmerston was out of office for the first time in over twenty years. This suddenly made him much freer to criticize "the stupid old Tory party, who bawl out the praises of Pitt while they are opposing all the measures and principles which he held most important". One of these was Catholic Emancipation, a subject on which Palmerston, as an Irish landlord who had attempted to improve his estates, claimed to speak with some knowledge:

> If I wished to convince an impartial Englishman of the policy of abolishing these laws against Catholics I should bid him repair to the south of Ireland; to mix with the Catholic gentry; to converse with the Catholic peasantry; to witness the open and undisguised discontent of the former; to probe to the bottom the more concealed but not less deeply rankling passions of the latter; to see what a fierce and unsocial spirit bad laws engender....

This speech of 1829 created a bigger impression than anything he had done previously. A few weeks later he again spoke in the Commons with the same unwonted fluency and fire, now attacking Wellington's policy in Portugal and Greece, where Britain should have been supporting liberal causes but seemed instead to be going over to the reactionary enemy. The diarist Greville called this second speech "the event of the week". Palmerston had previously seemed a halting speaker—and, indeed, he was never to be an orator. His voice frequently trailed away. He hummed and hawed. A flourish of the handkerchief was liable to do service for a missing epithet. But these 1829 speeches put him back among the principal political contenders. When the Whigs came in at last under Grey in 1830 it was with the backing of the Canningite Tories. Their leader, William Lamb, Lord Melbourne, became the new Home Secretary, and his "illegitimate brother-in-law" Palmerston Foreign Secretary. Many said that Princess Lieven[2] had used her influence with Grey

---

[2] Princess Lieven, wife of the Russian ambassador, special agent of the Russian Foreign Ministry, society hostess, and close friend of Lady Cowper. Because of his well-known association with this fascinating intriguer, Palmerston was later accused of having been unduly influenced by her and of being himself in Russian pay. She finally broke with Palmerston when she failed to persuade him to annul the appointment of the anti-Russian Stratford Canning as ambassador in St Petersburg. She was (wrongly) convinced that Palmerston's enmity had brought about the Lievens' recall from the London embassy in 1833. But by 1840 she was back in London as mistress of the French ambassador, Guizot. Earlier the mistress of Metternich and then close confidante (at least) of Lord Grey, she can hardly have a rival for the variety and distinction of the international statesmen with whom she was intimate.

on Palmerston's behalf; certainly he was backed by powerful Whigs like Lords Lansdowne and Holland. Thus in November 1830 Lady Cowper, *née* Emily Lamb, found herself suddenly and surprisingly the sister of one important Cabinet minister and the mistress of another. The brother was soon to succeed Grey as Prime Minister; the lover (her second husband-to-be) was to dominate his country's foreign policies, either as Foreign Secretary or Prime Minister, for most of the next thirty-five years.

The year 1830 was a significant one in Europe's affairs; widely scattered revolutions severely jolted the post-Napoleonic settlement made at Vienna in 1814–15. This had survived intact until 1820; then during the twenties cracks had begun to appear, in Italy, in Spain, in Portugal, in Greece; but still the structure had in the main held. The alliance of the despotic Powers—Austria, Russia, Prussia —was still in operation, and the France of the restored Bourbon kings had been accepted back into their fraternity. Revolution, though always threatening, had been contained. But in 1830 the whole Vienna settlement was challenged. The Bourbon king was expelled from France; there were revolutions in various parts of Germany and Italy, soon followed by others in Belgium and Poland. Palmerston thus came to office at the end of a year which had seen the whole edifice of the despotic Powers, the "Metternich system", rocked and shaken. Earlier Palmerston's admired predecessor, Canning, had driven his wedge into several sizable cracks in the structure. He had declined to attend the anti-revolutionary European congresses; he had supported a liberal revolution in Portugal, paid at least lip-service to the liberals in Spain and to the Greeks fighting the Turks for independence; and he had recognized the rebel governments in South America. It may indeed be doubted whether Canning was quite such a liberal as Metternich thought him or he himself liked to be thought; but certainly Palmerston regarded him as mentor and pattern. Like the Canning he partly invented, Palmerston too would be happy to flout the despots and succour the cause of liberty all over Europe.

A few months before his arrival in office the Bourbon Charles X had fallen in the Paris Revolution of July 1830; the next month a revolution in Brussels started a further chain of events which gave Palmerston his first test of statesmanship and provided him with his first great success.

In the intention of creating a strong northern barrier to France the

Powers at Vienna had merged Belgium with Holland in a United Kingdom of the Netherlands. It had not worked. Belgians considered that they were the victims of economic, legal, and political discrimination. They resented the official status of the Dutch language. As Catholics they were hostile to the Dutch Calvinist Church. As Belgians they lacked all loyalty to the House of Orange. In particular the French-speaking Walloons were susceptible to the strong French campaign in favour of the return of Flanders to France. When the revolt of August 1830 succeeded in pushing the Dutch forces out of Belgium there was jubilation in France, but alarm among the despotic Powers at this new bogy of revolution, and strong possibility of another European war.

Palmerston wanted an independent and neutral Belgium under a constitutional monarch, and was prepared to force the Dutch king to accept such a settlement. France must be prevented from occupying Belgian Flanders, nor must a French prince be allowed to accept the new throne. It was not likely, he considered, that there would be a European war over Belgium unless the hotheads in France had their way, but the situation must be squarely faced. "It is no harm", he remarked, "that the French should think we are a little upon the alert with respect to our Navy." When the Belgians proposed to invite the Duke of Nemours to be their king—a son of the French King Louis-Philippe—Palmerston bluntly threatened war and meant it. Similarly he was ready for war if France attempted to take any Belgian territory. But the *emphasis* of his policy was all the other way, on co-operation with the moderate elements in France to knock sense into the stubborn head of the Dutch king. And in this he found a willing response among leading Frenchmen: Talleyrand, now French Ambassador in London, "Old Tally", as Palmerston called him, still as shrewd and prudent as ever; the chief minister in Paris, Casimir Périer; Louis-Philippe himself. To the mortification of the French patriotic party the Duke of Nemours was restrained from accepting the throne; the French government settled instead for a more 'international' candidate, Leopold of Saxe-Coburg, who was widower of George IV's daughter Charlotte, uncle of the future Queen Victoria, and son-in-law of Louis-Philippe.

Things looked menacing when 50,000 French troops invaded Belgium to throw out the Dutch, who had broken the armistice. "*One thing is certain*," said Palmerston at this point: "*the French must go out of Belgium, or we have general war, and war in a given number of days."* The French were reluctant to withdraw, but at length withdraw they did; and when, after all was settled, the Dutch king still proved obstinate and failed to yield up Antwerp it was actually with Palmerston's approval that a French army again invaded Belgium and expelled the Dutch. A British fleet co-operated by putting an embargo on Dutch shipping and blockading the Scheldt. Eventually the five Powers, Austria, Prussia, Russia, France, and Britain, gave their blessing to the new state and guaranteed its neutrality. Both war and partition, one or the other of which had always seemed likely, had been avoided. "It is an immense thing done", wrote Palmerston with justifiable self-congratulation. *"Parmi tous,"* said Talleyrand, *"c'est Palmerston qui est le véritable homme d'état."*

If Belgium provided a triumph Spain, Portugal, and Greece all disappointed. Ever since 1820 these countries had been engaged in struggles which were characteristic of the age—in Greece a war of national liberation from the Turks, in Spain and Portugal civil wars which typified the ideological rivalries of the time; struggles of liberals and constitutionalists on the one side (followers in Portugal of Donna Maria and of Queen Maria Cristina in Spain) against, on the other, Catholic absolutists (supporters of Dom Miguel in Portugal and Don Carlos in Spain). In all three countries the domestic strife, or in Greece patriotic war, was infinitely complicated by international ramifications as the great Powers of Europe—Britain, Austria, France, Russia—pursued their private interests in these quarrels.

Here were causes which Palmerston could throw himself into with enthusiasm. In 1832 he declared in the House of Commons that constitutional states were Britain's "natural allies". He left the Holy Alliance Powers and "that consequential political coxcomb" Metternich under no possibility of illusion: by the same token they must be Britain's natural enemies. Frequently, indeed, the tone of Palmerston's communications with Metternich overstepped in their cool insolence the bounds of normal diplomatic courtesy. When Metternich proclaimed that every upsurge of liberalism anywhere in Europe endangered peace and order Palmerston argued that on the contrary it was reactionary despotism itself that provided the danger by stifling the people's natural desire for liberty. As he wrote to the British ambassador in Vienna:

Not that we want all other countries to adopt our Constitution of King, Lords and Commons, or fancy that because such institutions are good here, they must necessarily answer *at once* everywhere else, and least of all do we want, as the Absolutists *affect* to think we do, to see *revolutions* spread everywhere. But we do think that the maintenance of good order, no less than the happiness of mankind, is promoted by redressing admitted grievances and remedying acknowledged evils, and we think that the policy which consists in prescribing the bayonet as the sole cure for political disorders to be founded in ignorance of human nature, and to be pregnant with the most disastrous consequences. But this is Metternich's creed.

All seemed to be going well in both Spain and Portugal by 1834. "To defeat the Holy Alliance in the arena they themselves have chosen would be no common victory," said Palmerston; the support he had given the constitutionalists had been much more overt than Canning's—every means short of official war. When the Holy Alliance renewed their agreements at Münchengrätz in 1833 Palmerston pushed energetically on: "The great object of our policy ought to be now to form a Western confederacy of free states as a counterpoise to the Eastern league of the arbitrary governments." By 1834 he had enlisted France into this "confederacy" of Spain, Portugal, and Britain to form a short-lived Quadruple Alliance. "I reckon this to be a great stroke," wrote Palmerston; "a capital hit and all my own doing." That same year (1834) saw the defeat and exile of Dom Miguel (the leader of the absolutist faction in Portugal), who retired to Rome. Don Carlos, the corresponding figure in Spain, had already been defeated and shipped off to England.

The triumph was brief. Don Carlos returned to renew the Spanish quarrel. Portugal lapsed again into civil strife. In Greece, too, where Palmerston had laboured to plant the seed of constitutional monarchy, he had no success. The soil of these countries apparently did not favour the growth of those British-style institutions of whose virtue and wisdom Palmerston was so cerain. The conservatives at home were constantly telling him so; and so, soon, was one of his severest critics, Queen Victoria: "these southern countries", as she comprehensively described them, were simply unfit for constitutional rule. Palmerston, unimpressed by such opinions, continued the fight, sending a British Legion and a half a million muskets to Spain, blockading the coasts held by the Carlists, promoting another liberal rising in Portugal when the absolutists again won control, stubbornly maintaining that the 'English Party' in Greece was certain of ultimate triumph. Unfortunately in the incompetent and obstinate Otto of Bavaria, his nominee for the Greek throne, he had backed a very poor horse, as he himself was forced to admit, and by 1837 he reluctantly conceded that Greece was "virtually handed over to Austria and Russia". As late as 1846 he was still sending British troops to Portugal to enforce constitutional government. He was nothing if not an optimist. Right, which he equated with the influence of Britain, would conquer; and when his opponents accused him of mischievous foreign meddling he always countered them with sanguine confidence and was quite unconvinced by the 'unfit nation' argument:

> For my part I believe that if any nation should be found not fit for constitutional government, the best way to fit such a nation would be to give it to them.

He by no means applied the full logic of such an argument to affairs at home. No radical would ever convince him, for instance, that the best way to fit the 'unfit' British working man for the vote was *to give it to him.* The support which he gave, as a member of Grey's Government, to the 1832 Reform Act was faithful but a little casual; like Grey himself and most of the aristocratic Whigs, he was deeply conservative over matters of social change. Important minor adjustments might with advantage be made in the political structure, such as abolishing rotten boroughs and giving the vote to ten-pound householders, a minority of the well-to-do. Similarly, humanitarian reforms ought to be supported—the Factory Acts, for instance, that Lord Shaftesbury (his wife's son-in-law) campaigned for. When in the eighteen-fifties Palmerston became for two years Home Secretary he proved quite a vigorous and enlightened administrator. But on the subject of the natural supremacy of the privileged classes he never entertained any doubts. A liberal he might be—abroad at any rate, where it behoved foreign nations to strive for *their* Glorious Revolutions (and in the process they might reasonably hope for help from Britain)—but a democrat he emphatically was not.

Neither did he believe (as, for instance, Napoleon III did) in the principle of nationalism. The cause of a united Italy or united Germany, the national struggles of the Hungarians or Poles or Czechs, meant little to him except in so far as he saw peoples fighting tyrants for their liberty. And even for liberty he was no knight errant. Every foreign cause was to be judged strictly by the criteria of British interests and the balance of power. It would not do, for instance, to assist too far the disruption of the Austrian Empire, or the floodgates might be down for Russia. And whether the Sultan of Turkey was a tyrant or not was irrelevant if weakening him meant strengthening the Tsar.

British interests; by Palmerston's time these spanned the globe. Though he was not an imperialist in the sense of a deliberate empire-builder, he took the expansion of British trade and the greatness of the Empire for granted as part of the natural order. When, for instance, the Chinese refused to open their ports to British trade and enter into relations with Britain (or any other European country) it seemed to Palmerston perfectly reasonable that they should be persuaded to do so by the presence of British gunboats. As it happened, Britain's demand that her East India merchants should be accorded greater freedom of trade coincided with an effort by the Imperial Chinese Government to end the importation of Indian opium, payment for which was causing a severe drain of silver currency. Two high-handed governments thus clashed head-on. That of China was fortified by the rightness of its cause and contempt for the "foreign barbarians". That of Britain had the more immediate advantages of modern firearms and the Royal Navy. It was not therefore surprising that the so-called First Opium War, an unequal contest, ended in 1841 with the British demands substantially conceded and Hongkong annexed. The humiliations and indignities heaped before the war on British traders and representatives and the righteous wrath that this roused in Britain succeeded in cloaking the essentially aggressive nature of the war.

It was the Tsar, and the threat which he was generally reckoned to pose to communications with and interests in India, that gave Palmerston his sharpest anxieties in the early thirties. (By contrast France at this time, once the Belgian question was settled, seemed quiet and amenable.) These were years when Russia was fast extending her authority, southward towards Georgia and Armenia, south-eastward towards Persia and Afghanistan, and eastward into Turkestan and Central Asia. The constant preoccupation of the British statesmen was the north-west frontier of India, the historic gateway of invasion. The Russians, having already penetrated Persia, had in 1837 prompted a Persian attack on the Afghan city of Herat. There seemed only one way to stop them—to replace the 'unreliable' ruler of Afghanistan by one upon whom the British could depend. "If the Russians try to make [the Afghans] Russian," said Palmerston, "we must make them British." In 1839, therefore, an Army of the Indus, 9500 strong, set out to take Kabul. However, their position there—they were attempting to set up a puppet ruler acceptable to Sikhs, but not, as it turned out, to Afghans— soon became untenable. On the terrible retreat all but three of the white troops were cut down by the tribesmen. Not for the last time in these remote bastions of empire (where the British Navy was unfortunately powerless) disaster was eventually succeeded by an expedition of revenge and repair. But little satisfaction could come to the British Government from this attempt to meet the Russians "as far off from our Indian possessions as may be convenient or advantageous to us".

Not only the north-west frontier but also the sea-and-land routes to India provided a constant anxiety. Apart from the all-sea journey *via* the Cape, there were three traditional ways to India, in these days before the Suez Canal: that through the Suez isthmus and the Red Sea; the ancient road through Damascus and the Persian Gulf; and the route *via* Constantinople and the Bosphorus. All these demanded a stable Near East; but the Sultan of Turkey appeared at this time to be a declining force. In the twenties he had lost Greece, and in the thirties he was being challenged by his ambitious vassal, the "Napoleon of the Near East", Mohammed Ali, Pasha of Egypt. At first Palmerston hesitated; it seemed questionable which of the two, the Sultan and the Pasha, offered a better prospect of an undisturbed and non-Russian Near East. Any doubts, however, were dispelled by the indications that in Mohammed Ali's service there was a large and growing body of Frenchmen; ever since Bonaparte Egypt had offered to the French a dream and an opportunity. Very soon Palmerston was a confirmed supporter of the Sultan Mahmoud: "The mistress of India", he declared, "cannot permit France to be mistress directly or indirectly of the route to the Indian dominions." It was not that Britain herself coveted Egyptian territory; Palmerston's opinions on this were put with his usual force in a letter written some years later:

> We do not want Egypt any more than any rational man with an estate in the north of England and a residence in the south, would have wished to possess the inns on the north road. All he

could want would have been that the inns should be well kept, always accessible, and furnishing him, when he came, with mutton chops and post horses.

The Sultan was Palmerston's innkeeper and postmaster in chief.

In 1831 Mohammed Ali, failing to gain his reward from the Sultan for help rendered in the Greek War of Independence, had sent his son Ibrahim to invade Syria. After two conclusive victories the road to Constantinople seemed to lie open. Intervention by Britain would have been Palmerston's reply to this situation, but his more cautious Cabinet colleagues, conscious that the Navy was already involved in the Portuguese and Belgian conflicts, would not agree to undertake further unknown risks. So the Sultan Mahmoud, "a drowning man clutching at a serpent", turned instead to Tsar Nicholas for help—and received it, by the Treaty of Unkiar Skelessi in 1833. It seemed to Palmerston that his colleagues had let down both him and their country; Britain's imperial position must inevitably be weaker now that the Russians had advanced to the Bosphorus and the Sultan had promised "to consult with the Russian government on all affairs of his Empire". Surprisingly, however, the Tsar seemed not after all to desire the destruction of Turkey. He apparently preferred a weak Sultan dependent on Russia. Thus during the late thirties Anglo-Russian relations, though always prickly, temporarily improved a little. When in 1839 Mahmoud, itching to settle scores with Mohammed Ali, attacked Syria and was once more defeated, it was French ambitions rather than Russian which perturbed Palmerston. Mohammed Ali was now fully in league with the French. His victory was received with excited enthusiasm by the French Press. Louis-Philippe likened him to Alexander the Great; and the French government, led on by public opinion, found it quite impossible to fall in with Palmerston's proposal that a settlement should be *forced* on Mohammed Ali by the Powers.

Regardless of France, Palmerston moved quickly to sign a convention with Austria, Russia, and Prussia to bring the overweening Pasha to book. Again, some members of the British Cabinet—Lords Clarendon and Holland in particular—sought to undo his policy, sending their own dissentient memorandum to the Queen and openly hobnobbing with the French ambassador Guizot. But this time Palmerston managed to rush his somewhat anxious colleagues along with him, threatening resignation to gain his way.

"For God's sake, gentlemen," protested the harassed Prime Minister Melbourne, "let there be no resignations."

Palmerston was convinced the French would not fight for Mohammed Ali. How could they? If they took on Britain they would lose their fleet and much more besides. And could they "help Mohammed by marching on the Rhine?" he asked. (Prussia was a signatory of the Convention, and feeling there was high against France.) "*And would they not be driven back as fast as they went?*" "My opinion", he said, "is not that we shall have war with France, but that we ought to make our minds up to have it any time. . . . Let the French say what they will, they *cannot* go to war with the Four Powers." As for Mohammed Ali himself, he must be "made to disgorge". If he resisted, then he would "just be chucked in the Nile".

He was in his element now. The Navy was sent to cut the sea communication between Syria and Egypt. Acre was taken. Soon Ibrahim's army had abandoned Syria, and his father proceeded to surrender his fleet and unconditionally submit. (It was in fact the *Turkish* fleet, which had earlier deserted to him.) The man of the hour was Palmerston; and even Queen Victoria, who had been critical of his harshness with the French, conceded the point. The integrity of the Turkish Empire had been upheld. In France the Prime Minister Thiers had fallen, and there was bitter resentment generally. Thiers himself described Palmerston as the leading statesman of his age. Greville, the diarist, a hostile critic, admitted that Pitt the elder could not have done better. Even Princess Lieven, "woman scorned" though she was, conceded that the success and glory were "Palmerston's alone". The man in the street, who knew nothing of the Ottoman Empire or the routes to India but always took a simple patriotic pleasure in seeing the 'froggies' beaten, thought 'Pam' a fine fellow. Imperturbable as usual during the crisis, he took his daily ride in Hyde Park and his dip in the Thames, lost no sleep and missed no meals—unlike his brother-in-law the Prime Minister, who professed he could "neither eat, nor drink, nor sleep". Lady Palmerston expressed her feelings as well as her husband's: "It is a great pleasure to see all our enemies floundering in the Mud."

It was the Whig government itself that was in the mud a few months later; Peel and the Conservatives came to office in 1841 and remained there till the Corn Law crisis of 1846. For Palmerston these were years both of relaxation and of opportunity. He was free to spend time on his estates, shooting and riding and hunting down in Hampshire and on the Cowper lands in Hertfordshire; racing his horses, supervising the replanting of his woodlands and flower-gardens. He could also revisit Sligo to see how his improvements were faring and take brief benevolent notice of his 900 Irish tenants. He could travel abroad, which a Foreign Secretary in those days had no time for. But these pleasures were not enough for a man as voracious for power as Palmerston. "I don't at all conceal that I think it is a great bore to go out [of office]", he said in 1841. "I like power and I think power very pleasant." (There had been sighs of relief, however, among his subordinates at the Foreign Office; never before had a minister worked his juniors so hard.)

In opposition he was all belligerence. Aberdeen, the new Foreign Secretary, cautious, conciliatory, and colourless, he regarded as an old woman. From the Opposition benches Palmerston could still bang the drum for England and for liberal causes abroad—even louder now that he did not have the responsibilities of office.[3] It was in these years too that he established that close connection with the Press which he was to make such good use of in the future. He was in any case by force of personality a popular figure and the patriotic emotions that he appealed to were of a kind that easily commanded public approval; but there was another reason why some newspaper articles were so loud in his support. Some he actually wrote himself, and many more were directly inspired by him. His prose style was as vigorous as the man himself and proclaims itself from many an anonymous leading article.

These five years in opposition did a great deal for him. When Melbourne resigned in 1841 it was generally assumed that Lord John Russell would succeed him as Whig leader, and so he did. But he had no appetite for long years in opposition, and he frequently absented himself from Westminster. It was often Palmerston who became the effective leader of the Opposition. He carefully cultivated the powerful Whig 'managers'—Ellice, for example. That his attitudes and activities were not acceptable to all the old Whigs is seen in 1845. At the close of that year Peel first resigned

[3] He did not, however, oppose indiscriminately. When Peel raised a storm by giving a grant to Maynooth College in Ireland, for the training of Catholic priests, Palmerston supported him. "We must not forget," he said, "as some men in their zeal seem to do, that Roman Catholics are Christians."

and Russell began making his cabinet. Grey (son of the Reform Act Grey) refused to join a government that included Palmerston. It was not only that his views seemed dangerously belligerent; he was, further, only a Whig by marriage and convenience, and could easily prove a cuckoo in the Whig nest. In 1845 Grey prevailed, Palmerston was blackballed, and Peel returned to repeal the Corn Laws. By 1846, after the fall of Peel, there was no question about it: Palmerston was *in*, Foreign Secretary in Russell's ministry and the most powerful personality in the Government.

Among those who were sorry to see him there were the Queen and Prince Albert. The Conservative Foreign Minister, Aberdeen, had been held in their highest esteem. He had conducted relations with France on the basis of his personal friendship with Guizot, chief French minister from 1840. Aberdeen had peacefully settled the troublesome North American border quarrel upon the 49th parallel—according to Palmerston "a disgraceful surrender to the American bully". "Our dear Aberdeen" and "our valuable Peel" had been markedly more pacific and accommodating, and far less critical of the crowned heads of Europe—so many of whom were Victoria's relatives—than the vocal and intemperate Palmerston. Now, therefore, when he was back in office he had strongly disapproving critics at the Palace, and in the five years before his dismissal in 1851 relations between Court and Foreign Secretary grew steadily more strained. Albert and Victoria frowned upon many of Palmerston's policies, upon his manner of pursuing them, upon his propensity for acting independently without the prior approval of the Crown, and finally upon the man himself. Lord Palmerston was "to take care that this does not happen again. . . . The Queen must remark upon the sort of proceeding of which this is not the first instance and plainly tell Lord Palmerston that it must not happen again."

On his return to office he ran into immediate trouble again with France. In 1846 he had visited Paris with his wife, and tried hard to charm away the impression that he was inveterately hostile. But to Louis-Philippe he always remained "*l'ennemi de ma maison*", and the desire to pay off old scores was strong. When a chance arose in 1847 secretly to arrange royal marriages in Spain that would favour the chances of a future French succession, Louis-Philippe and Guizot seized it. Queen Isabella was to marry a Spanish prince reputed to be sexually impotent, while her sister was to marry a Frenchman, the Duke of Montpensier, whose heirs therefore might reasonably expect to come to the throne in good time. This crafty scheme, which ran counter to assurances previously given to Britain, created chuckles of satisfied amusement in France and offered a tit-for-tat for the Mohammed Ali fiasco. "Bad faith, unscrupulous ambition and base intrigues," said Palmerston. Queen Victoria was equally outraged, since Louis-Philippe had earlier given her his personal word, when she had visited France a few years back, that such a French move would not take place. Still, declared the Queen, knowing how Palmerston provoked the naughtiness of the French, "if our dear Aberdeen was still at his post the whole thing would not have happened". This may well have been true; but, since the Queen of Spain proceeded to have children and at least there was no evidence that these were not by her husband, the whole affair proved no more than a storm in a tea-cup.

The revolutionary storms of the following year (1848) were a good deal more than this. Metternich and the European Conservatives—and Victoria—were united in seeing Palmerston as the source of a good deal of trouble. "We see the English Cabinet", said Metternich, "everywhere allied to the parties which desire revolution." This was only a half-truth, and did Palmerston a good deal less than justice. He did think that Austria should in the long run abandon North Italy, where he would have liked to see a neutral union of liberal states dominated neither by France nor Austria; but he never at this time contemplated a united Italy. He certainly did not wish to see the downfall of the Austrian Empire, which, he said, if it had not existed, would have had to be invented. It was Europe's best guarantee against the dominance of Russia in the East, and France in the south and west of Europe; "the maintenance of the Austrian Empire is an object of general interest to all Europe". Thus, though he approved of the Hungarian revolutionaries winning a constitution in 1848, he gave no support whatever to the idea of an independent Hungarian republic, which, by weakening Austria, could only benefit Russia. And when the Hungarian revolution was defeated in 1849, Queen Victoria and Prince Albert were quite missing the point when (according to Greville) they saw "with great satisfaction the downfall of the Hungarian cause and chuckled not a little at the idea of its being a mortification to Palmerston".

Similarly on the subject of Italy, the Queen—that instinctive supporter of the powers-that-be—could hardly have misunderstood her Foreign Minister more completely or complained about him more shrilly. "She is ashamed of the policy we are pursuing. . . . The partiality of Lord Palmerston in this Italian question *surpasses all conception.*" The nub of his policy was in fact to prevent France intervening on her own against Austria and so obtaining the domination of North Italy. To stop France sweeping the board in Italy he was even prepared if necessary *to co-operate* with her in a war against Austria, not, of course, to destroy Austria but to rescue Italy. It did not come to that. The moderate elements in France again, as in the earlier days of the Belgian crisis, prevailed.

Palmerston had in 1848 refused to receive the representative of Kossuth's rebel Hungarian government, saying that the British Government had no knowledge of Hungary except as one of the component parts of the Austrian Empire. When, however, the victorious reactionaries in Vienna and Petersburg demanded from Turkey the extradition of the 5000 Hungarian and Polish refugees (including Kossuth) who had fled there on the collapse of the revolution in 1849, Palmerston had an opportunity to show the despotic Powers what he was prepared to do in defence of freedom. To him, as to liberals generally, it seemed monstrous that these men should be handed back to be victimized, or possibly executed, by governments whose vindictive instruments were already shooting ex-rebels *en masse.* When Russia threatened Turkey with war if she did not surrender the refugees the British ambassador at Constantinople (that same Stratford Canning who had been the occasion of the breach between Palmerston and Princess Lieven) called in units of the Fleet *on his own responsibility* to give stuffing to Turkish resistance. Palmerston gave support to him, though advising him to encourage nothing extravagant that might provoke the Tsar to war. Again the Queen disapproved: "What business have we to interfere with Polish or Hungarian refugees in Turkey?" she demanded. But Palmerston had judged both the diplomatic situation and the national temper better than she. The Tsar's ultimatum was allowed to lapse; Austria was obliged, in Palmerston's words, "to forgo her bowl of blood"; the refugees were not sent back to their torture or death; and Palmerston was once more the darling of the British public. When later the Austrian General Haynau, who had been one of those responsible for the executions and

floggings in Italy and Hungary, visited England and was uncere-
moniously chased over some Thames barges by a group of brewers'
draymen, Palmerston stuck to his guns, refused to apologize to
the Austrian Government, and privately (but not too privately)
added that Haynau was "a great moral criminal" whose visit was
an insult to Englishmen. The draymen ought not indeed to have
struck Haynau, "which, however, they did not do much". They
should instead have "tossed him in a blanket, rolled him in the
kennel [gutter], and then sent him home in a cab", first paying his
fare. It was certainly undiplomatic comment for a statesman; it disgusted the Queen and Albert; it delighted the Radicals, who had
been thundering against "General Hyena", flogger of high-born
ladies; and it vastly pleased the general public, who enjoyed having
a Foreign Minister who talked straight and told the world what
Englishmen thought. For Russell and the Cabinet the Haynau
business was enough, and when Kossuth came on from Turkey to
England and received a hero's welcome Russell, prompted by the
Queen, "positively requested" Palmerston not to receive him. "I
do not choose," replied Palmerston, "to be dictated to as to who I
may or may not receive in my own house"; but he bowed all the
same to Russell's wishes, contenting himself with receiving a
Radical deputation who complained of "the odious and detestable
assassins" of Russia and Austria.

The cause of political refugees might generally be regarded as a
good one. However, Palmerston chose to make his most celebrated
stand of all in a cause which was somewhat more questionable. A
Portuguese Jew, Don Pacifico, who being Gibraltar-born was a
British subject, claimed that an Athens mob had sacked his house
and destroyed valuable vouchers 'proving' a very suspect claim of
£27,000 against the Portuguese Government. Palmerston took him
at his word, and instructed the British fleet returning from its mission in Constantinople to extract apologies and compensation from
the Greek authorities. It was not the first occasion on which British
subjects had been maltreated in Greece; and Palmerston in general
felt very bitter about the Greek King and his government—a corrupt and incompetent crew, he judged, to whom a smart lesson
would do no harm. Entering the Piraeus, the British admiral
accordingly seized Greek merchant-ships and cargoes as security. In
the *brouahaha* which followed, Palmerston was privately attacked
by Victoria and Albert as the cause of England's being universally

detested and mistrusted, and publicly assailed in a four-day Commons debate, by men of many shades of opinion, for his high-handed interference in the affairs of foreign states. Before the debate Russell, while justifying Palmerston to the Queen and Albert, conveyed to him a plain hint that he might be asked to resign, or at least transferred to the Home Office. Palmerston's reply was an oratorical triumph which for the time being made him unassailable. It was not Pacifico but a principle that he claimed to defend. A closely reasoned, and, for him, unusually eloquent speech, defending every aspect of the Government's policy, culminated in the famous peroration:

> . . . as the Roman, in the days of old, held himself free from indignity when he could say *Civis Romanus sum*, so also a British subject, in whatever land he may be, shall feel confident that the watchful eye and strong arm of England will protect him against injustice and wrong.

No other speech by a British statesman in the whole century had a more resounding effect. In Parliament and the nation alike it swept the board. Peel the Conservative and Bright the pacifist Radical from their opposite ends both conceded its brilliance. The hostile Greville called it claptrap, but magnificent claptrap. Even Albert, whose feeling towards Palmerston was not far short of hatred, admitted that it was a masterpiece. Don Pacifico had brought about the biggest single *event* of Palmerston's career. For a while, on the crest of a wave, he could be sunk neither by the Queen nor by Russell.

He did not enjoy his conflicts with the Court. He presented his views and countered those of the Queen in long, respectful memoranda. "Viscount Palmerston presents his humble duty to your Majesty and has the honour to receive your Majesty's communication. He would humbly venture to suggest . . .", and then would follow pages of reasoned argument. His prose, his patience, and his command of the details of the European situation were all equal to the task; but the Queen, with Albert over her shoulder, remained ever critical and sometimes heavily censorious. She had, in fact, by 1850 become quite obsessed with her dislike of Palmerston. Everything, anything, was dug up against him—his Italian policy, his Greek policy; his insults to foreign monarchs and their representatives, his constant mischief-making and interference; his failure to give support to Prussia's claims to Schleswig-Holstein

(Victoria and Albert were strong partisans of German unification); even a disreputable incident—so Albert told Russell—of ten years earlier, when an amorous Palmerston was alleged to have given chase to one of Victoria's ladies-in-waiting and hammered importunately but unavailingly on her bedroom door.

The Queen had many times pressed Russell to dismiss Palmerston. An off-the-cuff speech he made to the radical deputation that he received when he was warned off from entertaining Kossuth nearly finished him, but he survived. Immediately afterwards, however, he made a move which delivered him into the hands of his watchful enemies at Windsor. On December 2nd, 1851, Louis-Napoleon, Prince-President of the French, had seized full powers in Paris. Palmerston, judging that the alternatives were Louis-Napoleon or anarchy, expressed his pleasure at the *coup d'état* without waiting for a measured Cabinet decision. The Court pounced. Russell saw his opportunity to jettison the minister who had become a constant embarrassment to him; and the fact that on the French issue Palmerston was out of step with his liberal and radical admirers robbed him of alternative support. Russell's letter of dismissal accused him bluntly of "violations of prudence and decorum too frequently repeated". The Queen could hardly express her relief at being rid of the man who had "embittered our our whole life". In Vienna, Prince Schwarzenberg gave a ball in celebration. In the Commons debates Russell scored heavily and Palmerston was completely discomfited. "There *was* a Palmerston", said Disraeli. "Mamma England's spoilt child" would be able to do no more mischief for a while at least.

Within a few weeks, however, "Mamma England" recovered from the shock of seeing Palmerston support the enemy of the French liberals. Then, in a Commons debate over a militia bill, Palmerston sided with the Tory Opposition and Russell's Whig Government was defeated. "I have had my tit-for-tat with John Russell," Palmerston wrote to his brother, "and I turned him out on Friday last." The Tories having no real majority, it was the Peelite, Victoria's "dear Aberdeen", who eventually formed an all-party ministry. Its chances of survival would have been nil opposed by Palmerston; at the same time, after all his breaking of European crockery over the past few years he was not to be thought of at the Foreign Ministry. He accordingly became Home Secretary and proved a good and conscientious one, busying himself with problems of prison administration, sewerage, conditions of work in factories, London's smoke nuisance, and problems of vice, disease, and drunkenness. (He disliked the practice of liquor being drunk on public-house premises, considering that the Englishman should buy his pints as his wife bought the groceries, and take them home to consume in the bosom of the family.) "I have never known a Home Secretary", wrote Shaftesbury, "equal to Palmerston for readiness to undertake every good work of kindness"—a significant testimonial for the old rip from the pious humanitarian.

He was approaching seventy now; gout and deafness troubled him sometimes, and there were some who began to write him off. About this time Disraeli amused himself at Palmerston's expense by describing him as "an old painted pantaloon with false teeth which would fall out if he did not hesitate and halt so in his speech". Yet he was upright and active; his appetite was good, his constitution resilient, his humour sprightly. To "the man on the Clapham omnibus" he was "old Pam"; but the 'old' signified affection rather than years. Somewhat sensitive, however, on this matter of age and liking to be thought an evergreen, he wore his side-whiskers dyed; but the contrivance was generally held to be unconvincing. As a septuagenarian he still managed to take his morning gallop in the Park, and then ride on to the House.

During 1853 Britain's perennial quarrel with the Tsar was re-opened. Nicholas had claimed the right to 'protect' Orthodox Christians within the Turkish Empire in much the same way as the French Empire maintained a claim to protect the Catholics there. This Russian move followed repeated overtures to the British over the previous decade suggesting a partition of the dominions of the Sultan, whom the Tsar had more than once referred to as the "sick man", or "sick bear", of Europe. In the carve-up Russia would have occupied the northern Ottoman lands, including Constantinople, and Britain Crete and Egypt. But all parties in Britain, and the liberals and radicals especially, feared Russians even when they brought gifts. It was generally agreed that the Turkish Empire must be sustained; and when Turkey sheltered Kossuth and his fellow-refugees against Tsar Nicholas, the Sultan rather ludicrously began to appear, to British eyes, not as an antiquated and inefficient Muslim despot, but as a knight in shining armour, a defender of liberal and even Christian principles. Led on by a Press which saw in Nicholas the personification of everything evil, public opinion rumbled mightily and righteously against the Tsar's malefactions and the British Government's seemingly too mild reactions to them. Foreign policy was, of course, no longer the official business of Palmerston, the Home Secretary, but of Clarendon, the Foreign Secretary, and Aberdeen, the Prime Minister. Aberdeen was too sensitive, perhaps too honourable, and certainly not incisive enough to make a success of such a situation. As a young man he had seen too much of war's unpleasantness (he was present on the field of Leipzig), and now he laboured long and conscientiously to avoid a repetition of it. But he was carried helplessly along by Russian moves and the counter-moves demanded alike by the Press, public, Parliament—and, in private, Palmerston. Similar anti-Russian pressures were at work in France.

When the Tsar's troops crossed the River Pruth and occupied what is now Rumania the Turks, encouraged by the British ambassador, Stratford Canning (now Lord Stratford), declared war. The British fleet was moved up, first to the Greek archipelago, then to the Dardanelles, then to Constantinople, finally to the Black Sea itself. Louis-Napoleon, now Napoleon III, who had so recently promised " *L'Empire, c'est la paix* ", also prepared for war.

In all this Palmerston seemed to be the man of destiny, like Pitt in 1756 or Churchill in 1940. When the Russians sank the Turkish fleet at Sinope in December 1853 almost under the nose of the 'protecting' British fleet British public opinion exploded almost as violently as if the Royal Navy itself had been attacked. And when, at just the same moment, Palmerston briefly resigned (actually over the question of parliamentary reform, which he opposed) it was generally assumed that he was dissociating himself from the Government's 'feebleness', and also that the Palace had mounted another intrigue against him. Prince Albert, wrongly taken to be the villain of the piece, was the object of virulent attacks in newspapers, broadsides, and pamphlets. Then, when war came, amid demonstrations of astonishing enthusiasm, and when it quickly led to frustrations and scandals, the newspaper cry for Palmerston to replace Aberdeen became vociferous. The *Morning Advertiser* and *Daily News* were strong for him; so too was *The Times*, previously hostile; so, less surprisingly, was the *Morning Post*, which was under his own immediate guidance. If the public was shocked at the revelation of the Crimean disasters Aberdeen himself was conscience-stricken. He felt that with better judgment he might have avoided war altogether, and told John Bright that "his grief was such that he felt as if every drop of blood would rest upon his head". Such self-accusation remained with him for the rest of his life.

When he was defeated in Parliament early in 1855 the Queen might wriggle to escape from Palmerston—offering first Derby and then Russell the Premiership—but Palmerston was, as he commented with natural satisfaction, "*l'inévitable*". Apologetically Victoria wrote to her Uncle Leopold, "I had *no* choice." For nine of the remaining ten years of his life he was her Prime Minister, and at least it can be said of their mutual relations that on the whole they slightly improved with the years. When the Crimean War was at last brought to a (moderately) successful conclusion she even allowed herself to bestow upon him the rare honour of the Garter.

He was an energetic war Premier, but hardly a great one. He failed to unclog the antiquated administrative machinery that so infuriated Florence Nightingale. Lord Panmure remained at the head of the War Office, that "choked conduit". Luckily for Palmerston's reputation, Sevastopol, so long and frustratingly beseiged, fell at last. This should not, however, mark the end of the war, he considered—rather the beginning. The allies would now proceed to the conquest of Georgia and the capture of Kronstadt (the island base near St Petersburg). But the French had had enough of the war, and Britain's plans got short shrift from her allies. Victor Emmanuel of Sardinia described Palmerston as "some sort of mad dog from whom all the others should flee". The Austrians[4] too, not without threats, urged peace, and Palmerston was obliged to abandon hopes of martial triumphs and to conclude the Treaty of Paris (1856). The ultra-patriotic party, vocal as usual, were less than ordinarily pleased with their hero.

Nobody emerged from the Crimean War with much gain or credit. It could be held that the Ottoman Empire's integrity had been upheld and Russian expansion countered; yet the erosion of Turkish authority continued steadily. The Danubian principalities, whose invasion had occasioned the war, emerged from it as the independent state of Rumania—thanks very largely to the support of Napoleon III, who believed in applying the general principle of

---

[4] They had occupied the Danubian principalities with the approval of the allied Powers, but had not so far taken part in the war.

nationalism in a sense that Palmerston never did. What Palmerston did believe in, and strongly, was the persuasive influence of the Royal Navy, and when the Russians appeared to be slow in surrendering Kars to the Turks in accordance with the provisions of the peace treaty the dispatch of four battleships to the Black Sea (which had under the treaty been declared forbidden water to Russian warships) produced the required effect.

In similar manner, when in 1856 a ship flying the Red Ensign was arrested in the Canton river by Chinese officials and its flag torn down, Palmerston strongly supported the action of the local British Superintendent of Commerce, who ordered the blockade and later the bombardment of Canton. That the *Arrow* had pirates on board; that its licence to be regarded as a British ship had expired; in brief that the British case was weak in international law and weaker still in equity—all these were of scant importance to Palmerston, who could only see that the Chinese Commissioner had incited the Cantonese "to unite in wiping out the English villains".

British high-handedness was criticized from inside the Cabinet by Lord Granville and attacked in the Commons and the country by Gladstone, Disraeli, Russell, Cobden, Bright, and many prominent men of all parties jealous of their country's reputation for honesty and justice. Gladstone, for instance, made the very reasonable complaint that Palmerston "systematically pandered to whatever is questionable or bad in the public mind". The Commons supported Cobden's motion of censure and defeated Palmerston; but the old man had swift and sweeping revenge, appealing to the decision of a general election, and setting the tone of the campaign before his own faithful constituents of Tiverton:

An insolent barbarian wielding authority at Canton has violated the British flag, broken the engagement of treaties, offered rewards for the heads of British subects in that part of China and planned their destruction by murder, assassination and poisons.

The election of 1857 was in effect a sort of national plebiscite. *Palmerston* was the issue—for "Pam" or against him. In the result, morality and moderation were nowhere; Palmerston won hands down. His opponents—Tories, Peelites, 'conscience' Whigs, pacifist Radicals: "a fortuitous concourse of atoms", he called them— were scattered like chaff before the wind. Significantly, all three of his leading opponents of the "Manchester School", Bright and

Milner Gibson in Manchester itself and Cobden at Huddersfield, lost their seats. Palmerston's personal triumph was complete.

It was some time before his policies in China ran their full course. Late in 1857, in collaboration with French, British forces took Canton and moved north to Tientsin. To save Peking China made large new concessions to the Western Powers. Then, when the Chinese seemed to be backsliding from these 1858 Treaties, Anglo-French troops renewed the war, captured Peking, forced the Chinese Emperor to flee, and (in retaliation for the violation of a flag of truce) burned to the ground his Summer Palace. The subsequent treaty of 1860 completed the humiliation of the Imperial Chinese Government and defined the basis of commercial relations between China and the West for a lifetime to come.

Between the two active phases of these Chinese operations had come the shock of the Indian Mutiny. To begin with Palmerston would not take it very seriously: it was a riot of a few sepoys—the Queen and the nation must not be over-anxious. The Palace did indeed criticize him for the lack of vigour and urgency, and blamed him of all people, when adequate troops *had* been dispatched to quell the Indian revolt, for running the domestic defences too low. Afraid that the French might agree with the Queen and "take advantage of that which was erroneously imagined to be our moment of weakness", he lowered the physical standards of entry to the militia, turned down Belgian and Prussian offers of assistance (in a characteristic sporting metaphor he said we must win in India "off our own bat"), and banged the drum as loudly as ever.

The same feverish patriotism that had determined the election issue of 1857 and accompanied the fears for the Indian Empire actually brought about Palmerston's temporary eclipse the following year. This ironical circumstance originated with the bomb attempt of Orsini to assassinate Napoleon III because of his failure to live up to his promises of assistance to Italy. French opinion was in one of its *perfide Albion* moods, complaining that Orsini had been harboured by the British, and demanding that such undesirable conspirators should be expelled; and Palmerston by general consent was actually proposing to go too far (in a Conspiracy Bill) to meet French wishes. His parliamentary speech in defence of the bill was at the same time feeble and violent (he lost his temper with the Manchester men and shook his fist at Milner Gibson), and for once Commons and country agreed that Palmerston was weak and

Palmerston was wrong. For the second time within the decade the country was briefly governed by a minority Tory ministry under Derby.

Palmerston had no relish for being out of power, and his setback was one of the principal factors bringing about a cohesive Liberal Opposition capable of forming an alternative government. A grand meeting of 280 politicians of varying and even opposite opinions, from the generally conservative-minded Palmerston at one end to the radical Bright and Cobden at the other, was held at the Willis rooms—whose *habitué* Palmerston had been as "Lord Cupid" fifty years before, when the place was still called Almack's. Russell was there, and the Peelites, including Gladstone, who was opposed to Palmerston's views on practically everything except hatred of foreign despotism and support for Italian independence. The coalition formed at the Willis Rooms meeting became not only the basis of support for the next administration, but in time the Liberal Party itself. When Victoria had to find a successor to Derby she was thus faced by a reconciled Palmerston and Russell. Hard as she struggled to have Granville as her Prime Minister and Clarendon as Foreign Secretary, it was in vain. Though she deplored "the bad effect Lord Palmerston's name would have in Europe" and found the prospect of Russell at the Foreign Office "most vexatious", she was obliged to accept "those two dreadful old men".

These terrible twins took office at a critical moment in the affairs of Western Europe. Jolted by Orsini's bomb and giving play at last to his pro-Italian sentiments, Napoleon III had gone to war in alliance with Sardinia-Piedmont, to expel Austria from Northern Italy. Queen Victoria, Prince Albert, and the outgoing Conservative profoundly mistrusted French ambitions, had no particular feeling for Italian liberty, and saw Austria as the injured party. On the other hand, Italy was the one subject on which *all* the Liberals saw eye to eye. Palmerston, Russell, Gladstone, Bright, Cobden—all of them, while looking warily at the French, wanted to see the Austrians go, and for that were prepared to throw the weight of Britain into the scales. "I am very Austrian north of the Alps," wrote Palmerston to Granville, "but very anti-Austrian south of the Alps. The Austrians have no business in Italy, and they are a public nuisance there."

A month after Palmerston had returned as Prime Minister in June 1859 Napoleon III suddenly abandoned the Italians, and made peace with the Austrians at Villafranca. While Victoria (which meant Albert too) was "relieved by the happy news", Palmerston feared it would perpetuate an Austrian stake in Italy. Although he continued to stress that he supported a strong Habsburg Empire, he argued that Austrian supremacy

> is not really advantageous to Austria herself; it exhausts her resources, adds nothing to her real strength . . . and makes her odious to all liberal and enlightened men throughout the world.

What he wanted to see was not indeed a fully united Italy—few seriously considered that possible—but an enlarged Sardinia-Piedmont embracing all North and Central Italy and strong enough to stand up to France. The Queen hardly had words enough to condemn her ministers' policies. As for the Prince Consort, his resentment overflowed:

> All Palmerston's old tricks of 1848 and the previous period are revived again. Having Lord John Russell at the Foreign Office, whose inefficiency in the office, love of Italy, and fear of Lord Palmerston makes him a ready tool and convenient ally, he tries to carry out a policy of revenge against Austria and to bind us to the Emperor Napoleon more than ever, regardless of all the interests of England or Europe, and if impeded by the Cabinet or the Queen he is violent and overbearing, and if this be of no avail, cheats and tricks. He has taken towards the Crown quite his old position of 1851 before he was dismissed. . . .

Actually it was the man who had then dismissed him, Russell— more strongly pro-Italian even than Palmerston—at whom the Court's sharpest rebukes were directed. He had sent Victoria a letter beneath whose generous liberal sentiments it was not difficult for her to hear the tone of reproach:

> The Liberation of the Italian people from a foreign yoke is in the eyes of Lord Palmerston and Lord John Russell an increase of freedom and happiness at which, as well-wishers of mankind, they cannot but rejoice.

The imputation that the Queen and Albert were *not* well-wishers of mankind caused a royal ton of bricks to descend upon Lord John Russell's head ("The Queen must demand that respect which is due from a minister to his sovereign"), and the royal susceptibilities were duly and dutifully soothed. On policy, however, Palmerston and Russell stood firm, even when the Palace uttered veiled threats of dismissal.

Surprisingly, it was the actions of Napoleon that restored some amity between the Prime Minister and the Queen. When France annexed Savoy and Nice as her price for helping Sardinia-Piedmont to gain Lombardy, and high indignation followed in Britain, at last Victoria, Palmerston, and the public could share a common emotion. Palmerston's earlier attitude of wary friendship towards Napoleon gave way to mistrust and hostility that continued for the rest of his Premiership.

> I have studied the French Emperor narrowly and have studied his character and conduct. . . . At the bottom of his heart there rankles a deep and inextinguishable desire to humble and punish England.

In short Napoleon stood for aggrandizement and war, and the British must be prepared to fight and defeat him as they fought and defeated his uncle. If Palmerston failed to carry all the Cabinet with him in this view he had, as usual, less difficulty in convincing the general public, and none at all in this matter with the Queen. The Volunteers were formed in 1859, and Tennyson, the poetic voice of Palmerstonian England, wrote *Form, Riflemen, Form* for them, with its hostile references to Napoleon III. Palmerston had no need to worry unduly about Gladstone's stubborn opposition in the Cabinet; after one of his Chancellor's many threats of resignation Palmerston reported to the Queen in his driest vein:

> Viscount Palmerston hopes to be able to overcome his objections, but if that should be impossible, however great the loss to the government by the retirement of Mr Gladstone, it would be better to lose Mr Gladstone than to run the risk of losing Portsmouth or Plymouth.

'Francophobia' remained strong, and round the southern coasts of England there stand to this day evidences of it in "Palmerston's follies", the fortifications erected to guard against supposed Napoleonic ambitions.

It was principally Russell who prevented the universal alarm from drifting into war. And when Garibaldi astonished the world and became Britain's greatest hero by liberating Sicily it was above all Russell's initiative that 'held the ring' for Garibaldi and prevented the united European Powers intervening against him. Russell's influence in the Cabinet at this juncture converted his colleagues, including his Prime Minister, to support full Italian unification. Palmerston had earlier considered it "wild and foolish" to think of uniting Northern Italy with the South; but when Garibaldi crossed from Sicily to the mainland to continue his sensational advance the British fleet was under orders to make no difficulties for him. Palmerston had rejected Napoleon III's suggestion of a combined Anglo-French move to stop him.

All these last Palmerstonian years, which marked the high summer of Victorian prosperity and self-confidence, were nevertheless overhung with the threat of wars. No sooner had the Government drawn back from a war with France than it was contemplating one with the Northern states of the U.S.A.; and when that fear was removed the danger of war with Prussia over Schleswig-Holstein grew at one moment very close.

In the American Civil War Palmerston, though he dispatched 3000 troops to Canada as a precaution, was at first determined to stay neutral. He recognized the Southern Confederates as belligerents and, despite their support for slavery, he was privately, like most of the British upper classes, biased somewhat in their favour. In any case, like Gladstone and Cobden, he thought the Southern rebellion was on such a scale that it must succeed; and he was not sorry to watch the misfortunes of the Yankees, who in his eyes represented a noxious combination of ill-gotten wealth and vulgar democracy, besides threatening British Canada and, as protectionists, British trade. The Anglo-American situation became explosive only when a Northern sloop stopped and boarded the British mail-steamer *Trent*, and forcibly removed from her two passengers who were Southern emissaries sailing to Europe.

The least that England demanded was that the North should give back the two men and apologize. In those days before the transatlantic telegraph the inevitable delays in communication kept public opinion in a state of bellicose indignation for weeks. Palmerston's own combination of complacent jauntiness and aristocratic contempt for Lincoln's Government shows in another of his letters to the Queen (December 1861):

> Nobody can form any reasonable guess as to the answer which the Federal Government will make to the British demands, because that Government is not guided by reasonable men. . . . Your Majesty's position is anyhow a good one. If the Federal Government comply with the demands it will be honourable for England and humiliating for the United States. If the Federal

Government refuse compliance, Great Britain is in a better state than at any former time to inflict a severe blow upon, and to read a lesson to the United States which will not soon be forgotten.

This heads-we-win-tails-they-lose attitude was not good enough for the painstaking and conscientious Albert. Ill as he was (it was thought to be nothing serious), he filled out Palmerston's "meagre" dispatch with a passage that permitted the Americans to escape from the situation without humiliation. Peace and sanity were preserved.

It was the Prince Consort's last act. The "cold" which the doctors then thought might be a gastric fever was recognized too late to be typhoid. Upon his death the Queen was prostrate with grief—and as the months and years went by it seemed that the extremity of her grieving would have no end. As Albert's character assumed in her anguished memory ever more angelic qualities, not the least of her Prime Minister's sins was to have crossed him so often.

As he approached his fourscore years Palmerston's own health, though intermittently as vigorous-seeming as ever, could hardly be what it had been. Granville reported seeing him at the close of 1861, "looking very well, but old, and wearing a green shade, which he afterwards concealed. He looked like a retired old croupier. . . ." More important than physical health, his intellectual grasp and political touch both began to desert him in these last years. His handling of affairs during 1863–64 was rather like the driving of a motorist who has taken too much alcohol: confident, but lacking in judgment and finesse. When the Poles rebelled in 1863 his attempts to bluff the Tsar into a withdrawal never looked like succeeding, and gunboat diplomacy could avail nothing in Eastern Europe unless he was really prepared for full-scale war against Russia. Even such a war, a second instalment of the Crimean, could have been undertaken only in collaboration with Napoleon III, who was at this time fully as much an object of public and Palmerstonian suspicion as the Tsar himself. Apart from sympathetic words, therefore, the Poles could hope for nothing.

Palmerston's tricks had been learned during the thirties and forties, and they were tricks made possible by naval power. Now in the sixties, he proceeded to use the same style of diplomacy in very different circumstances. What earlier had been seen as real threats backed by the ability to act had now declined into idle bluster.

When Bismarck in 1863 was pressing German claims to Schleswig and Holstein, Palmerston wrote him off as "that crazy minister in

Garibaldi
Engraved by W. Holl from
a photograph

Gladstone as Chancellor of
the Exchequer
Engraved by W. Holl from a
photograph by Mayall

256

Tsar Nicholas I

Tsar Alexander II

Bismarck, 1860

Gladstone, the aged Premier

Bismarck in old age
From a portrait by F. von Lenbach

Kaiser William II

Berlin". Prussia he considered "Austria's tool and Europe's scorn"; miscalculation could hardly go wider of the mark. "Little Denmark" to Palmerston seemed one more small country being threatened by bullying despotic Powers, and he rashly announced that if any attempt were made to overthrow Denmark's "independence, integrity, or rights" those making the attempt "would find in the result that it would not be Denmark alone with which they would have to contend". He could not see that for the Danes to rule German Holstein was as indefensible as it had been for the Austrians to rule Italian Venetia. In the earlier situation he had been in daily touch with the Italian colony in London and took care to be closely informed of the rapidly changing situation. By contrast his responses to the German–Danish crisis of 1863–64 were unrealistic and ill-informed.

Chief among his critics, as Bismarck well knew, was Victoria herself, not too distraught by this time to constitute herself leader of the Cabinet opposition and champion of the German cause. In this she was doing what *he* would have wished. The German national movement, which Palmerston failed to understand,[5] had always been near to Albert's heart. Now to her Prime Minister the Queen professed "alarm and astonishment" at the Government's pro-Danish policies. In reply he politely but pointedly suggested that it was she who was being pro-German. Victoria insisted on her criticisms being read aloud to the Cabinet (where Granville was her principal ally), and upon the language of the Queen's Speech being toned down. The long battle continued; about this time Victoria wrote to her Uncle Leopold (using their private derogatory German nickname for Palmerston): "Pilgerstein is gouty, and extremely impertinent in his communications of different kinds to me." Victoria was "well-nigh worn to nothing with vexation, distress, and worry"; but it was Pilgerstein who lost. A majority of the Cabinet voted in favour of caution and peace. For Palmerston impotence was a new and unpleasant experience.

Abroad, Bismarck; at home the Chancellor of the Exchequer,

---

[5] —or at least underestimated until rather late. A month before he died he wrote: ". . . with a view to the future it is desirable that Germany, in the aggregate, should be strong, in order to control those two aggressive powers, France and Russia . . . and a strong Prussia is essential to German strength." The predatory nature of French aggressiveness was well known; as for Russia, "she will in due time become a power almost as great as the old Roman Empire".

Gladstone. This "dangerous man" who inhabited a world Palmerston did not recognize had just made a Reform speech that called down a stiff rebuke from his chief:

> Your speech may win Lancashire for you . . . but I fear it will tend to lose England for you. It is to be regretted that you should, as you stated, have taken the opportunity of your receiving a Deputation of working men to exhort them to set on foot an Agitation for Parliamentary Reform—the Function of a Government is to calm rather than to excite Agitation.

Palmerston had throughout his Premiership stood solidly against any extension of the vote—indeed, against any programme of general reform. "What is to be done about legislation?" asked a visitor one day. His answer was in the authentic voice of the eighteenth century:

> "Oh," he gaily replied, rubbing his hands with an air of comfortable satisfaction, "there is really nothing to be done. We cannot go on adding to the Statute Book ad infinitum."

He who had been the arch-enemy of Metternich's "repose" in Europe was now the high-priest of "repose" at home. But like Metternich he too knew that his world could not last for ever. "When Gladstone has my place," he said, "there will be strange doings."

Despite gout, sleeplessness, diseased kidneys, and a head that now tended to slump chestwards, he had no intention, at eighty, of premature decease. In February 1865, at a public banquet

> . . . he ate two plates of turtle soup; he was then served very amply to cod and oyster; he then took a pâté; afterwards he was helped to two very greasy-looking entrées; he then despatched a plate of roast mutton. . . . There then appeared before him the largest, and to my mind hardest, slice of ham that ever figured on the table of a nobleman, yet it disappeared in time to answer the inquiry of a butler, "Snipe or pheasant, my lord?" Pudding, jelly, oranges and half a pear followed.

Ill and all but helpless later that year, he never considered resignation. One night he stole out from his deathbed to climb the railings at the back of the house, to prove to himself that there was life in the old dog yet. As for Christian ministrations, he was deaf to them, but enjoyed listening to a reading through of his Belgian Treaty. "Read the sixth article again," he said on the Tuesday; on the Wednesday, with an official dispatch-box by his side, he died.

He was the John Bull of his generation, as Churchill was of his. An essentially popular figure, whereas Churchill until 1940 was generally unpopular, the two men have characteristics strikingly in common: a powerful hatred of foreign despotism; the fighter's virtues of belligerence and courage, which brought them both to the Premiership in the midst of a war that was going badly; a political longevity unique in their generation; an aristocratic distaste for political and social democracy; a vivid and vocal patriotism and a corresponding dislike of pacifists and the over-virtuous; a common touch that could reach out across class differences; a darting sense of fun and mischief and a red-blooded relish for life. Even in their "blind spots" (a crudity of approach, for instance, to Asiatic peoples and problems) the two men present some similarities. Churchill was a more Olympian and versatile figure; on the other hand, Palmerston was nationally and internationally influential over a much longer span of years.

He never elevated the House of Commons or the nation. As one Member said, with his "Ha Ha style" he "educated us down to his own level." Bagehot complained that he left "no great distinct policy", no "noble teaching". "He had many valuable qualities, though many bad ones," wrote Victoria upon his death, trying hard to be fair. "We had, God knows! terrible trouble with him about foreign affairs. . . . I *never* liked him, or could ever the least respect him, nor could forget his conduct on certain occasions to my Angel. . . . still he is a loss!" Perhaps Trollope's epitaph was neatest and most just:

> His great merit as a governing man arose from his perfect sympathy with those whom he was called upon to govern; his demerit, such as it was, sprang for the same cause.

Table of Events

1848–49.   Revolutions in Europe; Palmerston's moral support infuriates foreign governments and British court.
1850.   Don Pacifico case; "Civis Romanus" speech.
1851.   Louis Napoleon's *coup d'état*; Russell dismisses Palmerston.
1853.   Home Secretary in Aberdeen's government.
1854–56.   Crimean War.
1855–58
and   } Prime Minister.
1859–65.
1856–60.   Second Chinese war extends treaty rights.
1860.   With Russell (Foreign Minister) supports Italian unification. Fortification of Channel coast.
1861.   *Trent* incident; death of Prince Albert.
1863.   Polish rebellion and German-Danish war (1864) bring rebuffs.
1865.   Death.

8

THIERS

(1797–1877)

Order and Revolution in France

All great revolutions are about ideas as well as economics, in the mind as well as the stomach; and the French Revolution is no exception. The great matters which it raised were not settled in 1795, or 1799, or 1804, or whenever the Revolution is held to 'end'. Instead of ending it rolled powerfully on; and French history of the nineteenth century (to say nothing of European and world history) is full of the great issues, emotional and economic, political and philosophical, which had come to a head in the closing years of the eighteenth century. Is liberty or order the greater good, and is dictatorship too high a price for order? What are the basic rights of man and in what sense, if at all, are men 'equal'? In particular, what rights have the middle and poorer classes of the community to a share in government? Are any special rights hereditary and vested in the nobility? How sacrosanct are the rights of property? Who owns the land? Are the people sovereign or the king, and ought France therefore to be a monarchy or a republic? If a monarchy, ought it to be absolute, by divine and hereditary right, or constitutional, by right deriving from and shared with the people? If a republic, conservative or radical? Ought the conservative, Catholic France of the countryside to be dictated to (as it was time and again) by a revolutionary, industrial, and predominantly anti-Catholic Paris? What power ought the Catholic Church to have in the state and in the education of the children? And as the century progressed many of these questions were made sharper by the growth of capitalist industry and an increasing consciousness among the industrial poor of the class war and the doctrines of socialism. The red flag joined the Bourbon lilies and the revolutionary tricolour among the hallowed and hated symbols of loyalty and rivalry.

The career of Adolphe Thiers is a sort of running commentary upon all this debate and turmoil. His fourscore combative years spanned ten régimes and half a dozen revolutions. Born under the First Republic, he always claimed to be a child of the Revolution, a "man of '89". He was never in doubt that Napoleon, Emperor while Thiers was at school, was the greatest of modern men. Coming to prominence as a rebellious liberal under the restored Bourbon monarchy, he did as much as any man to create the July Revolution of 1830, which gave France eighteen years of cautious, respectable, constitutional monarchy (though he himself as one of its leading statesmen was often far from cautious). After its fall in the Revolution of 1848 he became under the Second Republic a leading spokesman of middle-class conservatism scared by the new prospect of 'red' revolution. Underestimating Napoleon III, he was arrested in the *coup d'état* of 1851 and forced at first to lie low under the Second Empire (during which time—for he was historian as well as politician—he completed a large-scale history of France under the first Napoleon); but during the latter days of Napoleon III he became once more the principal champion of free parliamentary institutions and the spearhead of the opposition to the failing dictatorship. A fervent patriot, he was nevertheless against France's entry into the war with Prussia in 1870; the French defeat in that year brought him finally to the leadership of his country at the hour of her cruellest humiliation. He made peace with Prussia. Then, when Paris once more in the Commune of 1871 challenged the will of the majority of Frenchmen, it was Thiers who imposed that will on the rebellious capital. In the Third Republic which emerged as the smoke of these tragic events was clearing his pre-eminence was so unquestioned that the new régime was for a time simply "the Republic of M. Thiers". He made it so successful a stopgap that it came to be the longest lived of all France's many régimes since 1789. (It lasted till Hitler destroyed it.) For nearly half a century, from the twenties to the seventies, there are only brief periods when this gifted and assertive little man was not at or near the heart of French affairs.

Adolphe Thiers was born in 1797 at Marseilles of parents with whom he was later not very anxious to associate himself. His father was a good-for-nothing who begot a very miscellaneous progeny. Surprisingly he married Thiers' mother (an earlier wife dying opportunely) a month after the baby's birth; but soon deserted them both, only reappearing long after, in an unsuccessful effort to sponge on his by then famous son. The mother and her family took care of the boy's education and sent him eventually to one of the new Napoleonic military schools, the Lycée at Marseilles, of which he later reported:

Life was very hard, but the hardships instead of killing me, as they might well have, gave me in a couple of years an iron constitution.

He was a tiny fellow (all head and no body; he was never to grow beyond five feet one), but full of energy and determination and of shining intelligence. When he was eighteen—it was the year of Waterloo—his mother went with him to Aix-en-Provence, where he studied law, developed opinions on politics, literature, jurisprudence, and, indeed, everything else, was admitted to the Bar in 1818, and formed with his fellow-student (and later fellow-historian) Mignet a friendship which was to last a lifetime. Thiers was not made for easy friendship, still less for love: insignificant-looking as he was, and not given to generous gestures; always counting carefully the pence of his emotions. But, as small men often do, he developed a tough skin and a driving ambition to dominate. Determination, tireless energy, good fortune, and above all sheer intelligence saw him through. He arrived in Paris in 1821, and within a few months was taken on to the staff of the *Constitutionnel*, busying himself with articles on every kind of subject—the theatre, the arts, politics, travel. It was a liberal friend from Aix who had secured him his position; the *Constitutionnel* was a liberal paper; and since its liberal owners and contributors took to this brilliant young newcomer, generously secured his income, and began to introduce him to men of influence, Thiers soon 'arrived'—and 'arrived' as a liberal. But his liberalism never went very deep; there was always an element of opportunism in it, and he was to discard a good deal of it later when he came to a position of authority. His love of system and order, the Napoleonic virtues, was always stronger than his love of freedom.

Most influential of his new friends was Talleyrand, to whom the banker Laffitte introduced him in 1823. Always good at picking political winners and quick to recognize his own shrewdness in others, Talleyrand took the young man under his wing. Thiers became a person to take account of, even if aristocratic society, ladies in particular, looked down with a certain scorn upon this bespectacled dwarfish vivacious little monster.

The 1820's were a time when French liberalism was under severe pressure. The moderation of the Bourbon monarchy restored in 1814 was fast disappearing. The 'Ultras', embittered *émigrés* who had returned from exile determined to reclaim their property rights and reassert the full authority of Crown, Church, and aristocracy, had always despised the compromise monarchy that Louis XVIII had been content to accept. The Charter of 1814, with its guarantee of constitutional liberties, had for them been an evil to be only temporarily tolerated. In 1815 their vengeance had cut loose in the south; two to three hundred of their victims— republicans, Bonapartists, and Protestants—had been murdered in a "White Terror". A sporting crew, they had gone 'marshal-hunting' (as the grim humour of the Duke of Berry had it) and in 1816 saw their most famous quarry, Marshal Ney, judicially murdered. During the ministry of Louis XVIII's favourite Decazes, the King had managed to preserve a degree of tolerance and kept alive the hope that one day Frenchmen might unlearn their passion to pay off old scores; but in 1820 the assassination of the Duke of Berry, the King's nephew and leader of the 'Ultras', had precipitated the utmost bitterness. Decazes fell; "his feet have slipped in blood," gloated Chateaubriand, "and he is down." A baby, born to Berry's widow seven months after his death, was hailed by royalists, with more joy than reason, as the *enfant du miracle*. A new electoral law enhanced their power in the Chamber and reduced the liberals to a tiny band. Press censorship was tightened and universities increasingly subjected to clerical authority. In 1823 a French army with the Holy Alliance's blessing crossed the Pyrenees to overthrow the liberals in Spain and restore one of the worst despots in Europe. When Louis XVIII died in 1824 and his brother the Count of Artois succeeded as Charles X the party of the priests and nobles had in effect already been in control for two or three years. The medieval harking-back of Charles's grand coronation at Rheims, and new laws in 1825 facilitating the founding of religious communities and prescribing death for the offence of sacrilege (first the offending hand and then the head to be severed) confirmed the worst of liberal fears. To what end, they asked, had there been a French Revolution at all?

Thiers, the young liberal, chose his own way of providing an answer: his *History of the French Revolution*, published in several volumes between 1823 and 1827, established both his literary and his political position. The book was history-with-a-purpose; frowning on Jacobin fanatics, it stood clearly for all that was cleansing and constructive in the Revolution. It possessed all the ingredients of success—narrative skill, patriotic fervour, and a theme freshly relevant in a France that seemed to be falling anew into the hands of reaction. The book, together with Thiers' articles in the *Constitutionnel*, earned him simultaneously a modest financial success and the applause of the liberals, as well as some less welcome attention from the secret police.

Many Frenchmen were now convinced that their country was falling under the control of "hidden forces", of whom the Jesuits were the most deeply mistrusted (even by moderate Catholics and royalists—some bishops denounced them, and everywhere the Bourbon Government was criticized for encouraging them). Opposition papers like Thiers' *Constitutionnel* enjoyed a circulation three times as great as those supporting the ministry. "We must lock the Bourbons up in the Charter," wrote Thiers. "Confined thus, they must explode." And in August 1829 Charles X *was* misguided and overconfident enough to dismiss his relatively moderate ministers and call in the Duke of Polignac at the head of an ultra-Ultra ministry, which Thiers prophetically described as the prelude to a *coup d'état*.

Basking in the success of his *French Revolution*, he had been at this time contemplating a world tour as a preliminary to embarking on a universal history, but the promise of excitement at home brought a change of plans. In January 1830, together with Mignet and Carrel, he launched a new paper, the *National*. The heart of its message was parliamentary monarchy; in Thiers' famous phrase, *le roi règne et ne gouverne pas*. The paper lived dangerously, always on the verge of suppression, but from the beginning it lived up to its name and was a national force. The analogies of 1688 and the English Revolution were constantly in the background of its articles. There was such a thing, Thiers claimed, as a bloodless revolution, which could lead to a genuinely constitutional monarchy, a synthesis of King, Aristocracy, and People. Over the Channel it already existed, this happy state of affairs, under the "model" George IV—not an epithet, perhaps, that all his subjects would have cared to endorse. As for 1688, the parallel with the Stuart monarchs was plain for all to see: if Louis XVIII was Charles II, then plainly Charles X was James II, and due for removal. All that was needed was a William of Orange, and might not a candidate be ready to hand in Louis-Philippe, Duke of Orleans and friend of the people? Three times the paper was prosecuted in the courts, but public subscription readily paid the fines.

The attempt at a *coup d'état* forecast by Thiers came in effect with Polignac's Ordinances published at St Cloud in July 1830. His reply to the swelling discontent was to suspend the remaining liberty of the Press, dissolve the parliament, and deprive the bourgeoisie of the vote. And now it was at the offices of the *National*, with Thiers in the chair, that there was held the journalists' meeting that gave the signal for the revolution. "We must risk our heads," said Thiers; and the group of writers and lawyers agreed the statement drafted by him which appeared in bold type next morning in the *National*:

> Today the Government has lost the legal character by which it commands obedience.

This was on 27th July. On the 28th a single sheet appeared, plainly inciting revolution:

> Yesterday the Charter was torn in shreds, and those who found in it their guarantees lost them; yesterday everyone was made free to act according to his power, and now no-one should expect security except through using force.

Having penned this piece of sedition, Thiers (with Mignet) went to ground in the country; he did not believe in "risking his head" too gratuitously. That same day Paris rose in revolt and inflicted heavy casualties on the garrison, which Charles had recently and most foolishly put under the command of Marmont, a notoriously unpopular marshal who had betrayed Napoleon. By evening the tricolour was flying from Notre-Dame. Next day (July 29th) two of Marmont's regiments went over to the rebels, and the tricolour was over the Tuileries too. Polignac meanwhile relied on the Virgin Mary's loyalty to the Bourbon cause; and the King, although he consented to return from hunting at Rambouillet, refused to treat with the Deputies, seeking a compromise settlement. When at last he agreed to dismiss Polignac it was too late. The capital was in the hands of the revolutionaries, at a cost of about a thousand dead, civilians and military. A republic seemed imminent.

On the 29th Thiers and Mignet deemed it safe to return to Paris in time to influence the crucial decision. Thiers went directly to see Laffitte, Talleyrand, Périer, and General Sébastiani. None of these wanted a republic, but how were they to avoid it? It was Thiers who argued that they should commit the Duke of Orleans without consulting him; and next morning Paris awoke to find itself bombarded by Orleanist propaganda. The *National* came out with its famous proclamation in praise of Louis-Philippe, which all the billboards echoed:

> The Duke of Orleans has never fought against us.
> The Duke of Orleans was at Jemappes.
> The Duke of Orleans is a Citizen King.
> The Duke of Orleans has carried the tricolour under the enemy's fire; only the Duke of Orleans can carry it again. . . . It is from the French people that he will hold his crown.

Nobody, however, had yet actually invited him; and it was Thiers—lawyer, historian, journalist, revolutionary, and now most surprisingly king-maker—who was commissioned to ride off to the Duke of Orleans' summer residence at Neuilly to deliver the formal message. Louis-Philippe, however, was not at home; in fact, he was hiding, as befitted a prudent prince; but his sister gave fair replies. Eventually he arrived at the Palais Royal, still in some fear of his reception by republican Paris. But then on the balcony of the Hôtel de Ville there occurred the clinching formality. The aged General Lafayette, a legend in himself and the very embodiment of respectable republicanism, received amid plaudits the new King-to-be under the folds of the symbolic tricolour, and determined the issue with a public embrace. As Chateaubriand put it: "A republican kiss has made a king."

Thiers always considered 1830 *his* revolution; he was jealous of his reputation in it to his death. And if he had made the revolution, certainly it had completed the making of him. His career as a journalist was over; he was appointed by Louis-Philippe to be, first, Secretary-General of Finances, and then in 1832 Minister for Home Affairs. He identified himself with the group of rich bourgeois who, under the bourgeois monarch, had now become the real rulers of France—men like Laffitte, Baron Louis, and Périer; bankers, financiers, manufacturers, merchant princes. Now that he was one of them, he must have an establishment to match.

About 1822 the little lawyer from Aix, with his nasal Provençal

accent and his harsh determination to 'get on', had been introduced to the household of M. Dosne, a banker and industrialist,
who lived in fine style in the Place St Georges. Mme Dosne held a
salon there which Thiers frequented, and soon the two struck up
a friendship which, with Mignet's, was the most significant of his
life. Mme Dosne, domineering, ambitious, politically aware, but
rather shallow and vulgar, became Thiers' intimate confidante,
protector, adviser, backer—and eventually, though they were much
of an age, mother-in-law. Scandal-sheets and busy tongues found
more than interesting the ostentatious nuptials in November 1833 of
Adolphe Thiers with the sixteen-year-old Elise Dosne. Anxious to
get the consent of his mother in Aix, he had written: "I am to
marry a young person, lovely"—a pardonable and perhaps only
slight exaggeration—"amiable, *and raised for me with infinite
care.*" It proved a curious but in its way very successful *ménage*:
two women, mother and daughter, companion and wife. Three
women, in fact; his sister-in-law Félicie was a permanent part of
the household. Dosne *père*, on the other hand, slides away into
oblivion, a man of no consequence, whose principal function seems
to have been to provide his daughter with a rich dowry and Thiers
with a mortgage on a magnificent establishment—the Hôtel St
Georges. There they 'received' every evening. Mme. Thiers, delicate
and unpolitical, would retire early from the social fray; Mme
Dosne was the presiding spirit, indefatigable, avid for her Adolphe
and his fame—as avid, if that were possible, as he himself. Already
in 1834 he proposed himself for the Academy, and was received
among the Immortals.

"It is from the people of France that he will hold his throne"; so
Thiers had proclaimed of Louis-Philippe in July 1830. It was soon
apparent that this was mere rhetoric. It is true that a revised Charter
was announced, with a somewhat wider, though still narrow,
franchise. The tricolour was restored; the hereditary right of peers
to sit in parliament was abolished, and Louis-Philippe became King
not "of France" but "of the French". But Lafayette's proposal in
favour of universal suffrage was not seriously entertained, and when
republican unrest and violence continued Louis-Philippe and his
ministers soon showed that their well-advertised liberalism was the
reverse of democratic. Those many republicans who had grudgingly accepted Louis-Philippe as a stopgap king, a sort of bridge

between Bourbon monarchy and Second Republic, were soon disillusioned.

Thiers, as usual, had no doubts of his own position. He was one
of those known as the Party of Resistance (resisting, that is, further
revolution). While his old paper, the *National*, under his one-time
colleague Carrel, drifted away from him towards radicalism and
even socialism, Thiers became more and more "le petit roi des
commerçants", the head (with Guizot, his great rival) of the conservative bourgeoisie, the party of order. If the enemies of that order
on the Left were more numerous, those on the Right, the hard core
of Bourbon royalists, were still not to be ignored. 'Legitimist' rum-
bling continued in many parts of the country; and when the
Duchess of Berry, mother of the pretender 'Henry V', landed
secretly and proceeded to stir up a Bourbon rising in Vendée and
Brittany, Thiers, Minister for Home Affairs, learning of the existence of an informant, made a secret assignation with him, and paid
over a heavy bribe from the Secret Funds. He then pounced on the
Duchess and confined her in the Castle of Blaye—altogether a
successful and dramatic stroke. As it turned out, he need hardly
have bothered. The Duchess, having entertained a passion for an
Italian Count, was soon to be confined in a different sense, and
although she had in fact made a second and secret marriage, the
legitimacy of her new offspring was no comfort to the Legitimists.
Her baby of 1820 had been hailed as the *enfant du miracle*; this
one was rather the *enfant du débâcle*. The government of Louis-
Philippe was able to allow the Legitimists to weaken themselves
in internal squabbles for years to come.

On the Left it was a different story. The Revolution of 1830 had
not brought prosperity. The year 1831 was, in France, as in Britain,
one of unemployment and crisis. Like Britain, France at this time
was beginning to experience, not, indeed, an overall fall in the
standard of living, but a sudden expansion of a few large-scale
industries—textiles and metals in particular—with all the attendant
miseries of the early Industrial Revolution. The very expression
'Industrial Revolution' was first used by a Frenchman, Blanqui, at
this time; and for the first time, too, men now began to speak of
'socialists' and 'socialism'. Child and female labour, slum squalor,
uncontrolled hours and conditions, malnutrition and disease, were
the price paid in France as elsewhere for the blessings of economic
growth. To familiar hardships were added in 1831–32 the un-

familiar horror of cholera, which killed many thousands, the chief minister Périer among them.

"All the benefits of victory of 1830 should be for the people," Thiers' *National* had written; events turned out otherwise. Impatience and despair grew, and in 1831 the weavers of Lyons rose in revolt, enforced a workers' share in wage-fixing, and were briefly in collective control of this second city of France, until force dispersed the rebels and the principles of *laissez-faire* were reaffirmed.

Unrest, however, continued. There was a revival of republican clubs. Republican pamphlets were distributed by the million; radical papers raised their voices by the score and stretched their legs in new-found freedom, often advocating violence and rebellion. (Marrast's *Tribune* was nevertheless prosecuted 114 times within four years.) Eventually in 1834 both Lyons and Paris broke into fresh insurrection. Now was the time for Thiers, the pocket Napoleon, to show his teeth, and bring the mob *his* whiff of grapeshot. As Minister, he dispatched General Bugeaud to Lyons, where the rioters were shot down. In Paris he himself took command, and directed the battle (or massacre) of the Rue Transnonain. In his minister's uniform and a plain target for the insurgents, he was lucky; it was his secretary beside him who was hit. The heavy bloodshed of that day was never forgiven him by the Left. Neither, after Fieschi's attempt next year on the King's life, were Thiers' September Laws (1835), striking down the republican opposition while the iron was hot: special courts for summary trial, majority jury verdicts, judgment in the prisoner's absence, heavy fines for sedition in the Press. Only four years earlier Thiers had been himself the chief of campaigners for a free Press; now his own *National* was one of the papers to suffer by the new laws, and his own co-editor Carrel one of those to be arrested. Inevitably he reaped the reproaches of old liberal associates and confirmed the hatred of republican enemies. Being Thiers, however, he did not lack self-justification. Clemency would be regarded as weakness, and weakness would bring revolution. Order was everything. As for his 'treason', he cited a parallel, as he often did, from English history: "the younger Pitt was called a traitor in his lifetime. Today he has a statue at Westminster."

Not Pitt, however, but Pitt's enemy Napoleon, was Thiers' real hero, and in this he was a characteristic Frenchman of his day. Napoleon was the subject above all others that fascinated the France of Louis-Philippe: an idealized Napoleon, generous, far-sighted, titanic, triumphing over the foes of France. The songs of Béranger, the poems of Hugo, endless histories, novels, paintings, dramas, harped on the theme. By the side of the great Emperor, Louis-Philippe seemed humdrum and minuscule, with his bourgeois prudence, his submissiveness abroad, his commonplace manner, his umbrella on his arm—strolling like any other gentleman through Paris streets, excessively willing to have his hand pumped by the citizenry. The Crowned Pear[1] was inevitably contrasted with the Little Corporal. Yet seeking to identify themselves with the passion for things Napoleonic, Louis-Philippe and his ministers unwittingly helped to dig the pit in which they were eventually to fall. When the Napoleonic Column was restored to the Place Vendôme, and when the ashes of Napoleon were brought home from St Helena and reburied with pomp in the Invalides, Frenchmen were not merely indulging their nostalgia for glories past; unknowingly they were smoothing the path for another Napoleon to come.

In 1835 none of this was to be foreseen as the Minister of the Interior attended the grand unveiling ceremony at the Place Vendôme. The horse he rode that day was called Vendôme too— or *Vanndomme* in Thiers' Provençal accent. Everyone knew that Thiers felt an affinity for Napoleon—there was a topical joke that in good time he would have his own statue on the Place between Napoleon's legs—but on the day of the ceremony his horsemanship was not quite the equal of his ambition. The Prince de Joinville, one of the King's sons, was, as it happened, an admirer of Thiers, but he also savoured his more ludicrous aspects:

> The troops, the National Guard were under arms; the military band with drums and a magnificent drum-major at their head were massed at the foot of the column. We approached, *en grand cortège*, via the rue de Castiglione. In front of us was the column surmounted by the statue that was covered with a veil destined to fall at a given signal. Upon our arrival at the scene, Monsieur Thiers, *en grand uniforme*, wearing a hat with waving plumes and mounted on 'Vanndomme', spurred his horse, left the cortège *au grand galop* and passed before my father, crying shrilly in his high falsetto, 'I bear the King's orders.' He accompanied these words with a wave of the hat that unkind tongues declared he had copied from the pose of General Rapp in Gérard's painting, 'The Battle of Austerlitz', at the Louvre. At this gesture of his, the

[1] Louis-Philippe's pear-shaped head became the cartoonists' stock-in-trade.

drums began to beat, the band struck up, and the veil fell from the statue. But Monsieur Thiers was no longer master of 'Vann-domme', who, wild with enthusiasm, charged head down, upset the drums and the magnificent drum-major, and tore off with the little minister hanging on to him like a monkey at the Hippodrome.

On two occasions, in 1836 (February–August) and 1840 (February–October), Thiers became Louis-Philippe's chief minister (*Président du Conseil*); each time his spirited foreign policy threatened to run away with him as violently as his horse Vendôme; each time he was dismissed by the King for fear of the consequences of his rashness. In 1836 it was over Spain, where insurrections and civil wars between Liberals and Carlists rumbled confusedly on through the thirties. Thiers was determined that France should play a more militant part and intervene against the Carlists. Louis-Philippe was as strongly resolved to remain at peace, and when Thiers tried to rush him into action was glad to force his resignation. On the second occasion, over the Near Eastern crisis of 1840, Thiers was ready to go to war in support of Mohammed Ali and French interests in Egypt. It was his misfortune to run up against Palmerston at his most cocksure and masterly.[2] Britain faced France with a *fait accompli*, a treaty agreed between the other great Powers; France must like it or lump it. In any case Mohammed Ali was to be dealt with by the British Navy, and France must forgo her hope of empire in Egypt and Syria. Thiers, outmanœuvred and outgunned, nevertheless increased the strength of the fleet, prepared the fortification of Paris, and demanded war credits. The papers under his influence hummed with bellicose demands. But again Louis-Philippe chose the path of prudence. "Please moderate the tone of the newspapers," he wrote to Thiers. Privately he said, "I will not allow myself to be carried too far by my little minister. . . . He wants war and I do not want it. . . . I shall break with him rather than break with Europe." In the autumn of 1840 he was glad to replace Thiers by the more cautious and pacific Guizot, who remained in office for the rest of the reign.

Deprived of his opportunities to conduct Napoleonic policies, Thiers resumed work on the history of Napoleonic France that he had begun during an earlier period of opposition. He studied; he trod the sacred soil of Austerlitz, indefatigably noting. He filled his

[2] See pp. 237–239.

walls with huge copies of Italian paintings and his library shelves
with busts and bronzes—his somewhat ponderous *petit musée*; he
collected tropical plants and rare birds—and kept pet gazelles! He
directed from his house the editorials of the pro-Thiers Press. In the
Chamber he led the Opposition.

That is to say, he freely attacked those of Guizot's policies that he
disapproved, while maintaining his essential loyalty to the Orleans
monarchy itself. During the 1840's the régime was slowly foundering
in dullness; lacking any *réclame* abroad, Louis-Philippe and Guizot
attempted in 1847 a smart *coup* with their Spanish marriages and
succeeded only in infuriating the English.[3] At home it remained a
régime of the rich, resisting every effort to broaden the franchise.
Some Frenchmen looked longingly back to Napoleon, some beyond
him to the heroic days of the Revolution. Lamartine, poet and
romantic, turned (like Guizot, like Mignet, like Thiers himself) to
history, and scored a great success with his *History of the Girondins*.
Romantic revolutionism was in the air; men were ready for anything
but the dull monarchy of Orleans. The year 1847 was one of
economic slump, and socialist writers and politicians of the Left—
Louis Blanc, Odilon Barrot, Ledru-Rollin, Duvergier, Garnier-
Pagès—hammered away at the stubbornly inactive Government.
As for Thiers, he was a politician and he was in opposition. Circumstances and his own opportunism thrust him into alliance with the
reformist party. More men, he agreed, must have the vote; the
scandalously high proportion of deputies who were rewarded with
office must be reduced. But he saw the risks and he wanted no
revolution.

It was, however, on the way. The officers of the National Guard
were full of republican sentiments. It became the fashion to hold
banquets at which the toast was *Reform!*—and when Louis-Philippe
and Guizot forbade attendance many of the reformers defied the
ban. Even if "all the other deputies shirked their duties," promised
Lamartine, "I would go to the banquet with my shadow behind
me." Thiers, however, promised to keep *his* shadow away; he was
afraid, as he said, of "the *bonnet rouge* under the banquet table".

> The Government will resist; it could not do otherwise. If you
> try to brave its resistance there will be a bloody affray. . . . I
> do not desire your defeat or your victory. Hence I refuse the fight;
> I refuse the banquet . . . .

[3] See pp. 241–242.

On February 22nd, 1848, coming away from a meeting at the house of Barrot, where he had unsuccessfully tried to prevent the Left Wing from attempting to impeach Guizot and his ministers, Thiers walked home via the Place Louis XV, the Place de la Madeleine, the Rue St Florentin. Children and workmen, he reported, were tearing up the streets at a fantastic rate; they were beginning to build barricades. The crowds were shouting *A bas Guizot! Vive la Réforme!*; and when the National Guard were called in they too shouted the same cry, *Vive la Réforme!* The 1848 Revolution had begun.

Guizot fell and was succeeded by Molé. Immediately Molé fell and was succeeded by Thiers—a Thiers ready to try strong measures. When the house burns, he told Louis-Philippe, you must have someone to put out the fire. But Thiers on his own certainly could not put out the fire which was now burning—not even Thiers in conjunction with the radical republican Odilon Barrot. One day the crowd shouted "*Vive Thiers! Vive Barrot!*" The next day it was shouting only "*Vive Barrot!*" and Thiers was in danger of having his throat cut by the "sovereign people". He advised Louis-Philippe to invite Barrot to form a government, but it was too late. The barricades and red flags were up. The King's reception when he reviewed the National Guards was depressingly lukewarm. Then, as Thiers was breakfasting with the King, he learned that 20,000 workmen were advancing towards the Palace up the Rue de la Paix. It was the crucial moment; should the King stay or go? Thiers' plan (prophetic for 1871) was for him to retire to St Cloud and march from there upon the rebel capital; a siege would be better than a war on the barricades. But Louis-Philippe would not hear of it. Like Charles X in 1830, he preferred abdication in favour of his young grandson. On February 24th the seventy-five-year-old King followed in the steps of his predecessor and withdrew to England.

The Provisional Government set up under the presidency of Lamartine was an amalgam of liberals and socialists; among its members were Ledru-Rollin, leader of the radicals; Albert, a workman; and Louis Blanc, a socialist writer. It proceeded to abolish monarchy "of every kind" for ever, and to introduce universal male suffrage, which in a twinkling raised the number of voters from 200,000 to 9 millions. Even so, in the Assembly which they elected—France being in general rural and Catholic—the conservative parties predominated; middle-class republicans and royalists far outnumbered radicals and socialists. At Marseilles, however, Thiers himself was defeated—"by bankrupts, failed lawyers, and charlatans", according to his own indignant account. It was only a temporary setback; he was soon elected in five constituencies, opting to sit for Seine-Inférieure.

The revolution of February establishing the Second Republic was only the beginning of the 1848 Revolution. The elections were a bitter pill for the Paris radicals to swallow, and disturbances continued both in the capital itself and in the other big industrial towns of the provinces. The *other* revolution was beginning to rumble, the social revolution of the urban masses, of socialists against the bourgeoisie, of the poor against the rich. A month before Louis-Philippe abdicated de Tocqueville had warned the Chamber: "Can you not see that their passions, once political, have become social?" Privilege was still the enemy, but the privilege no longer of a feudal nobility but of a capitalist industrialism careless of the sufferings of its victims. To these new revolutionaries Thiers policy of "the middle way" (*le juste milieu*) was as cynical a mockery as Guizot's famous invitation: "*Enrichissez-vous!*" The Orleans monarchy had seen the triumph of the men of property; and what, asked Proudhon, was property? *Property was theft*: a simple but inflammatory diagnosis horrifying to liberals and conservatives alike.

In mid-May 1848 there was violent rioting in Paris. A mob invaded the Palais Bourbon, 'dissolved' the Assembly there, and marched off to the Hôtel de Ville to set up their own government, in which attempt they were foiled by the National and Mobile Guards; Blanqui and Raspail, of their leaders, were deported. A little later, after a crowd of four or five hundred had assembled outside the Thiers mansion and threatened to burn it down with himself inside, Thiers repeated to the Assembly the advice he had given to the King in February—retire outside Paris and systematically retake the capital. This got him short shrift. "If M. Thiers continues to make such suggestions," said General Cavaignac, "I'll have him shot."

Socialist writers, Louis Blanc especially, in the years of unemployment before 1848 made much of the poor man's "right to work"; unemployment was economically wasteful and humanly unforgivable. As a concession to this thinking the Provisional Government had hastily set up National Workshops, a parody of Blanc's ideas. 50,000 men were taken on; and since there was useful work available for perhaps a fifth of that number only, about 40,000 men were given pointless occupation and "might as well have spent their time bottling the waters of the Seine". To Thiers this was madness, and would have remained madness even if run as Blanc had intended:

> If the workman knows that the State will provide him with work at all times, he will never save. You will kill all the useful virtues. The only consequence of the National Workshops is the guarantee of an army of insurrection.

And in June the Government did provide such an army by suddenly deciding to end the expensive experiment. Bachelors between eighteen and twenty-five were offered the alternatives of dismissal or military enlistment.

The class war now exploded in the streets of Paris. On June 24th the Assembly voted General Cavaignac full powers. Train-loads of troops were brought in, and in three days of bloody fighting (the June Days), the "army of despair", men, women, children even, 100,000 strong, was crushed. The party of order, of the bourgeoisie and the peasantry, the champions of the "conservative revolution" of 1789—the party of Thiers—was victorious.

In those terrible days, said Lamartine (himself rapidly losing influence in face of Cavaignac and the conservatives), the Second Republic died; it now merely waited burial. But many who lacked republican enthusiasm still had no wish to bury it. Thiers for one; a moderate monarchist, he accepted the republic. Indeed, being Thiers, he confidently expected in time time to direct it. A republic, he said, in a phrase that was to be endlessly repeated, "is of all governments the one that divides us least." But although he grudgingly accepted universal suffrage, the republic must be, if he were to support it, moderate. Socialism was subversion, "an idle and slavish society", the negation of liberty. Nationalization—*i.e.*, National Workshops—meant "the poor paying the poor and the ruin of all the poor". Conscious, however, of the existence of the harshest poverty, he hastened to disclaim heartlessness; for the poor "everything must be done—except that they must not be allowed to decide great matters that concern the future fate of the country". These sentiments remained with him for the rest of his days; they were expressed in parallel circumstances after the second great defeat of the Paris workers in 1871. What Thiers wanted, each time, was "the Republic without the Republicans". Opinions like his, forcefully and even brutally expressed, were not likely to endear him to the working class. For a whole year he carried pistols in his pocket; and on at least two occasions during 1848–49 his person and his house were in danger from the infuriated Left.

The new Republic had to find its President, to be elected by the free vote of all Frenchmen. Cavaignac was a candidate, the man who had suppressed the June revolt; so were Lamartine and Ledru-Rollin. But the dark horse was Prince Louis Napoleon, nephew of the great Emperor and inheritor of the glamour of his fame; self-professing social reformer and author of *L'Extinction du Paupérisme*; heir and beneficiary of the Bonapartist legend. After the dull bourgeois calculation of the Orleans monarchy and the hate-laden disorders of mid-1848, Louis Napoleon seemed to stand for order and material progress, for glory, yet at the same time for peace. He had some appeal for nearly everybody. To the peasants he represented conservative tradition and good order; to the middle classes security from red rebellion; to the royalists a stopgap until their squabbling factions could unite round an undisputed candidate for the throne; to the urban workers a progressive alternative to Ledru-Rollin and obviously preferable to Cavaignac, the "butcher of June". Louis Napoleon's election in December 1848 was by a huge majority; it was "not an election but an acclamation".

Louis Napoleon himself professed liberal opinions, and he was certainly no Catholic; but he knew that no-one could hope to rule France without Catholic support. One of his first actions, therefore, was to restore the Pope to his throne; a French military expedition which had originally been sent to *assist* the anti-papal revolutionaries finished by crushing them instead. Louis Napoleon was grateful for the Catholic plaudits and salved his conscience by hoping—in vain, of course—to persuade Pope Pius to introduce liberal reforms. The once-liberal Thiers, "man of '89", as he still claimed to be, went a long way in support of this pro-Catholic policy. When the Prince-President brought in the Catholic royalist Count Falloux to prepare a new education bill Thiers, together with such Catholic intellectuals as Montalembert, played a large part in framing the details of the new dispensation. Accused of apostasy, Thiers defended himself. Circumstances had altered cases; he was more frightened now of the destructiveness of the Left than of the power of the Jesuits. The so-called Loi Falloux, which might as justly be called the Loi Thiers-Montalembert, broke the state monopoly of higher education and allowed the Church for the next thirty years to play a very powerful part in the nation's education. Thiers, more Catholic now in some ways than the Catholics themselves, had even suggested that *all* teachers should be appointed by the bishops.

The conservative reaction seemed so strong in 1850 that it began to produce its own counter-revolution, especially among the lower middle classes. When Paris elections in that year produced republican gains the conservative majority in the Assembly proceeded to pass a new electoral law which deprived 3 millions of their vote— a third of the electorate. In the future three years' continuous residence was to be a necessary qualification, and this inevitably discriminated against industrial workers, residentially the least stable class. Louis Napoleon had no part in this; it was the Assembly's work, and Thiers was as eloquent as any in its support. He feared the common man; he had become, in Gambetta's phrase, "*le chef de la bourgeoisie française*", and in his speech in support of the suffrage limitation he made use of an expression which his enemies never forgot—wishing to exclude, he said, not the poorer classes as such, but "the vile multitude". It was the sort of phrase a politician will spend a lifetime explaining away.

Although Louis Napoleon had won so resounding a popular victory in December 1848, he by no means impressed everybody as the new man of destiny. Mignet thought that years of exile had robbed him of the power of understanding Frenchmen. Thiers himself, in a letter to Disraeli, wrote off the Prince-President as "a nobody" (*un homme absolument nul*). With a little patience and political subtlety Thiers was confident that Louis Napoleon could be outmanœuvred and at the appropriate moment removed. But Louis Napoleon was at this stage to prove a cleverer politician than Thiers and his friends.

It was an era of continuing economic hardship and low corn prices. The Republic had brought no answer to France's problems, and if Frenchmen were disillusioned with it that was all to Louis Napoleon's advantage. Confident of the people, he asked the Assembly to restore full universal suffrage; it refused. Likewise it refused to amend the constitution to permit his re-election as President for a second term. Many—Flahault and Morny, for instance— were openly advocating a Bonapartist *coup d'état* as the only way of resolving the deadlock between President and Assembly. On the other hand, Louis Napoleon was convinced that Thiers and others were preparing a *coup* against *him*. And certainly Thiers in his own mind was playing for high stakes. In mid-1851, after a speech in the Assembly (during which he had praised liberty as practised in England, where the aristocracy held democracy in check), his characteristically self-flattering account of his own performance, in a letter to Mme Dosne, shows well enough how his thoughts were tending:

> I spoke for three hours and I watched the attentiveness, the enthusiasm, even the tears flowing, as I spoke of France, and Jules Favre shouted "There is the man who should be President of the Republic.". . . The feeling generally is that I surpassed myself.

Next to himself, the Presidential candidate that he favoured was the Orleanist Prince de Joinville; failing him, said Thiers, "the Empire is in the process of being made every moment".

He was right. Louis Napoleon had satisfied himself of his own position—with the army, with the police, and with the people—and decided, in his quarrel with the Assembly, to grasp the nettle. On November 30th, 1851, he spoke to his cousin Princess Mathilde as he escorted her to her carriage after a performance at the Opéra. Nodding in the direction of Thiers and another member of the Assembly a few yards away, he said:

> For a long time I haven't been able to take my eyes off these people, who would like to bring me down and throw me into Vincennes. Perhaps *they* will be in prison in a couple of days. . . . Everything in France will be lost if I don't act.

On December 2nd, the anniversary of Austerlitz, Parisians came out on to the streets on their way to work to find the town everywhere placarded with proclamations announcing the dissolution of the Assembly. Louis-Napoleon was 'saving' the Republic, "invoking the solemn judgment of the only sovereign I recognize in France . . . the people". At about the same time 78 policemen, each with his warrant from the Prefect of Police, were arresting the 78 politicians whose removal was most vital to Louis Napoleon. One of them was naturally Thiers, still in his night-clothes at 6.15 A.M. He was at first convinced that he was to be killed, and was about to make for the drawer where he kept his pistols. The *commissaire* was obliged to show him that he too carried arms, and pocketing those of Thiers ordered him to dress and get into the waiting carriage, which took him to Mazas Prison. Thiers was sure that he was about to be shot: "I see very well," he said, "you are taking me to my death." Back at the Hôtel St Georges, Mme Dosne was ill with vexation and indignation, but not so ill as to forget to burn any compromising documents. Sick and fearful in prison, Thiers was released on Louis Napoleon's orders, to return home under police surveillance. Two days later, still closely guarded, he was conducted *via* Nancy and Strasbourg to the German border and exile, restored to his usual stubborn good health despite a high degree of self-pity.

The *coup* had been carefully prepared and efficiently executed, but it was far from bloodless. Some staunch republicans, among them Victor Hugo, tried to rouse the eastern districts of Paris, and down in the south the Jacobin spirit had to be harshly quenched. About 15,000 were sentenced following these disturbances and 9000 deported; and for the next eighteen years, from his exile in the Channel Islands, the implacable Hugo thundered away against *Napoléon le Petit*, new dwarf tyrant, the caricature-mockery of Napoleon the Great.

From Brussels the exiled Thiers proceeded to London, where he was treated with delightfully flattering hospitality. Watching at the State opening of Parliament the aged Duke of Wellington holding the great Sword of State in trembling hands over the Queen's head, he had occasion to ponder the futility of his own "thirty years of effort" to give France this kind of monarchy, "the true Republic". Then and always he considered English liberty the truest, guaranteed as it was by aristocracy, unthreatened by the violence of utopianism, guarded by tradition and moderation. From England he went on to make an extensive tour through Italy and Switzerland, his observant eyes busily noting every feature of the scene—geographical, political, artistic, historic, literary. Surrounded by friends and by his faithful and admiring womenfolk, lionized wherever he travelled, he was still bored; bored and hungry for the power that he had been cheated of.

In December 1852 Louis Napoleon crowned the edifice and proclaimed himself Emperor Napoleon III of the French, but already in the preceding August he had signed a decree permitting the re-entry of Thiers. In the Tuileries gardens, taking the air the day after he arrived back, the returned exile enjoyed a respectful little ovation from the fashionable crowd promenading there; but he soon noticed how depressingly ready the *canaille* now were to cry *Vive l'Empereur!*—with just as much enthusiasm, he sourly observed, as they so recently shouted *Vive la République!* It seemed that it would be a long time before Monsieur Thiers could again hope to count for much in the nation's affirs.

The new men now by the Emperor's side were all Bonapartist either by blood or by long years of fellow-conspiracy: Persigny, the Emperor's companion from his earliest days, became Minister of the Interior; Morny, Talleyrand's grandson and the Emperor's half-brother, President of the Legislature; and Walewski, son of the first Napoleon by his Polish mistress, Foreign Minister. Of these, Morny has the highest claim to statesmanship; but he, like the others, had little real power. Napoleon III treated all his ministers impartially, like clerks.

Active politics were of necessity forbidden territory to Thiers. But his diminutive frame contained many men. He turned to business, and sat on the board of the large and prosperous coal and iron firm of Anzin, which eventually in 1869 made him its chairman. He became one of the great collectors and connoisseurs of pictures and sculptures. But his main activity during the first decade of the Second Empire was in the field of his "chères études", and above all in the task of completing his second major work, in twenty volumes, *The History of the Consulate and the Empire*, which he had begun to publish in 1845. In both the literary and financial sense it was a prodigious success, though little enough read now; and never, for a man with Thiers' thirst for power, as great as that of Napoleon I himself, could writing be a substitute for politics. He would give ten successful histories, he said, for one successful campaign: "writing is a poor thing compared with action".

France under the great Napoleon, the subject of his narrative, could hardly fail to excite Frenchmen in the early glittering days of his nephew; and in 1857 Napoleon III saluted Thiers as "the historian of the nation". His writing had the swift flow of the accomplished journalist; it was as clear and precise as the man himself. Sainte-Beuve, while ridiculing Thiers' presumptions in claiming to understand mathematics and philosophy (and he might well have added everything else as well), had the highest opinion of his gifts of exposition and persuasion:

> As he speaks or writes he involves you imperceptibly in his story and its novelty; he carries you along with him in a current

sometimes rapid, sometimes leisurely, and . . . unless you are careful, his conclusions, his impressions have become your own. . . .

Every day of his long life, to the morning of his death, Thiers rose at five. He read voraciously. In all his numerous travels he was noting, recording, analysing, reporting every detail of what he saw. The range of his interests was extraordinarily wide—politics, finance, business, history, painting, architecture, military science; even the physical sciences of geology, astronomy, and chemistry. (True, he did not always notice the sunset or the colours of the landscape. No-one could have been temperamentally farther removed from the romantic spirit that was the dominant influence in the arts of his day.)

Under the régime of Mme Dosne, that insatiable hostess, still 'promoting' Thiers indefatigably, the house in the Place St Georges with its sumptuous *haut bourgeois* décor saw constant and distinguished company. Among the throng the master came and went; he was happiest when he had retired to his sanctum, the spacious and lavishly adorned library with its 9000 volumes, a place of more than mere study, where he could talk with those few friends— Mignet and Victor Cousin in particular—who were almost part of the Thiers household, and here he would meet the leading political figures of his day and discuss those aspects of life in France that could not be freely ventilated elsewhere.

For although there was much in the France of Napoleon III to applaud, it was an authoritarian state and liberty was not among its blessings. No public opposition was tolerated. The Press was not officially censored at publication, but three warnings from the Government were enough to secure a paper's suspension or suppression; newspaper proprietors were thus given a powerful incentive to follow the Napoleonic line. The Prefect's powers and dignity in the Napoleonic tradition were much enlarged. He became an effective local despot, and among his functions was that of securing the return in the national elections of the "official candidate", nominated by him. In any case the Chamber had lost most of its powers, and not even its debates could be reported—merely the official summary. Republicanism, bereft of its public voice and of its leaders, was intimidated. The Church and aristocracy alike rallied behind a régime which took care to champion their interests, and which was generally regarded as the happiest alternative to social upheaval.

The numbers of the police were increased and those of the gendarmerie trebled (Bismarck in 1855 reported finding in Paris "more policemen than lamp-posts"), yet it would be inaccurate to call the Second Empire a police state in any modern sense. Neither was it a military dictatorship, despite the implications of the name Napoleon and a generous employment of colourful pageantry. France, during this first half of the Second Empire, remained in the control of civilians; but the control was firm, centralized, and illiberal.

In many respects Napoleon III was fortunate in the hour of his seizure of power. The year 1852 marked the beginning of a new and more prosperous era in the French (as in the British and the German) economy. In that year the Bank of France was able to lower its interest rates, a move which in itself would have been enough to promote rapid expansion. When it coincided with a rise in prices consequent upon the Californian and Australian gold discoveries the economic climate, harsh through much of the earlier decade, began to be sunnier. Investment and the rewards of investment grew. Eager to exploit the favourable situation, Napoleon encouraged and promoted railway development, a national telegraph system, the building of ports and markets, and public works of every kind, culminating in an ambitious and imaginative rebuilding of the centre of Paris, under the direction of its new Prefect, Haussmann. There were, it is true, agricultural troubles—poor harvests, for instance, in the mid-fifties and vineyards ravaged by disease—but by the middle years of the Second Empire (1858–62) the régime could point to prosperity as well as to good order—and even some military success in the Crimea and Italy—among its achievements.

The siesta in the public career of Thiers was therefore lengthy. There was obviously no place for him in the Napoleonic system so long as it was both flourishing and firm in its determination to admit no limitation on its powers. In 1857 a new Legislature was elected, promising to be as docile as its predecessor. Napoleon might reasonably hope that he had securely established his dynasty. It might be parvenu—indeed, he had underlined the fact that it was by taking for his Empress a commoner, the beautiful Spaniard Eugénie de Montijo. The families of the older aristocrats might still keep away from the upstart court at the Tuileries; but Napoleon could fairly claim to be a popular ruler, and the attempt of Orsini upon his life in 1858 only enhanced his popularity. He had, moreover, an heir, a son born in 1856. His armies had defeated those of Russia and Austria, and gained the territories of Nice and Savoy for France. Napoleon entered the 1860's in what seemed a very strong position.

He was, however, a man of contradictions. Deep in his heart he wished to be other than an autocrat. He reminded his ministers in 1859 that the liberal sentiments he expressed in that early book *Des Idées Napoléoniennes* (1837) were not catchpenny ideas but genuinely felt. "My convictions have not changed," he said. He longed to be a liberal; and, indeed, he truly was a sort of socialist and a humanitarian idealist. He would not for ever rest content with the authoritarian Empire of the fifties.

The increasing hostility of Catholic and conservative Frenchmen to the Emperor's Italian policies helped, after 1859, to propel him down a liberal path. It became clear that Napoleon, though he temporized and retained troops to defend the Pope in Rome, was committed to the principle of a united Italy, and therefore to a diminution, at least, of the temporal power of the papacy. The rift between the Emperor and the Catholic Church grew serious. The extreme Catholic paper *Univers* was suppressed and French publication forbidden to Pius IX's encyclical *Quanta cura* (with its ultra-conservative Syllabus of Errors). Was this, then, the moment, when Catholics were angry with him, for the Emperor to turn to his early promises and try little by little to implement them? In these years of 1859 and 1860 he could still grant concessions from strength, not weakness; and so perhaps "forestall the day when concessions would no longer be voluntary". Besides, as Thiers said, it was absurd for France

> to preach liberty, sword in hand to the whole world, to tell the Pope, the King of Naples, the rulers of Tuscany and Modena, and the Emperor of Austria himself, that they were perishing or would perish for having refused sufficient liberty to their subjects

—and then to deny this very liberty to the French. Moreover, Thiers suggested, the fears of red revolution so strong ten years ago had subsided; rigid authoritarianism, if it had been justifiable in 1851, was no longer so in 1860.

Already in 1859 Napoleon had taken the first step, an amnesty for political prisoners and exiles—contemptuously rejected by Louis Blanc and Victor Hugo. "When Freedom returns," said Hugo, "so shall I." But, whatever Hugo might say, during the sixties freedom did begin to creep back. The Chambers were given stronger rights of debate and more control of expenditure; the Press laws were progressively relaxed. Free trade too was introduced from 1860; forced arbitrarily in this case by the Emperor's decision upon French industries which were loath indeed to take on British competition in level fight. The free-trade treaty may have provided a cold douche that was in the long run salutary for French manufacturers, but it was certainly the most unpopular of Napoleon's liberalizing measures, and Thiers, like most of his businessmen friends, was very critical of it. It increased their pressure to demand not merely the right to criticize, but the right to influence society.

The elections of 1863 marked a further stage in Napoleon III's progress towards the Liberal Empire. They were the occasion also of the return of Thiers to active politics; he was elected for a Paris constituency ("*Ce sera un dialogue entre l'Empire et moi*") and in his very first speech stressed the "necessary freedoms" that France must have: the freedom of the individual from arbitrary power; freedom of expression; electoral reform; and the freedom of the electoral majority to govern. (For those with long memories this might well have sounded cool from the man of the Rue Transnonain 'massacre' and the September Laws.) Through 1864 and 1865 he made more such speeches attacking the still dictatorial nature of the régime and its expensive failures abroad—in Mexico particularly, where Napoleon's attempt to gain an imperial foothold was on its way to total and ignominious fiasco.[4]

Until his death in 1865, Morny pressed upon a hesitant Napoleon the impossibility of standing still. From the governmental side he was saying much what Thiers and the Opposition were constantly repeating:

> The elections of 1863 have left only two forces facing one another, the Emperor and democracy. The forces of democracy will grow steadily; it is urgent that we should satisfy them before they carry us away.

This was rather too drastic and too radical for Napoleon, though in 1864 he did press through the legislature a bill legalizing trade

[4] The Mexican adventure was a characteristically Napoleonic attempt to have the best of both worlds: while making liberal concessions at home and displeasing the Catholics, he might simultaneously win back Catholic support by setting up a great Catholic, 'Latin' Empire to set against the dominance of the Protestant 'Anglo-Saxons'.

unions, and there was now infinitely more chance for the Opposition to get its views generally heard. In that Opposition, composed of both conservatives and republicans, Thiers was pre-eminent. Elder statesman now, he was still brimful of confidence and ambition. When he spoke men listened; and he spoke often, denouncing the Government's failures in foreign policy and especially the miscalculation culminating in the Prussian victory of 1866 and the union of fifty million north Germans under Prussian domination, a worse disaster in his eyes even than the union of twenty-five million Italians under the royal house of Savoy, or the loss of lives, money, and prestige in Mexico. In the matter of Italy he sided wholeheartedly with the Catholic party. The House of Savoy had always been France's enemy, and France should never abandon the Pope to its ambitions or "shelter behind Protestant Europe to consummate the ruin of the Catholic Church". No speech he had made since the "vile multitude" outburst of 1850 so endeared him to conservative opinion. More and more over these years Thiers was being heard not merely as a conservative, but as the mouthpiece of a consensus of anti-governmental opinion; even the Left were prepared to forget his record of earlier years and applaud when now he declared:

> We are free, you say? I say to you, we live under dictatorship.

Yet briefly in that winter of 1869–70 it did look as if Thiers might make his peace with the régime after all, for in January 1870 the Liberal Empire seemed at last to have arrived. The administration of Emile Ollivier, inaugurated that month, promised to be the first of Napoleon's governments to enjoy real ministerial responsibility, and Thiers, it seemed, was going to accept this peaceful revolution entire: "The opinions that I represent," he said in the Chamber, "are seated there on the Government benches." But Napoleon's anxiety to rush through another popular plebiscite, his insistence on his own right to appeal to the people over the heads of his ministers, and doubtless, too, the Government failure to make any friendly response to Thiers himself, threw him back with Gambetta among the Opposition. "Between the 1848 Republic and the Republic of the future," shouted the fiery Gambetta to the ministers opposite, "you are merely the bridge, and it is we who will pass over it." And when, the following month, in June 1870, the ailing Emperor, his ministry, and the great majority of the Assembly's members rushed like the Gadarene swine into their war with Prussia over the Spanish quarrel and the Ems telegram,[5] Thiers and Gambetta were among the few who opposed it. It may well be that by his constant public harping on the loss of French prestige abroad he had done as much as anyone to create an excited nationalism that now infected French public opinion. Still, he deplored the declaration of war. Noisily interrupted by the 'patriotic' party, and insulted by the Government's supporters, Thiers pleaded for prudence and for peace. Only the representatives of his erstwhile enemy the Left—men such as Jules Favre, Ernest Picard, Léon Gambetta—applauded him. France, intoxicated by a chauvinistic popular Press, feverish with fear and hatred of the Prussians, ill-led by a weary Emperor and his war-minded advisers, plunged over the precipice into the "terrible year", while outside the house in the Place St Georges the vile but patriotic multitude threw stones at the windows and shouted *A bas Thiers! A bas le Prussien! A bas le vendu!*

The disaster was so sudden that it seemed at the time incredible; afterwards, inevitable. The French armies were numerically inferior, inferior in artillery, inferior above all in leadership. It was unthinkable that, bearing such a name, Napoleon could be anything but commander-in-chief; but he lacked military judgment and in any case was too ill to wield in practice the leadership that was his in theory. When, after early defeats in Alsace and Lorraine, he abandoned his command, he chose as his successor the popular Bazaine rather than the capable Lebœuf; and Bazaine allowed himself to be outmanœuvred and surrounded in Metz. MacMahon in Châlons, his moves determined as much by political as military considerations, was warned that Paris was on the verge of revolution and could countenance no more retreats. He aimed to come to Bazaine's relief, but was overwhelmed at Sedan, 84,000 French troops being taken prisoner, including MacMahon and the Emperor himself. "I never dreamt," wrote Napoleon to the Empress, "of a catastrophe so appalling." Tormented by severe pain, he preserved a grave dignity amid the disaster.

It was September 2nd, the anniversary of Austerlitz and the *coup d'état* of 1851. The following day, Napoleon's telegram announcing the army's capture reached Paris; the day after that, Eugénie,

[5] See pp. 389–392.

officially Regent, fled to Deauville, and so to England. Nobody in Paris questioned the inevitability of revolution. It was merely a question of how, and in whose name. The mob shouting for a Republic invaded the galleries of the Palais Bourbon, but were persuaded by Favre and Gambetta to withdraw and yell themselves hoarse at the Hôtel de Ville. In the Assembly Thiers proposed that, "since the throne was vacant", they should set up a Committee of National Defence. In his view two things were imperative: order in the capital must be preserved, and peace must be made with the enemy. "I cannot approve of any violence, but I cannot forget that we are facing the enemy and that he is near Paris." Like Thiers, Gambetta had resisted the declaration of war, but now he became the leader of those who wished to fight it out to the end. Soon, when the Germans advanced to the outskirts of Paris and invested it, this vigorous and eloquent Radical escaped in a balloon to Amiens and thence to Tours, to organize an Army of the Loire, rouse the provinces, and attempt the unlikely glory of delivering Paris. Thiers, an older, sadder, and soberer man, argued that an immediate peace would prove less crippling than one imposed after a prolonged struggle, which could only end in defeat. Yet while there was a ghost of a chance—if there was a ghost of a chance—to save France, he would try to seize it. In October, therefore, this old man of seventy-three set out on a diplomatic mission which took him in forty days to London, Vienna, St Petersburg, and Florence in a last despairing bid to shake the Powers from their neutrality. Of course he drew a blank. Bismarck had made sure of the Tsar; Gladstone and Granville were unimpressed by Thiers' argument that by her neutrality Britain was repeating in 1870 France's own mistake of 1866. The Italian authorities were happy that French troops had at last been withdrawn from protecting the Pope in Rome, and received Thiers' plan for a Franco-Italian alliance with no interest. Immediately upon his return he obtained a safe-conduct from the Germans to proceed through their lines to Versailles. He had just gone thousands of miles across land and sea, exhausting enough for a septuagenarian, but, he said, this short journey to Versailles, on such a mission, to prepare the ground for an armistice, travelling through burned villages and by shell-pitted roads, was the most painful of all his long life. Rowed back over the Seine close by the damaged Pont de Sèvres by a single infantryman, the tough little man was in tears.

To fill the cup of woe, Metz fell, setting free 200,000 more German troops for other tasks; and although Gambetta roused futile hopes and salved some wounded pride by capturing Orleans, the end came implacably closer. Besieged Paris was beginning to go hungry, and the bombardment was becoming serious. Gambetta might continue to preach *nil desperandum*: "If we do not despair we shall save France"; Jules Favre might proclaim "Not an inch of our land, not a stone of our fortress!" but the Germans were in the riding-seat. They proclaimed their new *Reich* at Versailles in January 1871. The disparity in military strength was now overwhelming, and most Frenchmen inclined to agree with Monsieur Thiers that nothing was to be gained by prolonging the agony. He took no joy in it, but, as he said, he had the misfortune to be right twice, once in July to say there should be no war, and now to say that there must be peace.

On January 28th, with the citizens of Paris shivering in an Arctic temperature and on the verge of starvation, the armistice was signed by Bismarck and Jules Favre. Down in Bordeaux, which was in the process of becoming the temporary seat of French government, Gambetta and his supporters considered that he and France had been betrayed. There was much pressure upon him to set up a patriotic dictatorship, but he went no further than resigning from the Government. Thiers' verdict was hasty and uncharitable: Gambetta he declared to be "a raving lunatic".

Elections were held immediately for a National Assembly to meet at Bordeaux, and it was soon confirmed that the nation's support was for Thiers, not Gambetta. It voted for peace, for a quiet life, for picking up the pieces. It voted for monarchy (whether Orleanist or Bourbon) and against Bonapartism, against republicanism, against heroics. Thiers himself was elected in 26 constituencies (he opted for Paris), and was immediately chosen by the Assembly as "Chief of the Executive Power of the Republic"—President in all but name.

If ever a man went "naked to the conference table" it was Thiers in February 1871 when he met Bismarck, this time to negotiate peace. Altogether 600,000 French troops were prisoner or interned; in France 120,000 remained to face 800,000 Germans. And although Bismarck had his own troubles, Thiers had for months been pressing for peace, so that any threat he might make to renew the war could hardly sound very realistic. Favre accompanied him, but from the French side it was Thiers who led, and Favre afterwards paid him handsome tributes:

> I see him now, pale, agitated, jumping up and down in his seat. I hear his voice choking with vexation . . . his accents at once suppliant and proud. . . . He bore the insolence of M. de Bismarck with incomparable calm and dignity. To him we owe Belfort; I would never have obtained it. . . .

For, when Bismarck proved implacable over Metz, Thiers fought and fought for Belfort (a city which had not yet fallen to the German forces); and when at last Bismarck offered him the choice, Belfort or no victory march into Paris, Thiers had no hesitation: above all, save what territory could be saved, and see the hated invader quickly from the soil of France. In the indemnity negotiations, too, he managed to bring Bismarck down from six thousand millions to five, and flatly refused the insidious offer of a German loan to pay them. France would manage her own debts—and, indeed, one of the triumphs of the Thiers period of power (1871–73) was to be the ease with which a buoyant French economy saw the very large indemnity paid off. What could be done had been done. Resistant during the negotiations, Thiers broke down (Favre tells) and wept in the carriage as they returned.

At this moment he was on a pinnacle of personal prestige. He was the embodiment of good sense, the "necessary man" of conservative France: of the middle and upper classes, of the peasantry, the Catholics, the monarchists and the moderate republicans. All these together constituted the great majority of Frenchmen; there was, however, an important minority who still had a score to settle. This was made up of those among the Parisian working class who had never forgotten the June Days, the closing of the National Workshops and the bloody defeats of 1848; socialist followers of Blanqui and Proudhon (and to a lesser extent Marx), embittered enemies of the bourgeoisie and the Catholic Church; the republican patriots who, harking back to the heroic defence of Paris in 1792, saw Thiers and his government as defeatists and traitors. In any case Paris was Paris. Victor Hugo had written: "She goes her way alone, France follows. . . . Paris decrees an event; France, suddenly summoned, obeys." On March 1st the pride of the great revolutionary city was painfully insulted by the ceremonial entry of German troops; they paraded down a deserted Champs-Elysées draped with black flags. Paris, so recently half-starving, was now seething. There was already existing in the capital an unofficial left-wing Central Committee (soon to adopt the alarming title of the Commune), whose loyalty Thiers had grounds for mistrusting; and when troops that he dispatched to Montmartre to bring back the guns "stolen from the state" fraternized with the mob (who shot a couple of generals), he decided to do what he had once long ago advised Louis-Philippe to do, and what the Austrians had successfully done at Prague in 1848—retire from the capital and subdue it from outside. So began the bitterest and bloodiest of all Paris's many revolutions, and the only one in which the capital failed to impose its will upon the rest of the country.

Thiers was prepared to be ruthless, and he was certainly efficient. He persuaded Bismarck to accelerate the release of French prisoners of war, and accumulated a large army of 80,000 men at Versailles, hurrying on the preparations with strenuous energy. On April 2nd this Army of Versailles attacked, shooting its prisoners. The Commune retaliated by arming itself with hostages; among them the President of the Supreme Court and the Archbishop of Paris (whom Thiers refused to exchange for the socialist Blanqui). Priests and nuns were the object of the Commune's special suspicion and hatred. On the other hand, for 'socialists' (of a sort), the Communards were strangely content to leave alone the Bank of France. They did adopt the Red Flag and the revolutionary calendar, but they were never an organized party, and courage proved no substitute for unity; cleavages among them soon began to appear. Thiers, moreover, had his own numerous army of 'fifth columnists' in the city, especially among the better-off in the western suburbs. The Communards, scenting treason all around them and increasingly desperate, made violent gestures. The Hôtel St Georges was first stripped of those treasures that Thiers had left there (Mme Thiers had taken care of some of the most precious) and then destroyed. (The Assembly later voted a million francs towards its rebuilding.) The column in the Place Vendôme—that symbol of militarism— was pulled down. Far worse was to come from both sides. The Versailles troops, having gained unopposed entry to the city by a gate 'treacherously' opened to them, began on March 21st the systematic reduction of the capital and slaughter of its defenders. During the 'Week of Blood' that followed, not fewer than 20,000 were killed. Thiers' bombardment destroyed much; the Communards added to the ruin by themselves firing the Tuileries, the

Palace of Justice, the Hôtel de Ville, and many more of the finest buildings in Paris. Fifty-six of the hostages were shot, including the Archbishop. "It was a magnificent sight," wrote an eye-witness; "these traitors stretched on the ground made you feel the power of the Revolution. We felt that we were doomed already. We wanted to die in our turn but to avenge ourselves first. . . ."

On their side the Versailles troops, fed on stories of atrocity true and false, took fearful vengeance, slaughtering many of their prisoners out of hand:

> Startled spectators saw with increasing horror the streams of blood that ran without stopping from the barrack gates, and listened to the endless rattle of rifle-fire. . . . The men caught on the barricades expected and received no quarter.

Those prisoners that were not shot or did not have their brains beaten out with rifle-butts were marched, men and women, frightened, bewildered, or insolent, to Versailles where

> smart ladies lined the streets to jeer, to strike the vanquished with their umbrellas, to behave as the gutter women had behaved in Paris. . . .[6]

As *The Times* wrote, a paper as a rule friendly to Thiers:

> The laws of war! They are mild compared with the inhuman laws of revenge under which the Versailles troops have been shooting, bayoneting, ripping up prisoners, women and children during the last six days. . . . The triumph, the glee, the ribaldry of the 'Party of Order' sickens the soul.

In addition to those who had died in the Week of Blood, 36,000 were arrested, 13,450 sentenced to terms of imprisonment, and 7500 deported. No-one could accuse Thiers of softness. It had been an appalling victory.

However, it had been a victory, and Thiers was not one to be apologetic or diffident about it. At Longchamp on the reviewing stand, with his personal escort of cuirassiers, his white hair blowing upright in the breeze, he took the salute of his victorious troops with the keenest relish. He enjoyed supremacy and proposed to hang on to it, whether as first minister of a constitutional king or as president of a Republic. Thiers would rule, rule efficiently and hard-headedly, as a thrifty bourgeois should. For the time being he

---

[6] D. W. Brogan, *Development of Modern France, 1870–1939*, p. 73.

remained a republican among republicans, a monarchist among monarchists; but always he was a Thiers man first and foremost. He held court at Trouville, in his black frock-coat and his small-rimmed spectacles, with his neat short figure and his busy, no-nonsense manner, like a king in his own right. Bismarck called him Adolphe I. Meanwhile the 'legitimate' king, the Bourbon 'Henri V', displayed a lofty inability to come to terms with the national temper of his era. When in July 1871 by-elections were held, the republicans made significant gains. Above all, the republic, as Thiers said, *existed*. It had proved that it could rule, and rule firmly. And perhaps the best defence of all against an extremist republic—the chief bogy of Thiers and of most Frenchmen—might be a prosperous conservative republic: "the republic will be conservative or there will be no republic".

The "Republic of M. Thiers" showed the greatest vigour. A new military law was put through, which was to provide the basis for the French Army until 1914. To meet the challenge of the German system of three years' compulsory service Thiers adopted a five-year term (he would have liked seven or eight)—but with exemptions operated by lot. Those drawing lucky numbers did short service only, and students, priests, and seminarists were exempt altogether. In the economic field Thiers followed typically bourgeois policies; he rejected proposals for an income tax and began the retreat from Napoleon III's free trade towards protectionism. As for prosperity, the record proved astonishing. The disasters of 1870–71 seemed to have had no effect; business confidence could hardly have been stronger. When Thiers, the perfect bankers' minister, announced a 5 per cent loan to pay off the first 2000 millions of the war indemnity it was oversubscribed two and a half times. When in 1872 he came forward for the remainder it was oversubscribed fourteen times. Thus the principal task that he set himself, to see the enemy off the soil of France, was completed: Thiers' proudest title was "liberator of the national territory".

He was, in a sense, too successful. In 1870 he had been "the necessary man". Now his very success quickly rendered him less necessary. A symbol of recovery becomes expendable when recovery is complete. When the urgency of national crisis lessens, the luxuries of party battle grow more attractive. Moreover, the conservatives, for whom Thiers had once represented a guarantee against radical revolution, were by 1873 becoming alarmed at the apparently growing *rapprochment* between him and the party of Gambetta. Thiers, by this time, on pragmatical grounds, had declared firmly for the Republic. For the radicals, little as they liked him, he was the guarantor of the Republic's very existence—since a majority of the Assembly's members were monarchists.

Thiers, monumentally self-confident and self-satisfied, was himself convinced of his indispensability. The President, when he was M. Thiers, *reigned and governed*; there was never a personal power as personal as his, complained a critic. And who, after all, was there to supplant him? There was an Orleanist candidate, Louis-Philippe's son the Duke of Aumale—but then Thiers, as Louis-Philippe's old minister, was a very acceptable substitute for an Orleanist himself. There was Marshal MacMahon, descendant of an Irish refugee and devout Catholic, commander-in-chief in 1871, and a royalist; but by the side of Thiers he was a political simpleton. "He will never accept," said Thiers. "They have no-one."

By 1873, however, the royalist majority had had enough of Thiers. First they removed his presidential power of participating in the Assembly's debates. Then, led by the Duke of Broglie, they contrived his defeat on a motion condemning the government for its insufficient conservatism. And Marshal MacMahon, being persuaded by his wife and the royalists that it was his duty, did to Thiers' chagrin accept the Presidency after all.

With a royalist as President and a royalist majority in the Chamber, nothing now prevented a Bourbon restoration except the stubborn rigidity of the Count of Chambord, who flatly refused to accept the "dishonourable" tricolour, the flag of the Revolution. The moment passed, never to return. "No-one will dispute," said Thiers, "that the founder of the French Republic is *Monsieur le Comte de Chambord*." A republic; it was, after all, as he had long ago said, the form of government that divided Frenchmen least. His misfortune was that at its head sat not Thiers but MacMahon; the paradox, that the basic law of the Third Republic, the Constitution of 1875, was voted with reluctance by a predominantly monarchist Assembly.

Thiers, like Bismarck, that other "indispensable" minister soon to be in a similar situation, never accepted his fall as final. For the remaining four years of his life, combative and cocksure as ever, he schemed to come back, determined to have his revenge on Broglie and MacMahon. More and more in the last years he came to rely on his understanding with Gambetta and the radicals; at least they shared common enemies on the Right. And Thiers looked forward confidently as ever, this impish, perky, and pugnacious man who had begun political life as the *protégé* of the indestructible Talleyrand, to a new tenure of power in which he would be President and Gambetta Prime Minister. But on September 3rd, 1877, suddenly, at the age of eighty, he died.

The contradictions and ironies that had pursued his long career remained with him to the grave. This most redoubtable enemy of the "vile multitude" was buried in that same Père Lachaise cemetery where the last Communards had faced the firing squads six short years before. On its way thither the body of the man who had so pitilessly destroyed them, and whom they had held guilty of every crime, was borne through the working-class quarters of Paris with dignity and honour. A million Parisians lined the streets to pay tribute to this great Frenchman; patriot, savant, and statesman; "liberator of the soil of France; king of the French Republic". He had long been in his way a sort of national monument. The history of the previous age he had written; that of his own he had done more than any other Frenchman to make.

Table of Events

1797.	Thiers born at Marseilles.
1799– 1814(15)	⎱ Rule of Napoleon I.
1814(15) –1830.	⎱ Bourbon restoration.
1823–27.	Thiers' *French Revolution.*
1830.	July Revolution; Louis Philippe of Orleans king.
1834.	Thiers suppresses unrest in Paris and Lyons.
1840.	Support for Mohammed Ali threatens war; Guizot displaces Thiers.
1845–57.	Thiers' *History of the Consulate and Empire.*
1848.	Fall of Louis Philippe; Second Republic; Louis Napoleon President.
1850.	Loi Falloux.
1851.	Louis Napoleon's *coup d'état.*
1852.	Second Empire established.
1854–56.	Crimean War.
1859.	Franco-Austrian War.
1859–70.	Progressive liberalization of Napoleon III's régime; re-emergence of Thiers.
1870–71.	Franco-German War; "Republic of M. Thiers" established.

1871.	German Empire proclaimed at Versailles. Thiers suppresses Paris Commune and negotiates peace.
1873.	Thiers ousted by royalists.
1875.	Constitution of Third Republic approved.
1877.	Death of Thiers.

9

GLADSTONE

(1809-98)

And Victorian Liberalism

Gladstone entered Parliament in 1832, the year of the Great Reform Act, which he fought and feared; he left it in 1894, the most revered and vilified statesman of his age. For sixty-two years he reflects the turmoils and torments of that Victorian Age which is so mistakenly pictured as a period of stability and repose. As a young man he thought he knew the answers to the problems of his day: a stern front against political radicalism and parliamentary reform; the maintenance of the Corn Laws and protectionism; an unbending hostility to all forms of religious observance other than the Church of England, to which (though he was Scottish on both sides of the family) he was intolerantly devoted. But his mind, like that of his master Peel, was too honest and receptive to be confined within rigid political dogmas. The times were rapidly on the move; intellectual and social climates were changing faster than ever before. Political attitudes had therefore to change also. Thus the young man whose maiden speech was made in justification of the slave owners was already voting in 1833 on the side of the slavery abolitionists. The rigid Anglican of the early days, who declared that if the Church of England was good enough for the English it must be for the Irish too, became the man who spoke out against the anti-Catholic panic of 1851 and later disestablished the Anglican Church in Ireland; the man who in 1834 voted against a parliamentary motion to admit nonconformists to the universities survived to rid the universities in 1871 of religious bars. "We cannot," he discovered, "change the profound and resistless tendencies of the age towards religious liberty.... To endeavour to turn them backwards is the sport of children done by the hands of men." The young protectionist became, first under Peel and then after Peel's death, the principal parliamentary architect of free trade in Britain. The opponent of the first Reform Act became the instigator of the second and third, which enfranchised the working class. The man who entered Parliament in 1832 as the Duke of Newcastle's nominee for the semi-rotten borough of Newark was forty years later to extinguish the last traces of landlord control by the Secret Ballot Act. In short, the "rising hope of the stern and unbending Tories" lived to become "the people's William".

Religion and morals were from the beginning his dominant interests. While he was still at Eton he felt that he had a call to enter the Church, and it was his father, a wealthy Liverpool trader and West Indian slave owner, who deterred him, thinking the law provided a career more suitable for the fourth and most brilliant of his sons. (Between John Gladstone and William there existed the closest of bonds; "it tortures me," Gladstone once said, "to think of an inclination opposed to my beloved father.") A resplendent career at Oxford, marked by violently Tory speeches in the Union debates and crowned by a 'double first' in classics and mathematics, helped to propel him into politics. The Duke of Newcastle, by offering him Newark, clinched the issue. At twenty-two the House of Commons claimed him, but this was far from meaning that religion had lost him. For the next decade, inside Parliament and out, Church affairs came first. He earnestly examined both himself and the world and found much to criticize, much to question. Amusements, for instance. There were

> indulgences not essentially linked with sin but opening up many channels of temptation—balls and assemblies for example.

Ever methodical and exhaustive, he proceeded to list in his private diary thirty-nine reasons—a good Anglican number—why such relaxations might be permitted. When he travelled in Italy it was the local sermons rather than the antiquities or scenery that absorbed his critical attention. When one of his brothers proposed to marry the daughter of a Unitarian banker he was beside himself with anxiety and censoriousness. When his sister Helen turned Catholic —and incidentally also became a drug addict—he passionately urged his father to throw her out of the house. (The old man's heart was softer.) His closest friends were men such as Hope-Scott and Manning, who like himself had grown up amid the pieties of Evangelicalism and were now turning towards the High Church and the Oxford Movement. Religion was, as he said, the pole-star of his existence, and his highest ideal was to impregnate politics with morals. He contemplated secular affairs "chiefly as a means of being useful in Church affairs".

So serious and puritanical a young man, strong and handsome as he was, with his deep, flashing eyes and wonderfully well-tuned voice, found courtship difficult. In debating chamber or the House of Commons his majestic periods rolled magisterially forth, but confronted by ladies who were the object of his devotion he was reduced to conducting negotiations through brothers or fathers. To begin with these were abortive. Caroline Farquhar thought "Mr G's ideas with regard to religion more strict than I should like to embrace", while Lady Frances Douglas was reported as reciprocating none of his feelings. At last on holiday in Italy, he laid timid but determined siege to Catherine Glynne, whose family owned Hawarden[1] Castle in Cheshire and had connections with some of the most famous families in England, Grenvilles, Stanhopes, Wyndhams, Stanleys, and Nevilles among them; her ancestors included five Prime Ministers. Gladstone's letter of proposal to his "dear Miss Glynne" deserves to rank as a self-parody of his early style at its worst—all convolution and parenthesis, pomposity and primness. The second paragraph may illustrate:

I seek much in a wife in gifts better than those of our human pride, am also sensible that she can find little in me: sensible that, were you to treat this note as the offspring of utter presumption, I must not be surprised: sensible that the lot I invite you to share, even if it be not attended, as I trust it is not, with peculiar disadvantages of an outward kind, is one, I do not say unequal to your deserts, for that were saying little, but liable at best to changes and perplexities and pains which, for myself, I contemplate without apprehension, but to which it is perhaps selfishness in the main, with the sense of inward dependence counteracting an opposite sense of my too real unworthiness, which would make me contribute to expose another—and that other!

Catherine Glynne, though her answer to this opaque communication was a discreetly temporary negative, was soon, as she claimed, learning by heart (amor vincit omnia) passages from Gladstone's newly published book The State and its Relations with the Church, a severely intolerant, largely unintelligible, and wholly unreadable treatise, which led The Times to call its author a menace to the

[1] Pronounced Harden.

Church and "a repository of puerile and discreditable bigotry".
Gladstone himself later admitted that his mind had been "a dark
place" into which the light had "filtered slowly".

A more direct approach to Catherine Glynne at a Fulham
garden-party elicited a positive response, and in July 1839 the pair
were married, together with Catherine's sister Mary to George
Lyttelton, another scion of the "grand Whiggery". Gladstone's
proved the happiest of marriages: Twenty-one years later his wife
was writing to him—

> I am longing to be with you and look after you. . . . I seem
> to live upon your letters for indeed it is trying to be from you
> especially in your anxious labours

—and at the end of the letter describing the summer beauties of
Hawarden to her husband pent up at Westminster:

> Oh, come down! Not even this loveliness does without you,
> my darling.

Every day when he was away from home he wrote to her, sometime two or three times a day. For fifty-eight years they shared
family happiness and griefs (they had eight children), political
triumphs and disasters. He had found a treasure. Catherine Gladstone was a woman of great sympathy and generosity of spirit.
Lively, warm, humorous—even a little impulsive and eccentric as a
blue-blooded aristocrat could afford to be—she nevertheless shared
essentially all her husband's seriousness, without his solemnity.
There is no doubt that it was she who helped to rub down the sharp
edges of his religious extremism. But her loyalty and admiration
never wavered, and always, good Victorian that she was, she
deferred ultimately to his masculine judgment. Sometimes this involved quite extraordinary difficulty. One of Gladstone's self-
imposed tasks of Christian endeavour was to go out into the streets
of London's West End at night, or into its brothels by day, accost
prostitutes, and try to persuade them to give up their sinful life.
Often he would bring them home, where perhaps Mrs Gladstone
herself would welcome them and assist in the work of rescue. She
never rebelled against the proceedings, which repeatedly led to misunderstanding and scandal—even to violence and blackmail. In
view of the danger to his reputation his colleagues repeatedly
begged him to abandon the work; Mrs Gladstone did not. In any
case she would have known that to ask would be fruitless. On

entering politics he had set aside his opportunity to embrace the full religious life. He must have some alternative or equivalent; nothing, therefore, could make him give up this godly if politically reckless undertaking. In office and out, against all worldly advice, he continued and expanded the work until almost the end of his days.

In 1841 the Whigs were at last 'out', and Peel, so long resisted by the young Queen Victoria, was positively 'in'. Of all Gladstone's predecessors and contemporaries, it was Peel who gave him most, whom he most respected, and in many respects most resembled. They were, both of them, rich sons of the commercial-industrial aristocracy, Britain's new masters. Both were prize scholars at school and university; both were described as "Oxford on the surface, Liverpool below". Each of them, beginning as the strictest of Tories, was hammered by events (economic and Irish events particularly) and by the workings of his reason and conscience into something very different. Both men, in their relations with foreign Powers, disliked the aggressive patriotism of their opponents, Palmerston and Disraeli in particular, and aspired towards peace and conciliation.

Disraeli and Gladstone were generally regarded at this time as the most brilliant of the younger Tories. It would be difficult to conceive of two men more sharply contrasted. Disraeli—Anglican Jew, social and political adventurer, novelist and dandy, charmer and eccentric, 'outsider' who hobnobbed with the landed aristocracy and was eventually adopted by them as leader—was a multi-coloured bundle of contradictions and surprises; verbally subtle, intellectually flirtatious, superficially flippant and cynical; the romantic odd-man-out among Victorian statesmen. He inhabited the same party and parliament as Gladstone, but was of an entirely different and alien universe. Gladstone adjudged him to be without morals, a mountebank. Indeed, his mistrust and hatred of Disraeli was to become permanent and even obsessive, influencing his whole career. (Catherine Gladstone shared her husband's feelings, and the Gladstone children must have heard much family talk about this detestable ogre. Little Mary Gladstone was once playing with another child, who asked, "Is your father a Whig or a Tory?" "I don't know," she answered, "*but Dizzy is a beast.*")

Both Disraeli and Gladstone were hoping for office in Peel's 1841 government, but Stanley (later Lord Derby) refused to serve in the same Cabinet as "that scoundrel" Disraeli, who was therefore cold-shouldered, although both he and his wife wrote begging letters to Peel asking for an appointment. Gladstone, although he fared better and was given office, was nevertheless somewhat disappointed. He was made *Vice*-President of the Board of Trade, with no seat in the Cabinet, and grumbled a little at being "set to govern packages" rather than men. However, working a minimum of twelve hours a day and learning fast, he was soon President of the Board and became in effect Peel's right-hand man in the long and tedious work of reforming and simplifying the nation's taxation. The customs duties on 605 articles were abolished—over half the total—and those on most of the remainder reduced. Thus Peel's and Gladstone's remedy for the prolonged economic depression of 1839–42, the crisis period of the Chartist revolt, was to cheapen the cost of living, and increase consumption. Peel's notorious 'interim' innovation of a small income-tax to tide over the loss of customs revenue was not approved of by Gladstone, though he accepted it as a purely temporary measure.

In all this four years' activity at the Board of Trade the zealot had found that "packages" too were important. He had, moreover, made an immense impression in Parliament and was commonly spoken of as a future Tory Prime Minister. As well as assisting Peel to reform the tariff in the direction of free trade, he had taken through the Commons two important acts which asserted the principle of state supervision of railways and regulated the affairs of railway companies for many years to come. They must run at least one train a day on every line and provide at a penny a mile adequate third-class accommodation with covered seating. To emphasize his concern for the less wealthy passenger (often before this herded in with goods and livestock), and perhaps to satisfy his own passion for thrift in little things (he was an inveterate hoarder of candle-ends and bits of string), Gladstone would often travel third-class himself. So, on occasions, did his wife, to the amazement or amusement of her friends.

The most important budgets of Victoria's reign, marking the transition of Britain from protection to free trade, were those of 1842, 1845, 1853, and 1860. Gladstone was concerned in all of them, in the forties in the Board of Trade and in the fifties at the Treasury as Chancellor. The Budget of 1842 had made his reputation; for Peel's second great Budget of 1845 he again did the preparatory work, and used to say that he regarded it as one of his greatest achievements; but before it was actually introduced he had resigned from Peel's Government. The zealot had again briefly got the upper hand of the financier.

Peel had decided to increase from £9000 to £30,000 the grant which Parliament voted annually for the training of Catholic priests at Maynooth College in Dublin—a grant which Gladstone had already attacked in his luckless book. He now proceeded to wrestle with his conscience, write personal explanations to Peel which Peel could not understand, and make eloquent speeches which, as his speeches so often did, left his hearers exceedingly impressed but quite uncomprehending. "It is always difficult," said Sir James Graham, "through the haze of words to catch a distant glimpse of Gladstone's meaning." The upshot was that he did resign, after much delay, *and then voted, finally, for increasing the Maynooth grant.* The sophistication of his reasoning defeated most, then as now, and did not even impress Gladstone himself in later life: his resignation, he agreed, had been absurd.

Disraeli had written off the career of Gladstone as finished after the Maynooth business, but he was already back in office under Peel for the climax of the Corn Law crisis. Corn and sugar had always been excluded by Peel and Gladstone from their free-trade reforms, sugar to mollify the West Indian planters (Gladstone senior for one) aggrieved by the abolition of slavery, and corn because the protection of agriculture was a fundamental article of belief for a Tory party of landed gentlemen. But Peel and Gladstone, although their wealth had *made* them landed gentlemen, were not wholly and essentially so. They were of Lancashire, and they understood the language of Cobden, Bright, and the Anti-Corn-Law Leaguers. Already, before the failure of the Irish potato crop in 1845, Peel had envisaged the ultimate repeal of the Corn Laws. What the terrible Irish famine did was to deprive him of time—a commodity politically vital to him—time to convert his own followers as Cobden had been recently converting him. There was already, however, a strong element in the Tory party mistrustful of the tenderness shown by Peel and Gladstone towards the manufacturing interests, and Peel's repeal of the Corn Laws (1846), carried with the support of Whig votes, brought the revolt of the true-blue Tories into the open. Led by the racehorse-owner Lord George Bentinck, who "joined in the attack on Peel as though he were a dishonest jockey" and by the Jew Disraeli, whose scathing assault had back-benchers roaring their approval, the country gentlemen turned on Peel and destroyed him.

In a purely economic sense all the hullabaloo about the Corn Laws proved to be much ado about very little. Both sides in the great dispute had apparently been wrong: after repeal the farmers were *not* ruined and the price of bread was *not* significantly reduced. Everything proceeded much as before. But in a political sense 1846 marked a most important new point of departure. The Peelites, those 'liberal'-minded Tories loyal to Peel in his defeat, chief among them Aberdeen and Gladstone, were left as a third party between Whigs and Tories—and the British political system is unkind to third parties (unless like Parnell's Irish Nationalists they are all-conquering on their own territory). Hence within a decade or so there came about a new alignment: on one side the Tories, now properly called Conservatives; on the other the Liberals—that is, the union of the Peelites and the Whigs—with some radical support. The full regularization of the new situation had to wait for the death in 1865 of the Whig leader, Palmerston, who in domestic affairs was sharply conservative. By then the House of Commons was back on its straight-line axis, and W. S. Gilbert was briefly right:

> That every boy and every gal
> That's born into the world alive
> Is either a little Liber-al
> Or else a little Conserva-tive

Until first the Irish and then the Labour Party upset it, it was true. The unquestioned leader of the Conservatives was "that beast Dizzy", and of the Liberals the Peelite ex-Conservative Gladstone.

In 1846 these developments lay some way in the future. For six years after the defeat of Peel, Gladstone, while remaining a Member of Parliament, was out of office. Over this period private affairs occupied most of his time. He always maintained that his five-year-long attempt to extricate the Glynne family from financial disaster provided a tough and valuable apprenticeship for his future work as Chancellor. He never subscribed to the comfortable orthodox view that a finance minister need know nothing about finance.

Mrs Gladstone's brother, Sir Stephen Glynne, head of the family and proprietor of Hawarden, also owned a small farm in Staffordshire which turned out to lie over useful seams of coal and ironstone. There were hopes of fabulous profits, but the company formed to exploit the minerals was ill-managed and it foundered in the 'boom and bust' of 1847–48. Stephen Glynne, a good medievalist and antiquarian, was a wretched businessman, and he had unwisely pledged his Hawarden estate as security for the Staffordshire enterprise, which was now bankrupt with liabilities of £450,000—no mean sum even set against the fortunes of Gladstone and the Glynnes. They agreed to put everything into the struggle to avoid selling Hawarden. For a time it did have to be closed, and some of its land was sold off, but after years of financial retrenchment and contrivance Gladstone managed to save the property, secure the interests of the Glynne family, and put Hawarden itself in trust— Stephen Glynne being a bachelor—for his own eldest son, William. Thus his wife's old home became by dint of his efforts (including the expenditure of £267,000 of his own money) his own home too, by right as well as by adoption. He loved the place almost as much as she, and much of his open-air relaxation came among its thousand acres of park, especially from wielding the axe among his woods and copses. His health was astonishingly good, and so remained throughout his long life. He had muscular strength, as well as apparently unquenchable energy both in private and public affairs. He would think little of a twenty-mile tramp across country in the course of a busy day's work, or sometimes on less strenuous family walks he would like to prove his powers by carrying four of his children on his back.

While Gladstone was busy saving Hawarden he was almost as busy trying to rescue his difficult and unstable sister Helen from the clutches of opium and the Roman Church. (Of the two, Gladstone seemed to have considered the second more dangerous.) Again, his energy was ferocious. At one period his sister, terrified of him, tried to escape into a convent. At another she signified her opinion of the Protestant theologians with whom he pursued her by using their pages for toilet-paper, and Gladstone's outraged tones of protest, on making the discovery, are richly Victorian:

> My dearest Helen, I write to you with the greatest reluctance on a most painful subject . . . circumstances which admit of no doubt as to the shameful use. . . . You have no right to perpetrate these indignities.

Worst of all, Helen Gladstone claimed to be cured of her opium-taking and psychological crises by a Catholic "miracle". In

Gladstone's view his sister had been the victim of a trick which had occasioned "one of those delusions which seduce some minds into superstition". And unfortunately it was not only his sister who strayed from the Anglican path. His two dear friends Hope-Scott and Manning followed Newman on the road to Rome: "dismal events", Gladstone called them; he thanked God that his own Anglicanism remained unshakable. As for his sister, she lived abroad for thirty more years, a mild eccentric, and he never saw her again, but on her death he was careful to claim back her remains for Anglican burial.

Anguish and frustration over the condition of the Church of England, sorrow at the defection of friends, grief following the death of one daughter, worry over the illness of another, wearisome concern over the Hawarden finances—a multiplication of such troubles sent Gladstone off with his family in the autumn of 1850 on what was intended to be a recuperative holiday. It turned out to be much more—more even than the exhaustive summarizing and criticizing of many sermons, which still made up a large part of the Gladstonian recipe for relaxation. He discovered in Italy more than sunshine and sermons; he heard the groans of injustice and smelt the stink of corruption, and his moral indignation was mightily aroused. The Pope's régime was "a foul blot upon the face of creation", that of the Neapolitan Bourbons "the negation of God erected into a system of Government". He attended a political trial and heard the prisoner given a sentence of twenty years in chains. He then managed to visit this same victim, to see with his own eyes and smell with his own nose something of the condition of Naples' dungeons. For a long time he could think of nothing else but the judical crookedness and torture and the "profanation of public religion". Back in England he exploded into print with his *Letter to Lord Aberdeen*, which met a sensational success with liberals and radicals and a corresponding hostility from the "party of order" abroad. Palmerston was so pleased with it that he had copies dispatched to each British representative at European courts with instructions to pass on a copy to his host government. Yet although the shock of Gladstone's Italian discoveries undoubtedly pushed him nearer to his ultimate Liberal destination, his Tory attitudes were still strong. He despised the "impostor" Palmerston, with his demagogic jingoism. He was not even in favour of Italian unity at this stage: it was too abstract a proposition, he wrote to an Italian acquaintance, and "if there are two things on earth that John Bull hates, they are an abstract proposition and the Pope".

However, there was nothing abstract about cutting customs duties, and by the close of 1852 he was back as Chancellor of the Exchequer in Aberdeen's new coalition Government at the practice of that aspect of liberalism—free trade—that he had fully embraced. The Budget of 1853 abolished duties on 123 articles and reduced them on 133 more. Peel's much-disliked income-tax was to be whittled down by stages and got rid of altogether within seven years. Every item of state expenditure, especially military, was strenuously inspected and cheesepared where possible. Low taxation, extreme public economy, unaggressive policies abroad, high prosperity at home: these were the simple principles of Gladstonian finance in those high Victorian days of private enterprise, when the state was thought to have no business with business, except to get off its back and let wealth "fructify in the pockets of the people". On the whole, everybody agreed, with varying degrees of emphasis, proviso, and qualification. Gladstone himself was not *wholly* committed against state intervention in private business—his railway acts are sufficient evidence of that—and the power of the state should be used, he conceded, "to ameliorate social anomalies", in factory acts, for example. These, however, were only some necessary exceptions to the general rule of *laissez-faire*.

Meanwhile the Corn Laws were largely forgotten as, for a generation, the Tory farmers and landowners did better under free trade than they had been doing previously under protection. Fortunately for his financial reputation, perhaps the highest of all among British politicians, Gladstone's era at the Treasury roughly coincided with the last days of unchallenged British mastery in world trade and industry. Britain could afford free trade and, thanks to her preponderant but relatively inexpensive navy, could afford to dispense, on the whole, with large military expenditure. Had it not been for the Crimean War (1854–56), towards which he was less than enthusiastic, the Chinese wars (1856–60), of which he wholly disapproved, and the great Napoleon III scare of 1860, when he stood out strongly against expensive new armaments and fortification,[2] Gladstone might have succeeded in abolishing income-tax altogether. He was still hoping to do so as late as 1873. As for the later, largely socialist, complaint that even under mid-

[2] See under *Palmerston*, p. 254.

Victorian prosperity the nation's wealth was allowed to "fructify" in the pockets of *too small a proportion* of the people, such an argument cut no ice with Gladstone. He many times condemned what he called the "pet idea" of Socialism. He believed in riches, in the opportunity to make them, and in the right to inherit them. (This did not stop him in 1853 extending the legacy duty to include landed property, the first step of many to bring violent protests against him from the great proprietors.) It was not that he was indifferent to poverty, and he certainly considered the wealthy had a duty to be charitable; but the poor's best hope, in his view, lay in a flourishing economy, as little taxed as possible.

He took further important steps in his Budgets of 1860 and 1861, which included a repeal of the paper duties, the so-called "taxes on knowledge", against the strong opposition of the House of Lords and some inside the Cabinet itself. These Budget triumphs, of 1853 and 1860 especially, were grand parliamentary occasions, with their four- or five-hour orations (fortified by Mrs Gladstone's egg-and-wine); and the succeeding plaudits of Members, Press, and public put him right at the centre of the national stage.

In 1853 Gladstone had been a Conservative Chancellor; by 1860 he was a Liberal. The transition had come in 1859, when Palmerston offered him any office he cared to name. As a Peelite who had strong objections to *both* the leaders of the two main parties in the House of Commons he had been in a predicament. If he had loathed Disraeli less he would almost certainly have accepted office under the Conservatives in 1858, but he could stomach him at no price. Palmerston in Gladstone's eyes was little better, but the two of them had one thing at least in common, a desire to aid Italian freedom, and this, said Gladstone, was what first pushed him into the Liberal ranks. "Why, if he can swallow Pam, couldn't he swallow Dizzy?" asked young Lucy Lyttelton, Gladstone's niece. "I don't pretend to be able to answer this."

However, cynics and sceptics—and Gladstone's profuse expression of virtuous and godly sentiments always produced many such —thought they could. Palmerston was seventy-four, Russell sixty-seven; how could Gladstone, an ambitious fifty, fail to become Liberal Prime Minister on their death or retirement? The Conservatives had Disraeli, a mere fifty-four. But even if the motive of self-advancement was there Gladstone was the sort of man who could never have admitted such a thing even to himself. His constant self-examination, however anxious, invariably elicited favourable responses.

By 1859, then, Gladstone was a Liberal, one of the 'triumvirate' (with Palmerston and Russell), never quite accepted by the old Whigs and never fully at home with the Nonconformists.[3] His Liberalism was still in many respects deeply conservative (in that very year 1859 he defended rotten boroughs as the "nurseries of statesmen"); yet his newly found passion for liberty was sincere, and, as Palmerston noted, he genuinely wished to identify himself with "the people". But when in 1864 he made his celebrated declaration that

> every man who is not presumably incapacitated by some consideration of personal unfitness or of political danger is morally entitled to come within the pale of the constitution,

the general principle was so hedged around with Gladstonian qualifications that the speech could be interpreted to mean almost anything or almost nothing. In his speeches he usually managed to leave such loopholes and lines of escape. Was it political craft, or the lingering of inborn conservatism, or the refusal of a subtle intellect to over-simplify? It was all these things at once. Gladstone's speeches were all labyrinth and convolution, parenthesis and proviso. His friend Bright once remarked that they "never sailed boldly from headland to headland", preferring "to hug the coast and follow to its source any navigable river which he encountered". But in 1864 nobody worried about those broad estuaries of qualification; few bothered to read the 'small print'. Gladstone had apparently committed himself to giving the working man the vote.

[3] Sir Philip Magnus in his *Gladstone* (pp. 141–142) quotes a hostile aristocratic view of the Hon. Emily Eden which exactly puts its feminine finger on what so many of the upper classes felt about him:

"I daresay he is very clever, and he is good-natured, doing his best to bring his mind down to the level of mine; but he fails. He is always above me; and then he does not converse—he harangues—and the more he says, the more I don't understand. Then there is something about High Church people that I can't define, but I feel it when I am with them—something Jesuitical—and they never let themselves go. And to complete my list of things, there is an element of parvenuism about him, as there was about Sir Robert Peel—something in the tone of his voice, and his way of coming into a room, that is not aristocratic. In short he is not frivolous enough for me. If he were soaked in boiling water and rinsed until he were twisted into a rope, I do not suppose a drop of fun would ooze out."

Palmerston's death in 1865 cleared the decks for action. When Russell succeeded as Prime Minister, with Gladstone Leader of the Commons, the new parliamentary reform bill promised at first to be only a timid step, involving no redistribution of seats and merely a few modest additions to the franchise. It was the obstruction of the measure by the alliance of Conservatives and conservative Whigs that made of Gladstone something of a popular hero. When Russell resigned, the Derby-Disraeli ministry that followed, aware of the surge of public opinion in favour of giving the vote at least to the male head of the household, decided to "dish the Whigs" (*i.e.*, the Liberals) and introduce their own Reform Bill. This proved to be full of Disraelian subtleties and safeguards, with 'special' franchises to secure Parliament against the dominance of the working-class vote. However, Gladstone in opposition now seized the chance to outmanœuvre Disraeli and so 'dish the dishers' —to the delight of the Radicals and horror of many traditional Whigs. Both Gladstone and Disraeli were more reform-minded than a large body of their followers, and each was to find 'educating' his party a delicate business. Disraeli now, to the disgust of the Tory aristocrats, accepted one Liberal amendment after another and thus transformed the bill. By the time it became law Gladstone and Disraeli between them had by this so-called Second Reform Act (1867) almost doubled the electorate and enfranchised all borough householders.

One by-product of Gladstone's growing liberalism was the severance of his political connection with Oxford University which he had represented for eighteen years. "A dear dream is dispelled. God's will be done!" he wrote in his diary. He found instead a seat nearer home, in South Lancashire, and both there and in the provinces generally he made great efforts to understand and be understood by 'the people'. Until Gladstone's day no leading statesman had ever considered it necessary, or indeed proper, to make speech tours and address mass audiences; that had been left to agitators or to propaganda organizations like the Chartists or anti-Corn Law Leaguers. But now Gladstone in a sense realized those youthful aspirations of his to be a priest and preacher; most of his great popular speeches were in fact secular sermons. And although Queen Victoria might frown and the old politicians disapprove, Gladstone established what every modern politician takes to be axiomatic—that where there is mass voting there must be mass appeal. Gladstone, lacking television, went on circuit and was a huge success. 'The people' loved him, and he succeeded in convincing himself that he loved and understood the people.

On Russell's retirement in 1868 and Disraeli's defeat in the general election Gladstone became for the first time Prime Minister. On the one side his Liberal administration included the Radical John Bright, the very voice of the Nonconformist conscience; on the other, Robert Lowe, the most prominent critic of Gladstone among the old Whigs. Yet it was not a divided ministry; with a large Parliamentary majority and a vigorous leader, it was the strongest government since the defeat of Peel.

The issue on which Gladstone had chosen to fight the election was the disestablishment of the Protestant Church of Ireland; and it was the troubles of Ireland, together with foreign affairs, that were to dominate the remaining quarter of a century of his active political life. The woes of Ireland were ancient and bitter, built upon religious discrimination and economic exploitation. A country five-sixths Roman Catholic (and the remainder mainly Presbyterian) was subjected to the rule and tithe-system of an Anglican Church that represented the merest handful of the population. Land-hunger drove up rents, and landlords, both resident Irish and absentee English, milked the nation of its wealth.[4] Then in the great famine of 1846–47 the Irishman's salvation, the potato, had betrayed him. In that terrible time over three-quarters of a million had starved, and afterwards two millions more, nearly 30 per cent of the population, had emigrated. The landlords' attempts to solve the agrarian crisis by the creation of larger and more viable farms had in turn produced new miseries, new grievances, and new violence. 'Clearances' meant evictions, with no redress; evictions meant despair; despair meant revenge. "Ireland, Ireland," wrote Gladstone to his wife as early as 1850, "that cloud in the west, that coming storm, the minister of God's retribution upon cruel and inveterate but half-atoned injustice." ("Half-atoned"; even in his letters to his wife Gladstone did not "sail boldly from headland to headland"; his wish to be scrupulously fair to his fellow-countrymen mitigates, even in such a letter, the severity of his judgment.) In the sixties his conscience and his intellect both

---

[4] Not all landlords, however, were rich. Many had mortgaged their lands for cash—but of course mortgagees, and agents too, were often more ruthless with troublesome tenants than landlords were.

began to wrestle with these great matters, and for thirty years more they were to continue to be locked in the struggle.

The serious outbreaks of anti-English violence in the mid-sixties—the time of the 'Fenian' disturbances in Ireland, England, and America—made the matter more urgent than ever, and Gladstone worked ferociously at getting to know what the "Irish problem" really was. Among his fellow-Englishmen he found only what John Morley called "a huge and bottomless ignorance". Before the 1868 election he had become certain of one thing: the pre-eminent position of the Anglican Church in Ireland, which he had earlier so passionately defended, was indefensible. It must be disestablished and disendowed. This, he told the electors, was to be the last great stroke that would topple the "upas tree" of Ireland's troubles, "the tall tree of noxious growth poisoning the atmosphere of the land as far as its shadows can extend". He skilfully soothed the Queen's anxieties on the subject, avoided an outright clash with the House of Lords by accepting a compromise on disendowment, and so, finally, disestablished the Church of Ireland. But the poison-tree of Ireland's bitterness was far from being toppled. On the contrary, agrarian outrages increased, and it soon became clear that the Church question had been only one branch, not the trunk, of the tree. Gladstone as a man of religion had perhaps been inclined to overestimate its importance. Certainly if, as he had said on coming to power, his "mission" was to pacify Ireland, then so far his mission had failed.

He turned to agrarian reform. All the many acts passed since the Union of 1800 had been in the landlord's interest; but it became clear to Gladstone—though he had immense difficulty convincing doubters in the Cabinet, landlords themselves, and *laissez-faire* Liberals generally—that the Government must now intervene on the other side, to protect the tenant against the landlord. Again, Queen Victoria was among those difficult to persuade:

> To this great country [he wrote to her] that state of Ireland after 700 years of our tutelage is an intolerable disgrace, and a danger so absolutely transcending all others that I call it the only real danger to the noble Empire of the Queen . . . .

Twice (1870, 1881) Gladstone endeavoured by agrarian reforms to give the Irish peasant a fairer deal. Until 1870, if a tenant made improvements on his holdings and was subsequently given notice to quit, the whole betterment value of the improvement went to the landlord. The tenant faced a dilemma from which he had no escape: either to pay an increased rent or to be evicted. Gladstone's two Land Acts attempted to give him the legal 'ownership' of his improvements and to protect him from eviction except for the non-payment of rent. However, the act of 1870 was a total failure because it did not attempt to fix 'reasonable' rents; such a concept seemed wildly radical to the Liberal mind with its almost religious belief in the sanctity of free contract and its horror of state inter-vention. But in 1881 Gladstone, drawn much further down the road of economic reform than he could earlier have thought possible, did set up government land courts to try to assess fair rents. His Land Act of that year was the most complicated measure that had ever come before Parliament, but he failed again. Unhappily, by that time feelings in Ireland were running so high, distress was so acute, opposition so concerted, violence so endemic, that the scheme never had a hope of working. It is doubtful in any case if it could have done, even if there had been political calm. Gladstone was in effect trying to achieve an end that has since baffled all non-totalitarian governments (and many totalitarian)—how to hold down the cost of a commodity in short supply but heavy demand. In Ireland that commodity was land. Even when the land court fixed a low rent, ways were found to circumvent the decision—for instance, by charging the incoming tenant extortion-ately for his predecessor's improvements. The most fruitful solution of the Irish land question proved in the long run to be the one advocated by Bright in 1870, but rejected by Gladstone and most Liberals as too revolutionary—state loans to farmers to enable them to cease being tenants and become proprietors. It was left to the Conservatives in 1903 to carry through this eventually success-ful piece of public enterprise.

The old walls of aristocratic and ecclesiastical privilege had been dented on many occasions from 1832 onwards, but never breached; Gladstone's first ministry of 1868–74 was now to tear some further very sizable holes in the defences. The Church of England, the Army, the landlord class, the House of Lords, the Civil Service —all these strongholds of birth and privilege felt the blow. It was not privilege itself that offended Gladstone; he was, after all, richly born and in many senses one of the privileged class himself. He approved of democracy only in so far as it would enable the best to emerge from any class; in that sense he always supported the principle of aristocracy, 'the rule of the best'. Moreover, he had none of the passion for social improvement that drove on men like his contemporary Shaftesbury. The 'social problem' left him somewhat indifferent. Destitution concerned him far less than prostitution. The problem of popular education absorbed him only when the vital interests of the Church of England became involved —thus Forster's vital Education Act of 1870 really was Forster's and in no way Gladstone's. As for the great social evil of drunkenness, Gladstone was "against it" in much the same way that Calvin Coolidge was "against" sin; but when it came to steering between the financial interests of the brewers on the one side and the campaign of the strongly Nonconformist temperance movement on the other, it was the Home Secretary, Bruce, who was left in sole charge. "I cannot get him really to interest himself in the subject," complained Bruce. Hence the Licensing of Public Houses Bill, a highly unpopular compromise, was his alone, though Gladstone managed to share with him the unpopularity it provoked. Slum clearance, factory legislation, the position of trade unions, public health, the improvement of sewerage and of water supplies— even where such matters as these were tackled by his administration, they remained departmental matters. Irish and foreign affairs apart, the questions that engaged Gladstone's formidable energies had to do either with religious and moral principles or with the efficiency of government. What disturbed him about the Army and the Civil Service, and about the Church's stranglehold on the universities, was not simply that they were based on privilege, but that the privilege was indefensible: it made for a bad Army, for academically deprived universities, and for a Civil Service unable to perform its vital tasks.

For Gladstone, the first thing about the Civil Service was that it had to be paid. Its numbers should therefore be kept as low as possible, and he was ruthless in cutting them. By age-old tradition its higher posts were in the patronage of upper-class families; Whitehall provided at the public expense a comfortable and not unrespectable haven for cousins unsuited to the Church, or unmilitary nephews, or younger sons without overmuch ability. Not surprisingly, therefore, the Civil Service, where "heavy swells with long whiskers lounged in late and left early", was a byword for inefficiency. To tackle complicated jobs able men often had to be brought in from outside. It had been on Macaulay's recommendation in 1853 that, first, the Indian Service was thrown open to public competition. This "pedantic eccentricity" of competitive examination was then first extended to Whitehall in a small way in 1855. Now in 1870 Gladstone made it the general rule: career was henceforth to be open to talent. Much may be said against examinations, and much has been said against the Civil Service, now swollen to a size that would have left Gladstone amazed and horrified; but it is unlikely that over the past century many reforms in Britain have done more than this one to promote good government.

University reform followed. Oxford and Cambridge had long resisted all parliamentary interference, but since 1852 they had been increasingly obliged by public and parliamentary pressure, and by liberal-minded academics inside the universities, to listen to criticism and accept change. By the time of Gladstone's premiership non-Anglican undergraduates could be allowed to take a bachelor's degree, but until 1871 all lectureships and fellowships remained a Church of England monopoly. The young Gladstone defended this situation; the elderly Prime Minister of 1871 took the final decisive step and abolished all religious tests at the universities.

The British Army a century ago was still living under the *ancien régime*; it could hardly have been farther removed from the spirit of equal opportunity. Its officer ranks were recruited overwhelmingly from gentlemen; it demanded wealth and social status; it revolved round tradition and the rules of etiquette. Not only did commissions have to be bought, but when an officer was promoted he had the right to offer the rank he was leaving to the highest bidder among his subordinates. And although promotion by merit was not altogether unknown, it normally had to be accompanied by purchase—a custom which did rather more for the tone of the officers' mess than for fighting efficiency. Public misgivings had begun with revelations of muddle and incompetence during the Crimean War and grown with the Napoleonic scare of the 1860's; by the time of the Franco-German war there was alarm. By that time (1870) Gladstone's War Minister, Edward Cardwell, had put forward his schemes of reform which, besides proposing to abolish the purchase of commission and rank, made the Commander-in-Chief for the first time subordinate to the political authority of the

Minister of War, introduced a shorter term of service (a lesson from Prussia), and made financial economies by the reduction of colonial garrisons. These reforms were stubbornly resisted by the Army itself, by its Commander-in-Chief the Duke of Cambridge, by his cousin Queen Victoria, and by strong forces in both Houses of Parliament. It soon became plain that the Lords, though they might swallow most of Cardwell's proposals, would never accept the abolition of purchase. Determined to have his way, therefore, Gladstone adopted a tactic which brought upon him many accusations of unconstitutional behaviour: he circumvented the Lords by persuading the Queen to exercise her power to issue a royal warrant. Purchase had been originally legalized by George III's warrant; it was now abolished by Victoria's, whose lingering doubts over the reform itself were more than cancelled out by her pleasure in exercising her royal prerogative. The officers were duly compensated for their loss of 'rights'. So, in Gladstone's phrase, the nation bought back its own army from its own officers.

Friction with the Lords arose again over the secret ballot. For forty years radicals had been demanding a form of voting which would safeguard the weaker against the stronger elector, the tenant against the landlord, the workman against his employer, the shopkeeper against his rich customer, the churchgoer perhaps against his priest. To this reform also, more pressing now that so many workmen had been given the vote, Gladstone was a tardy convert, but once converted he pressed hard. The "people's House", as he called it, must not be obstructed; and the Lords, having once rejected the bill—partly on the interesting ground that secret voting would mean the end of the monarchy—bowed at the second moving. Nobody, it seems, foresaw what the bill would mean to Ireland, where tenants could and did vote in the ballot booths for the new Home Rule Party without fear of landlords' reprisals. Gladstone was putting great power into the hands of the Irish at Westminster just at the time when they were about to gain a new and dynamic leader, Parnell. And when in the following decade Gladstone's second ministry proceeded by the Reform Act of 1884 to enfranchise the *county* householder and thus again to increase the weight of the Irish vote, the effect was profound: the Irish Nationalist Party, bitter, determined, well disciplined, and over eighty strong in the Commons, could make its voice heard with a vengeance.

This later stage of the Irish struggle still lay in the future. Between the two long Gladstone governments were to come the six years of Disraeli (1874–80). Years before his electoral defeat in 1874 Gladstone's first ministry had run into severe unpopularity. Widespread reforms had engendered hostility equally widespread. Nonconformists were angry that the Education Act had buttressed the status and finances of Church of England schools; the powerful drink trade (though they had succeeded in defeating Bruce's original intentions) were angry at the Licensing Act: "better Britain free than Britain sober", especially when sobriety was so bad for business. Trade unionists were resentful that Gladstone's government had re-enacted the most stringent provisions of the 1825 Act forbidding "molestation" and "obstruction" and had left the unions still at the mercy of the law of conspiracy. And every other reform that this reforming administration had fathered had left behind it a wave of resentment from those dispossessed of their old privileges. There were squabbles too within the government ranks, minor ministerial scandals, brushes with the Queen. By-elections were going heavily in favour of the Conservatives, and Disraeli—still the literary romantic even when scoring political points—likened Gladstone and his colleagues on the Front Bench to

one of those marine landscapes not very unusual on the coasts of South America. You behold a range of exhausted volcanoes. Not a flame flickers on a single pallid crest. But the situation is still dangerous. There are occasional earthquakes, and ever and anon the dark rumblings of the sea.

Aware of lost ground, Gladstone decided to take the Exchequer into his own hands again and repeat the wizardry of earlier years with what he called a "palpably beneficial" Budget to win a general election with. Income-tax stood in 1874 at threepence in the pound. With rigorous cuts in military and naval spending, he promised to repeal it altogether and at the same time further to reduce indirect taxes.

The electorate, however, remained unimpressed. Gladstone was, as he wrote, "borne down in a torrent of gin and beer"—blaming principally the Licensing Act, and then the Education Act, for his heavy defeat. He might perhaps have added his foreign policies: he had in general shown an unpopularly pacific and accommodating spirit. Russia had been allowed, under cover of the Franco-German War, to refortify her Black Sea bases in defiance of the 1856

Treaty of Paris, and over three million pounds had been paid to
the U.S.A. Government for the damage done by the British-built
Alabama during the American Civil War. Palmerston and Disraeli
would certainly have drummed up threats of war, if not war itself,
on the first issue, and few but Gladstone would have accepted the
hostile findings of an international court of arbitration on the
second. Reasonableness, internationalism, the avoidance of futile
and expensive gestures of war—such things were all very fine, but
they did nothing to feed the public's hungry patriotic ardour or win
elections.

The defeat of 1874 depressed him. He himself had only just
squeezed in at Greenwich, which he took very hard. He was in
fact as out of love with politics as the electorate was with him.
The grapes were sour: perhaps he should finish with politics. Was
not the "real battle" being fought elsewhere, "in the world of
thought"? The hosts of Midian prowled and prowled around; the
very "belief in God and the gospel of Christ" was being called in
question. Was not his mission now, in his declining years, to carry
the banner for true religion and campaign against the iniquities of
atheism and the Pope?

Gladstone took to religious controversy as some other men take
to drink or women. These were the years when the great evolution
debate was at its height, and Gladstone on that issue was in no
doubt at all; as a fundamentalist Christian he abhorred Darwin,
and still more "Darwin's bulldog", Thomas Huxley. Bishop Wilberforce, the most vocal of the anti-Darwinians, was one of Gladstone's closest friends, and Gladstone rushed vigorously into the
fray. Twelve years later, when he was Prime Minister once more,
he was still engaged in fierce disputation with Huxley and publish-
ing articles to maintain the literal truth of the Genesis story of the
Creation. Then there was the ever-present threat of Roman
Catholicism, against which he wrote an emphatic pamphlet following the "monstrous" declaration of Papal Infallibility in 1870.
(The sales exceeded 100,000.) And there was always Homer, an
area of study which only a Gladstone would have involved in
Christian theology. On this subject, one of his lifelong hobby-
horses, he held views which were at once learned, profuse, and
wildly unorthodox. Incredibly, he held the Greeks to have been
"the secular counterpart of the Gospel", and a chosen people no
less than the Jews. At the Flood, as he claimed to prove from

Biblical texts, they had been spared by divine prescience. In Gladstone's unique judgment the Greeks were the forerunners of Christianity, and the doctrine of the Trinity was clearly adumbrated in Homer. This was a subject on which a very large number of scholars inclined to agree with the famous Dr Jowett of Balliol, who declared that a man who could see the doctrine of the Holy Trinity foreshadowed in the persons of Zeus, Poseidon, and Hades must surely be crazy. But if, in this (to him) vital matter the academic world thought Gladstone a crank he remained an unrepentant and voluminous one.

These classical and theological pursuits and the work of moral rescue which never ceased (and never ceased to put his friends' hearts in their mouths) presented challenging counter-attractions to a defeated politician aged sixty-five. He managed to convince himself, moreover, that his health was in decline, though his doctor pronounced him sound as a bell and he was still capable of felling heavy Hawarden timber and of walking thirty-three miles in a day over the Scottish countryside. In her letters his wife tried to rally him out of his defeatism ("however my poor opinion is so little worth having, so perhaps I need not have said anything"). In January 1875 he positively announced his retirement—upon which the Church of Rome (that "Asian monarchy: nothing but one giddy height of despotism and one dead level of religious subservience") felt the lash of a second vehement onslaught.

This pursuit of "high and sacred ends", punctuated by an occasional elder statesman's intervention in the House, might have remained Gladstone's lot for his declining days. He had, for instance, prepared a substantial packet of theological notes on the subject of Retribution. They remained and remain notes. Methodical always, he wrote on the outside of the bundle: "From this I was called away to write about Bulgaria."

British statesmen of the nineteenth century faced by the 'Eastern Question'—the question of what to do about the disintegration of the Turkish Empire—were obsessed with the fear of a Russian takeover. Turkey must be supported, they felt, because the alternative to a Turkish Constantinople seemed to be a Russian Constantinople. They were not unaware of the inefficiency and cruelty of the Sultan's rule, or unsympathetic to the desire of the Balkan national groups to achieve independence; yet the fear of Russian expansion and hatred of the Tsar's tyranny were such that it was always easy to experience, or to rouse, anti-Russian feeling, while the misrule of the Turks was regarded with indulgence.

During the 1875–76 the Turks' Balkan dominions, from the Adriatic to the Black Sea, were once again disturbed by national revolts, but the characteristically harsh repression that followed was this time reported upon by the London *Daily News*, and official inquiries confirmed that about 10,000 Bulgarian men, women, and children had been slaughtered. This was what took Gladstone from his notes on Retribution. In September 1876 he wrote *The Bulgarian Horrors and the Question of the East*, finished in three days while he was in bed with lumbago. Its message was simple, its success instantaneous. The Bulgarians were Christians; Britain was Christian: a Christian country should have a Christian foreign policy, and Turkey should be forced to give her Balkan provinces independence.

> If anyone asked me [he said in a speech at Blackheath] how I would distribute the spoils, my answer would be this—I would not distribute them at all. These provinces were not destined to be the property of Russia, or of Austria, or of England; they were destined for the inhabitants of the provinces themselves.

For the first time for many years, he felt, there was "a virtuous passion" in the tide of British politics. He caught it at the flood, to the embarrassment of Disraeli's Government, which, though it was itself divided, was certainly more 'Turk' than 'Russian'. Disraeli would have preferred to be able to ignore the Bulgarian atrocities, and when in 1877 Russia declared war on Turkey, defeated her, and approached Constantinople he considered that European peace could be preserved only by Britain threatening Russia with war. Faced by this torrent of Gladstonian indignation Disraeli was not allowed to sweep the moral issue under the bed. The personal antipathy between the two men, always present, was at this time intense. Sometimes Disraeli (now Lord Beaconsfield) attacked with elaborate sarcasm; sometimes his hatred overflowed, as when he wrote to Lord Derby of

> that unprincipled maniac Gladstone—extraordinary mixture of envy, vindictiveness, hypocrisy, and superstition . . . whether preaching, praying, speechifying or scribbling—never a gentleman.

The domestic political passions aroused in Britain by this Near Eastern War crisis were as powerful and prolonged as those generated by any foreign-policy crisis of the past century. (Perhaps only the Suez affair of 1956 divided the nation as fiercely.)

One effect was further to embitter relations between Gladstone and the Queen. In the early days these had been tolerable—loyal respect on Gladstone's side, graciousness on the Queen's. Things had begun to change when Gladstone tried, perhaps tactlessly, to prise his monarch out of her retirement in the Isle of Wight, where she indulged her widow's grief and self-pity for what seemed to him an unwise and inordinate time after Albert's death. Republican sentiments, which Gladstone abhorred, were growing apace, and one of the things that he tried to do was to persuade Victoria to allow the Prince of Wales to become Viceroy of Ireland. The Prince, he thought, might well play on his mother's behalf a bigger part in public life generally. The Queen felt she was being lectured and took offence. According to Victoria, Gladstone could "never understand". He was "tactless", "obstinate", "tiresome"— especially so by contrast with the flattering charmer Disraeli. Now, with Gladstone's intervention in the Balkan dispute, these adjectives were inadequate to do justice to the Queen's feelings; he was "shameful", "disgraceful", "a mischief-maker and firebrand", a "half-madman". "Tyrannical" too:

> The Queen must say . . . that *she* has felt that Mr Gladstone would have liked to *govern* HER as Bismarck governs the Emperor.

Victoria was, of course, passionately pro-Disraeli and pro-Turk. She expressed a shrill desire for a sharp, successful war against the Russians. "Oh," she wrote, "if the Queen were a man, she would like to go and give those Russians, whose word no one can believe, such a beating." And Gladstone seemed to be falling over himself to defend them: by attacking Turkey, he claimed, they were performing a duty which the other European Powers had shirked—an attitude that seemed immoderate not only to his enemies but to many Liberals as well. When Disraeli forced Russia by threat of war to forgo the fruits of her military victory over Turkey and to submit the whole Balkan question to a conference of the European Powers he seemed to have won both at home and abroad a famous victory. Russia's "Big Bulgaria" had been cut down to size and the remains chopped into parts; Cyprus had been taken for Britain; Turkey (once more) had been induced to promise reforms; and a complicated balancing operation completed between great-power rivalries and little-power nationalism in the Balkans.[5] To Gladstone it seemed like Palmerston all over again, only worse: Disraeli had taken the wrong side, cynically exploited the nation's jingoism, taken the country to the brink of war, and had his false triumph acclaimed as Peace with Honour.

Dilke at this time noted that "the ordinary Sunday afternoon diversion of the London rough" was "going to howl at Mr Gladstone" outside his London house. Yet it was Gladstone rather than Disraeli who won the next round, despite Disraeli's Congress of Berlin success, his Garter from the Queen, and his apparent triumph with Press and public. As Disraeli (Beaconsfield) now pressed ahead with his 'forward' imperialistic policy in Afghanistan and South Africa—he had already snapped up a 44 per cent holding of Suez Canal shares, set up a virtual Anglo-French protectorate of Egypt, and presented his monarch with the imperial crown of India—Gladstone threw his daemonic energies into a great onslaught on "Beaconsfieldism", with its "false phantoms of glory". The methods and weapons he used were at that time unprecedented. Rejecting the offer of a safe seat in Leeds, he set his sights on capturing Conservative Midlothian, in his ancestral Scottish Lowlands. His canvassing did not wait for the dissolution of Parliament; disdaining the traditions of gentlemanly electioneering, he hurled at audiences along the railway line from Liverpool to Edinburgh, or in his prospective constituency (and next day, *via* the newspapers, at all Britain), the thunderbolts of his indignation. Disraeli had betrayed justice and Christianity; every voter had it in his power to strike a blow against the impostor and for a more Christian Europe. Beyond Europe, indeed, for a more Christian world:

> Remember the rights of the savage, as we call him. Remember that the happiness of his humble home, remember that the sanctity of life in the hill villages of Afghanistan among the winter snows, is as inviolable in the eye of Almighty God as can be your own.

It was assumed, after the election of 1880 which the Liberals

5 See pp. 363–364 and 401.

won so handsomely, that it was Gladstone's Midlothian campaign that had convinced the electorate and turned the tables on the Conservatives. Disraeli himself thought otherwise, and he was probably right. As he wrote to Lord Lytton, "the distress of this country is the cause and the sole cause of the fall of the government over which I presided". It was the economic depression, he considered, which had betrayed him; the great Victorian boom had given way at last. Business was sagging; unemployment was high; farmers were facing ruin. In such circumstances in a free country governments do not win elections. Even from the Liberal side it is arguable that as much was done by Joseph Chamberlain's new organization of the party machine as by Gladstone's moral crusade.

Whatever the reasons, Gladstone had won, and the Queen's distress was great. She struggled hard to avoid accepting as Prime Minister this man who was now odious to her. Approaching Lord Granville and Hartington, however, she soon discovered that, disapprove as they might of the extremer aspects of Gladstone's recent opinions and behaviour, no prominent Liberal would dare, or even wish, to supplant this leader of theirs who had 'retired' five years back. So Victoria had to put up with her "half-madman". As he was about to set out once more to kiss the royal hand at Windsor on his appointment his wife asked casually if there was anything she could do for him while he was away. His simple answer—"Pray for me"—would seem improbable or insincere on the lips of any other British Prime Minister.

The new government was at first able to show that "Beaconsfieldism" was at an end. The 'forward' policies in South Africa and Afghanistan were reversed. Even when a small British force was defeated by the rebellious Boers at Majuba in February 1881, Gladstone refused to listen to the popular cry for an expedition to wipe out the disgrace. Instead he restored independence to the Boer republics of Transvaal and Orange Free State which Disraeli had earlier annexed. Hopes of reconciliation and amity, however, were ruined by the discoveries of gold, the rush to exploit them, and the restrictionist policies of the Boers.

In the Nile Valley, Gladstone would have liked to pursue a similar policy of retrenchment and disengagement, but events defeated him and in the end played a large part in bringing down his ministry. He had earlier condemned both Disraeli's purchase of the Suez Canal shares and his acquisition of Cyprus, and when anti-European riots broke out in Alexandria in 1881, with 59 killed, he at first tried hard to associate other European Powers with Britain in the restoration of order, much as they were in fact to act in concert later in the parallel 'Boxer' riots in China. Nothing was more un-Gladstonian than a British naval bombardment of Alexandria, followed by a military expedition to crush the Egyptian nationalist revolt; yet this was exactly what he became responsible for. The French, who had collaborated with Disraeli, now withdrew, and no other Power would be involved in the business. Willy-nilly by the fleet's bombardment and General Wolseley's subsequent victory at Tel-el-Kebir in 1882 Gladstone became involved in the processes of "Beaconsfieldism". The impetus of imperialist expansion was too strong to be halted by a mere change of government at home; and, indeed, Gladstone, unlike Bright (who resigned on this issue), was far from being a thoroughgoing pacifist on religious grounds. He even managed to declare in the House of Commons. "We have carried out this war from a love of peace." Humbug and hypocrisy? Self-deception and sophistry? For once it was difficult for the Conservatives to press such criticisms, since it was their policies, largely, that he was carrying out. However, he did continue his refusal to announce a formal British protectorate over Egypt and struggled vainly over the following years to extricate his government from deeper involvement in the Nile Valley. The awkward fact remained that British economic and imperial interests were henceforth more and more concerned with Egypt, where Englishmen were now the real rulers.

The stirrings of Egyptian nationalism had proved not difficult to suppress, but up among the heat and dust of the Sudan a movement was already astir, hostile to Cairo and Christianity alike, fanatically devoted to the Mahdi, or Messiah, of the desert Muslims. An Egyptian army sent to deal with him was annihilated without trace. Accordingly Gladstone's government decided that it would be prudent to withdraw the Egyptian garrisons, totalling 32,000 men, that were scattered vulnerably in these vast and remote areas, and chose General Charles Gordon to reconnoitre the situation and prepare the withdrawal. The appointment was actually made while Gladstone was absent sick at Hawarden, and he personally never saw Gordon, but, of course, his ultimate responsibility as Prime Minister was inescapable. No choice could have been worse, as he freely admitted in later years:

> Gordon was a hero, and a hero of heroes; but we ought to have known that a hero of heroes is not the proper person to give effect at a distant point, and in most difficult circumstances, to the views of ordinary men. It was unfortunate that he should claim the hero's privilege by turning upside down and inside out every idea and intention with which he had left England, and for which he had obtained our approval.

An established popular hero, personally brave and adventurous, politically over-sanguine, accustomed to going his own road, and in his own evangelical-Christian way almost as fanatical as the Mahdi, Gordon slipped dangerously out of the control of his political superiors in Cairo and London. Communications between Egypt and Khartoum, and hence between Gordon and Gladstone's government, broke down. Gordon, instead of sticking to his essentially pacific instructions, began to see himself as a Christian knight-errant; he developed plans for "smashing the Mahdi", and ended by getting himself stranded at Khartoum, while the force that Gladstone at last felt obliged to send to his relief (reversing his previous decision) arrived just too late.

> My own opinion [wrote Gladstone in 1890] is that it is harder to justify our doing so much to rescue him, than our not doing more. Had the party reached Khartoum in time, he would not have come away (as I suppose), and the dilemma would have arisen in another form.

Gordon was dead; and between a dead hero and a living Prime Minister there was not much doubt which way the balance of popular sympathy would swing. Gordon became a martyr and Gladstone a murderer overnight. The Queen, who had earlier been secretly urging Lady Wolseley to persuade her husband the Commander-in-Chief to have a public showdown with Gladstone, was so beside herself with indignation that she sent her Prime Minister a telegram of protest without observing the invariable custom of secrecy (that is, not in cipher but *en clair*). Such venom and hostility coming from such a source used to depress him more than anything else, with the single exception of the condition of Ireland. Already in 1882 he had remarked to his wife, "The Queen will never be happy until she has hounded me out of office", and the next year he confided to Granville—always one of the closest of his friends: "The Queen alone is enough to kill any man."

She was his opponent during this Gordon year of 1884 on another issue—his bill to extend the vote to the householder in the county constituencies, in other words to a large proportion of the rural labourers. The Lords predictably resisted the reform, and the Queen as predictably took their part; they reflected the country's opinion, so she told Gladstone, more truly than the House of Commons. When he continued his Midlothian habit of 'whistle-stop' speeches on his railway journeys Victoria expressed herself as "*utterly* disgusted with his *stump* oratory". But conciliation on this occasion prevailed. Inter-party talks smoothed out points of difference, and the Conservatives were mollified by a second bill (1885) redistributing the parliamentary seats. Thus the 'Third Reform Act' which had at first threatened so ominously, ended with smiles and graciousness all round, and another great step had been taken towards political democracy. The Radicals, who had pressed Gladstone hardest for it—Dilke and Chamberlain in particular—were pleased; both they and the Conservatives stood to gain from the redistribution of the seats. Only the old Whigs were the losers, and hence were increasingly disgruntled with Gladstone. The surprising thing is that nobody seemed adequately to recognize the immense accession of weight that the reform would bring to the Irish vote—which was suddenly trebled.

Ireland; always it was Ireland over the years. After the agricultural depression of the late seventies her anger had grown more bitter, her misery more violent and desperate. As the number of evictions rose the number of agrarian outrages rose too, only more steeply. By 1880 'Captain Moonlight' was in command, with rick-burning, cattle-maiming, and arson over almost the whole country. In that year there were 10,457 evictions and 2590 outrages. Funds were pouring in from emigrants to America and Australia for Davitt's Land League; Parnell was urging what came from its first victim's surname to be known as the 'boycott': anyone taking over a farm from which the tenant had been evicted "should be isolated from his kind as if he were a leper of old".

Forster, Gladstone's Chief Secretary for Ireland, and Lord Cowper, the Viceroy, pressed for a strong Coercion Act and got it, though not without a long and noisy tussle in the House of Commons—Parnell's Irishmen used obstructionist tactics to such effect that one session of the House lasted forty-one hours. The Act, which gave the Viceroy's government power to arrest and detain upon suspicion for an indefinite period, was answered by a rent-strike promoted by the Land League; in its turn this produced the arrest of Parnell and the League's leaders. It was amid such unpropitious circumstances as these that Gladstone's second Land Act went through, with its promise of fair rents assessed by rent-courts and of security against arbitrary eviction. Parnell and the Land League were not unaware of its merits; but they calculated that if so much had been obtained by rebelliousness, yet more concessions could be extracted by still more rebellion. Hence despite the Land Act extremism grew and the tally of political murder rose. After secret negotiations, therefore, a deal was done. Parnell was released from prison in return for his undertaking to try to make the Land Act work. This alleged weakness on Gladstone's part caused the resignation of Chief Secretary Forster, and in his place Gladstone chose Hartington's brother (and the husband of Mrs Gladstone's niece), Lord Frederick Cavendish, a man of liberal principles and one to whom Gladstone was affectionately attached.

On the afternoon of his arrival in Dublin in May 1882 he was stabbed to death in Phoenix Park by political gangsters; murdered, ironically, not because he was Cavendish, the new Chief Secretary (the assassins were unaware of his identity), but because he tried to protect his companion, the Permanent Under-Secretary, who was the man that the gang had marked down. For Gladstone the Phoenix Park murders were a double blow: personal (the family connection was intimate) and political. The hope of pacification in Ireland—the "mission" he had set himself fourteen years before—receded almost beyond hope of attainment.

By Christmas 1884 Gladstone knew in his own mind that Ireland would have to have Home Rule, but this potentially dangerous private decision remained private. Secret communication with Parnell led nowhere; the Irish leader seemed consumed by a cold hatred of the "hypocrite" Gladstone, and calculated that, in any case, even if Gladstone were genuinely converted to Home Rule, his party would never follow him. So it was Irish votes that brought the Liberal government down in 1885, and for a time Parnell had higher hopes of the Conservatives than of the Liberals. Just as Peel had sold the pass on the Corn Laws, might not Salisbury now concede Irish self-government? It was a delusion: Salisbury also remembered Peel in 1846, and had no intention of being knifed by a second Disraeli (in the person perhaps of the ambitious Lord Randolph Churchill). During 1885 Gladstone still hoped, over-sanguinely, for an all-party agreement on Home Rule; he was fully aware of the political dynamite involved in the prospect of a Liberal leader opting for it on his own. Chamberlain visited him at Hawarden and returned unconvinced; eventually it was Gladstone's son Herbert, M.P. for Leeds, who publicly referred to his father's conversion and thus unintentionally cast the die.

In February 1886 Gladstone, after a brief Conservative interlude, was Prime Minister for the third time, wholly absorbed in Irish affairs and committed to a policy which frightened most British opinion, including much Liberal opinion, on grounds both political and religious. To give a large measure of independence to a hostile Ireland was felt to be folly on the grand scale, and to give Catholic-ism free political rein ran counter to the religious prejudices of most Anglicans and Nonconformists; Home Rule would mean "Rome rule". In any case had not the Irish by their very ungovernability shown themselves unfit to govern?

Even so, with Chamberlain as ally the thing might have gone through—through the House of Commons at least. But Gladstone had unwisely slighted Chamberlain, much as Peel once slighted Disraeli: Gladstone refused Chamberlain the Colonial Office, which he had asked for. As for Hartington and many of the older Whigs, they had already given warning of their dissent. Old John Bright was hostile too. All Gladstone's eloquence and energy could not carry the Commons or the country with him, or win the general election that followed; and, with Chamberlain leading a breakaway group of 'Liberal Unionists', the Liberal Party was split by the Home Rule issue as the Conservatives had been split by Corn Law repeal forty years before.

Under Lord Salisbury and his nephew Balfour the Conservatives proceeded to give Ireland not Home Rule but resolute rule—coercion on a more or less permanent basis. Gladstone, however—the "old man in a hurry", as Randolph Churchill had called him—had not yet abandoned the struggle. When the Liberals won a small majority in the 1892 election their eighty-two-year-old leader, Prime Minister for the fourth and last time, attacked once more. This time the Commons saw the Home Rule bill through by 34 votes, but the Lords threw it out by a ten-to-one majority. Full of fire and fight, and increasingly radical in his old age, Gladstone would have taken to the electorate the issue of "the Peers versus the People", as Lloyd George was soon to do, but his colleagues had no enthusiasm for this particular fight. Indeed on the Irish problem at this time the People and the Peers were not so far apart. Another nearly thirty years—years, especially towards the close, of bitter revolutionary violence and counter-violence—had to pass before Ireland achieved its independence, and then, like India in the next generation, only at the price of partition.

Even without a House of Lords crisis, Gladstone's unpopularity among the upper classes did not fall far short of Lloyd George's in 1910. Right into his old age the wildest and most malicious rumours continued to circulate concerning his work for moral rescue, and all in all "the upper ten thousand" (as he described them) hated him more positively than ever in this last decade of his authority; socially to a large extent they ostracized him. Yet his radicalism, however genuine, was always limited. The idea, for instance, of a graduated death duty, being proposed by his col-league Harcourt, shocked him, as did all new-fangled measures smacking of socialism. His was an older brand of radical thinking, respecting free enterprise and the rights of property, seeking low public expenditure and low taxation, detesting jingoism and foreign adventures, revering above everything religious and political liberty. On a visit to Kiel he watched with foreboding the young Kaiser reviewing the newest German battleships, but alone in his Cabinet refused to support the spending necessary to modernize the British capital fleet. The prospect of a naval armaments race appalled him, and as for Rosebery's wish to send an army into Egypt to overawe the Sultan, he would "as soon set a torch to Westminster Abbey".

Friction mounted. His Cabinet colleagues, while regarding him with the awe proper to the Grand Old Man, were in the main out of sympathy with his views and wished to see him go—though they "blubbered", said Gladstone, when he finally announced his retirement; and, as for the Queen, she left him in no doubt that she would be delighted to be shot of him. She did not consult him about his successor (choosing Rosebery), and her farewell letter, though polite, was cool and curt. At least she was too honest and 'outright' for humbug, but the taste in Gladstone's mouth remained bitter. Even when he died, after five years of retirement and mounting in-capacity, she could not bring herself to express regret in the

Court Circular, and rebuked her son, soon to become Edward VII, for helping to bear his coffin. Mrs Gladstone (who was to outlive her husband by two years) was according to Victoria's Journal "very much upset, poor thing" at her farewell audience in 1894, and

> asked to be allowed to speak, as her husband "could not speak". This was to say, which she did with many tears, that whatever his errors might have been "his devotion to Your Majesty and to the Crown were very great." . . . I am convinced [added Victoria] it is the case, though at times his actions have made it difficult to believe . . . .

"I have no doubt," wrote Sir Edward Grey, the future Foreign Minister, "taking force of character, energy, and intellectual power combined, that Gladstone was the greatest man in whose presence I have ever been"; and the historian Acton considered that of all modern statesmen, "in the three elements of greatness combined—the man, the power, the result—character, genius, and success—none reached his level." In no other period but the Victorian could a statesman of just such pious fervour have flourished; his abundant moral energy throws back a heightened reflection of the spirit of the age itself. His enemies at the time and his debunkers afterwards often declared him a hypocrite, a charge that the morally earnest man must always be exposed to—and neither as ambitious politician nor as party leader could he, of course, be wholly above manœuvring for advantage. Labouchère once said that although one did not mind him having the ace of trumps up his sleeve, one did resent his claim that it had been put there by Almighty God. He was conservative and 'old-fashioned' in much, and in scientific matters ignorant or even obscurantist—which provoked H. G. Wells to jeer that he was "educated at Eton and Christ Church, Oxford, and never recovered from the process". As a classicist he was learned but eccentric. As a politician he had blind spots. But the principles and the worth of Gladstone the man may no more be smiled away than the achievements of the statesman. Even in Ireland, where during his lifetime events defeated him, in the long run his judgment was justified. No other British Prime Minister has ever towered so long and commandingly over his age.

Table of Events

10

TSAR ALEXANDER II
(1818-81)
Reform and Frustration in Russia (with an introductory account of the reign of Nicholas I)

In his last years Tsar Alexander I (1801–25), once upon a time the champion of freedom and enlightenment, the ruler whose first decree had been to abolish torture, who had dreamed of educating the people of Russia and reforming her creaking institutions, had succumbed to religious mysticism and a paralysing fear of political anarchy. He had, as he said, "got to know God and become another man", but not even Metternich had deemed him a *better* man, however much he found the Tsar's conservatism convenient for his purposes. A succession of religious fanatics such as the Baroness Krüdener and the Archimandrite Photius had him under their spell. He propounded the Holy Alliance, threw Russian troops into the quelling of liberal revolutions in Italy and Spain, recast the Russian censorship, and began to reconstruct higher education on all-embracing religious principles. (University teachers of physics and chemistry were to take a strictly "biblical view" of their sciences, and mathematics must advance religion similarly—the triangle, for instance, could be used to demonstrate the mystery of the Trinity.) All young liberals, such as the Tsar had himself been twenty years before, were now obliged to take their ideas underground. Some of these men were Guards officers, members of the minor nobility mostly, who had long discussed the possibility of setting up a constitutional government, of liberating the serfs, and of freeing Russia from the strangleholds of bigotry and obscurantism. Some were freemasons; some were dreamers; a few were republicans. They had no firm political programme, but they had decided on a first step—the assassination of Alexander on the occasion of his coming south to attend a troop review in the summer of 1826. The event did not materialize; the Tsar was taken ill in the autumn of 1825 and passed quietly, but from the conspirators' point of view prematurely, from the scene. New plans had to be hastily improvised.

On Alexander's death a situation arose of characteristically Russian confusion. He had left no legitimate son to succeed him; he had, however, two younger brothers, Constantine and Nicholas. Unknown to Nicholas, Constantine (much the elder) had on contracting a morganatic marriage renounced his right of succession, and from Warsaw, where he was Viceroy, he now proclaimed his brother Nicholas as Tsar. Nicholas, on the other hand, began by proclaiming his allegiance to Constantine, but on being fortified by the dead Tsar's unsealed instructions proceeded to claim the throne for himself. He was not unaware that conspiracy was afoot. There had been leakages and defections, and on December 24th (December 12th according to the unreformed calendar), two days before the officers were due to take their oath of allegiance, Nicholas wrote: "The day after tomorrow I shall be either a sovereign or a corpse." On December 26th the rebels formed up two or three thousand of their uncomprehending troops in Senate Square, St Petersburg, where all morning and afternoon the men stamped their feet to keep warm while their officers waited for the 'insurrection', such as it was, to spread. Some shouted for "Constantine and the Constitution!" (It was said that many thought 'Constitution' to be Constantine's wife.) Meanwhile, a little apart, were lined up other, more numerous, regiments loyal to Nicholas. At last, as December's weak daylight began to fade, one of the rebels broke the delicate stalemate by mortally wounding the military governor of St Petersburg with a pistol-shot, and the arguing gave way to force. With the greatest reluctance Nicholas brought up cannon and cleared the square with grapeshot. There were some scores of dead, including civilians drowned under the broken ice of the Neva, and the first and last attempt in that century at a liberal Russian revolution came to a forlorn end almost before it had started. Over a hundred of the conspirators were exiled to the colonies and mines of Siberia;[1] thirty-six were condemned to death, though five only

[1] In view of their high birth, Nicholas grudgingly permitted them the privilege of being accompanied by their wives if these consented, and

were actually hanged. Had their palace revolution succeeded these men would not have been agreed on what to do next; the whole affair—romantic, idealistic, and naïve—was about as far from Lenin and 1917 as could be. Yet the Decembrists, as they came to be called, developed an importance in the years that followed. They gave birth to a legend. As heroes and martyrs they entered the Russian imagination and became part of the intelligentsia's quest for a freer and nobler nation. And their pathetic rebellion confirmed the new Tsar, a man of parade-ground mentality, in his resolve to rule according to the most rigid principles of autocracy. In his thirty-year reign Russia was confined into a strait-jacket, or, as a contemporary French observer put it, subjected to "the discipline of the camp—it is a state of siege become the normal condition of society."

The mind and character of Nicholas I (1825–55) had none of the contradictions of his father's. He was straightforward, honest, and conscientious; a wintry man, living in lonely austerity within the sombre grandeur of his St Petersburg Winter Palace; in many ways less Russian than Prussian—as, indeed, by birth he predominantly was. It was the military virtues that he assumed to be the highest—courage, obedience, respect for discipline and order. He possessed a powerful sense of occasion, of rising to the challenge of history, and of his own transcendent rôle. When, for instance, in 1831 cholera struck St Petersburg he personally confronted a rebellious and panic-stricken mob and ordered them to submit on their knees to their God and their Tsar, and they obeyed. December 1825 he never forgot. He had personally interrogated the conspirators awaiting death or deportation in the fortress of St Peter and St Paul and extracted confessions from them. Convinced that he was rescuing Russia from disruption and anarchy, he set about locking and double-locking the doors upon the spirit of freedom so that no escape would ever be possible.

The organization of Russia's police under the notorious 'Third Section' of the Imperial Chancellery was at the heart of Nicholas's system of government. The police were of two kinds: one, a uniformed gendarmery organized throughout the whole Empire on military lines; the other, a secret force, the ancestor of a long line of instruments of tyranny that have disfigured Russian history over the

many devoted women did follow their husbands into their grim exile. Nicholas by special decree bastardized any children born to them in Siberia.

succeeding century and a half. Nicholas's spies and informers, women and even children among them, moved everywhere; and the broken remnants of the Decembrist societies were soon hunted down.

Under Nicholas the censorship was all-pervasive—he himself acted as a kind of supreme censor-overseer—yet it was inevitably powerless to stifle either thought itself or the imaginative breath of literature. Every movement of overt criticism was indeed pounced upon, yet poets, novelists, and political philosophers, though they might live dangerously, could never be wholly silenced. Some like the radical Alexander Herzen who lived abroad in exile[2] could in any case not be reached; those like Lermontov who stayed at home were in constant danger, and when he published a passionate poem denouncing the death of Pushkin, who was hounded to death in a duel, he was arrested, court-martialled, expelled from the Guards, and exiled to the Caucasus for a year. When he was killed in 1841 (also tragically in a duel) his collected works were published only in a heavily mutilated form. The novelist Dostoyevsky (a member of a mild idealistic socialist group) was not only condemned to death, but suffered the ghoulish pantomime of being lined up before the firing-squad expecting death, before the reprieve came. He still did five years for 'conspiracy'. When Chaadayev wrote that Russia existed in a kind of no-man's-land between West and East, possessing no distinctive culture of her own, the Tsar on his own personal authority had the author declared insane. It is true that Nicholas laughed at Gogol's *The Government Inspector*, a play which dared to satirize the corruption and extortions of the bureaucracy, but the author did not escape the Tsar's personal censure; and when Turgenev on Gogol's death published a too favourable obituary he also was banished from the capital. The Tsar's Minister of Education, Uvarov, expressed the situation concisely: his business, he said, was to "build intellectual dams to hold up the flow of new ideas into Russia". Ironically, Nicholas I's reign marks the beginning of a golden age of Russian literature and politico-philosophic speculation—the era that began with Pushkin, Gogol, and Belinsky, and ended with Tolstoy and Chekhov. Indeed, Western ideas—liberalism and socialism among them—were so strongly

[2] From 1847. His fortnightly periodical *Kolokol* (*The Bell*), published in London between 1857 and 1865, was smuggled into Russia, where it considerably influenced the progress of reform.

championed that they provided their own reaction among the Russian intelligentsia. 'Westerners' were countered by 'Slavophiles', those who saw hope of national salvation and regeneration in specifically Russian institutions and Russian culture. But they equally with the 'Westerners' condemned the corruption and injustices of their time and were strong for their own brand of change. The dam against new ideas never stood much chance.

Under Nicholas the scope of Russian officialdom was vastly expanded. Uniformed (as also were some other sections of the population, professors and students, for instance) in attire specially designed by the Tsar, the bureaucrats became, with the police, the principal agents of the Tsarist system. There were half a million of them, "a thieving, bullying Tartar horde", as one disgruntled nobleman described them, that "plundered all classes" and produced general discontent. From 1835 they were in complete control of education. They staffed the lawcourts and the offices of censorship, tax-collection, and land-survey. Most of them were wretchedly paid —there is a story concerning two honest provincial clerks who reported for duty only on alternate days, since they had but one pair of boots between them; yet, wielding the state's authority, the bureaucrat had ever-present opportunities for dishonesty and extortion. The courts were a byword for delay and corruption—the more protracted the case, the bigger the chance of bureaucratic profit. Remedy for abuses was unobtainable since legal actions were in secret, and public criticism, except of the oblique literary kind, impossible. Paper-work mounted and cases became self-perpetuating; ten wagon-loads relating to one suit alone once disappeared for ever (with the wagons) on the road from St Petersburg to Moscow. With both police and bureaucracy, the cruellest abuses of power often occurred among those of the Tsar's subjects who constituted religious or national minorities—Jews, Finns, and Asiatics of various races. Officials would consider it worth paying their superior a premium to be sent to Finland; they could still make a good profit on their outlay:

> If the land-surveyor is travelling on business and passes a native village, he never fails to stop there. He takes the theodolite off his cart, drives in a post and pulls out his chain. In an hour, the whole village is in a ferment. . . . The elders come to pay their respects: the surveyor goes on measuring and taking notes. They ask him not to cheat them out of their land, and he demands

twenty or thirty roubles. They are glad to give it and collect the money; and he drives off to the next village of natives.[3]

During the reign of Nicholas the landowning gentry were themselves brought under the jurisdiction of state officials. Many landowners, indeed, were taken into the direct employment of the state, and local initiative and independence were discouraged. This had a beneficent aspect, at least in intention, and Nicholas repeatedly insisted on the obligation of the masters to respect the law in their treatment of serfs; his publication of the massive new code of jurisprudence prepared by Speransky brought to public notice what had long been forgotten or ignored—that although serfs were chattels, they did have legal rights, however slight. It was unlawful, for instance, to punish serfs severely enough to cause death (though many had so perished), and private owners were reminded that for major crimes serfs must not be punished without the knowledge of the Tsar's officials. Nicholas also attempted to further the slow progress of emancipation by mutual consent of serf and master, whereby the better-off peasants by purchasing their freedom could sometimes lighten the weight of mortgage round the landlords' necks, and at the same time by migrating to the towns provide much-needed labour for the workshops of Russia's infant industrial revolution. Again, Nicholas endeavoured to improve the lot and status of the many millions of serfs (some 18,000,000 counting dependants) on his Crown lands. But all these good intentions came to very little.

Serfdom had lain heavy on the conscience of thinking Russians ever since Radishchev had portrayed its inhumanities in the 1790's. The spirit of the Enlightenment ventured tentatively across Russia as it did over the rest of Europe; the French revolutionary ideals of liberty and fraternity struck strong chords in the sensitive Russian soul, and not least in those early days in the soul of Tsar Alexander I himself. The literature of the times is heavy with the consciousness of wrong. And if most of Russia's 100,000 landowners dug in their heels to defend their property rights, many were uneasy. Few would have gone as far as Kropotkin:

---

[3] Quoted in W. E. Mosse, *Alexander II and the Modernization of Russia*, pp. 22–23. Similar instances of blackmail are quoted—for example, when police carted the same corpse from one Finnish village to the next, extorting at each a payment for *not* holding an inquest to discover the murderer.

These were things which I myself saw in my childhood. If, however, I were to relate what I heard of in those years it would be a much more gruesome narrative: stories of men and women torn from their families and their villages and sold, or lost in gambling, or exchanged for a couple of hunting dogs, and then transported to some remote part of Russia for the sake of creating a new estate; of children taken from their parents and sold to cruel or dissolute masters; of flogging 'in the stables', which occurred every day with unheard-of cruelty; of a girl who found her only salvation in drowning herself; of an old man who had grown grey-haired in his master's service and at last hanged himself under his master's window; and of revolts of serfs, which were suppressed by Nicholas I's generals by flogging to death each tenth or fifth man taken out of the ranks, and by laying waste the village, whose inhabitants . . . went begging for bread in the neighbouring provinces, as if they had been the victims of a conflagration. As to the poverty which I saw during our journeys in certain villages, especially in those which belonged to the imperial family, no words would be adequate to describe the misery to readers who have not seen it.

Although serfdom and slavery in Russia had originally been two separate conditions, both law and practice had long blurred the distinction, and the eighteenth- or nineteenth-century serf was in fact the outright property of his master. He could be bought or sold like any other property, pledged as a security for loan or mortgage, given as a present to a mistress, or gambled away over a game of whist. He must pay for his existence either in money or in work, or more probably in both. In areas where labour was scarce in relation to the arable acreage (mostly the good grain areas) the emphasis was on payment in labour; where it abounded, as among the poverty-stricken northern forests, serfs paid more heavily in cash, but had more freedom to farm their own holdings. In the village council (*mir*), where it still continued to function, the peasants were inevitably overawed or dominated by their social and economic superiors. And despite the reforms of Nicholas, masters continued to have virtually total jurisdiction over the 'souls' that they owned. For wrongdoing punishment might vary from a mild flogging to the most extreme brutality; even worse, it might mean surrender to the authorities for deportation to Siberia or a twenty-five-year term in the Army, where discipline was always harsh and sometimes savage. 'Widows' of such unfortunates might remarry after three years; the children were likely to be sent to a special school in preparation for a life—one might say a life sentence—in the Army. Serfs' marriages were at best by the consent of their lords, and often by their direction, for they had, of course, an immediate interest in the processes of natural increase—and not infrequently themselves assisted in them through the persons of the younger women and girls; "half the landowners killed by their serfs," wrote Herzen, "die for their valour on the fields of love." And there was violence in plenty; desperation of one sort or another—land-hunger was probably the greatest single cause—drove many serfs to acts of rebellion, and over seven hundred peasant risings were officially notified in the thirty years of Nicholas's reign alone, half of them needing Army units to be called in before they were put down.

Nicholas revered the memory of his brother Alexander I and was fanatically dedicated to the maintenance of the European system of 'legitimacy' that Alexander had hoped to perpetuate with his Holy Alliance of Christian monarchs. For Nicholas the rôle of Russia was to stamp out the flames of revolution before they could set light to the sacred order of things as they were; to make the world safe for autocracy. When in 1830 the 'legitimate' rulers of France and Belgium were overthrown by revolution Nicholas did not hesitate to propose armed intervention to his brother monarchs, and when they held back was proposing to intervene alone until another revolution nearer home in Poland deterred him. When Russian authority had been forcibly reimposed there and the rebellious forces, led by Polish counterparts of the Decembrists, had been crushed, Nicholas proceeded relentlessly towards 'russifying' the legal, educational, and administrative system of Poland. At conferences held at Münchengrätz and Berlin in 1833, in company with Metternich and his father-in-law of Prussia, he recreated the Holy Alliance and reaffirmed his brother's principles. The revolutions of 1848, when the long-threatening thunderstorms burst all over Europe—the only thrones not threatened were Victoria's and Nicholas's own—gloomily confirmed him in the rightness of his judgment. He was with difficulty dissuaded by his advisers from launching an army of 400,000 across Germany to the destruction of the latest French revolution. His manifesto of March 27th, when all Germany, France, and Italy were in turmoil, ends with the sort of rebuke which had once brought the St Petersburg mob to their knees: "Submit yourselves, ye peoples, for God is with us." For some months the threat of a one-man crusade against democracy

persisted; he warned the Prussians that the establishment of a republic would mean invasion, and in the following year (1849) his
armies did invade Hungary, overthrow the revolution there, and
return the kingdom to the rule and punitive reprisals of the Habsburgs—an action which, he calculated (events proved wrongly),
had earned him Austrian gratitude.

Inside Russia repression and censorship were now redoubled to
the point of suffocation. Newspapers were unable to make any
comment at all on news. Even the Slavophiles, the most 'Russian'
and patriotic of the would-be reformers, were put under permanent
police surveillance, and arrests and deportations were intensified.
More and more, innovations and prohibitions took on a ludicrous
character: for instance, a commission was charged with the task of
examining musical scores to search for conspirators' codes. One
learned work was commanded to remove the phrases "forces of
nature", with its explosive connotation, and another to apologize
for the expression "movements of minds". For Nicholas minds were
not to move—only to learn, respect, and obey.

Since he never fully trusted anyone and found it difficult to delegate authority, he drove himself as hard as any of his subordinates
in the pursuit of his mission. Up early, he would be on the parade-
ground or receiving foreign diplomats by mid-morning, going on to
visit a school or hospital, perhaps, or to grace some public function,
before settling down to the principal business of the day—eight or
nine hours reading state papers or preparing dispatches. He was a
man exhausting himself and his servants in underpinning his vast
house and repairing its ever-widening cracks.

It was the Crimean War that closed Nicholas's age of ice and sent
Russia forward on the turbulent waters of change. The opportunities
and prospects afforded to Russia by the increasing feebleness of the
Ottoman Empire had occupied the diplomacy of the reign almost
equally with fears of European revolution. On his accession
Nicholas had inherited the problems presented by the Greek War
of Independence against Turkey. Throwing overboard his father's
hesitations, he had sent his rickety navy to co-operate with the
Franco-British fleet which destroyed Turkish naval power at Nava-
rino, and the following year his southern armies—or those among
them that survived the scurvy and dysentry and the inefficiencies of
the supply system—defeated the Turks, obtained effective control
of the lands that were later to become Rumania, and eventually

enabled him to ratify Greek independence by the Treaty of Adria-nople (1829). Constantinople appeared now to be within Russia's grasp. But Nicholas's policy during the 1830's was to act as the Sultan's 'protector' (for instance, against the attacks of Mohammed Ali in 1833), rather than by military conquest to realize the old Russian dream of the capture of Constantinople; to have Turkey as a dependent state rather than as a military enemy who might be capable of acquiring such powerful allies as Britain and Austria. During the second "Mohammed Ali crisis" of 1839–40[4] he recog-nized in good time the dangerous implications of a war with Britain and prudently collaborated with her (and with Turkey, Austria, and Prussia) to the discomfiture of Mohammed Ali and his backer, France.

However, Turkey was undoubtedly in Nicholas's view "the sick man of Europe", and a visit to London in 1844 convinced him that the Sultan would get no active support from Britain if Russia were to give him the *coup de grâce*. The Tsar now began to speak re-peatedly of this "sick man", reviving once again the old notion of a partition of the Ottoman Empire between the Powers. Britain, however, was not to be drawn. The Tsar was by this time, and especially after his suppression of Hungarian independence in 1849, the big, bad bear of Europe, an object of all good liberals' hatred. In Britain, Palmerston's Britain, the very mention of the tyrant's name was sufficient to throw pacifist radicals into a belligerent frenzy. As to France, Nicholas was quite unable to accept the idea of the upstart Napoleon III as Emperor, and refused to address communications with the time-honoured "*Monsieur mon frère*". *Monsieur et bon ami*" was as far as he would go—which added offence in high places to the already widespread French hostility. Another quarrel, hardly less piffling, arose between the Russian Orthodox Church and the Catholics (in this case French) over the guardianship of the Holy Places in Jerusalem, and was allowed over the years 1851–53 to escalate into a full-scale Russo-French squabble. Finally, the claim was pressed by Nicholas that his was the right to 'protect' all the Orthodox Christians within the Turkish domains.

Step by step he stumbled slowly towards the Crimean War. First, as the protector of the Christians, he moved his forces for-ward into Moldavia and Wallachia (the 'Danubian principalities'

[4] See pp. 237–239 and 272.

—modern Rumania). In reply, Britain and France sent their navies to the Dardanelles, and Turkey, urged forward by the British ambassador, declared war on Russia. Still Nicholas found it inconceivable that his Holy Alliance allies and fellow-monarchs of Austria and Prussia would fail to support him in his rôle as protector of Christians. In particular Austria; he had subjugated Hungary for her in 1849 and supported her against Prussia in 1851,[5] and he considered he had a reasonable claim on her gratitude. It was not forthcoming: Austria went over to Russia's enemies. Still, if Nicholas had not by this time involved his own pride in the quarrel, and if Britain and France had not been deprived of sane judgment by popular attacks of patriotic war fever, a reasonable settlement could easily have been negotiated. Both sides, however, took up positions from which retreat became difficult, and both sides blundered into a war which, amid much suffering and heroism, was to expose their various military machines as creaking anachronisms. The lack of any railways south of Moscow, the swindling by military contractors, and the general inefficiency of the Russian administration proved in the end more powerful factors than the ineffectiveness and poor leadership of the Anglo-French armies. It turned out that supplies and reinforcements could reach the Crimea more quickly from Britain and France than from Moscow, and "if thousands of British and French soldiers perished of cold and disease in the trenches before Sevastopol, the tracks leading from the centre of Russia were marked by the bones of Russian dead". It has been estimated that altogether 600,000 Russians perished in this war. The scale of the losses, and in particular the failures of organization in the Army, the Tsar's chief pride, struck him hard.

At the onset of the war Nicholas had remarked that Russia's best ally would prove to be the severe winter, as it had been in 1812 against the other Napoleon. "Generals January and February" would be fighting on Russia's side. By February 1855 both armies were indeed suffering harshly. The Tsar that month caught a chill, refused to take proper care of it, and within a few days was dead. Some thought then, and some think still, that he was the victim of despair and hastened his end with poison. However that may be, General February had "turned traitor".

From his deathbed Nicholas, the officer going off duty, handed

[5] See pp. 242–244 and 375–376.

over in correct military fashion to his successor Alexander. "I deliver to you my command"—he habitually referred to the Russian Empire as his command—"although I bequeath you many labours and anxieties." Few monarchs can have been so conscientiously prepared by their predecessor for their future task. Alexander had long had to attend meetings of the Council of Ministers, and become thoroughly familiar with the details of the civil and military administration. He had sat on several of the secret committees—in all Nicholas appointed nine—to inquire into the problems of serfdom. (In general Alexander had taken a landowner's conservative view and given no inkling of what he was later to perform.) Again Nicholas had insisted on his heir undertaking an arduous tour of thirty provinces of the Empire so that he might acquaint himself with conditions of life in "all the Russias" over which he was to rule. It was on this tour that the well-meaning Alexander met some of the surviving Decembrists in their Siberian exile, and afterwards intervened with Nicholas to improve their lot.

The new Tsar was aged thirty-seven at his accession, a tall, rather anxious-looking man, full-moustached and side-whiskered after the mid-century fashion; with the look of a soldier about him, and an honest, soulful expression. Everybody seemed to be agreed upon his character: as the Englishman Granville reported home, he was amiable, he was well intentioned, but he was "weak as water". Though his father had taken care of his education and his tutors had given him a fair command of history and languages, he had grown up lacking interest in things scholarly, or artistic, or 'serious'. His inclinations were towards outdoor pursuits—bear-hunting later became a passion—and he was absorbed in the trappings of military life: parades, reviews, and the rest. Some of this worried his principal tutor, the poet Zhukovsky:

> Madam forgive me [he wrote once to the Empress] but an over-developed passion for the art of war, even if indulged in on the parade-ground, would cripple the soul and the mind. He would end by seeing his people as an immense regiment and his country as a barracks.

Zhukovsky, idealist, liberal, and romantic, laboured passionately to implant in his pupil the seeds of humanitarian endeavour and moral integrity, to despise luxury and flattery, to hate the cruelties of war and the sins of the flesh. That such a man could remain for so long to mould the mind of the heir to the throne says something for the Empress's protective influence, for in most respects Zhukovsky's ideas were remote indeed from those of Nicholas. On one matter, however, they could agree—the need for a Spartan simplicity of life. There is something both ludicrous and heroic in the spectacle of first Nicholas and then Alexander, Emperors of All the Russias, living out their godlike lives amid the ornate splendours of the St Petersburg Winter Palace or the lavish magnificence of Tsarskoye Selo, sleeping habitually on their simple camp-beds in their stark bedrooms, like officers on a hard campaign. The 'regimental' side of Alexander II is hardly surprising in view of his upbringing and ancestry; there was after all far more Prussian than Russian blood in his veins. Even if he were no intellectual, neither was Alexander a boor. He was generally thought to be inclined to indolence and wilfulness, but he had plenty of good sense as well as good intentions. At the same time, there was a strong strain of emotionalism in him (tears came frequently), and a tendency to bouts of melancholy.

On a visit to Germany made when he was twenty Alexander had fallen heavily in love with the fifteen-year-old Princess of Hesse-Darmstadt.[6] Since she was not in fact the daughter of the Grand Duke, but only accepted as such to minimize scandal, Nicholas for a time resisted his son's resolve to marry her, only giving way when Alexander threatened to renounce his succession rights.[7] So once more a German princess came to the Russian court (being received into the Orthodox Church and 'russified' as Maria Alexandrovna) and gave a yet further Teutonic injection to the bloodstream of the Romanovs. Alexander's marriage was at first everything a marriage should be, and he was much in love with this wife to marry whom he had had to fight so hard. Her portraits show an intent, serious-faced woman of distinguished beauty. Like that other imported German spouse, Victoria's Albert, she was often suspect as having intellectual pretensions and the wish to influence matters of state. She was for a time both Alexander's 'right-hand man' and prolific wife; strongly reinforced his liberal ideals; fell

---

[6] Hesse-Darmstadt is the ancestral family of the Battenbergs or Mountbattens.

[7] This account of Nicholas's opposition is strenuously challenged by E. M. Almedingen, in her *Emperor Alexander II*, as lacking documentary support. Her version is that Nicholas opposed the match because he thought he had reason to suspect congenital malformation which would prevent the princess from having children. In the event she had eight.

out of favour when Alexander's infidelities grew too much for her to stomach; climbed back by learning to suffer them silently; and finally, a sick and slighted woman, was to end her days the object of general sympathy.

Although there was much talk upon Alexander's accession in 1855 of a new age dawning and intense hopeful speculation concerning the new Tsar's intentions, in particular over the future of serfdom, his immediate tasks were strictly military. Peace talks in Vienna had broken down, and the position of the defenders of Sevastopol grew desperate. At first Alexander insisted on the place being held. When it could no longer be, and the Russians retired to positions outside the fortress, still he insisted on the rest of the Crimea being held. Appealing to the "spirit of 1812"—falsely so, for he refused to allow the enemy to be enticed into Russia's dangerous open spaces, and hence comparisons were idle—he did everything he knew to remind his countrymen that, two years after Napoleon had taken Moscow, Russians had entered Paris in triumph. "We are the same Russians still, and God is with us." But God was with no-one in this wretched war. Prussia, and even Sweden, threatened to join the ranks of the Tsar's enemies; Finland might be lost, or Poland; the Caucasus was in danger of falling to the Turks; and if the fighting continued bankruptcy seemed likely. For months Alexander resisted his advisers' counsel; he refused to accept the available peace terms, which were "dishonourable". In the end, however, there was no escape, and the Treaty of Paris was accepted in March 1856. Russia lost territory at the mouth of the Danube (Bessarabia); the Black Sea was denied to her warships and she was to maintain no fortifications on its shores.

Humiliation in war provides very frequently a prescription for radical domestic change, and on three occasions within a lifetime military disaster switched the course of Russian history. In 1917 the Bolshevik Revolution succeeded the convulsions and agonies of the First World War. Earlier, abortive revolution and subsequent reform had followed hard on the reverses of the Japanese war of 1904. And it was the shock of the Crimean defeat that pinpointed Russia's weaknesses and anachronisms and ushered in the so-called era of the "Great Reforms" of Alexander II.

Even before the war was over there were straws in the wind: permission granted for foreign travel; relaxation of restrictions within the universities and of censorship generally; mitigation of the persecution of religious minorities. In April 1856, as a coronation gesture, there came tax concessions, a three-year suspension of recruiting for the Army, and sundry other signs that heralded a thawing of Nicholas's ice. Yet serfdom remained, "the question of questions, the evil of evils, the first of all our country's problems".

What would this "amiable" Tsar do? It was agreed that he was easily led, but the question was in which direction, and who would win the privilege of leading him? Although immediately after the war ended he released a flood of liberal optimism by declaring to an assembly of the nobility that it was "better to abolish serfdom from above than wait until it begins to abolish itself from below", it remained for a time doubtful whether his will would be radical enough or his resolution sufficient to see this great reform through. Alexander indeed continued to give support to the general idea of emancipation at some unspecified future date, but it was remarked that, in the early days of the reign, the 'old guard' at court, both the previous Tsar's conservative ministers and the new one's hunting companions, continued to enjoy favour, whereas the Empress, who sided with the reformers, by this time did not. She had lost authority by complaining of Alexander's affair with one of her maids of honour, Princess Alexandrine Dolgoruka, and for the first but not the last time there was a complete rift between Empress and Tsar. He had broken the conventions by marrying for love; now he was reverting to them by adopting the traditional diversions of monarchs in general, and Romanovs in particular. Even Nicholas I, that austere man, good husband, and conscientious parent, had taken for granted his right to a succession of mistresses, casually adopted and as casually discarded. What was eventually to cause the St Petersburg court the deepest outrage was not a similar series of infidelities on Alexander's part but his stubbornly long-lived, and it was thought besotted, infatuation for one woman (who also bore the name of Dolgoruka). To marry for love was dangerous; to take, and keep, a mistress for the same reason was both ridiculous and shocking. He was eventually able to make her his second wife, but at this time (1857) when Alexander first met her, she was as yet only a child of ten.

Man of pleasure though he was and remained, Alexander did not lack a sense of responsibility, and, at least in the short run, it was the reformers who won the battle for the Tsar's mind. A majority of his ministers were strong conservatives ("planters", as the exile

Herzen had christened them), but it was the minority who carried the Tsar with them, and the key man among the minority was Lanskoy, Minister of the Interior. Others—Nicholas Milyutin, Rostovstev, and many more—were influential figures behind the scenes, but Lanskoy was the greatest of the ministerial architects of the emancipation. There was a partial reconciliation too with the Empress, always an advocate of the reform; so, as it happened, was her rival Alexandrine Dolgoruka. And both the Tsar's aunt-by-marriage, the Grand-Duchess Helen (another German), his brother, the Grand-Duke Constantine, a much more convinced liberal than Alexander, provided additional stiffening for the royal resolution.

A voluntary, agreed emancipation—Alexander's original conception—soon looked to be an idle hope; the serf-owners were too numerous and entrenched. Alexander accordingly undertook a long campaign of pressure. He himself in 1858 went on a tour of important provincial towns to bring home to the local landlords his determination—that it was not a matter of *if*, but only of *how*, and that he expected them to co-operate in arguing out the formidable complications.

For the abolition of serfdom presented not one problem but a hundred. Economic conditions and legal obligations varied enormously from region to region. Some landowners whose property was expensively mortgaged to the bank were positively anxious to exchange their serfs for cash to repay their loans. Others, those, for instance, in the rich black-earth areas of the south, foresaw ruin. Some were prepared to accept the ending of the legal status of serfdom but firmly against making the freed serfs any grants of land (the Government early made it clear that this idea was unacceptable). And over the whole complex of problems hung an economic imperative: until serfdom *was* ended, and labour made more mobile, the industrialization of Russia must lag far behind that of the world's leading nations. So Russia must abolish serfdom, or remain what the Crimean War had shown to be a forlorn contradiction—a nineteenth-century great Power with a medieval economic and social system, a colossus with feet of clay.

The stifling secrecy of earlier years had given place to a great public debate, and for five years deliberations continued. The conservative owners grumbled and stalled and feared the worst; the Tsar painstakingly dragged them forward, and in 1859 a start was made on the vast task of drafting the statutes of emancipation. By

March 1861 they were complete; the Tsar who had been diagnosed as all amiability and weakness seemed to have confounded prophecy: he would henceforth be known to the world as the Liberator.

The emancipation was a vital step, and its impetus carried Russia forward to further important developments; nevertheless it gave too little, it came too late, and in many respects it proved a failure and a fraud. There were, of course, great gains, men and women[8] were no longer chattels to be bought or sold, or married off against their will, or punished at the whim of their owner. They could in future own property and in theory at least go to law. Even their freedom in law, however, was incomplete, and emancipation gave them something a good deal less that civil equality. Ex-serfs still existed as a legal class on their own. They, and among civilians only they, could still receive corporal punishment. They still could not move at will about the country, being bound by the internal passport system to the *mir*, or village commune, which might refuse permission if they wished to migrate from their locality, or at least might insist on their continuing to pay their local dues. And if they did stay on in the village they did not own the freehold of their new lands; legal ownership lay in the hands of the commune itself, whose business it was to regulate crop rotations, collect taxes, and generally supervise the local economy. Indeed, these old-established peasant communes, which the Slavophiles saw as beautifully and uniquely Russian, gained a new lease of life from the emancipation, taking over much of the rôle that the serf-owner now abandoned; but their influence proved in the main cramping and conservative, and it was a blessing when in 1907 the reforming minister Stolypin at last enabled peasants freely to leave their ancestral villages.

To have abolished slavery was a thing not to be sneezed at, and if the economic terms of the liberation proved disappointing and their consequences sometimes crippling it ought to be remembered that Alexander and his ministers were in no position to distribute largesse. The essential damage had been done in the wasted years before 1861. Russia was poor. Farming was medieval, a struggle for the barest existence; industry was stunted, communications primitive. In much of Western Europe capitalist farming and industrial development had torn up the old subsistence peasant

---

[8] 45 million of them if we include state-owned serfs, emancipated by subsequent edicts of 1863 and 1866.

economy by the roots—often painfully—yet in the process had increased wealth manyfold and laid the foundations of a general benefit to come. But in Russia the feudalism that remained till 1861 made such capitalist expansion impossible. The peasant on the soil, the landowner on his estate, each imprisoned in his own social mould, was each pursuing a way of life which was age-old but in the context of the nineteenth century dangerously unproductive. Alexander's liberation was to give the serfs their lands—or, more accurately, sell it to them. It could not bring them prosperity. In fact, by carving up land still further into smaller holdings it wrote a prescription for chronic undernourishment and perpetuated peasant poverty. Neither was the landowner to benefit; his lands dwindled and his debts soon began to grow again. As for the peasant, the terms of his emancipation so loaded him with indebtedness that he was condemned, apparently for ever, to raise cash by selling cheap grain for export to advanced countries, in order to keep up his payments. So Russia became one of the granaries of Europe while the Russian peasant half starved for lack of bread.

In total, about one-half of the land was allocated to the freed serfs, and in order that the deprived serf-owners should be promptly compensated the state advanced to them four-fifths of the value of their lost property (over half of this sum had been mortgaged to the banks in any case and simply went to wiping out debts), while the peasant paid them the other fifth. The peasant then had to repay to the state the four-fifths that it had advanced, plus $6\frac{1}{2}$ per cent per year interest, from his earnings over the next forty-nine years. The whole arrangement was much like a modern hire-purchase transaction. The purchaser was the peasant, who made a down-payment followed by a very long series of regular payments; the vendor was the landowner; and the state acted as finance house. Where the peasant could not muster his 20 per cent down-payment, he might instead earn his freedom by continuing to serve his master for 30–40 days a year. These proved harsh and bitterly unpopular terms. To make things worse, the ex-serfs had to pay too much for their lands in terms of its actual 1861 value, and they obtained on average no more than four-fifths of the acreage they had previously farmed; in the fertile south only two-thirds. Some four millions were left with no land at all, and many of these went to the towns to work long hours for wretched wages in conditions typical of early unregulated industrial development. It is not surprising that many of those that stayed in their villages felt cheated—in the first four months after liberation there were officially reported 647 cases of peasant rioting, and 499 times during 1861 troops had to be called in. Some thought that things were so bad, the good Tsar must intend a *second* liberation to put things right, and Alexander was obliged to issue a discouraging statement:

There will be no emancipation except the one I have given you. . . . Work and toil. Obey the authorities and the landowners.

But rural discontent rumbled on, and was eventually to play a vital part in the great revolution to come. The standard of living had been desperate enough before 1861; afterwards, especially as the numbers of the rural population continued to rise rapidly, it not only failed to improve but actually deteriorated.[9]

Alexander had twenty more years to live after promulgating the edict for freeing the serfs. They were on the whole years of frustration both for him and his subjects. His accession had engendered, particularly among the liberal intelligentsia, wonderful hopes that could never be fulfilled. Consequently what for decades had been suffered with a shrug of the shoulders as part of the nature of things—the bribed official, the busybody censor, the ignorant jack-in-office, the superstitious priest, the servile peasant, the boorish landowner, the corrupt contractor, the eternal thwarting of intelligence and enterprise and idealism—all this was increasingly found to be intolerable. The ferment of the first year or two of the new reign was turning sour even during the long deliberations over serfdom; the disillusionment that followed, if not stronger among students and intellectuals than among peasants, was certainly more articulate. Underground radical movements in the Army and universities, secretly published journals and pamphlets, even public demonstrations (of sympathy with the Polish nationalists, for example), produced an intensity of anxiety and resentment in Alexander that began to affect his equilibrium. One must be calm, he wrote to his brother Constantine:

[9] Some progress was made in agrarian reform under Stolypin just before the First World War, but land hunger remained unsatisfied. And it was this aching land-hunger of the Russian peasant that took command of the revolutionary situation in the countryside in 1917. Lenin and the Bolsheviks might disapprove of another 25 million peasants seizing their plots, but there was little at that time that they could do about it. Their costly struggle to get the peasants back under state control in collective farms was to come later.

Unfortunately I know from my own experience that this is difficult; I am often seized by an internal trembling when particularly stirred. But one must exercise self-control, and I find that prayer is the best means to this end.

He tried hard to be on the side of the angels, and resisted the more violent suggestions of some of his ministers, who wished, for example, to teach the intelligentsia a lesson by closing the universities for a period. The ringleaders of the student demonstrations at Moscow and St Petersburg were sent to Siberia, but simultaneously Alexander appointed as his new Education Minister Golovnin, one of Grand-Duke Constantine's liberal protégés. These men, Golovnin, Reutern, the brothers Milyutin, over the next few years did their best to transform the major branches of Russian life—education, the legal system, local government, the Army. Perhaps their task was hopeless, and liberal reform was a graft that would never grow on the Russian stock, rooted as it was in autocracy. Perhaps they would have succeeded better if they had had more consistent support from the Tsar. But he was a torn man and vacillated between the opposing camps that were always to be found in his Imperial Council. There would be occasions when the reformers seemed to have his full support; then a change of ministers would signify that the conservatives were again winning influence. There were many reasons why he should worry. There was a general unrest following the emancipation, culminating in a peasant massacre by troops at Bezdna. In Warsaw in February 1861 there were open demonstrations, with many thousands singing patriotic songs in the streets and with students tearing up the cobblestones to hurl at the Russian troops. There began to be talk of what Turgenev, in his novel *Fathers and Sons*, was the first to call "nihilism", the revolutionary gospel of "denial and destruction" so that the country could be built anew. The first widespread and alarming evidence of nihilism came in May 1862 with an epidemic of great fires all over Russia, assumed to be the work of organized incendiaries. In St Petersburg alone two thousand buildings were gutted, and although such destructiveness could only have the effect of deflecting resentment away from the government to the unknown fire-raisers themselves, the general consequence was to heighten the sense that the years of honeymoon between Tsar and people were over. A few months earlier had come the first political trial of the reign, of a poet accused of spreading seditious literature. And, as in the days of the Decembrists, there were elements, it was clear, of disaffection among the officer corps, especially in the junior and middle ranks— in 1862 four officers were sentenced to death for slandering the Tsar and spreading subversive literature, and an N.C.O. for similar offences was given the traditional punishment of being flogged through double ranks,[10] with a twelve-year sentence of hard labour in the mines to follow. The day before the death sentences were to be carried out, Alexander, attending a cadets' passing-out parade, suddenly after a few conventional words astonished his audience and perhaps himself too by spitting out words of warning to these young officers lest they should ever be seduced into disloyalty. One of them recorded how the Tsar's face was full of "blind rage" and "distorted with anger". His words failing, "he violently spurred his horse and galloped away".[11]

The Polish troubles mounted. Alexander, not without justification, regarded himself as a true friend of Poland, and desired 'moderate' reform there as he desired it in Russia. On his accession in 1855 there had been a sudden freshening of the atmosphere, a relaxation of repression, a reaction from Nicholas's relentless russification. Yet, Tsar of Russia, he was also King of Poland, and he repeatedly reminded Poles that so he intended to remain. Any attempt to break away, as the Polish gentry dreamed of doing, would be implacably resisted. *"Point de rêveries!"* Alexander warned them. With the rest of Europe he had recently watched Italians winning their independence from Austria and the Bourbons of Naples. Garibaldi was the most famous of living heroes, and the Poles celebrated his triumphs almost as enthusiastically as the noble failure of their own hero Kosciuszko (crushed by Russia and Prussia in 1794) or the martyrs of the 1831 rising. Alexander's problem was how to be generous without losing the whole Russian empire in Poland. For a time under his representative Wielopolski a genuine effort was made to respect the Polishness of Poland. Elections were arranged for local assemblies and district councils;

[10] The treatment was frequently lethal. A thousand men in two ranks facing inward, armed with sticks "the thickness of a little finger" beat the victim as he paraded between them, once, twice, or perhaps half a dozen times, N.C.O.s watching to see that maximum force was used. The strict rigour of the regulations, still observed during the reign of Nicholas, required the prescribed total of blows to be completed if necessary upon the corpse.

[11] Quoted in W. E. Mosse, *op. cit.*, p. 130.

new Polish secondary schools were to be set up, and a 'Main School' (in essence a university) was established in Warsaw. But this was not nearly enough for the Polish gentry, who dreamed of full independence and the pre-partition frontiers of 1772. Nationalist demonstrations and street disorders began to be almost daily occurrences in Warsaw. Alexander, well meaning but scared, and almost persuaded that immediate martial law was the only sensible policy, made one last effort to reconcile moderate Polish opinion, sending his brother Constantine to Warsaw as Viceroy with Nicholas Milyutin as chief administrator. (Constantine himself thought that this office should have been given to a Pole, but Alexander would not hear of the suggestion.) God apparently did not fashion the Poles to be moderates: they greeted Alexander's representatives with threats and attempted assassinations. Constantine, hoping to make a clean sweep of the worst trouble-makers, ordered a call-up of those young men known to be revolutionaries. They did not wait to be conscripted, but fled to the forests and started the revolt. By 1863 the Polish upper classes, unsupported, however, by the mass of the peasantry, had mounted a full-scale rebellion, which soon settled down to a sort of guerrilla war. Alexander's policy of limited liberalization had failed; nothing remained for him—since to submit to Polish nationalism was unthinkable for him—but to defeat the insurrection first and then to return to his father's policies of repression and russification. Lands confiscated from the rebel gentry were distributed among the Polish peasants. Those of the Catholic clergy who had escaped exile or the gallows officiated under the eyes of the police. Russian Orthodox churches were built in the towns. All instruction and litigation was conducted in Russian. The very name of Poland disappeared from the map; it became the Vistula Region.

The early years of Alexander's reign, once the Crimean defeat was swallowed, had seemed a time of hope and promise, despite the looming difficulties. The achievement of emancipation marks a watershed. After prodigious effort the top of the hill had been reached, and the remaining twenty years, before the violent tragedy that ended them, constitute a dispiriting downhill journey. Yet before frustration finally took hold and the powerful impetus of reform was altogether dissipated, a further set of measures was enacted that did go some way towards renovating and modernizing the old Russia. On paper, indeed, they seem to go a long way; in intention they added up to a considerable revolution; but in practice they were constantly obstructed by conservatism in high places and by fears of opening the floodgates to liberalism and revolution. As with the liberation of the serfs, contradictory forces were at work both in the commissions that prepared the reforms and in the officials who administered or frustrated their working; both in the Tsar's Imperial Council and—most vital of all—in the divided mind of the Tsar himself.

These contradictions are seen in the best known of Alexander's 'great reforms' following emancipation—his creation of a new system of local government intended both to fill the gap left by the alteration of the old squirearchy's status and to undertake tasks that had previously been done wretchedly or not at all—repairs of roads, provisions of village schools, relief of the poor, insurance against fire (important in a land of wooden houses), and the establishment of rudimentary hospital and veterinary services. The new creations (1864) were the *zemstvos*, councils to be elected at both district and provincial level. (In 1870 a parallel system was instituted for the towns.) Alexander's liberals wanted voting power to be shared equally between peasantry, town-dwellers, and landowners, but the conservatives prevailed, and the *zemstvo* voting system became dominated by the landowners. Further, since these councils had no jurisdiction over police or government functionaries, they were always to see their work thwarted by the opposition of hostile officials. The *zemstvo* schoolmaster was liable to find his arrival in the village and his spreading of the light hampered by local men of influence who regarded him as a dangerous innovation and a source of liberal or socialist ideas. Moreover, the *zemstvos* were set up only in some of the provinces of Russia; they never grew into a universal system of genuine self-government. Even so they achieved something, and certainly in their early days they enlisted the enthusiasm of progressive men. They built roads, hospitals, and lunatic asylums; they improved the breed of cattle and horses; above all, they enabled Alexander's reign to show a trebling of the number of village schools—at least a scratching of the surface of peasant ignorance. In the towns too the new councils made progress: in St Petersburg alone the expenditure on education was multiplied by ten during the seventies. And of course all these councils were *elected*, however weighted the voting; inevitably, therefore, they prompted the question: if in local, why not in national affairs?

Must the government of Russia always remain in the hands of a God-given autocrat?

The autocrat's own answer to this was quite unyielding; it must. For one thing, who would protect the poor against the rich if not the Tsar himself, the father of his people? For another, Alexander was sure—and grew surer still as the threat of assassination mounted—that the Tsar's absolutism was the only guarantee against dissolution and chaos.

> I suppose [he said to a reformer] that you consider that I refuse to give up any of my powers from motives of petty ambition. I give you my imperial word that this very minute at this very table I would sign any constitution you like if I felt this would be for the good of Russia. But I know that, were I to do so today, tomorrow Russia would fall to pieces.

Apart from the introduction of *zemstvos*, the principal reforms put through during the sixties by Alexander and his ministers[12] concerned justice, higher education, and the Army. At the same time came also the first important developments in Russian state-assisted railway construction (660 miles of track at Alexander's accession, 14,000 at his death) and the creation from virtually nothing of a banking system. Nicholas's iron curtain blocking off Russia from Western thought and progress was breached all along the line, despite the activities of so many powerful influences in government, police, and Church filling in the breaches.

For centuries justice in Russia had been secret, corrupt, harsh, and arbitrary, and Alexander from the start of his reign had made clear his intention: to institute "just, merciful, and impartial" courts. When Emancipation came it meant that the landowner lost his earlier position as dispenser of justice in his own court; in the rural areas, therefore, magistrates were now to be elected by the *zemstvo* assembly. There was to be trial by jury in criminal cases; judges were to be secure from governmental interference; preliminary examination by magistrates, after the French style, was to take the place of the earlier intimidation by the police. All this ought to have meant a vast leap forward; at last there was in theory equal justice for all, and evidence that it was not merely theory lies partly in the large increase in the number of cases heard. But again the improvements were neither complete nor altogether lasting.

[12] In particular Golovnin (education), Reutern (finance), and Dmitry Milyutin (Army).

Administrative interference with court decisions began to creep back with the years of renewed repression to come, and some of the reforms never reached outlying areas, many of which (Poland, for example) were never to know trial by jury under the Tsars.

The military reforms of Dmitry Milyutin—brother of the Nicholas Milyutin who did so much to prepare the Emancipation—pressed home the lessons of the Crimean failure at much the same time as those of Cardwell pressed home parallel lessons in the British Army. Behind Cardwell stood Gladstone; behind Milyutin, and giving him similarly stubborn backing against the opposition of the aristocratic old guard, stood Alexander. First, in 1863, he signed an edict forbidding the more barbarous forms of corporal punishment. Later edicts reorganized Army training for officers and reduced the length of service in the ranks to fifteen years—six in the active army and nine in the reserve. Conscription, instead of being as before a kind of capricious life-sentence, falling only on "serfs and the lower class of town-dwellers", now became a universal liability, though with the actual call-up depending on a lottery, and with a human system of exemptions and reduced terms of service much favouring the educated classes. Moreover, it was in Milyutin's new army that the illiterate masses at last had an opportunity of learning to read; many more peasants did so from the ranks than from the sparse new village schools. Until Alexander's day it could reasonably be said that the Russian Army was a vast penal institution; not the least of his achievements was to alter all that.

The mid-sixties marked a turning-point for Alexander in his private as well as his public life. It was during 1865 that he, a man now of forty-seven, first laid siege to his eighteen-year-old ward Catherine Dolgoruka. This apparently icy beauty, in whose welfare at the Smolny Academy[13] the Tsar had long shown a more than guardianly interest, he now succeeded in persuading (though not till after lengthy resistance) to become his mistress. She was to prove no ordinary "creature of the hour" of the sort that had consoled him on frequent earlier occasions. From the beginning it seems that he promised to marry her if the Empress (who was tubercular) should not live. Catherine was henceforth his "wife before God". And when after a time she was persuaded into leaving him and lived for a while abroad he sought her out on a

13 This was a school for daughters of the nobility; in 1917 it was to be commandeered as the Bolshevik headquarters in the Revolution.

visit to Paris in 1867, brought her back to St Petersburg, and installed her there. From then he considered himself bound to the Empress only by the demands of etiquette and the necessity of making joint public appearances. Catherine Dolgoruka was later created Princess Yuryevskaya; bore the Tsar three children, all accepted and provided with princely titles; became the source of much bitterness between him and his legitimate children, who flew to the defence of their slighted mother; was blamed, as the "Tsar's gold-haired witch", for half the ills that befell Russia; but remained, aloof to the world, adoring and adored by the Emperor, whose joy and necessity she continued to be during the later, increasing sombre, years of his reign.

In 1865 Abraham Lincoln, that other Liberator, was assassinated, and the event caused Alexander genuine shock and sorrow. Lincoln "was a beacon to the whole world", he wrote; "nothing but courage, steadfastness, and the desire to do good". The following year, as Alexander was stepping into his carriage, an expelled university student named Karakazov fired a shot at him from close range. Luckily, as he fired, his arm was knocked up by a bystander. He was arrested and hanged. Next year (1867) the Tsar visited Paris—it was the occasion when he was rejoined by Catherine Dolgoruka—and while he was driving back with Napoleon III from a military display at Longchamp there was a second attempt upon his life, this time by a Pole. The pressure of these events and the realization that there existed, even among the upper class (Karakazov was of the lesser nobility), a sizable number of would-be assassins provided powerful reinforcement to those influences steering Alexander away from his genuine but always fragile liberalism. He continued to support Dmitry Milyutin, and the vital Army reforms proceeded, but Golovnin was dismissed from the Ministry of Education, and in general from 1867 the conservatives and the police were in the driving-seat. Zamyatnin, the liberal Minister of Justice, was replaced by a police administrator; local magistrates unacceptable to the police were frequently dismissed; ever-mounting restrictions were placed on newspapers and magazines; from 1874 all political cases were tried in special courts, and eventually in courts-martial.

Most of Alexander's constructive work was, then, over and done by the mid-1860's, and a good deal of it was subsequently reversed. It may well be that a liberal autocracy was an inherent contradiction in any case, and it may be argued whether diehard conservatism or murderous terrorism was the greater obstacle to progress in Russia over these years. What is certain is that Alexander, though he was no coward, was never to enjoy security or peace of mind again, or even much privacy, except when he could snatch it with his mistress. When once he protested that even the very words of his private family quarrels were apparently known to the police the answer came: "The words and opinions of His Majesty must be known to our department. . . . Rest assured that the Emperor is the most closely watched person in all St Petersburg."

In the early 1870's some idealistic reformers, many of them university students,[14] inspired by the writings of such men as Pisarev, Lavrov, and Bakunin, and concerned for the sufferings of the peasantry, decided to "go to the people"—hence their name of *narodniki*, or 'populists'—living among them and preaching the gospels of nihilism or anarchism or one of the other current variants of socialist belief. They were greeted with total incomprehension. Sometimes the countryfolk, unable to appreciate teachings which advocated the abolition of private property, of the family, of organized religion, of the state itself, themselves rounded up their revolutionary well-wishers and handed them over to the police. The high-minded 'reason' of these enthusiastic radicals was to cut little ice against the innate conservatism of poverty-stricken peasants. For them the one topic that really mattered was the land, and there private property was the very thing they did want—their own fields at a price that could be afforded. What the missionary 'men of the people' saw as entrenched superstition was to the people themselves simple piety. In so far as the 'state' meant anything beyond tax-collectors—and these they certainly might like to abolish—it must mean the Tsar, who was as remote and mysterious as God himself and as incapable of evil. How could it be right or even conceivable to abolish God or the Tsar?

God and the Tsar; religion and nationalism; these couplings were inextricable. Alexander II's reign, which had begun with the

[14] Or excluded students. Golovnin's successor at the Ministry of Education, Count Dmitry Tolstoy, using compulsory classics to counteract such dangerously modern studies as history, geography, and science, required the curriculum at the gymnasia (or grammar schools) to consist overwhelmingly of Greek and Latin—and the universities recruited exclusively from these schools.

national disaster of the Crimean War, was one of intense national assertiveness and imperial expansion. Defeat in the Crimea was followed immediately by victory in the Caucasus, where the patriot-hero Shamyl and his stubborn guerrillas were finally overcome by 1858, and a conquest that had begun long ago with Catherine the Great was thus completed. But the requests of the Viceroy, Prince Bariatinsky, for men and money to repair the ravages of the long war and develop the potential of the Caucasus fell on deaf ears. Alexander wanted cheap conquests; the imperial finances could not afford Bariatinsky's constructive imperialism. The Caucasus once conquered, Russian expansion took the line of least resistance. In much the same way as Austria's 1866 defeat by Prussia helped to steer her imperialism eastward, so the Balkan blockage enforced by the Crimean defeat diverted Russia's expansion towards Asia, and during Alexander's reign the imperial borders moved forward from the Caspian Sea almost to the Himalayas, and right across Siberia to the Pacific Ocean and the Chinese border. The Khanates of Central Asia could offer scant resistance. Japan had not yet entered the imperialist race, and the outlying northern provinces of the decadent Chinese Empire provided easy prey. Britain with her Indian possessions did constitute a barrier, but north-west of the Himalayas Russian colonization could flow rapidly forward, like a tide coming in over level stretches of sand. So long as the exchequer was not too seriously affected, Alexander was enthusiastic for these developments. As early as 1850 he had sided with the Far Eastern expansionists against Nicholas's more cautious ministers, and his intervention as Tsarevich had served to tip the scales. Soon came the foundation of Vladivostok and, by the Treaty of Peking, the cession by China of the whole region of the Amur and Ussuri rivers. During the 1860's and 1870's, while some Russian forces advanced to the borders of Persia, others succeeded in mastering the whole of Turkestan and occupying the approaches to Afghanistan.

It was here that Alexander's simple delight in the expansion of Russian power had to be qualified by a due regard for the susceptibilities of Britain. Russell and Clarendon, British Foreign Secretaries of the sixties, repeatedly tried to extract undertakings from the Russians that a halt would be called, and mistrust grew as Gorchakov, Alexander's Foreign Minister, justified each new annexation (on much the same grounds, incidentally, that the

British had adduced for their own advance in India)—hostile tribesmen to be subdued, order to be maintained, *et cetera*. Sometimes
the reassurance that no further conquests were contemplated
had already been belied by events before it was received in
London; this was not so much cunning deception on Alexander's
part—he was no Bismarck or Cavour—as further evidence that
he was not himself wholly in control of events. Generals on the
spot acted; Alexander half approved; explanations to soothe
London could follow later. The last thing he wanted was a major
confrontation.

If Britain had been alarmed by the Russians' progress towards
India she was incensed by their *coup* of 1871, when they made use
of Europe's over-riding concern with the Franco-German war
quietly to annul those clauses of the 1856 Treaty of Paris that
demilitarized the Black Sea. This they did in order to "re-establish
their sovereign rights . . . the better to preserve the safety and
dignity of the Empire". Gladstone found the Russian explanation
on this occasion "silky" but "unsatisfactory". Victoria professed
herself "concerned and alarmed", and some newspapers clam-
oured for another war. Alexander, however, very soon had the
backing of a victorious Prussia—now at the head of the new
German Empire—and Gladstone was ready enough, given a face-
saving agreement regulating the size of Alexander's Black Sea
fleet, to accept his *fait accompli*—hailed as a triumph throughout
Russia. The following year Alexander was visiting his uncle in
Berlin to set his country's seal upon the new League of the Three
Emperors (the *Dreikaiserbund* of Germany, Austria, and Russia).
His uncle William I of Germany he liked and respected; towards
Francis Joseph of Austria he entertained both dislike and mistrust
—which would have been greater still had he known that Bismarck
was secretly promising Austria assistance in promoting her
(necessarily anti-Russian) schemes of expansion towards the
Balkans. Anti-British sentiment was as strong in Russia as anti-
Russian sentiment in Britain. It was something of a shock, therefore, for both courts and both publics when Victoria's son, Alfred,
Duke of Edinburgh, fell in love with and persisted in wishing to
marry Alexander's only daughter, Maria. "Was greatly astonished",
wrote Victoria; "felt quite bewildered." So too did Alexander, and
hostile too; but the unlikely marriage went through. The Queen
reported: "I took dear Maria in my arms and kissed her warmly

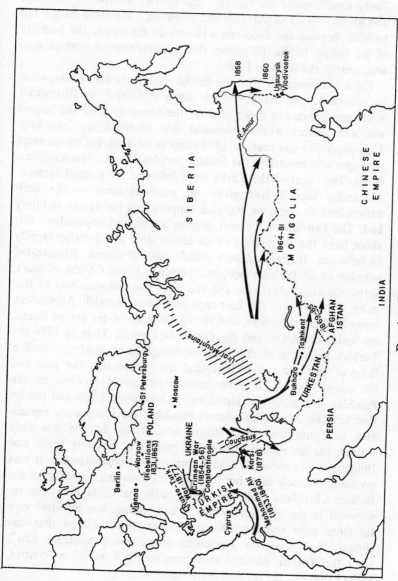

Russian Expansion

several times." Alexander himself came to England in 1874—
"very kind", wrote the Queen, "but terribly altered . . . so thin,
and his face looks so old, sad, and careworn". He could hardly fail
to note, beyond the decorous welcome of the court, the hostility
of the British public, for whom this well-intentioned worried man
was, simply, the Russian Bear.

For a brief space in 1875 the British thought better of him, when
he intervened personally with his uncle William I—to Bismarck's
acute annoyance—in order to deter the Germans from the further
war with France which it seemed that Bismarck was planning.
That particular war scare of 1875 came to nothing, but in the same
year sporadic revolts of the Balkan peoples—Serbs, Montenegrins,
Bulgarians—against the Turks were followed by general turmoil.
Alexander himself had given no encouragement to the Serb
nationalists to count on Russian support, but his agents certainly
had. The Pan-Slav movement, a more active and imperialistic off-
shoot from the Slavophiles of an earlier day, was growing rapidly
in influence. It dreamed of a grand—and, of course, Russian-led
—union of all the Slav peoples, Russians, Poles, Czechs, Slovaks,
Serbs, Croats, Bulgarians, and the rest. The Empress was of this
party. So too were the heir-apparent (the Tsarevich Alexander),
many of the newspapers, and strong elements of the armed forces,
the world of letters, and the Orthodox Church. Then in 1876 the
Turkish massacre of thousands of Bulgarians[15] produced such a
flood of patriotic and ecclesiastical indignation that the Tsar and
his ministers were, however unwillingly, swept forward on the
Pan-Slav stream. It *was* unwillingly. Conventional Russian patriot
that he was, Alexander was no Pan-Slav. He indignantly repudiated as "pure nonsense" British accusations that he was only
waiting for an excuse—under the pretext of rescuing Serbs and
Bulgarians—to move his troops forward to Constantinople. It was
no doubt honestly said; but for a host of Russians liberation of the
Balkan Christians from the Turk, with the Orthodox faith re-
crowned in the city from which it had sprung, was an ideal very
far from pure nonsense. Kaiser William I considered that one
should "feel sorry for Alexander—one cannot condemn him".
since the Russian national movement had got out of his control,
in the hands of "the revolutionary element".

[15] The 'Bulgarian atrocities'. See also pp. 319–322.

To him there remained but one island of refuge—the house on the English Quay, where his "wife before God" could well understand his helpless anguish, and it was to Catherine that Alexander turned again and again through those difficult days when his country went well-nigh mad in welcoming a catastrophe as though it were God's choicest gift.[16]

When in 1877 the Tsar declared war on the Turks the crowds in St Petersburg were jubilant; not so Alexander. As usual he had steered rather unhappily between opposing extremes. He had at first refused to accept the resignation of his pacific Finance Minister Reutern, who argued that Russia's shaky exchequer simply could not stand a war, yet he entered the war apprehensively and with "deep sickness of heart".

The campaign itself showed all the old inefficiencies. The high command was inept and split by disputes, the hospital and commissariat services not much better than in the Crimean War. The men "died with the rugged simplicity of their forefathers". Alexander knew his own limitations better than to take strategic command, but he went south to Bulgaria with his armies. His asthma, an old enemy, was troubling him, and he was ill besides with insomnia and anxiety; Todleben, the Crimean veteran in charge of the siege of Plevna, was as shocked by his appearance as Queen Victoria had earlier been—the Tsar looked "so thin and old".

By the time that the Russians had taken Plevna and moved on to Sofia, Adrianople, and the approaches to Constantinople, it was too late. The European Powers, and in particular Britain, were moving in to frustrate the hard-won victory. The Treaty of San Stefano, which Russia imposed upon the Turks, leaving them Constantinople but little else in the Balkans and creating a large Russian-dominated Bulgaria that stretched to the Aegean Sea, became very soon a dead letter. A British fleet entered the Dardanelles; Britain was swept, as Russia had been two years earlier, by a wave of jingoism; war fever infected all ranks of society, from the excitably militant Queen downwards (Victoria thought Russia "really a most despicable military power"); and at last, at the Congress of Berlin, before which Russia was obliged to submit her conquests, half of them were snatched back from her. In Asia she managed to keep Kars, Batum, and Ardahan, and in Europe Bessarabia at the mouth of the Danube. But Bulgaria was

[16] E. M. Almedingen, *The Emperor Alexander II*, p. 288.

trisected, the southern third being restored to Turkish administration; and Britain and Austria successfully insisted on sharing the fruits of Russia's victory—Austria in Bosnia and Hercegovina, Britain in Cyprus. ("Trust the Englishman", ran one Russian comment, "to land a good fish out of troubled waters.") Alexander and his ministers tried hard in public to sustain the notion that Russia had won what she fought for—after all, the full independence of Rumania, Serbia, and Montenegro was upheld by the Berlin Treaty. But few were deceived. The Balkans had plainly not been freed yet from the Turk. The British and Austrians had been able to threaten and win, turning Russia's expensive military victory into a humbling diplomatic defeat. Alexander reported to Todleben that he was "cumbered with many cares".

He had indeed good reason to be a worried man. All that year of 1878 political murder was rife throughout Russia—of policemen and government functionaries in particular. Through the summer Alexander stayed with Catherine Dolgoruka in St Petersburg, and when in the autumn he travelled by train from the capital to Moscow, the route had to be thick with military precautions:

> All along the route [wrote one of his sons] we saw bayonets and uniforms; at night, thousands of camp fires were lighting the way. . . . Father could not disguise his worry. . . .

By 1879 the most active of the violent nihilist groups, which called itself "The Will of the People" (*Narodnaya Volya*), proclaimed unequivocally that the Tsar, as "the personification of arbitrary, cowardly, and ever more violent despotism", merited death. In April one of these nihilists, a provincial schoolteacher named Soloviev, shot at the Tsar while he was out walking. It made the fourth assassination attempt against Alexander, who was saved only by the quickness of his reactions and prompt evasive action. Again it was a dangerously near thing: a bullet tore a hole in his clothing. Twice during 1879 Alexander went south to Livadia in the Crimea to escape, in what measure he could, with Catherine and their three children, from the strain of existence in the capital. But "The Will of the People" were not idle. When Alexander left Simferopol in November on the long journey back to St Petersburg, telegrams sent by watchful observers read: *Price of flour two roubles, our price four.* These code messages, one for the conspirators in Alexandrov, one for another group farther up the line in

Moscow, signified that the Tsar was travelling in the fourth coach of the second train. (It had become normal practice to dispatch a 'false' imperial train ahead as a precautionary measure.) Zhelyabov, the nihilist leader at Alexandrov, had managed to bury under the line eighty pounds of dynamite connected by leads to a portable battery, and precisely as the fourth coach of the second train passed over it he pressed his switch. It failed to work, and the task was therefore up to Moscow. There the "Will of the People" group, led by Zhelyabov's mistress, Sophia Perovskaya (who was the daughter of a Governor-General of St Petersburg), had burrowed a perilously flimsy tunnel from the cellar of Perovskaya's lodgings to the railway-tracks. At her signal the charge was fired and the second train duly blown to pieces, with severe loss of life. But the Tsar after all was not on board; impatient of delay in repairs to a locomotive, he had instructed that the order of the trains should be reversed at Kharkov. He was already safely in the Kremlin when news of the explosion reached him.

The plotters grew yet bolder. Another of the Zhelyabov group succeeded in penetrating the Winter Palace itself. Given the inefficiency of Tsarist security, nothing was impossible. He obtained employment with a building firm doing structural repairs, managed actually to get engaged to the daughter of one of the Palace gendarmes; and little by little built up in his bedroom a store of a hundred pounds of dynamite, two storeys underneath the royal dining quarters. On the chosen evening the Tsar's guests were a little late, so that when the wing was wrecked by the explosion, again with many deaths, he was only at that moment descending the stairs. Catherine came rushing to discover if the Tsar was safe. His wife was in no position to do so—she was on her deathbed, and in a coma.

Alexander had affronted public (and especially court) opinion by installing Catherine and her three children in the suite immediately over that of the ailing Empress in the Winter Palace, with a connecting lift for his own ease of access. He now outraged society by remarrying straightway upon Maria Alexandrovna's death, with only the minimum interval prescribed by the Orthodox Church. One must remember that he was a man pursued by the perpetual threat of death. He longed, moreover, to legitimize his second family, and had in any case always vowed to Catherine that he would marry her immediately it proved possible. He had waited fourteen years, he said: "Remember, I am the only one who can judge what I have to do." The decision seems to have instilled in him a kind of defiant gaiety; years later one of his young nephews remembered him presenting his second wife (now officially Princess Yuryevskaya) for the first time to an implacably hostile royal family:

The Emperor walked in briskly with a strikingly attractive woman on his arm. He gave a gay wink to my father and then sized up the massive figure of the Heir-apparent. . . . The nervousness [of Princess Yuryevskaya] was obvious. Frequently she turned to the Emperor, and he patted her hand gently. She would have succeeded in conquering the men had they not been watched by the women. Her efforts to join in the conversation were met by polite silence. I felt sorry for her and could not comprehend why she should be so ostracized for loving a handsome, kind, and cheerful man who happened to be the Emperor of Russia.

The boy's elders understood differently, however. The Heir-apparent—the future Alexander III—criticized his father openly. The unpopularity of the man once hailed as Liberator was now general, and even a palace revolution to overthrow him was by no means out of the question.

When the Winter Palace attempt failed, the Tsar's luck had held against the terrorists for the sixth time. It was plain that the repression, though fierce, was signally failing to deter. One last effort, therefore, was to be made to conciliate progressive opinion. The Armenian, Loris-Melikov, a protégé of Catherine, was given authority to prepare a new decree, under which the great judicial reforms would have been made at last to operate as originally intended, and delegates from the *zemstvos*, irrespective of class, would have been allowed to enter a radically reformed Council of State. By Saturday, February 28th, 1881, the Tsar's signature was on the decree, which was sent to the printer's ready for publication on Monday morning. But Monday morning was a new reign.

Zhelyabov himself had just been arrested—at last. However, he did not betray his confederates, who, much depleted, were now led by Sophia Perovskaya. They had mined at least two of the St Petersburg thoroughfares used by the Tsar. They had bomb-throwers ready should the mines fail, 'suicide' volunteers ready to move in on the Tsar and finish him off if necessary; their devotion to the 'people's will' was total. For three weeks Catherine had succeeded in persuading Alexander not to attend the Sunday-morning ceremonial parades that he so enjoyed. This Sunday he changed his plans. First he was not going; then he decided to, after all; he could not become a prisoner, he said. He did attend the parade and began to return as usual by a route previously unannounced. This rendered the mines and tunnels useless, but there were still the volunteers. One of these, as the Tsar passed at a deliberately smart pace along the quay by the Catherine Canal, threw a bomb which wrecked the royal carriage, and killed and wounded two of the Cossack escort, three horses, and an errand-boy. As for Alexander himself, once again he had survived. He got out from the wreckage unscathed and walked back to help tend the victims, but at the moment that he was about to get into the escorting police sledge a second terrorist ran out and hurled his bomb at point-blank range, annihilating himself in the act. The Tsar's legs were shattered, his clothes ripped off, and the upper part of his body terribly damaged. On the journey back to the Palace he lost consciousness and never recovered it.

Zhelyabov, Perovskaya, and three others of "The Will of the People" group were tried and hanged. "Have you been following the trials?" wrote Karl Marx from London to his daughter; "they were sterling people through and through . . . simple, businesslike, heroic . . ."; a reminder, this name of Marx, that although that particular nest of terrorists was finished with, and a chapter of history closed with the tragic happenings of March 1st, 1881, other less "simple" and more scientific revolutionaries, the followers of Marx, would soon be taking the nihilists' place. The Loris–Melikov liberal decree of 1881 was, of course, never published, and the reign of Alexander III was to be one full of reaction and redoubled repression.

"What were his failings compared with his virtues?" wrote one of Alexander's severest critics a month after his death. "He lived by his resolve to do good to the people, so let us not argue about him." History nevertheless insists on arguing. No-one, certainly, will claim the autocrat Alexander II to have been an unqualified success. Indeed, it was as an autocrat that his failure was greatest. Within Alexander, Kropotkin wrote, "two individuals warred". His misfortune was to become to a great extent the plaything of contrary currents both in his country and within himself. Although his education had persuaded him towards liberal ideals he remained in essence a conventional conservative, and of course his inheritance had made him inescapably a despot—in theory. He meant well and tried to do good, but it is difficult to see him now as as anything but a victim. He was bequeathed impossibilities. He instituted great and necessary moves towards the modernization of his country, yet almost all of his reforms proved incomplete, or they were thwarted in the administration, or (like the Liberation) were vitiated by the harsh facts of economics. Hostile circumstances and the infinite difficulties inherent in governing the Russia of his day blasted the early hopes of his reign. He ended by becoming less the referee than the football of events.

Table of Events

1801–25.	Reign of Alexander I.
1818.	Birth of future Alexander II.
1825.	Accession of Nicholas I. Decembrist conspiracy.
1830.	Revolutions widespread in Europe.
1831.	Revolt in Poland followed by 'russification'.
1833.	Russia 'protects' Turkey against Mohammed Ali.
1840.	Russia joins Britain and European Powers to thwart Mohammed Ali and France.
1848.	Revolution general in Europe.
1849.	Nicholas intervenes to subdue Hungarian revolution.
1854–56.	Crimean War.
1855.	Accession of Alexander II.
From 1858.	Russian expansion in Caucasus, Turkestan, and Central Asia.
1861.	Emancipation of the serfs.
c.1862.	Beginnings of 'nihilism'.
1863.	Polish revolt.
1863–70.	Reforms in Army, education, finance, local government (zemstvos, 1864).
1871.	Remilitarization of Black Sea.
From 1872.	Rapid growth of 'populist' groups (narodniki).
1877.	Russo-Turkish war; battle of Plevna.
1878.	Treaty of San Stefano; Treaty of Berlin.
1881.	Assassination.

II

BISMARCK

(1815–98)
And the Ascendancy of Prussia

In 1815, the year of Bismarck's birth, 'Germany' was a term having mainly geographical, linguistic, and cultural significance. Politically it had little importance, indeed, only a shadowy existence; 'Germany' was a very loose Confederation of 39 independent states under the primacy of Austria. Yet when Bismarck died at the close of the century Germany, having excluded Austria and defeated France, was united under the Empire of the Prussian Hohenzollerns, the strongest and most prosperous state on the continent of Europe, bursting with pride in its achievement and impatient to move forward. In 1895, on Bismarck's eightieth birthday, every German prince, every German city, every German university, the armed forces, the newspapers, the entire nation,[1] combined to honour the man who had come to symbolize German greatness. His achievement had indeed been impressive, and it was inevitable that his reputation should grow to giant size. The legend of Bismarck the wonder worker, the master of timely wars, the supreme champion of diplomatic chess, lingered long after his death, and the follies and blunders of his successors threw into relief his shrewdness and relative moderation. In retrospect he even seemed to have had a sort of clairvoyance: Jena, he said, had come twenty years after the death of Frederick the Great; twenty years after *his* departure would come "the great crash".

The "crash", in fact, came by instalments: first the defeat of the

---

[1] Not quite the entire nation. His old enemies among the political parties combined in the Reichstag to defeat a motion of congratulation. The parallel and contrast with Churchill, that other doughty warrior and national symbol, is instructive. Similarly lionized in his old age, Churchill, a notably more magnanimous man than Bismarck, was honoured even by his bitterest foes. But of course Churchill was a House of Commons man, Bismarck an aloof stranger in the Reichstag.

German Army, followed by the Revolution of 1918—the end of Bismarck's Reich; then the inflation and slump of the twenties and early thirties; and at length, after the fevered and short-lived triumphs of the Nazi era, the collapse of 1945. By 1945 all Bismarck's work lay in ruins. The mighty German Army had been crushed, the estates of the Junkers broken up. Large areas of previously German territory had been annexed by Poland and the U.S.S.R. Königsberg itself, the cradle of Prussian monarchy, where Bismarck in 1861 watched the coronation of William I, had become the Russian city of Kaliningrad. Bismarck's own Pomeranian estates were part of the communist 'Eastern Zone' of a partitioned and occupied Germany; symbolically, his own Schönhausen was razed to the ground by Red Army troops.[2] The state of Prussia had ceased to exist. Bismarck might well have argued, from the grave, that his successors had wantonly ignored his principles, distorted and perverted the nationalism upon which he built, and in the vulgar arrogance of their ambition invited the creation of that hostile coalition which must inevitably destroy Germany. 'Lesser Germany' had been enough for him, the Prussia-dominated Reich of 1871. His successors sought unlimited expansion, world status, and under Hitler the union of *all* Germans in a Greater Germany that would include Austria and more. Considered against the vagaries of Kaiser William II or the crimes and lunacies of the Nazis, Bismarck's ambitions seem sober and his achievement solid. But Prussian military prestige, the easy triumphs of 1866 and 1870, the humiliation of France, the denial of parliamentary government at home—these provided dangerous foundations on which to build a great modern state. Brilliantly successful though they were, Bismarck's methods carried with them promises for the future that boded no good either for Germany or for Europe in general.

He came from an old but not particularly distinguished Junker family—North German Protestant landowners, proud of their lineage (as good as the Hohenzollerns, Bismarck once said), military in their traditions, intense in their conservatism. Bismarck's birthplace, Schönhausen, where Bismarcks had lived since 1502, lay only just to the east of the Elbe, but the Kniephof estate in Pomerania to which the family moved in 1816 was true Junker

---

[2] His daughter-in-law, who was also his niece, shot herself as they approached.

country. These Junkers, or squires, were the modern descendants of the land-hungry colonizers who during the Middle Ages had moved eastward beyond the Elbe into Slav-populated country. Land was everything to them. They were not usually of the grand aristocracy, who might well have judged them uncouth and whose airs they frequently resented. Many of them personally worked their own estates. While maintaining a sturdy independence towards the demands of the King of Prussia, they still provided the sinews of his increasingly powerful state: above all they manned the officer corps of his army and the offices of his civil administration. Junkerdom was at the heart of the old predominantly peasant Prussia.

Bismarck was proud to be a Junker and inherited most of the Junker attitudes; but his brains are more likely to have come from his mother, the Berlin-bred daughter of one of Frederick the Great's high officials of state, who was a man of the Enlightenment and later held by some to be too sympathetic to Jacobinism. His daughter succeeded to his sharp wits and was ambitious to see them sharper still in her son Otto. She took him away from Pomerania at the age of seven and sent him to school in Berlin; at seventeen he proceeded to Göttingen University, where he soon abandoned the fashionable liberalism of the day and turned to hard drinking, strenuous love-making, and the traditional pursuits of an upper-class young 'blood' at college. In his first term alone he became mixed up in twenty-five student duels. He affected strange and flamboyant clothes and professed a lofty contempt for Göttingen's academics. After three terms debts obliged him to transfer to Berlin University, where he could lodge at home. Already he was the complicated amalgam of personalities that persisted for the next sixty years. One part of him, glorifying his paternal traditions, was hard-living, down to earth, brutally healthy, anti-intellectual and even boorish; but he was also his mother's son, articulate and subtle-minded, emotionally taut and prone to tears, a romantic. "Faust complains of having two souls in his breast", he said. "I have a whole squabbling crowd"; and then a characteristic political touch—"it goes on as in a republic".

When his mother died in 1839 the young Bismarck, while his father stayed at Schönhausen, went to run the Pomeranian estates with his brother, abandoning the Civil Service which he had briefly entered and found tedious. For eight years now Bismarck lived, first as the squire of Kniephof, and then, when his father died in 1845, of Schönhausen. They were riotous years. "The mad Junker" they called him; he was wild and arrogant. "In his love for women", one of his few close friends, Keyserling, baldly remarks, "he followed his natural instincts without scruples." He over-ate and over-drank. Bismarck himself later spoke with conventional remorse of "his blind appetite for pleasure", of squandering his gifts and his health. Actually his health was remarkably able to stand up for itself. Tall, powerfully built, with (in those days) reddish-blond hair and beard, his eyes already somewhat puffy and staring, his carriage rather stiff, he had the constitution of an ox. (The surprising thing about him was the gentleness of his voice.) But the life of a country squire—drinking bouts and nocturnal adventures notwithstanding—proved in the end a bore; neither did serious reading and foreign travel satisfy for long. He rejoined the Civil Service and left again within a fortnight, unable, he said, to put up with his superiors. He fell at last genuinely in love with the gentle, pious, and beautiful Marie von Thadden, the daughter of a neighbouring landowner. She, however, married another, and then died at the age of twenty-six. Bismarck's turbulence was somewhat sobered by these experiences: the volcano became quiescent. Watching Marie die in Christian resignation, he found himself in the unaccustomed exercise of prayer. On her deathbed she begged him to turn towards religion, and formally he did; from that time he never ceased to call himself a Christian. Yet never in any very spiritual sense was he a religious man. Certainly he did not question that God existed (and the German people would not have had such a good Chancellor, he said later, if he had been less of a Christian). "I do not understand", he wrote later, "how a man who reflects on himself, and still knows and seeks to know nothing of God, can endure his life for contempt and weariness." But he never found reason to doubt that God's interests were essentially those of the Prussian monarchy; "I believe that I serve God when I serve the King." It was a little like Cromwell's "God has revealed himself, as his manner is, first to his Englishmen."

A by-product of Marie's death was Bismarck's marriage to a friend of hers, a quiet, devout girl, Johanna von Puttkamer. "I like piety in women", he said, "and have a horror of feminine cleverness." Certainly Johanna was not clever, but she was stable and well suited to him; Bismarck's marriage to her in 1847—he was thirty-two—brought him half a century of domestic happiness. That same year, 1847, took him also into half a century of politics.

During the years when he had been living on his estates political events had been on the move in Prussia. The 'quiet years' during which despotism and reaction had ruled largely unchallenged—the age of Metternich, with the Prussian monarchy in step with him—were coming to an end. From 1840 the new King of Prussia, Frederick William IV, though he was firmly absolutist and profoundly conservative, had by his actions and speeches encouraged liberals to live in hope. He had relaxed the censorship, released some political prisoners and given voice to a wealth of progressive-sounding eloquence. In 1847 he sought to kill two birds with one stone. He decided to convene a sort of Estates of the Realm by holding a united session of all the provincial Assemblies (Diets), and having gathered them all together to persuade them to vote a loan for promoting a railway to East Prussia. But he never intended this United Prussian Diet to have any effective parliamentary power. Its petitions to the Crown were numerous, its debates eloquent, but its achievements slight; even the railway loan came to nothing.

The majority in the United Diet was liberal; but one member who was emphatically not so, and made for the first time something of a name for himself by his brusque opposition to the liberals, was Otto von Bismarck. He spoke, it was said, with an offhand arrogance, as though he were carrying on a conversation with himself. Only chance had brought him there at all. His fellow-Junkers in Pomerania had not made him a delegate, merely a reserve should one of their number fall ill. When one did Bismarck had gone in his stead to Berlin and so edged on to the stage of politics.

Less than a year later Germany, like half Europe, was in a state of ferment. In January 1848 there had been a revolution in Italy; in February the French monarchy fell. On March 13th, Metternich, the very symbol of the old order, was overthrown in Vienna. This was followed immediately by street fighting in Berlin and disturbances throughout Germany. Everywhere men were demanding a wider franchise, a free Press, more power for the assemblies, an amnesty for political prisoners, trial by jury, an end to tithes and feudal dues—in a word, freedom. Some, more extreme, were ready to fight for a socialist republic. In Berlin the sensitive and well-meaning Frederick William, shocked by the bloodshed, ordered a partial withdrawal of troops from the capital; in error they were all withdrawn, and the defenceless King was forced to salute the paraded corpses of those who died in the rioting. In mental turmoil he then rode through the streets, wearing the people's tricolour, the black-red-gold of the national revolution. The liberals, it seemed, were victorious. Even a German national state, perhaps, might not be far off.

All this was horrifying to Bismarck. His first reaction was to try raising a peasant army to rescue the King from the rebels; his second, equally wild, was to promote a *coup d'état* which (since the King was clearly a prisoner of the revolution) would have set up the Regency of his sister-in-law Augusta until her son should come of age and assume the throne. Soon calmer views prevailed. The revolution was perhaps a flash in the pan, the work of a few well-to-do liberals, whom it would be wise not to overestimate. A little toughness, a stiffening of the King's resolve to stand up to them, and they could be defeated. Bismarck snorted with contempt for them, the more so since so many of them were 'new' Prussians coming from the Westphalian and Rhine provinces that had been Prussian only since 1815. For Bismarck these men were almost as foreign as Bavarians or Württembergers or Austrians; for him 'Prussia' meant the historic fatherland, the Prussia of Frederick the Great. How could these "commercial travellers in Rhenish wine", these prosperous liberal-minded business men from the west, value the heritage of the Prussia of the Junkers and Frederick the Great? Their ancestors were in any case fighting on the other side.

In May 1848 the Prussian National Assembly met in Berlin, and its deliberations continued until December in a city at best in revolutionary confusion and at worst in bloodshed and anarchy. The King retired to the palace of Sans Souci at Potsdam. By October the Habsburg Government had subdued the revolution in Vienna and was soon completely to regain control in all the old imperial dominions. In November Frederick William, encouraged by these signs and the ebbing of the revolutionary tide, felt strong enough to dismiss his parliamentary ministers in Berlin and appoint in their stead men who unmistakably signified the defeat of liberalism and a resumption of authority by the old Prussia—by the monarch, that is, and by his faithful army and Civil Service. Bismarck had been considered for a minor post—all summer he had been urging firmness upon the King—but Frederick William thought him too violent a reactionary, one to be made use of, he said, "only when the bayonet is in full command".

The King finally dissolved the protesting Assembly on December 5th, and although he promulgated a new constitution, the essentials of monarchical government were retained. The new Chamber (*Landtag*) had to be content with the shadow of power; the substance lay, and continued to lie until 1918, with the King and his ministers, responsible to the King alone.

In 1848 there were revolutions, mainly abortive, throughout the many states of Germany; but there was in addition and simultaneously an all-German revolution, the attempt to set up for the first time a united German state. 550 delegates assembled at Frankfurt in the *Paulskirche* to formulate the fundamental rights and laws of the new Germany: civil and religious equality, trial by jury, freedom of the Press, an end to feudalism. All that was lacking *was* the new Germany. Those wishing to set up a federal republic were outnumbered. Those, in the majority, wishing to establish a constitutional monarchy found the King of Prussia unwilling to accept the imperial crown they proffered; to him, held fast in his world of Divine Right, such a crown, lacking God's authority, could only be "a crown of shame". Those supporting a Greater Germany found no answer to the problem of how to deal with Austria's non-German peoples. The Little Germans, a majority, found themselves up against the objection expressed by Frederick William that "Germany without Austria would be a face without a nose". By the middle of 1849 the Frankfurt Parliament had petered out, and during 1850 Austria and Prussia each fell to making rival unions of states. When the showdown came, with the threat of a major inter-German war, it was Prussia that gave way. By the Olmütz settlement of 1850 the Prussian (Erfurt) Union was dissolved and Prussia returned to the fold of the German Confederation, in which Austrian primacy was confirmed. On the surface, at least, nothing at all had been achieved; it was "back to 1815".

Many Prussians regarded the Olmütz agreement as a humiliation; not so Bismarck. For him it was simple realism. Why should Prussia risk her very existence in an Austrian war which would set her, even if she won it, on a basis of mere equality with such states as Bavaria or Württemberg—fellow-members of the Union but every bit as foreign, as far as Bismarck was concerned, as Austria? Bismarck knew only one fatherland, Prussia. Only Prussia's honour and wellbeing mattered. For him at this time, and for long afterwards, German nationalism was the sort of moonshine suitable only for corrupt Rhinelanders and "South German children of nature" infected by French ideas. For him it was "the German swindle. . . . Prussians we are, and Prussians we will remain."

Bismarck's support for official Prussian policy at Olmütz was rewarded by his appointment as Prussian envoy at the restored Confederation Diet at Frankfurt. He went, ironically enough, as the man who had stood for reconciliation with Austria; once at Frankfurt, however, he made it his business to challenge every Austrian assumption of superiority. At Frankfurt he came to hate Austria. His uphill work of asserting first the equality, then the supremacy, of Prussia now began. It was customary for the presiding Austrian, but no-one else, to smoke at council meetings; very well, then, Bismarck would light up his cigar. The Austrian President of the Diet received Bismarck in his shirtsleeves; Bismarck, therefore, must strike a blow for Prussia by remarking upon the heat and removing his own coat. (These famous and perhaps childish episodes lost nothing in the telling by Bismarck in later years.) He was conscientiously and patriotically cantankerous on points great and small, and Austrian diplomats, their nerves frayed, came to look forward to a quieter life elsewhere.

It was Bismarck, too, as Prussia's negotiator, who held out against Austria's admission to the German Customs Union (*Zollverein*) which had been building up ever since 1819 and was steadily making the "German swindle" no swindle at all, but an economic fact.[3] It is unlikely that Bismarck fully understood what was happening, but in promoting Austria's economic exclusion from the newly developing Germany he was helping to make a decision quite as vital as the military decision that was to follow in 1866.

These years provided Bismarck with his first experience of dip-

[3] Austria's attitude to the *Zollverein* has parallels with Britain's to the E.E.C. a century later. Austria was German yet not fully German, Britain European yet not fully European. The position of both Powers was complicated by their decaying but persisting imperial connections. Each began by resisting the common market; tried then to set up a rival to it; applied later to join it; and was refused admission.

lomacy. To begin with he hated Frankfurt, that cosmopolitan and un-Prussian town, a place, he complained, of "lies and intrigues". But already by 1853 he seems to have been preferring his existence there, with its invigorating wrangles and its generous choice of friends, to some aspects of Berlin; the Berlin parliamentary debates, for instance, he found "immeasurably shallow and undignified". (He was for some time a member of the Lower Chamber of the Landtag as well as representative at Frankfurt.) "There is something very demoralizing in the air of the Chambers; it makes the best people vain without their knowing it." This low opinion of parliaments and parliamentarians he never found cause to change.

Politics and family life had between them somewhat transformed "the mad Junker". He certainly liked to think of himself as a reformed character and talked of the "folly of his former days". God, his wife, and the children, he said, had made life endurable. The American historian Motley, who saw much of the Bismarcks during these Frankfurt years, wrote in the summer of 1855:

> The Bismarcks are as kind as ever. . . . It is one of those houses where everyone does what he likes. . . . Here there are young and old, grandparents and children and dogs all at once, eating and drinking, smoking, piano-playing, and pistol-firing (in the garden) all going on at the same time. . . . Every earthly thing that can be eaten or drunk is offered you. . . .

In September 1857 Frederick William's mental powers, long unstable, deteriorated further. A succession of strokes robbed him of the power of speech, and he therefore in 1858 appointed his brother William to act as Regent on his behalf. This brought various changes; liberal ministers took the place of the conservatives who had governed since the overthrow of the 1848 Revolution, and Bismarck, whom the Regent judged to be a firebrand and too implacably hostile to Austria, was promoted to the ambassadorship at St Petersburg. The promotion was rather nominal; Bismarck knew that he had been, as he said, "put on ice". With some anxiety he watched from afar the explosive events of 1859 as Piedmont with French aid fought Austria and won Lombardy from her. He feared that feelings on German solidarity might take Prussia into the Austrian camp. Prussia, he thought, should keep her hands free, as she had during the Crimean War, or even take advantage of Austria's troubles to extend the Prussian frontier "either to Lake Constance or where Protestantism ceased to predominate".

If Prussia should ever want allies there was always Russia. He had offered this opinion back in 1854, and his stay at St Petersburg (1858–62) confirmed the judgment. It was Russia's vastness that most impressed him—"the great white bear" that had broken Napoleon, the giant whose vast potential power must never be forgotten in any calculation of risks. All his subsequent actions were qualified by this conviction.

His years in Russia were punctuated by a severe illness following an accident and incompetent doctoring. After he recovered and could take his family back with him; he liked Petersburg well enough. He got on well in court and diplomatic circles, and there was always enjoyable hunting in the Russian forests—but Petersburg was still "the ice". He felt cut off, and sometimes even pretended that he would be content soon to settle down quietly at Schönhausen "and set about having my coffin made". This was sour grapes. In fact he took care to come frequently to Berlin, where he was not displeased to have his more outrageous remarks repeated. "If you want a war," he said, "appoint me your undersecretary of state. I undertake to deliver you in four weeks a civil war of the very highest quality." He contrived to be talked about as a dark horse, a man of downright, uncompromising, and belligerent views, a self-advertised enemy of Austria abroad and liberalism at home, a politician with a future.

William, Prince Regent until January 1861, King William I from that date, had none of his brother's imagination, idealism, or instability. He was an upright, simple soldier first and last. For him, next to the crown itself, the Prussian Army was the holy of holies. His first task, therefore, must be to strengthen its basis and increase its manpower. Ever since 1815, despite a rising population, its annual intake of conscripts had stayed at 40,000; William, therefore, and his Minister of War, Roon, proposed now to increase the number of regiments to permit genuinely universal military service, an institution long dear to Prussian traditions. The liberal majority in the Landtag, as patriotic as any, did not contest the need for universal service, but they wished to make the term two years instead of the three insisted on by William, Roon, and the Army chiefs. They also objected to Roon's attempts to strengthen the position of the regular army, with its Junker officers, at the expense of the Landwehr, or citizen army, whose officers came largely from outside the nobility and in Roon's words "lacked genuine soldierly spirit". The quarrel, then, was between a traditionalist King and a Junker-dominated regular army on one side, and on the other a liberal Chamber unable to control King or dismiss Ministers yet possessing the vital power of the purse.

The Army crisis simmered steadily for two years (1860–62). Roon, a friend of Bismarck's, kept him posted upon developments, and constantly advised the King that Bismarck was the only politician tough enough to see the battle with the Chambers through, if necessary by unconstitutional means. William resisted. He did not like Bismarck. The man was wild. His foreign ideas were embarrassingly anti-Austrian, and he talked alarmingly of a *French* alliance. Several times William came to the brink of inviting Bismarck to form a ministry, but every time he found an objection.

Early in 1862 the Lower Chamber of the Landtag refused to pass the budget, and there was deadlock. Still William would not have Bismarck, though he did transfer him from Russia to France, where he was closer to hand. It was in France, therefore, during the summer of 1862, that Bismarck waited for the call, and while he waited fell perilously in love with the young wife of the elderly Russian ambassador to Brussels. Bismarck was forty-seven, Catherine Orlov twenty-two; he wore her onyx medallion on his watch-chain for the rest of his days. But he was not the man to allow his emotions to get out of control, and his wife's worries could safely subside.

On September 16th a telegram arrived from the Prussian Foreign Minister, advising Bismarck to return to Berlin immediately. He ignored it. On the 18th William forbade Roon to offer the Landtag a compromise. The crisis was at boiling-point. Roon wired Bismarck to hurry home, and on the 20th he reached Berlin. On the 22nd he saw the King at Babelsberg Palace, near Potsdam, and persuaded him to tear up the act of abdication which he had prepared—not that an abdication would have solved anything, for the Crown Prince also was determined to have the Army reforms. Within a fortnight Bismarck had received the appointments of both Prime Minister and Foreign Minister; obduracy had brought its reward and he had power on his own terms. Or almost his own terms: Bismarck, the royalist, had not failed to give a promise that he "would always submit to the King's orders in the last resort".

The Army reforms went through; Bismarck spent what had never been voted, and the constitution was ruthlessly violated. In his speech before the Landtag—or "House of Phrases", as he scornfully called it—the terrible new minister uttered the best-remembered words of his whole career. To him their truth seemed self-evident; to his critics and enemies they came to stand for all that was most dangerous in the Prussian tradition:

> The great questions of the day will be decided not by speeches and parliamentary votes—that was the great mistake from 1848 to 1849—but by iron and blood.

At the time these sentiments shocked not only the Landtag but the King, who was still frightened by his new minister's tendency to say in public what he really meant. And it was not only the King who was mistrustful. The Queen had never forgiven Bismarck for his extraordinary behaviour during the 1848 Revolution. The Crown Prince, a liberal, and still more his censorious English wife, Victoria, thought him unscrupulous and disreputable. When Bismarck followed up his defeat of the Landtag with a decree allowing the suppression of any newspaper or magazine that gave offence, the Prince created a stir by publicly deploring the action. Meanwhile relations between Bismarck and the Landtag went past the stage of being merely bad; they became so desperate as not to be serious. Year after year the Lower House threw out the Army budget. It made no difference; the docile Prussian taxpayer paid up. The newspapers toed the Bismarck line. There were no demonstrations.

Certainly he was unpopular. After a year of office he said that he felt fifteen years older. He suffered from headaches, from facial neuralgia and twitching, and from sleeplessness. Nothing in fact could be further from the truth than the image of Bismarck as a stark man of impassive nerves, a man of granite, the "Iron Chancellor". He certainly practised to wear an impassive front, but control came at a heavy cost. In 1863, against the whole weight of public and court opinion, he fought to persuade William not to attend a Frankfurt conference (promoted by the Emperor of Austria and thirty German princes) to discuss reform of the German Confederation. At the end of the argument both men's nerves were exhausted; Bismarck's grip broke the door-handle as he left the room. But he gained his point and confirmed his moral ascendancy: the King did not attend. This meant that Bismarck had wrecked the conference, and with it the last chance of uniting Germany by consent under Austrian auspices.

In foreign affairs too his first great steps were widely condemned. In 1863 the Poles rose against their Russian masters, and all over Western Europe, including Germany, the weight of public opinion was as strongly on their side as it had been in their earlier and equally futile revolt in 1831. Bismarck, however, had a Junker's view of the Poles. They were, after all, a subjugated 'native' population. The only way to treat such subjects was to hold them down—in a letter to his sister he even wrote "exterminate them". Elsewhere his language was a shade less brutal:

> No-one could doubt that an independent Poland would be the the irreconcilable enemy of Prussia and would remain so till they had conquered the mouth of the Vistula and every Polish-speaking village in West and East Prussia, Pomerania, and Silesia.

Bismarck had further motives in this Polish affair. He wished to build up a credit balance with the Tsar, and therefore he even offered an army to help in suppressing the revolt. Nothing came of the gesture except a howl of execration from lovers of liberty throughout Germany and Europe; but Bismarck was by now inured to unpopularity. He even affected to relish it: "nobody despises public opinion as much as I do". Possibly he was comforted by his own opinion of his fellow-countrymen: "If you let the Prussian poke his big snout at the world beyond, you can do what you like with him in his own country."[4]

It was the Schleswig-Holstein dispute of 1864 that provided Bismarck with the first of his many strokes of good fortune. "Man", he once said, "cannot create the current of events. He can only float with it, and steer." And his steering from now on, as for the next seven years he shot the rapids of diplomacy and war, was hair-raising but brilliantly adroit.

Holstein was a German duchy, and part of the Confederation. Schleswig was in population half German and half Danish; it was a fief of the Danish Crown. The King of Denmark was Duke of *both* duchies much as the King of England had earlier been Elector of Hanover. In 1848–49 there had been a revolution supported by Germany and led by an Augustenburg prince, demanding independence from Denmark; in 1852 an international settlement wound up the resulting war and sustained the Danish claim to sovereignty

[4] Ziekursch, *Geschichte des neuen deutschen Kaiserreichs*, pp. 26–27, quoted in W. Richter's *Bismarck*.

over the Duchies, although the German Confederation was not a signatory to this agreement. In 1855 the King of Denmark annexed Schleswig but allowed Holstein home rule. When in 1863 he died childless his heir, succeeding through the female line, could become King of Denmark without question; but could he also succeed to Schleswig and Holstein, where German (Salic) Law forbade inheritance through females? It was all diabolically complicated, yet in one sense for Bismarck sweetly simple. He meant to have the two Duchies, and have them not for the Augustenburg prince and not for the German Confederation as a whole, but simply and exclusively for the Prussian Crown. If for nothing else, the advantage of gaining Kiel, and the possibility of linking the North and Baltic Seas by a canal through Schleswig, made the prospect enticing.

His chances of success seem to have been so slight that only one with a relish for the impossible would have made the attempt. Denmark would plainly fight for her rights. Britain and the signatories of the 1852 treaty would be against Bismarck's game (though he remained justifiably confident that Britain would protest a good deal, bluff a little, but never go to war for Denmark[5]). German public opinion would be against it; the King of Prussia would be against it on the grounds of its immorality; the Confederation would be against it. Above all, Austria surely would not allow Prussia to get away with such daylight robbery.

The thing was so preposterous that it had to be done by stages. First he had to get Austria's support for an ultimatum to Denmark. It was thus an *Austro*-Prussian army which, under the watchword "Forward with God", advanced to an early victory over the Danish forces, with lively effects on German national feeling and the King of Prussia's military pride. Bismarck next had to seem to agree to the succession of Frederick of Augustenburg, who was not only a friend of the Crown Prince and like him a man of liberal-nationalist persuasion, but also popularly supported throughout Germany. He then played upon the Austrian Government's fears of liberalism, persuading it to abandon support for Augustenburg by threatening him with having to pay for the cost of the war fought on his behalf. Throughout 1865 Prussia and Austria haggled over what to do with the conquered Duchies. Eventually Bismarck

---

[5] Bismarck once said that if the British Army landed in Germany he would send the police to arrest it.

reached another stage on his journey when it was agreed that Prussia should rule Schleswig and Austria Holstein (Treaty of Gastein, August 1865).

The last stage proved the most stubborn. Even Austrian statesmen like Rechberg and Esterhazy, three parts hynotized by Bismarck and weakened by their fears of democratic revolution and Napoleon III, were not going to sign away their country's rights to Holstein. When pinpricks and irritants failed to move them Bismarck finally took in his own mind the crucial step, which he had so long contemplated—war. The reforms in the Army had gone through; new weapons, like the rapid-firing needle gun, were in its hands; there was reason to think the Prussian Army the finest in Europe. But if it were to come to a war it would not simply be a war for Holstein. A Prussian defeat of Austria could mean that all Germany north of the Main, all Protestant Germany, would be under the domination of Prussia. The Confederation would be broken and Austria expelled. Germany would have been conquered by Prussia.

He felt certain of the neutrality of Russia and Britain. Conquering his distaste for King Victor Emmanuel of Italy—"the bandit chief", as he liked to call him—he negotiated a treaty with him, by which, in return for military assistance, Italy would gain Venetia from Austria. Only France remained. Three times between 1862 and 1865 Bismarck had had secret conversations with Napoleon III, whose goodwill he had always—to William I's horror—been careful to cultivate, and who had shown himself not averse to Prussia taking Holstein and southern Schleswig, or to her making war upon Austria, provided that France was rewarded for her neutrality. It did not seem likely that France would make common cause with Austria.

Thus by the autumn of 1865 the world knew that Prussia was determined to have her German Civil War, and not unreasonably considered that (like the American Civil War just ending) it would be bloody, long, and exhausting. Bismarck in November instructed the Prussian authorities in Schleswig to exploit every possible complaint against the Austrians in Holstein. He was continually nervous that his plans would be thwarted, if not by German public opinion, then by his King's moral scruples, or a general conference of the Confederation, or even an international congress. As he was walking in the Unter den Linden in May 1866 he was shot at by a young student determined to rid his country and Europe of this war-monger. Missing, the young man was leaped upon and soon made helpless by his intended victim, who then calmly resumed his walk home. When, however, for a few days the danger of war receded he became quite ill, having to take to his sofa with violent pains in the legs.

Austria's position over these years was acutely difficult. She knew that her position both as an Italian power and as the leader of Germany was threatened. She had already lost Lombardy, and was so alarmed by the prospect of losing Venetia that she would probably, with reluctance, have ceded to Bismarck Prussian domination of the Duchies and of Germany north of the Main, if only he had been willing to guarantee her position in Venetia. The Austrian Emperor Francis Joseph and his ministers were uncertain whether to pursue traditional Metternichian policies of anti-liberalism and 'repose' or whether to try to spike Prussia's guns by championing the German national movement and themselves promoting reform of the Confederation. And all the time the economic tide was running against them and in favour of their rivals in Prussia. (It is ironical that Bismarck was able to find the money to govern without a parliamentary budget from 1862 to 1866 only because of the buoyancy of the Prussian economy. Thus the wealth which was largely the creation of the liberal middle classes provided the very means by which Bismarck could defeat them.) The desperation of the Austrians was such that in 1866 they actually signed a treaty with Napoleon III promising to cede Venetia to him, and thus through him to Italy, if he would hold off from intervening in their impending war with Prussia.

History calls it the Six (or Seven) Weeks War. In fact it was effectively over in a fortnight. Prussia was ranged against all the other states of the German Confederation, but within a week north-west Germany, and in particular Hanover, capitulated. The Austrians defeated the Italians at Custozza, but in Bohemia were themselves destroyed by the Prussians at Sadowa (which the Germans call Königgrätz). Bismarck was himself present on the field of battle, with the War Minister Roon, the Army Chief of Staff Moltke, and the King; and the slaughter of that day was not without lasting effect on him. Like most men of his day, he regarded war as a necessary instrument of national policy, but he was far from a power-mad monster, and despite the military tunic that he came to affect he was deeply sceptical of military men. Looking down on one of the dead at Sadowa, he said, "It makes me sick at heart to think that Herbert [his son] may be lying like this one day." Wars must be; but they ought to be economical. And now Bismarck, who had been anxious to have this war, was anxious to get out of it quickly, before France or Russia could intervene, by agreeing terms that would spare Austria humiliation. She was to lose no territory other than Venetia to Italy. On the other hand, William I, who had been reluctant to engage upon war, now stubbornly insisted on a punitive peace and a Prussian march of triumph through the streets of Vienna. There followed another prolonged emotional tussle between the two men, with Bismarck in his best prima donna vein, shedding tears of frustration, slamming doors in his rage, and even threatening to throw himself from a high window—until at last the Crown Prince persuaded his father to give his temperamental but prudent minister best.

The fact is sometimes brushed aside that Bismarck, who in the end 'unified' Germany, did so only by partitioning her. After Sadowa by the Treaty of Prague he destroyed the old Confederation. The Germans of the Austrian Empire were permanently cut off from his Germany; the new North German Confederation comprising all the twenty-two states north of the Main was essentially an extension of Prussia, which in any case contained five-sixths of its total population. Prussia gained five million new subjects; Hanover, Schleswig, Holstein, Hesse-Cassel, Nassau, and the Free City of Frankfurt were all gathered in under the Hohenzollern wing. Bismarck had, it seemed, achieved his aim; he himself thought his work finished. As he wrote to his wife, "There is nothing more to do in our lifetime." He had no ambitions directed towards South Germany. As for Austria, he had left her still one of the great Powers, whose friendship, moreover, Prussia might some day be glad of. Austrians as rivals he would not have, still less as superiors. Austrians as allies—that was another matter: "we shall need Austrian strength for ourselves later".

"It is France who is defeated at Sadowa," said Thiers; and certainly Napoleon, who had thought to intervene to France's territorial profit when the war was well advanced, seemed to have missed the boat. Bismarck, riding the wave of his success, proceeded to reveal to the South German states (Bavaria, Baden, Württemberg and Southern Hesse) certain demands Napoleon had earlier put forward to territory on the Rhine, including Mainz. The scare was too valuable to miss exploiting, and these states previously hostile to Prussia were alarmed into concluding military alliances with her. It was not that Bismarck had basically changed his views on German nationalism; but German nationalism was, of course, chronically anti-French, and he was quite prepared to make use of it for Prussia's purposes. "We shall need the national swindle later," he commented, "as protection against French demands."

There was a further by-product of the victory over Austria. In the national jubilation the old liberal enemy split, and the National Liberal group, seeing in the once-hated minister a potential unifier of the nation, were ready for reconciliation. Borne along on the popular patriotic current, they became the most numerous party in the North German Parliament (Reichstag) and later in the Imperial Reichstag; they dutifully voted a budget nine-tenths of whose expenditure was for the Army. Though they extracted some concessions from Bismarck as the price for their support, any British-style parliamentary government, with ministers accountable to parliament and liable to dismissal by it, was out of the question. There was one surprising respect in which they had no need to extract concessions: Bismarck astonished everybody in 1866 by championing universal suffrage. This, however, proved rather too subtle a ruse. His motive had been *anti-liberal*, for he calculated that the conservative vote of the peasants would prove a counterpoise to the liberal vote of the bourgeoisie. It was not to work out quite so simply as that.

Bismarck, now Federal Chancellor of North Germany, remained essentially the King's Minister. The two men, king and minister, knew that they were mutually indispensable as a man and wife who have been through the fire together, but this did not make them compatible—Bismarck adventurous in mind and action, subtle, unscrupulous; William stiff and constrained, conventional, the soul of honour. The tension between them did not lessen as the respect grew. Five times between 1869 and 1877 Bismarck used the ploy of a threatened resignation; five times he got his way. In public he remained sternly loyal; in private he grumbled constantly. William was "hard as stone". "I took office," said Bismarck, "with a great fund of royalist sentiment and veneration for the King. To my sorrow I find this fund more and more depleted."

Bismarck's Germany

In the Reichstag Bismarck was the King's lone representative.

> He sat aloof on the minister's bench, the more aloof in that he was for many years the sole German minister. He never had social dealings with the politicians on their own ground. . . . They had to come to him—to the beer-evenings which he gave with the same conscious condescension as is shown by the headmaster, entertaining the senior boys.[6]

The beer-evenings were at his inconvenient and untidy house in the Wilhelmstrasse, where it was remarked that the only adequate and well-provided rooms were the cellars, which housed prodigious supplies of beer, wine, and spirits. All his life Bismarck was a very heavy drinker, particularly of champagne. In his 'mad Junker' days he had sometimes consumed a bottle with his lobster breakfast. A speciality of his was "black velvet", a mixture of champagne and stout. He smoked mountains of cigars. He ate hugely, especially late at night.

Whenever he could, and more and more as the years progressed, he would escape from Berlin to the country. After the victory against Austria he bought a big estate at Varzin, in Pomerania, with the 400,000 thalers the Prussian Landtag honoured him with. Then, after the victory over France in 1871, William I presented him (by that time a Prince) with an estate much larger still at Friedrichsruh, near Hamburg. The daily courier kept him in touch with one of his two worlds, the great world of European politics, and he would work late on the dispatches through the quiet country nights and rise late in the mornings. The other world, one of whose particular attractions was its blessed remoteness from the first, was that of his family, his timber forests,[7] his dogs and horses, his well-loved countryside where peasants were still peasants and great landowners could still play God. The worlds of modern thought, modern art, 'good taste', were closed to him. (Wagner, for instance, was "a monkey".) Polite society was not for him; in the country he entertained little. Of the new Germany growing so fast around him, whose new power he in a way personified, he knew very little at first hand. He never saw a coal-mine or visited the Ruhr. He claimed to know nothing of economics, though he later laboured to

[6] A. J. P. Taylor, *Bismarck*, p. 100.
[7] He established a successful paper-mill, and was furious when the authorities tried to tax him on it. A secret order from the King had given him immunity from taxation.

overcome the defect. In literature and history, by and large he retained the tastes of his youth. When William I presented him with the Grand Cross (in diamonds) of the Hohenzollern Order he said, "I'd rather have had a horse or a barrel of good Rhenish wine."

The triumphs of 1866, the reconciliation with the National Liberals, the unchallengeable dominance of Prussia in Germany, and the personal supremacy of Bismarck himself all combined now to produce a gradual change in his attitude to the "German swindle". The text-book legend that Bismarck resolved to unify Germany and to that end planned three neat wars, with Denmark, Austria, and France, could hardly be further from the reality. The truth is rather that "floating with the current of history and steering", he was carried forward after 1866 towards an unplanned war with France and the absorption of South Germany into his Greater Prussia. It is true that there was nearly a war with France as early as 1867, over the complicated Luxemburg question, but good sense and moderation on both sides prevailed over the hotheads. It is also true that Napoleon III was casting around during these years for an alliance with Austria and Italy, but this was routine diplomatic probing, not a preparation for war. With Napoleon III Bismarck had always been on good terms—unlike William I, who thought him a revolutionary upstart; at the Paris exhibition of 1867 Napoleon and Bismarck continued the series of amicable *tête-à-têtes* begun at Biarritz in 1862. If South and North Germany were to be united it had no need to be through a Franco-German war.

Imperceptibly over these years 1866–70 Bismarck did come to accept that the southern states would one day join the new German Confederation. In one respect they already had: there was an all-German Customs Parliament in being, though three-fifths of its Southern members, Catholics suspicious of Prussia, were hostile to unification. Full unity would take several decades, Bismarck considered that we can put our watches forward," he said, "but time doesn't go any faster."

Time might not; but events suddenly and unpredictably did. In September 1868 the dissolute Queen Isabella of Spain was expelled from her country, whose government was taken over provisionally by her war minister. The throne lay vacant; who was to be invited to occupy it? Already Bismarck had sponsored one of the South German Hohenzollerns to the new throne of Rumania; Rumania's king had a brother, Leopold, who possessed qualifications which might recommend him strongly for the Spanish throne; he was a liberally inclined Catholic not only connected with the Portuguese royal house but also descended from the Murat and Beauharnais families. The fact remained, however, that he was undeniably German; and, well as Napoleon III liked the young man personally, no French government was going to approve of a German king in Madrid related to the Prussian king in Berlin. Mischievously, on the principle that a little diplomatic trouble for the French could do no harm, and without fully gauging the consequences of his actions, Bismarck in 1869 joined in the secret intrigues being busily forwarded in Madrid and promoted Leopold's candidature. He had hard work persuading Leopold to stand, and harder still wringing out of William I his reluctant consent ("with a heavy, very heavy, heart"); but the nomination stood. Bismarck tried later to disclaim responsibility, but there is not the least doubt that Leopold went forward only at his insistence. Success, he said, would be worth two army corps to Prussia in the event of war.

Not unexpectedly, when the secret came out there was indignation in France, where a strongly warlike line was taken by the Foreign Minister, Gramont, and others of Napoleon's ministry. (Napoleon himself was severely ill and in constant pain from his bladder disease.) The Press in both France and Germany did much to embitter relations, and in July 1870, to the King of Prussia's relief, Leopold withdrew his candidature. In France the joy was great; she had scored her biggest diplomatic victory since the days of Napoleon I.

All this time Bismarck had been in the country at Varzin; he was taking Carlsbad waters after an attack of jaundice. By now he was deeply depressed; talking of resignation, he hurried to Berlin. His Spanish intrigue had boomeranged, and Prussia appeared to have been soundly rebuffed. He would soon be back at Varzin, he said—a private citizen and glad of it. It was at this stage that Napoleon and Gramont, thinking that they had their man down, grew foolishly over-confident. Gramont instructed Benedetti, the French ambassador to Prussia, to seek an interview with King William, who was taking the spa waters at Ems; Benedetti was to demand that William apologize for what had happened and never permit the Hohenzollern candidature to be revived. The two men chatted on the promenade, with the band playing in the background and bystanders able to catch fragments of conversation. It was as amicable and seemly as the circumstances permitted; no public rebuff, no high words; but of course William refused to give any apology or commitment. Later in the day a routine telegram was sent by an official in the King's name to inform Bismarck of what had passed. "I rejected this demand somewhat sternly as it is neither right nor possible to undertake engagements of this kind à tout jamais."

Bismarck was in Berlin with Moltke and Roon. All three were in the dumps, feeling Prussia's humiliation and their helplessness in the situation. A war now could only be a war of naked aggression, seen as such by all Europe, and particularly by the South Germans. But on receiving the official telegram from Ems the resourceful Bismarck saw how it could be 'improved'. Omitting some passages, rearranging others, he contrived to make it sound as if the King of Prussia had been publicly affronted and had then brusquely sent the French envoy packing. The edited version of the telegram, together with other inspired material, was communicated first to Bismarck's tame Press (the *Norddeutscher Allgemeine Zeitung* distributed special free editions), and then, on Bismarck's instructions, to the principal European capitals.

It was the improvisation of a man who *now* certainly did want a war. The French in their folly gave it to him, and it was possible for Bismarck afterwards (while contradictorily denying that he had sponsored Leopold's original candidature) to claim that the whole sequence of operations had been devised to trap the French and so to unify Germany by a military triumph. To the ageing Bismarck of *Reflections and Reminiscences* it may even have seemed so.

Even now, in July 1870, Napoleon III could have avoided war. His Prime Minister Ollivier was a man of peace; the British Government offered mediation; and Napoleon himself was far from a fire-eater. But he was dragged forward to the destruction of his Empire by the war party in his cabinet led by Gramont, by his wife Eugénie, and by chauvinistic journalists and parliamentarians. Outnumbered in manpower as they were, two to three, the French declared war on July 19th. When King William took the train back from Ems to Berlin his journey, he wrote, was like a triumphal procession; he was "terrified by this enthusiasm".

As the Prussian armies under Moltke now advanced towards their second great triumph in four years Bismarck moved in for the diplomatic kill. He arranged for the editor of the London *Times* to be shown a French draft of a projected Franco-German treaty assigning much of Belgium and some of Rhenish Bavaria to France; this made doubly sure of British opinion, already predisposed against the French, and at the same time it conveniently alarmed the South Germans. Italy was happy to take advantage of Napoleon's misfortunes by occupying Rome. As for Austria, she was held back from any serious contemplation of a war of revenge by her own Hungarian troubles and by fear of Russian intervention.

As in the war of 1866, Bismarck was by his King's side during the military campaign. With his steel-spiked *Pickelhaube* on his head, cuirassier's boots reaching to the top of his thighs, and blue cavalry greatcoat, he looked the complete military man; but in letters home to Johanna he cursed the generals for their disregard of their men's lives. "It's all fists and no heads," he complained, "—and still we're winning." None of the General Staff, he grumbled, "except good old Moltke", could stand up to critical inspection. Most vexing of all, for a long time they would not let him sit in at their conferences.

He was at Sedan when Napoleon's army corps of 84,000 surrendered. The last time he had met him it had been in the Tuileries; and now it was in a workman's cottage by the side of the road after the battle, with Napoleon begging for better terms than the military were ready to grant. Bismarck refused; it was to be capitulation. But he treated the sick Emperor with more consideration and courtesy than was popular back home.

As it turned out, there was a revolution in Paris and it proved necessary to continue a costly war all through the winter of 1870–71, which (Paris being under siege) Bismarck spent at Versailles. It was thus at Versailles that the new German Empire was finally forged. In South Germany there had been a powerful movement of patriotic war enthusiasm, but it is not true that the South German states simply jumped on to the band-wagon of victory. Their rulers, and in particular the Kings of Bavaria and Württemberg, were, not surprisingly, reluctant to lose their thrones, and Bismarck was prepared to grant them sizable concessions in order to bind them to the German Empire that he saw it was now in his power to create. He saw, too, that a quick settlement with the South German princes would ensure their continuing in the war, which looked likely to prove tiresomely protracted. He absolutely rejected the Crown Prince's policy of simply coercing the South German governments by main force: "Your Royal Highness, a prince perhaps can act in this way; a gentleman like myself cannot." (He always liked to score over the Crown Prince, "this stupidest", he said, "and vainest of men".) There was a further reason why Bismarck had to obtain the approval not merely of the South German people but of the princes: William I, like Frederick William before him, refused to accept an imperial crown "from the gutter"; it must come from Germany's rulers.

So in the Versailles Hall of Mirrors in January 1871 the Second German Reich came into existence. It was a tense occasion for both King and Chancellor, who spent the preceding day bitterly arguing whether William was to be 'Emperor of Germany' (a territorial title which Bismarck refused to allow) or 'German Emperor'. "This Kaiser-birth has been a difficult one," Bismarck wrote home to Johanna; he wished he could have got his hands at the throat of the "damned parson" who preached the sermon, and he was still fuming against the General Staff. The Emperor, angry at being publicly hailed merely as 'Kaiser William', ignored Bismarck's proffered hand of congratulation as he stepped off the daïs. But of course the public at home knew nothing of these birth-throes, and received the proclamation of the new Empire with un-alloyed delight.

Franco-German hostilities ended at last, with an armistice—not before Bismarck's frustration at the delays had betrayed him into some untypical attitudes. Starving Paris must be mercilessly bombarded; all *franctireurs* should be hanged; French colonial troops taken prisoner should be shot. Even this severity could not match that of his wife, whose emphatic vision of Paris was characteristic of pious nineteenth-century Protestantism in both Germany and Britain: "I would gladly have thrown in many thousands of fire-bombs, shells, and mortars," she wrote to Bismarck, "until this accursed Sodom has been utterly destroyed for ever."

The Kaiser, Moltke, and the military men all insisted that Germany must have the whole of Alsace and Lorraine as the spoils of victory. Bismarck was less sure. In the peace negotiations with the French he insisted on the full severity of the German demands; but with his own side he pleaded that at least the French claim to Metz should be conceded, "if they paid us another thousand million. . . . I just don't like having so many Frenchmen in our house who don't want to be there." Strasbourg, largely German, was another matter. This proved one of the few occasions when he did not get his way—and perhaps it was partly because he was not himself wholly convinced of the wisdom of his own arguments. Perhaps it would be impossible to conciliate France; perhaps "they will simply fall on us the moment they think themselves strong enough". If so, the only answer was force, and the generals were right. Certainly they won the argument in 1871. The wholly French fortress city of Metz went to Germany to make doubly sure that a French war of revenge could not succeed. Bismarck's judgment insisted that it *was* a mistake. Thus at a significant moment of history the last word in Germany rested not with moderation but with aggrandizement, not with Bismarck but with Moltke. Germany made it impossible for the French ever to forgive or forget their humiliation.

Bismarck was not in general a statesman of principles. He had only two consistent touchstones of policy: before 1871 the expansion and greatness of Prussia; after 1871 the maintenance of European peace. Everything else was calculated according to the shifting currents of the hour. He was a great contriver and balancer, a master of expedients, supple, elastic, pragmatical. Anti-democratic, he introduced universal suffrage and the secret ballot, thinking thereby to confound the essentially middle-class liberals. Contemptuously anti-liberal until 1866, he co-operated with the National Liberals over the next decade to pass some highly progressive legislation affecting the judicial system, local government, and trade. In the early seventies he was bitterly attacked by conservatives, and especially by his own class of Junkers, when he removed from them their police powers and forced the reform through the Prussian Upper House by getting William to create new liberal members for the purpose. He persecuted Roman Catholics in the seventies, but was pleased to ally with them against the liberals and socialists in the eighties. When there was an attempt on the Emperor's life in 1878,[8] his first reaction when the very serious news was brought to him was not one of shock and concern but of zestful anticipation

8 It was actually the second and more serious of two attempts made in the Unter den Linden within a few weeks of one another. The would-be assassin was an impoverished intellectual, Dr Nobiling. He acted entirely on his own, but the opportunity to 'smear' the Social Democrats was too good for so political an animal as Bismarck to neglect.

at the opportunity the crime gave him of 'dishing' the liberals and crushing the socialists. His first words were "Then we'll dissolve the Reichstag!"—and in the ensuing election the National Liberals lost heavily. He fully acknowledged this quick, instinctive reaction of his to events:

> I have often acted hastily and without reflection. . . . I have never been a doctrinaire. . . . Give me a strong German state, and then ask me whether it should have more or less liberal furnishings, and you'll find that I answer: Yes, I've no fixed opinions; make proposals and you won't find any objections of principle from me. . . .

This sounds a long way from the views of the violent reactionary of 1848, who was to be called on "only when the bayonet is in full command".

Only on one issue, the place of the Roman Church in the new Empire, did he show something of the old rabid spirit. Prussia had once been an entirely Protestant state. It was first her new Polish subjects and then after 1815 her Rhinelanders who had begun to create for her a Catholic problem; and the chief reason why Bismarck after 1866 had been chary of absorbing the mainly Catholic South German states had been that they were ill-disposed to the Protestant North. Now suddenly in 1871, 37 per cent of the citizens of the Empire were Catholics, and Catholics at a time when Pope Pius IX and the First Vatican Council had just set the Roman Church upon the course of militant conservatism that had culminated in 1870 with the proclamation of Papal Infallibility. Rome, moreover, had sympathized with Prussia's enemies both in 1866 and in 1870. And now the new Centre Party founded at the time of the Franco-German war was proving to be a rallying point not only for the Catholics of Prussian Poland, Alsace, and South Germany but also for any political group disgruntled with Bismarck's policies—the supporters, for instance, of the deposed King of Hanover. For Bismarck all these opponents were the *Reichsfeinde*, enemies of the Empire, which was another way of saying 'enemies of Bismarck'. Already Pius IX had declared liberalism incompatible with Catholicism, but in any case German liberals were Bismarck's natural allies in this particular battle. With their support he set about crushing the Catholics.

In fact every German bishop at the Vatican Council had voted against Papal Infallibility, and a small but distinguished group of

German 'Old Catholics' refused to accept it. When the Catholic bishops (a great majority of whom fell into line) made a demand for the removal of the 'Old Catholics' from teaching posts, Bismarck's government refused it. Here was an issue for him to get his teeth into: a defence of German civilization (*Kultur*) against foreign contamination, of the German state against the infiltration of Rome; "a struggle for power", said Bismarck, "as old as the human race . . . between king and priest." He would defend the Empire against enemies internal or external. The anti-Catholic laws which now followed were severe. The Catholic clergy were debarred from inspecting primary schools. Priests who had not been educated at state schools and universities, or who were not Germans, were banned. The teaching of the monastic orders was put under state supervision. Jesuits were expelled from the country. It was an offence to preach in a manner likely to endanger public order. Civil marriage became compulsory (although Bismarck had earlier declared strongly against it). Many of the bishops and priests who resisted this legislation went to prison, and a time came when nearly half the Catholic parishes of Prussia—including most of those in the Polish districts and Alsace—were without their priest.

This 'struggle for the German way of life' (*Kulturkampf*) was Bismarck's most resounding failure. He had defeated Austria and humiliated France; but the Roman Church proved altogether too much for him, and he succeeded only in making martyrs. Having built national unity, he was now in danger of destroying civil unity. The Reichstag elections of 1874 gave the Centre Party as many as 95 seats. That same year a young Catholic tried to assassinate Bismarck, and there was white-hot hatred in the Chamber when he attempted to pin responsibility on the Centre Party. The atmosphere was such that many even of his Protestant conservative supporters, including William I, thought they saw the danger developing of a *general* attack on religion; compulsory civil marriage especially alarmed them. Stubbornly throughout 1875–76–77 Bismarck persisted, persecuting Catholics, frightening conservatives, offending many Junkers by condemning the backwardness of their attitudes, and still leaning on National Liberal support. He even offered to appoint one of their leaders, Bennigsen, to the post of Prussian Home Secretary, but Bennigsen declined unless Bismarck would appoint two of his fellow-leaders to ministerial posts. Nothing more, therefore, was heard about the matter.

His personal troubles multiplied too over these years. His health deteriorated; he had an alarming collection of stomach, kidney, and nerve disorders. His bulk, always large, grew enormous. He slept badly and was formidably irritable. Even now only just over sixty, he had been talking of himself for a decade as an old man; he was, he said, "weary of life". In March 1877, having first offered to resign, he retreated to his estates. Sick or well, he was indispensable; he knew it and he expected everybody else to recognize it. During the next ten months in the country he thought many things out afresh, and his return to Berlin in April 1878 signalled several switches of policy. The 'liberal' era was over.

Breaking with the National Liberals, he abandoned his earlier intention of allowing the new Germany to become, as Britain had become, a free-trade country. Henceforth, with the approval of the Centre Party and the conservatives, and of Junkers and industrialists alike, Germany was to be more firmly protectionist than before. New industries were insulated from the full severity of foreign competition; farmers and landowners were sheltered, as in free-trade Britain they were not, from the drastic effects of unrestricted grain imports from the New World and Russia. Grasping now the support of his old enemies of the Centre, he began winding up the *Kulturkampf*, being eased in his retreat by the death of Pius IX and the conciliatory gestures of his successor Leo XIII. (By 1887 Leo was able to pronounce the chapter of conflict closed.) At the same time, and again with the support of the conservatives and Centre, he moved against the force that he had been coming to see as a more dangerous enemy than either Catholicism or liberalism—the rapidly growing party of revolutionary socialism. By the the Socialist Law of October 1878, renewable triennially, all meetings, societies, books, or pamphlets aimed at overthrowing the existing political or social order were banned. Agitators could in future be expelled from their home towns; districts were empowered in severe circumstances to proclaim a state of emergency. (Social Democrat members nevertheless continued to sit in the Reichstag.)

Here was an issue even more crucial than that of religion. The conflict of Protestant versus Catholic was an old one; the rules of the battle, the ways of the enemy, were known and understood. But the social problems involved in the birth of modern industrialism were new and uncharted. Explosive forces were forming among the mines and steelworks of the Ruhr, the docks of Hamburg and shipyards of the north-coast ports, the tens of thousands of factories taking Germany rapidly forward to the industrial leadership of continental Europe. The new socialist theories of collective owner-ship were a fundamental challenge to existing conceptions of society—whether the Junker, agrarian notion which was basically Bismarcks' own, or the capitalist conception of the businessmen and liberal intellectuals, which Bismarck distrusted—even hated—but had gone along with during the seventies.

Socialism must be killed; the question was whether by kindness or harshness. In the forty years between 1878 and the revolution of 1918 both methods were tried. Both failed. The strength of the German Social Democrat Party grew impartially in fair weather and foul until after the First World War its destiny was to preside over the collapse of Bismarck's Empire. Bismarck's own predilection was for severity. The ideas of socialism were as abhorrent to him in the eighties as the ideas of liberalism in the forties; and now, after his flirtation with the liberals in the seventies, he was back on a course that came more naturally to him. In his words socialists were "the menacing bands of robbers with whom we share our largest towns". Like Metternich, he now visualized himself as "a rock of order"; and in due course the break with Kaiser William II that led to his dismissal was to come upon this very issue of harsh-ness to the socialists.

Bismarck, however, would not have been Bismarck if he had not also subtler and more imaginative schemes. Together with repres-sion came welfare; a policy of "whips and sugar plums", as the Social Democrats scornfully described it. In 1884 came legislation for compulsory state insurance against sickness and industrial accidents; five years later (and twenty years before Britain) old-age pensions. Benefits were low; but the principle was new and radical; Bismarck is one of the most surprising grandparents of the Welfare State. But as a counter-attraction to socialism his insurance schemes must be reckoned a total failure. The workers swallowed the sugar plums but still voted in increasing numbers for the Social Democrats.

After 1871 Germany was, in Bismarck's words, "a satisfied state", and the object of all his subsequent diplomacy was to keep things as they were. This meant above all two things: first, to pre-vent France from building up an anti-German alliance that would allow her to wage a war of revenge; and, second, to prevent the inevitably opposed interests of Russia and Austria-Hungary from breaking out into a war which would upset the balance of power in Eastern Europe. European peace, then, was what Germany needed once she had created her Empire.

Although the German generals did not fear France on her own, even the rapidly recovering France of the early seventies, Bismarck in 1875 did promote some dangerous-sounding talk of a second war against the French. "The cause of peace is not assisted," he told his Emperor, "if France is assured that she will in no circumstances be attacked whatever she may do." The idea of a preventive war, however, was greeted with such outspoken hostility from Russia and Britain that no more was heard of it; it is in any case improbable that Bismarck ever seriously contemplated it. Over the next decade, in fact, Franco-German diplomatic relations steadily improved, with Bismarck losing no opportunity of encouraging France "everywhere in the world except at that little corner on the Rhine". The more busily Frenchmen were engaged in expanding their empire in Tunis, in central Africa, in Egypt, or in Indo-China (Vietnam), the less anxious became Germany's watch on the Rhine. But when in 1887 France seemed to be under the spell of another of its men of destiny, General Boulanger, with much heady talk of revenge for 1870, Bismarck could not resist exploiting the situation. His generals assured him that they were not afraid of France, and the chauvinistic Boulanger soon proved a broken reed; but since for Bismarck foreign and domestic affairs were always part of one and the same matter, the chance to play the Boulanger scare against "the enemies of the Reich" was too good to miss. A great hullaba-loo was raised of "the Fatherland in danger", and at the 1887 general election the parties hostile to Bismarck were slaughtered. Until now he had striven fruitlessly to get his new Army Law through the Reichstag (it was to run for seven years), and the situation had become uncomfortably reminiscent of the original Army crisis of 1862. Now, thanks to Boulanger ("he happened very conveniently," Bismarck admitted) the Army vote went through with a massive majority.

This ability of the old master-tactician to use foreign issues to promote his own domestic advantage can be seen too in his attitude towards the acquisition of colonies. Bismarck did not want colonies for Germany. He castigated "the greed of the colonial jingoes". Colonies would prove costly to the taxpayer—and this they certainly did prove to be. Moreover, for so 'continental' a Power as Germany they were a distraction and an irrelevance. "Your map of Africa is very nice," he once said, "but my map of Africa lies in Europe. There lies Russia and there lies France, and we are in the middle. That is my map of Africa." Yet suddenly in the eighties Bismarck's often repeated opposition to colonies seemed to melt away. In South West Africa, in West Africa, in East Africa, and in New Guinea, Germany acquired territories which appeared to be direct challenges to British imperial interests. Despite appearances Bismarck had not changed his views, and he certainly had no intention of becoming involved in a war over colonial issues; but for electoral purposes in 1884 a quarrel with Britain was likely to be highly convenient. It could provide a stick with which to beat the Social Democrats and the Progressives, who could be made to seem anti-national—for at this time feeling in Germany was running strongly in favour of colonies and against the British. Gladstone— "Professor Gladstone", as Bismarck was pleased to sneer at him —was British Prime Minister over these years, and a tiff with Gladstonian England was almost worth having for its own sake. The Crown Prince, moreover, whom Bismarck recognized as his arch-enemy (he was bound to be Emperor very soon) was an admirer of Gladstone, and it would be useful for Bismarck to have in reserve a popular nationalistic policy to use against a 'pro-British' Emperor. This last was Herbert Bismarck's explanation of his father's about-turn on colonies. The old man's own was balder: "The whole colonial business is a swindle, but we need it for the election."

"There lies Russia, and there lies France, and we are in the middle." Russia was never absent from Bismarck's calculations; but there too lay Austria-Hungary, still a great and even expansionist Power, her ambitions turned (once she had lost her key position in Germany and Italy) south-eastward towards the Balkans. Bismarck accepted as axiomatic that Russia and Austria must clash in the Balkans; his most constant anxiety after 1871 was to keep these two 'natural' enemies from war. (An Anglo-Russian war would be different; the more damage Russia and Britain did to one another the better.) Between 1866 and 1871 Bismarck had had the benefit of Russian neutrality. After 1871 the main weight of his diplomatic energies was directed towards making Germany secure on her eastern frontiers.

Between 1875 and 1878 there was a prolonged Balkan crisis, with the Christian subjects of the Turk in revolt. Russia, coming to their aid, defeated Turkey and threatened Constantinople. Britain and Austria then forced Russia under threat of war to deny herself the fruits of her military victory and come to the conference table. In all this Bismarck's concern was to prevent a general war if possible, but in any case to keep Germany out of the quarrel. Over and over again he said that the whole Balkan question was not worth the bones of a single Pomeranian grenadier—a revealingly *Prussian* sentiment.

So it came about that Bismarck presided at the vital European conference that met in Berlin in the summer of 1878, ten days after Nobiling's attempt on the Emperor's life. Germany herself, he stressed, had no sides to take or claims to make; she was simply the peacemaker, the "honest broker" in the settlement. The Russians for their part were not at all convinced of this, and resented what they considered to be Bismarck's part in the final treaty, which constituted a sharp diplomatic defeat for Russia. In fact Russo-German relations were deteriorating throughout the 1870's, to the serious alarm of William I. The Tsar Alexander II was his nephew, and blood was thicker than water. It was the apparently wilful and off-hand hostility of Bismarck that puzzled and pained him.

As host and chairman of the Congress of Berlin Bismarck was in his element, forcing things along at a cracking pace so that he "could get off to Kissingen for the cure", not bothering to conceal his distaste for the more tedious or pompous speakers (Gorchakov, the Russian, for instance), going out of his way to be charming to the Frenchman, Waddington, gormandizing like Gargantua himself at the numerous banquets. As for Disraeli, Bismarck was highly taken with him; "the old Jew," he kept saying, "that's the man." And plainly there was something about the artfully receptive Disraeli that encouraged the outrageous side of Bismarck. Reporting back to Queen Victoria, Disraeli wrote:

> In the afternoon at six o'clock great dinner at Prince Bismarck's. All these banquets are very well done. There must have been sixty guests. . . . I sat on the right of Prince Bismarck and, never caring much to eat in public, I could listen to his Rabelaisian monologue; endless revelations of things he ought not to mention. He impressed on me never to trust princes or courtiers, that his illness was not, as people supposed, brought on by the French war, but by the horrible conduct of his sovereign, etc., etc. . . .

Disraeli, knowing his Queen Victoria very well, did not neglect to add how different was the conduct of *his* sovereign, etc., etc.

But the Chancellor was not all outrageous lovability. Some of the more unpleasant aspects of his character grew upon him in old age. When, for instance, in 1881, his son Herbert wished to marry Princess Carolath, whom Bismarck disapproved of (principally because she was related to a courtier he hated), the old man showed a distressing vindictiveness and torrents of almost pathological temperament. Appealing alternately to pity and fear, he threatened to kill himself and to ruin his son's career. The Princess, who was already married, was divorced because of Herbert Bismarck, but then he did not go through with the match. The parental bully in Bismarck won his rather scandalous victory, and Herbert continued to climb the ladder of his career. Bismarck never forgot a slight or forgave his enemies; when, for example, the Liberal politician Lasker died in the U.S.A. he refused to pass on to the Reichstag the Congress's message of sympathy. Roon complained that he treated him "as a rebellious and inefficient subordinate". He was excessively rude to officials who could not answer back. Even his son Herbert, an important minister, would be snubbed in public with *Quatsch nicht*—"Don't talk drivel." He could be mercilessly unforgiving; Count von Arnim, German ambassador in Paris, whom he saw as a possible rival and imagined to be intriguing against him with the Empress Augusta, was hounded by Bismarck, even to the extent of criminal proceedings and effective exile.

Living much of his time on his estates in crusty, solitary, majesty, he admitted that he often lay awake all night just *hating*. He tyrannized over his assistants and changed them (said Holstein) "like knives and forks after every course". He had his cronies and confidants, a fairly small circle, Count Henckel, Bleichröder his personal financial adviser, Bucher, Count Rantzau. He had himself long been *Prince* Bismarck, but when members of the old aristocracy came to visit him they found his Varzin and Friedrichsruh households more than a little unprincely and eccentric. Great dogs cluttered up the rooms and like their master were liable to bite. Two of Bismarck's doctors declined to go on treating him or his family because they would not put up with the conditions of service. It was not until a very direct fellow arrived, a certain Dr Schweninger, that Bismarck at long last consented to follow any medical advice. Schweninger was tough. "I don't like being asked questions," said Bismarck. "Then get a vet," said Schweninger; "he doesn't question his patients." Under his care half Bismarck's chronic ailments improved or disappeared. Dieting reduced his weight from eighteen stones to fourteen. Plainly many of his troubles had been due to gluttony and alcohol. Mentally he did not age; his intelligence was as keen, his tongue as blistering, as ever.

After the Congress of Berlin William I, visiting Russia, did his utmost to set things right with his nephew the Tsar, but Bismarck, against the Emperor's wishes and during his absence, almost casually made the most far-reaching of all his diplomatic decisions. The result was the Austro-German Dual Alliance of 1879, bitterly resented by William and carried through by Bismarck only after more hoisting of storm signals and, once again, threats of resignation. "Let those who have forced me to take this step answer for it above," said the Emperor. "My whole strength is broken," he wrote to Bülow; "I don't know what will become of me." Bismarck was far more concerned with what would happen to *him* when the Emperor died.

The Austro-German Treaty fashioned a new kind of alliance: one made in peace-time to meet hypothetical situations. Under its terms each ally would aid the other if attacked by Russia or would remain neutral if the other were attacked by any Power other than Russia—meaning plainly France. It was the first step towards the great system and counter-system of alliances aimed at securing the peace but ultimately leading to the 1914–18 war. Bismarck was aware of the dangers. He many times repeated that he would support no Austrian military adventures in the Balkans, and perhaps, had he still been alive and in power, he never would have tolerated the combination of muddle and recklessness with which the 1914 German Government did just that. (Even this is far from certain—there had been a good deal of muddle and recklessness on Bismarck's part in 1869–70.) All the same, with the Dual Alliance of 1879 the signposts are up, pointing to 1914. Soon joined by Italy (hence the Triple Alliance, 1882), it inevitably invited its own counterpoise, even by Bismarck's own logic of the balance of power. Plainly too the alliance was seen to be aimed against Russia and France. And since vital national interests have a way of ignoring opposed political systems and joining hands across chasms, it pointed directly towards the 'impossible' alliance between republican

France and Tsarist Russia, the war on two fronts, the German nightmare.

In order to forestall this and to hang on to what was left of Russian friendship, despite all the harsh words and the Austrian alliance, Bismarck in the 1880's constructed a super-subtle policy of 'reinsurance', for long hailed as his diplomatic masterpiece. In plain terms this famous Reinsurance Treaty (1887) meant making a secret agreement with Russia behind the back of his Austrian ally: double-dealing on the grand scale even though its motivation was peaceful. Its potential efficacy—for it was never put to any test—must be regarded as very doubtful, and his successors, judging so, immediately abandoned it.

When Emperor William I died at last in 1888 Bismarck, at seventy-two, was undoubtedly the leading statesman in Europe. He had imprinted his stamp upon Germany, upon Europe, upon his era, as no other statesman since Napoleon and Metternich. Assuming by now practically monarchical status, he even had an heir in his son Herbert, State Secretary since 1886. "I shall not go," he declared, "even if they throw me out." "They", of course, meant the contemptible enemy, the wishy-washy liberal, the man who mixed water with his wine and perhaps had some Gladstone or other up his sleeve, the Anglophile Crown Prince Frederick William and his English wife. Already, however, the Crown Prince was under sentence of death, stricken with cancer. Doomed also, though he could not yet know it, was Bismarck's own position. By 1888 the Age of Bismarck was all but over.[9]

Table of Events

1815.	Bismarck born at Schönhausen. German Confederation.
1840–61.	Frederick William IV King of Prussia.
1847.	Bismarck in the United Prussian Diet.
1848.	Revolution in Berlin and throughout Germany. Frederick William refuses German crown.
1851–58.	Bismarck represents Prussia at Confederation Diet.
1858–62.	Ambassador at St Petersburg.
1861 (–88).	William I, previously Regent, King of Prussia.
1862.	Constitutional crisis over Army reforms; Bismarck called to power.
1863.	Polish rebellion.

[9] For an account of Bismarck's dismissal and last years see the ensuing chapter, *Kaiser William II.*

1864.	Schleswig-Holstein dispute; war with Denmark.
1866.	Austro-Prussian ('Seven Weeks') War. Treaty of Prague. Bismarck Chancellor of North German Confederation.
1866–78.	Co-operation with National Liberals.
1869.	Supports Hohenzollern candidature to Spanish throne.
1870.	Ems telegram. Franco-German war.
1871.	German Empire proclaimed at Versailles.
1871–78.	The *Kulturkampf*.
1878.	First Anti-Socialist Law. Congress of Berlin.
1879.	Dual Alliance with Austria (Triple Alliance, 1882).
c.1884.	Acceptance of colonial expansion.
1884–87.	Social insurance legislation.
1887.	Exploits Boulanger episode to win election and secure new Army law. Reinsurance Treaty.
1888.	Death of William I and Frederick; William II succeeds.
1890.	Dismissal of Bismarck.
1898.	Death at Friedrichsruh.

12

KAISER WILLIAM II
(1859-1941)
And the Slide to World War

The death of Kaiser William I in 1888 signalled the end of an era for Germany. By all the accepted standards of the day it had been a great one. Under Bismarck Germany had achieved at least a sort of political unity, though at the cost of Austria's expulsion. The German Empire had arrived among the three or four greatest of the Powers. Her rate of industrial growth had been impressively rapid and was still increasing. Her army was the finest in Europe, yet under Bismarck's moderating hand had not seemed since 1871 to constitute a danger to the peace of Europe. The Austro-Hungarian Empire and Italy were Germany's allies; France and Russia had been kept from allying against her. Britain was so little hostile that Germany had even been able to acquire colonies and thus somewhat to satisfy her need for prestige with no more trouble than a few wrangles at the conference table.

Yet the appearance of stability was illusory. Germany, which after 1871 Bismarck had declared to be a "satisfied state", was far from that. She was a nation on the move, bursting with confidence and ambition. Her population was soaring. Her manufacturers were seeking new markets, her financiers new investments, beyond the German borders. There were, or were soon to be, a Colonial League, a Pan-German League, a Navy League, an Eastern Borders Association, and many more such ultra-patriotic associations bang-the German drum. The trouble was that if Germany sought expansion she must inevitably expand into others' zones of expansion. She had no elbow room such as France in North and West Africa, or Russia had in Asia, or Britain had the wide world over. To expand in Europe Germany must become a military aggressor; to expand overseas beyond the limits set by Britain she must challenge the British Navy.

In internal affairs also the Bismarckian Reich was far from stable. The great Chancellor's own personal ascendancy, his adroit manipulations and timely retreats, had for a time maintained its authoritarian structure against parliamentary and working-class pressures. By the eighties, however, Bismarck was running out of expedients. Concessions in social insurance for the labouring masses did nothing to destroy their appetite for more political and industrial influence. So long as William I was there, Bismarck's position appeared unassailable. Nevertheless, godlike as he seemed, he was finding it more and more difficult to maintain a majority in the Reichstag. In the elections of 1887 he rallied electoral support only by crying up patriotic fears for the safety of the Fatherland. Already he was contemplating the outlawing of the Social-Democrat Party. The Constitution of 1871 might have to be overturned: "We may well reach the point," he remarked in 1886, "where I shall be compelled to destroy what I have myself created."

Bismarck had nothing but contempt for the Crown Prince, soon briefly to be Kaiser Frederick: a well-meaning and liberal-minded man likely, Bismarck thought, to want to meddle with the established system and perpetrate the horror of horrors, a "Gladstone cabinet". In fact, as a National Liberal, Frederick approved of much that Bismarck had achieved, but disapproved of his methods, which he considered cynical. Mild-eyed, earnest and malleable, Frederick had an English wife. The moulding force behind him that Bismarck resented—indeed, hated—was the Crown Princess Victoria, Queen Victoria's eldest daughter and like her mother a woman of formidable will. Her father, Albert, whom she adored, had taught her long ago that Prussia was an illiberal country that stood in dire need of constitutional reform, and her married life as the Prussian heir's wife who never ceased to be an Englishwoman confirmed everything that she had been taught. Germans found her rigid, domineering, and hostile. On her side, revulsion against German ways became rationalized in righteous condemnations: of Bismarck, for his lack of principle and brutal use of force; of Prussia, for her lack of respect for justice and liberty. Though she intrigued against him, she could not shake Bismarck while he enjoyed the trust of the old Kaiser; but she intended, when William I died, to see that things were run differently.

As it turned out, Bismarck had no need to worry. Rather more than a year before the old Kaiser's death, Frederick developed cancer of the larynx; the doctors were able to prolong his life by performing a tracheotomy, but he never spoke again. There was a macabre race between him and his aged father to see who could cheat death the longer. When he did come to the throne, the shadow of a man, it was amid an unsavoury public controversy concerning the alleged incompetence of his English doctor. His first acts as Emperor were to decorate the new Empress with the Order of the Black Eagle and to pencil on a slip of paper his gratitude for being spared "to live long enough to be able to reward the courage and energy" of his wife.

Nothing had worked out as Victoria had planned. Her husband, acceding in March, died in June. Her eldest son, William, born in 1859, had had the ill luck to be a disappointment to his parents. He was partially crippled, with a left arm shrunken as a result of damage done at birth by the doctor's forceps, and his mother never ceased to lament and even exaggerate this misfortune, which, though it permanently handicapped him, did more damage perhaps to his mind than to his body. It did not prevent him, for instance, from becoming a proficient horse-rider, yachtsman, and shot. But he grew to resent his parents and to behave abominably both to his father, whom he despised, and to his mother, whom he considered a traitress to Germany. Bismarck, with an eye to the future, had not neglected to play upon this rift, paying serious attention to William's schooling in foreign affairs and the Bismarckian tradition. It was not that the young man lacked seriousness or application; he was almost too ready to assume his responsibilities. Rather, it was steadiness and judgment that were lacking. Charitableness, too, was wanting: even before his father's burial he asserted himself, putting a wing of the royal palace under Army supervision while he personally ransacked his dead father's tables and drawers for papers that would incriminate, so he thought, his mother. He then prevented her from entering the palace rose-garden to pick roses for the death chamber, and in the end she refused to attend the public funeral. The Prince and Princess of Wales, who did, were outraged by the behaviour both of William and the Bismarcks, father and son. It was the beginning of a long and eventful antipathy.

As soon as the funeral was over, Kaiser William II with gusto set about the business of ruling Germany. He was twenty-nine, keen-eyed, cocksure, sharp-minded, volatile, abounding in physical energy. He had positive and voluble, if not always consistent, opinions on every subject. He sped from one topic to another, from one ceremony or foreign visit to another, from one splendid uniform to another still more splendid. Of latter years Bismarck had made a point of serenely governing the country by remote control from his Friedrichsruh estate in the depths of the country-side. By contrast, with William everything was suddenly activity and drama. The margins of political dispatches were spattered with his excited commentary. Reviewing his troops, hunting, pheasant-shooting, opening the Reichstag, yachting, visiting his own small navy, inspecting the enormous British one (of which to his delight he was made honorary Admiral of the Fleet), attending torchlight processions of students, making innumerable civic speeches full of crackling phrases—he moved everything along at breakneck speed and with imperial panache.

If William had been content to be a spectacular figurehead, a public-display Kaiser who left the business of politics to the politicians, things might have turned out differently. But he had serious and high-minded political intentions, ideas of enlarging the Triple Alliance to include all the major Powers, dreams of uniting into a single-minded German people all the contending classes and factions. The loyalty of the rich landowners and capitalists, the almost religious patriotic fervour of Protestant liberals of the middle class —these would be easy to command. But he wanted also to be the adored Emperor of the Catholics and of the Socialists: a working-man's Kaiser, a "King of the Beggars". At the same time he held constantly before him the example of Frederick II, "the Great King". However, as his mother wrote to Queen Victoria, "a little modesty and self-understanding would teach him that he is neither Frederick the Great nor the genius that he imagines himself to be." William's own high valuation of himself was accepted dutifully by his admiring wife, the bigoted and primly conventional Empress Augusta Victoria. (She was almost *too* submissive; in the end her constant running after him was liable to exasperate him.) To his seven children the Kaiser was a remote and—to his six sons at least —a forbidding figure. And of course the whole official existence that he was born into was one where he could not enter a room without a springing to attention, a clicking of heels, and a curtseying of ladies.

He was the All-Highest; and in theory at least he was also the All-Powerful, King of Prussia, Emperor of Germany by divine right, and supreme War Lord of the Imperial Army. By the Constitution of 1871 he could determine foreign policy, make war and peace, conclude treaties, summon or prorogue the Federal Council and the Reichstag, and appoint or dismiss the Chancellor. The practice, however, was different. For a quarter of a century Bismarck had ruled by *his* divine right that sprang from his own success, and he remained confident of staying in power for the rest of his life, despite the Reichstag, despite Frederick and his constitutionalism, despite now the unpredictability of the "hot-headed, conceited, and wrong-headed" William. (The epithets were Queen Victoria's, but the sentiments were shared by Bismarck, and, indeed, by most who came into close contact with the young Emperor.)

The year 1889, in Germany as in England, was one marked by strikes, discontents, and agitation. For these troubles Bismarck and the Kaiser proposed opposite remedies. Bismarck was for limiting the franchise, abolishing the secret ballot, and crushing the Social Democrats. As for the Reichstag, he sought deliberately to provoke it by advancing two proposals—one for a very costly military budget, the other to permit the deportation of Socialist agitators. William, on the other hand, was for conciliation. He had already convened, to Bismarck's annoyance, an international conference in Berlin to discuss labour problems. He wished, further, to enact laws enforcing a Sunday holiday and limiting the work of women and children. For a time Bismarck thought that he had frightened the Kaiser into seeing the error of his ways. "No surrender", they agreed—or so Bismarck thought. When the 1890 Reichstag elections went against him—the pro-Bismarck parties lost 85 seats and the Social Democrats trebled theirs—he proposed more and more reckless measures; force, if need be: "the time for blood and iron" might well be coming again.

There was certainly to be a show-down; but it proved to be not between Bismarck and the Reichstag, not between Bismarck and the Social Democrats, but between the Kaiser and Bismarck. William, following some high words, instructed his Chancellor to rescind an old Cabinet order which forbade ministers to consult the Emperor without first consulting the Chancellor. Bismarck refused. The source of his power now suddenly became the source of his weakness. He had always claimed loftily to be independent of parliament or party, the master agent of the Emperor's will. This meant, however, that there was no parliamentary base from which to fight back when a new Emperor chose to brush him aside. He reaped what he had sown. (If only Queen Victoria had been able thus easily to get rid of Gladstone, whom she detested, and whose 'weakness' Bismarck had despised!)

Thus William dispensed with the indispensable minister, and at the same time with his son, deputy, and 'heir', Herbert Bismarck. Bismarck, though he had many enemies (some of whom, like Count von Waldersee, played a part behind the scenes in stiffening William's resolution), had come to most Germans to seem so essential a part of the natural order that it was thought necessary to preserve the fiction that he had retired through ill-health. Only privately could he affirm the truth, that he had been "sent packing". Neither could he publicly show his feelings about the man who, he considered, would "ruin the Empire"; but he did allow himself the gesture of taking three roses from the mountain of flowers sent him by his admirers and placing them on the sarcophagus of *his* Kaiser, William I. Then he retired to his estate at Friedrichsruh. He was seventy-five; but he was not the man to accept defeat. For the rest of his life he schemed to come back. He published innumerable articles in the Press, over a hundred during 1892 in one Hamburg paper alone. He raked over the past in his memoirs, and rearranged it where necessary to demonstrate his own unique wisdom. But the Kaiser, who had dared to put Germany at risk by dismissing him, never considered having him back; and to Bismarck it was remarkably galling how little he was missed.

Getting rid of Bismarck did nothing, of course, to solve Germany's social problems. Together with his new Chancellor, the Prussian general Caprivi, William for a time made much of his "New Course'. But their well-meaning intention to make the régime popular with the mass of working folk was of little significance so long as the political structure of the Empire remained undemocratic and effective power rested (or was disputed) between Emperor, industrialists, and the military aristocracy. William, claiming noisily that there was "only one master in the Empire—and that is myself", soon found his 'soft' domestic policy bankrupt. Before long he was threatening worse blood-and-thunder to the Socialists even than Bismarck had. A speech at Potsdam to new recruits revealed his usual bluster and tactlessness. (It was reading this speech that convinced Tolstoy that the Kaiser's mind was diseased.)

You have sworn loyalty to me. That means, children of my guard, that you are now my soldiers. You have committed yourselves to me body and soul. There is for you one enemy and that is my enemy. In view of the present Socialist agitation it may be that I shall order you to shoot down your own relatives, brothers, or even—which God forbid—your parents, but even then you must carry out my orders without a murmur.

Caprivi, though he came from the Prussian military aristocracy, displayed by contrast a patient leniency in his dealings with the Social Democrats and some obstinacy in coping with the wild fluctuations of the Kaiser. By 1894 William had had enough of him, and dismissed him—confessing nevertheless to his friend Count Eulenburg that he had "no idea whom he could call on next". The choice fell upon Prince Hohenlohe, a Bavarian Catholic of moderate views and an elder statesman of tact and long experience. Events, however, were never under his control.

Apart from the Kaiser's, the hand chiefly influencing the conduct of foreign affairs was not that of the successive Chancellors, but of Holstein, Counsellor at the Foreign Office continuously from 1878 to 1906. Bismarck had made use of his abilities for twelve years while disliking and despising him: "the man with the hyena's eyes," he warned William, "of whom you must be wary." In 1890 Holstein had the satisfaction of helping to bring about Bismarck's fall, and after that never felt quite safe until the old man was dead. From 1890, while the truculent and erratic Kaiser postured and thundered, Holstein, spiteful, eccentric, and remote, came to regard the formulation of policy as his own preserve. Even Bülow, the most important of William's ministers (Foreign Minister, 1897–1900, Chancellor, 1900–9), stood to Holstein rather in the position of pupil to master; it was indirectly Holstein's recommendation (through Eulenburg, the Kaiser's intimate) that had brought him to the fore. As for the Kaiser, Holstein regarded him as a meddler; he met him once only, and was of the opinion that, not being sane, he should be placed under restriction. This strange man Holstein, charming when he cared to be, inveterate but secret gambler on the stock exchange, was loved by none and trusted none. He always carried a revolver in his pocket, and on one occasion he challenged to a duel and wounded the editor of a humorous paper which had attacked him. He spent a lifetime in the Foreign Office working out the complicated equation of European diplomacy—and in the end got the answer wrong.

Holstein's policies, like his intellectual processes, were complicated, but at the heart of them was this theory: Germany must exploit the fact that the rivalries of her chief potential enemies, Britain, Russia, and France, were so deep-rooted as to render these states incapable of military co-operation. In particular, the clashing interests of Britain and Russia must ultimately involve them in war; this Germany ought to be ready to profit from. His consistent mistrust of Britain was the principal stumbling-block to the Anglo-German alliance which Joseph Chamberlain sought—and in his own inconsistent way the Kaiser too—between 1898 and 1901. The aggressiveness of Germany's own actions during the Holstein era in the end made possible the very alliance of France, Britain, and Russia that he thought impossible.

On Bismarck's dismissal in 1890 Holstein first discovered the secrets of the Reinsurance Treaty with Russia; it was due for renewal. But in Holstein's view it was too clever by half, and, if discovered, would be likely to endanger the Austrian alliance, the foundation stone of German policy. Holstein, Caprivi, and the Foreign Minister Marschall, therefore, together advised William against renewal of the Treaty. It was left to Bismarck in 1896 unscrupulously to reveal, as part of his private war on William and his new ministers, the secret of the Reinsurance Treaty. By then he could point to what had happened since the good old days when Bismarck was at the helm. France and Russia were now drawing together ominously for Germany. First (1891) there had been an exchange of naval visits, then military consultations, then (1893) a secret treaty of mutual assistance, finally (1897) a publicly acknowledged alliance. What Bismarck did not point out, though Caprivi justifiably did, was that France and Russia had begun to move towards an understanding well before Bismarck's dismissal. It is unlikely that he could have found any wizardry to prevent it.

If Russia and France were to make their alliances solid Germany's position between them was unpromising. The least the Kaiser could do was to try to exert his personal charm and influence on his cousin Nicky, the new Tsar of Russia (1894–1917). With the old Tsar, Alexander III, he had had no chance. "*Il est fou,*" the Tsar had said, "*C'est un garçon de mauvaise foi et mal élevé*" —and Bismarck had allowed him to see the Tsar's remarks, with the calculated intention to wound. But new developments in the Far East seemed to offer German opportunities. In the war between

China and Japan in 1894–95 China had been humiliated and seemed now to lie helplessly before the aggressor. Not only did Germany herself begin to think of acquiring a colonial base there; there seemed at the same time to be an excellent chance of diverting Russian ambitions and energies in a direction harmless to Germany. Thus the Tsar Nicholas II was encouraged to challenge Japan in northern China. This Japan neither forgot nor forgave. But William was quite unworried by Japanese resentment. On the contrary, he began to develop anti-Japanese sentiment into a kind of crusade. The Yellow Peril was much talked of in the nineties, and at one stage William even commissioned and caused to be sent to his cousin Nicky an allegorical painting showing the Powers of Europe, under the direction of the Archangel Michael, uniting to protect Christian civilization against "the attacks of Buddhism, heathenism, and barbarism". German liners travelling to the East displayed a copy, by order.

On the Chinese coastline there followed the inevitable clash between the European Powers; the 'scramble for China' was started. Russia took Port Arthur, France Kwangchow, Britain Wei-hai-Wei, and Germany—using the pretext of two missionaries murdered in Shantung—the port of Tsingtao, in the Bay of Kiaochow.

The Kaiser had developed a deal of Christian indignation over the missionaries; but two years later this was nothing to the frenzy of prolonged excitement that he suffered when the 'Boxer' nationalists rose in Peking, murdered the German Minister, and besieged the foreign embassies there. Peking, William announced, must be razed to the ground and the honour of German vindicated. Troops were prepared for the purpose. To the Kaiser's chagrin, however, an international force under a Russian commander was already on the march to Peking to relieve the beleaguered embassy staffs, and by the time the Germans arrived the job was done. That Germany should not be consulted roused him to fury. He was always given to making excitable speeches, but now they detonated all over Germany wherever there was a ship to be launched or a regiment to be addressed. "No great decision shall be taken without the German Emperor," he thundered. In an address to troops departing from Wilhelmshaven he made the most memorable and regrettable of all his many flights of public bombast:

> You are about to meet a crafty, well-armed, cruel foe. . . .
> Give no quarter! Take no prisoners! . . . Just as the Huns a

thousand years ago under their King Attila made a name for themselves that still strikes terror in story and legend, so through you may the name 'Germany' be stamped on China for a thousand years. ...

"Hun" as a synonym for "German" was too good for Germany's enemies to neglect; and the Allies in the coming World War certainly did not fail to make the burr stick. A little selective editing, and such an outburst could hardly be improved on as anti-German propaganda.

Relations with Britain had begun well after the new Kaiser's accession—rather too well for the ultra-patriots and the Colonial League. In 1890 a colonial agreement surrendered to Britain rights in Zanzibar and sovereingty over Uganda; in exchange Germany acquired a favourable frontier for her East African colony (part of modern Tanzania) and the North Sea island of Heligoland, British since 1807. From 1894 Anglo-German relations grew sourer. The emotions of the Kaiser himself were painfully divided about England. He genuinely felt himself to be, as, of course, he was, partly English. He visited annually, and spoke the language perfectly. Though his wife was German through and through, his children wore English clothes, played with English toys, and were brought up to speak English by English nursemaids. At Windsor he would point to the Keep and pronounce "From that tower the world is governed." But through his awe for the British Empire, for the Royal Navy, and for his redoubtable grandmother Victoria there ran a strong vein of envy that was half-way to hatred. His uncle Edward (Bertie), Prince of Wales, soon to be Edward VII, he detested. In his presence he always felt, more even than usual, the need to show off, to over-compensate for his withered arm with a greater than usual display of manly vigour. Competing at Cowes with his beloved *Meteor*, he threw himself so literally into the fray that the Prince of Wales feared, or perhaps hoped, that he might go overboard. The Prince's easy man-of-the-world assurance always acted as an irritant to William, and he was quick to lodge a complaint with the British Government when he considered that Edward had given him less than his due meed of deference as Emperor. Upon this, Victoria gave her 'insolent' grandson short shrift:

To pretend that he is to be treated *in private* as well as in public as "His Imperial Majesty" is *perfect madness*. ... If he had such notions he had better *never* come *here*.

But he did continue to come regularly, in particular for the racing at Cowes, where according to Edward VII he took command and turned "what was once a pleasant holiday" into "nothing but a nuisance".

These two men, William II of Germany and Edward VII of Great Britain, so dissimilar in temperament, nevertheless shared a world and a background in some respects strikingly similar. They were both eldest sons of conscientious, liberal-minded fathers and were both disapproved of by their fond and strong-willed mothers. Both in their youth were stuffed full of the majesty and dignity of their destinies. Both inherited and accepted that peacock world which expected of them half a dozen changes of uniform a day and assigned to their royal persons a semi-divine status. Sticklers for form, tradition, and etiquette, they gladly lived up to these exhausting requirements. But when with their chosen company they relaxed they were at opposite poles: the Kaiser strenuous and not a little crude among his Junker cronies, back-slapping and practical-joking on his all-male yachting cruises or his pheasant-shoots, a hearty among hearties; Edward self-indulgent with his ladies, or at his groaning dinner-table, or over the cigar-smoke at the gambling tables with his rich philistine friends; Edward a lover of France and things French; William, by contrast, a stern Prussian Protestant, seen in his own eyes at lofty moments as a modern Caesar sent to humble 'the Gauls'. This last was a term he was always using; for him all France's vaunted civilization amounted only to an unpleasant amalgam of superstitious Catholicism and free-thinking immorality. The Kaiser, more unstable emotionally than Edward, had a quicker brain; but it is noticeable how Edward in William's eyes (as also in the Tsar's) seemed always a mischief-making schemer rejoicing in Germany's humiliation (or, with the Tsar, Russia's) and plotting her downfall. "He's a Satan. You can hardly believe what a Satan he is!" exclaimed William at a 1907 dinner-party. (Britain was at that time trying to settle her quarrels with Russia.) Perhaps he had had reported to him Edward's recent comment upon *him*: "The most brilliant failure in history."

Queen Victoria, on the other hand, held William in the sort of affection that a naughty child is held, and of her he was at once genuinely fond and rather scared. "It was strange," wrote Eulenberg, "to see the Kaiser ill at ease and almost tongue-tied in the presence of the little Queen," but when she lay dying in 1901 he hurried over the seas to her bedside, gained golden opinions by his kind and sensible behaviour at the deathbed and afterwards, and returned to regale his unimpressed entourage with enthusiastic praise for British ways.

The most enviable asset of Britain was undoubtedly its large and splendid navy. "I take an interest in your fleet as if it were my own," he once wrote to Victoria. But why should he not have one of his own? The idea soon came to possess him. "Our future lies on the water," he was fond of saying, and his Chief of Naval Staff, von Tirpitz, found that with William he was preaching to the converted. In Tirpitz's view a large navy was vital to give Germany a bargaining counter, and to ensure that she would be treated as a Power of top status. This matched exactly William's strenuous desire to keep up with the Imperial Joneses in Britain. A navy would, moreover, be a novel acquisition: none of the German states had ever before possessed one of any significance. William, a passionate sailor, was entranced with the whole idea. The Navy League openly, and the big steel combines more discreetly, agitated for it, and William was not the man to be deterred by such comments as those of his friend Eulenburg:

The coming Navy Bill [of 1898] is looked upon more as satisfying your Majesty's sport than as being a necessity for Germany.

Edward VII too spoke slightingly of his nephew's "toys", and there was certainly an element of "sport" in the Kaiser's navy; there was an element also of big business in it; but above all it was a matter of prestige. Inevitably it was seen by the British as a challenge—even the suggested two-to-three ratio which Tirpitz (if not the Kaiser) might have been willing to settle for. Englishmen thought that if God had intended Germany to have a big navy He would have seen to it that she too was blest by being an island and the centre of a world empire. The big German navy must be either an unwarrantable luxury or a direct menace to Britain. Four-fifths of German trade was with Europe, two-thirds of Britain's with the world beyond; "it is existence to us," said Churchill, "it is expansion to them." On their side Tirpitz and the German big-navy school always claimed that they intended no hostility towards Britain. The theory was that Britain would be more inclined to pay a high price for the German alliance which it was assumed she must seek. At the least, German strength would buy British neutrality if war came between Germany and France.

"What about my ships?" the Kaiser asked Bernhard von Bülow before appointing him in 1897 as his Foreign Secretary. Yes, answered Bülow, it would be possible to get a Navy Bill through the Reichstag, but they would have "to beat the national drum". "Agreed, agreed," cried William; what a "splendid fellow" this Bülow was! As for Tirpitz, now promoted to be Minister of Marine, he was "the master".

So the first Navy Bill was introduced in 1898. The second, doubling the proposed construction, followed in 1900; and after that the battleship race continued right up to the outbreak of the War in 1914. From 1900 Tirpitz and the German Government deliberately accepted "a policy of risk", counting on sufficient European support if German naval building should provoke from Britain any sudden act of preventive destruction; European sailors had never forgotten Nelson at Copenhagen.

It was not only naval matters that poisoned Anglo-German relations; there was abundant mutual resentment in colonial affairs. The troubles in South Africa afforded special scope. Ever since the discovery of gold in Witwatersrand in the eighties there had been severe trouble in the Transvaal between the Boer President Kruger and the immigrants (*uitlanders*) who flooded into his country. Since the *uitlanders* were principally British and South African Dutch, this led to bitter quarrels between the Transvaal Government on the one side and the British and Cape Colony Governments on the other. The situation seemed promising for trouble-makers, and a hopeful flirtation developed between the German Government and Kruger, who was among other things encouraged to put a prohibitive tariff on goods from Cape Colony. "Small colonial concessions" might be acceptable, the German Foreign Minister Marschall suggested, as the price for persuading Kruger to abandon the tariff later. As the quarrel between Boers and British grew in intensity during the nineties Germany adopted the stubbornly anti-British Kruger as a sort of honorary Teutonic hero. Even Bismarck in his last years of disillusionment wondered whether Kruger was not a greater man than himself.

It was German assistance in 1895 that linked Pretoria, the Transvaal capital, with the coast. The Kaiser sent his congratulations. Two German warships made an appearance in neighbouring

Delagoa Bay. When the Jameson Raid occurred at the end of 1895, German public opinion was strongly indignant; news of its failure was greeted with satisfaction. The telegram of congratulations from the Kaiser to Kruger which raised such a storm was nothing to what William and his advisers had been contemplating —the dispatch of troops to aid the Boers, with the eventual goal of a German protectorate over the Transvaal. That dream did not last long, and the Kaiser was soon sending his grandmother Victoria (who had strongly remonstrated over the sending of the telegram) the most amicable, if unconvincing, explanation of his actions.

When the South African War came in 1899 all Germany sympathized vehemently with the Boers. By that time, however, official German behaviour was more cautious and correct. The unpredictable William left a Germany seething with anti-British feeling to visit England for the celebration of Victoria's eightieth birthday. At Windsor he was quite carried away by all the imperial excitements and, Boer War or no Boer War, thought they constituted "the most inspiring experience of my life". But back home in Germany he was soon able, like most of his fellow-countrymen, to extract some pleasure from the tale of Britain's reverses in South Africa.

Two other areas in these closing years of the nineteenth century seemed to offer opportunities to Imperial Germany—the southern Pacific and the Near East. In 1898 Spain was at war with the U.S.A. over Cuba; the Filipinos seized the moment to proclaim their independence from Spain. Here were beckoning prospects for Germany, and the Kaiser, together with Tirpitz and the colonial enthusiasts, began to dream (as the elder Pitt had in England long before) of rich spoils to be won from the dissolution of the Spanish Empire in the Pacific. William wired Bülow:

> Tirpitz is convinced that we must have Manila and that it would be of enormous advantage to us. As soon as the revolution has torn Manila from Spain we must occupy it.

The swift defeat of the Spanish Navy by the American soon dissolved the dream. The German naval squadron sent hopefully to the Philippines was in no position to challenge the U.S.A., and Germany was obliged to content herself with the purchase from Spain of the Marianne and Caroline Islands. Some protracted haggling over the Samoan group of islands ended with their partition between Germany, Britain, and the U.S.A.

In the Near East during the same year (1898) William made one of his most significant and spectacular personal interventions. The latest moves in the century-old "Eastern Question"—what was to happen to the decaying Turkish Empire—which Bismarck had declared to be not worth the bones of a single Pomeranian grenadier, now seemed to present his successors with chances they ought not to miss. Britain, long the support of the Turkish Empire against Russian attack, had under Gladstone and Salisbury shifted the emphasis of her policy. Whereas Disraeli in 1876 had officially played down the Turkish massacres of the Bulgarian Christians, neither the British Government nor the British public had any wish to ignore the bloody massacres by the Turks of their Armenian Christians (1895–96). Britain and Russia, though they were traditional rivals and enemies, worked together to save Greece from the full effects of her defeat in the Greco-Turkish War of 1897, and to free Crete from the Turks. At this juncture, when it was proposed that the Powers should combine to bring pressure against the "unspeakable Turk", the Kaiser chose to take Bülow with him on a tour of the Turkish Empire as the Sultan's honoured guests.

This was the culmination of a decade of German penetration into Turkey. It had begun in 1889, when the Kaiser, with his wife, paid a first ceremonial visit. When Sultan Abdul Hamid during the Armenian massacres became the moral outcast of Europe, Germany drove home her opportunities. While Salisbury sent the Sultan protests, the Kaiser sent him a birthday present of a signed photograph. German military experts began the modernization of the Turkish Army. The *Deutsche Bank* was established at Constantinople. German capital partly financed, and German engineers began to build, a railway through Anatolia to Ankara. The Kaiser's second visit of 1898 was ostensibly a celebration of the success of Turkey's new German-trained troops, but it became much more than that. William and Bülow proceeded from Constantinople to the Holy Places and Syria. In this Crusader country the Kaiser's chronically inflammable oratory ignited, and at Damascus, with Europe listening, he declared himself

deeply moved by the thought of standing where the great Saladin . . . had once sojourned. The Sultan and the three hundred million Muslims who reverenced him as Caliph may be assured that the German Emperor will ever be their friend.

France, with her North African Muslims, Russia with hers in Central Asia, and particularly Britain with hers numbered in scores of millions in Africa and Asia, could hardly fail to notice.

In 1902 the German Anatolian Railway Company signed an agreement to extend the Constantinople-Ankara line to Bagdad. "Berlin to Bagdad"; it was the German counterpart of Rhodes's "Cape to Cairo". The line was to run from Berlin through Vienna, Constantinople, and Ankara, to Bagdad, and even on to Basra; it could well become the main artery for German economic and political exploitation of the Near and Middle East and, if the project came about, would make possible a vast German-dominated trading area stretching from the North and Baltic Seas to the Persian Gulf, the strongest of challenges both to Russia and to the British Empire.

The tension arising from the opposition of rival alliances, the scrambles for Africa and China, and in particular the alarums associated with the Kaiser's "world policy", convinced politicians in Britain that the days of her "splendid isolation" were numbered. Ever since Castlereagh veered away from the Holy Alliance Powers at Troppau[1] Britain had turned its back on continental entanglements. But events since the fall of Bismarck increasingly suggested to British ministers the prudence of having allies on the Continent; and if ever Britain were to make a European alliance there was only one country, Germany, with whom it seemed possible.

Disraeli had once considered a German alliance, and Bismarck himself in the year before his fall had proposed to Disraeli's successor Salisbury an Anglo-German treaty, sending his son Herbert Bismarck to London to sound the possibilities. Both countries shared fears of Russia and France, but Herbert Bismarck found that the British Government considered the project unacceptable—indeed, unmentionable—to the British voter. On the British side, however, the idea of the 'natural' Anglo-German alliance persisted. Joseph Chamberlain, in particular, was its champion, and it was the turn of the British Government several times to propose it between 1898 and 1901. By that time it was Germany that would not commit herself. Holstein, Bülow, and the Kaiser were convinced that Britain could ally with no major Power *other*

[1] See pp. 81–82.

than Germany. There seemed to be no hurry: a few more years, a navy approaching parity with Britain's, and far better terms could be extracted. Bülow and Holstein, nervous of their man, bade the Kaiser on his English visit to be noncommittal; between Russia and Britain, his cousin and his grandmother, the Kaiser could one day be arbiter of the world's affairs. During the Boer War mutual Anglo-German suspicion grew deeper, public recriminations louder. Bülow and Holstein did not take Chamberlain seriously when he told them that a Britain rebuffed by Germany would turn to France. Even when in 1904 Britain and France came to a mutual agreement concerning their rivalry in Egypt and Morocco, Bülow (speaking in the Reichstag) professed no alarm; the Anglo-French entente fell far short of a military alliance. William himself was rather less confident; he felt a growing sense of Germany's isolation as Italy edged away from the Triple Alliance and Britain and France moved steadily towards one another.

During 1904–5 two conflicts dominated international politics —those between Japan and Russia in the Far East and between France and Germany in Morocco. To Bülow and the Kaiser both these seemed to offer Germany a chance of confounding her rivals and breaking up the diplomatic ring that was threatening to form around the Austro-German bloc.

In 1904 Russia was disastrously defeated by Japan on land and sea. Since 1902 Britain had been Japan's ally, and for some time the Kaiser had grounds for hoping that Britain would become embroiled in a war with Russia. In the North Sea a Russian squadron (on its way to annihilation by the Japanese Navy in the greatest sea battle since Trafalgar) had mistaken some Hull trawlers for Japanese torpedo-boats, and fired upon them. A howl of execration followed in the English Press, and William thought the moment opportune to heighten the tension and come to the aid of the Tsar.

> If you become involved in war with England [he wrote] I will put my fleet at your disposal and force France to go along with us.

This confident talk of "forcing France" was not mere words. The German Army, with the aggressive and politically influential Schlieffen as its Chief of Staff, was confident that it had more than the measure of the French; as for the British Army, after the Boer War it was held in contempt.

When the prospect of Anglo-Russian hostilities receded and France successfully used her good offices to calm the British wrath, William was disappointed but still not without hope of working upon his cousin Nicky. Given such favourable circumstances as those of 1905, the Tsar might well prove to be clay in the hands of the persuasive and dynamic Kaiser, who looked forward eagerly to a personal *tête-à-tête* with the susceptible and malleable Nicholas. In June their yachts made secret rendezvous (with the anxious approval of Holstein and Bülow) off the Finnish island of Björkö. As ever, William could not resist the prospect of a *coup de théâtre*.

> My guests' faces will be worth seeing when they suddenly behold your yacht. Tableau! What sort of dress for our meeting? *Willy*.

The Björkö meeting produced rather more than a social surprise for the Kaiser's guests aboard the *Hohenzollern*. There emerged a Russo-German treaty—as things turned out abortive—providing in the event of war for mutual assistance *in Europe*. This was to have been William's master *coup*. He wrote home to Bülow of how the Tsar's "dreamy eyes shone brightly" as he read through the document before signing. "My heart was beating so loudly that I could hear it." The following day William, his euphoric metaphors in a fine confusion, was writing to assure the Tsar that a cornerstone had been laid in European politics, a new leaf turned in the history of the world. At one stroke, so he thought, he had "freed his beloved Fatherland from the terrible pincers of Russia and France". Alas, Kaiser and Tsar proposed, but their advisers disposed. The Russians showed no willingness to desert the French alliance. Bülow objected that whereas the projected treaty might provoke an English assault on Germany, it would not commit Russia to attacking the British Empire in India. Using Bismarck's old technique, he proffered his resignation. The Kaiser was momentarily shattered; on the verge, he protested, of a nervous collapse. He even threatened suicide.

> I thought I had laboured for you and won an exceptional victory, and you send me a few tepid lines and your resignation.

The Björkö treaty was stillborn. Bülow was soon able to withdraw his threat of resignation and the Kaiser to bob back like a cork to the surface.

France's colonization of Morocco had been proceeding rapidly since 1900. The principal competition had first come from the British, and although by the agreement of 1904 Britain had been given the *quid pro quo* of a free hand in Egypt, the principle was laid down of the "open door", which in theory gave Germany too her place in the Moroccan sun. It was Holstein's calculation that a strong German demonstration in Morocco in defence of this "open door" would promote dissension between Britain and France— still unaccustomed and touchy friends—and, with luck, break up the Entente. The Kaiser himself was not convinced of Morocco's importance, and neither to begin with was Bülow. William, in fact, had only just informed the monarchs of Great Britain and of Spain that Germany had no ambitions at all in Morocco. However, Holstein worked upon Bülow, and Bülow eventually persuaded a genuinely reluctant Kaiser to participate in the Holstein strategy. Accordingly, during his Mediterranean cruise in March 1905 he was to make a surprise descent upon the Moroccan port of Tangier. A pinnace put him ashore, an alarmingly spirited white horse bore him briefly through the streets, and then before the Sultan's representatives he made a 'strong' speech affirming the "open door" and Morocco's independence. The gesture looked menacing to France, and was certainly theatrical in the best Kaiser manner. But the Kaiser had merely been acting his part; the script was by Holstein and Bülow.[2]

What did they gain? On the surface, apparently, a quick success. The French were alarmed, and, in an effort to appease, the French Prime Minister and Cabinet forced the resignation of the Foreign Minister Delcassé, who Bülow complained was anti-German. It looked as if France would be humbled, and to celebrate this expectation William promoted Bülow from Count to Prince. Nevertheless, at the international conference that met in Algeciras in Spain, on Germany's demand, she found that her toughness had succeeded only in bringing about (Austria apart) her diplomatic

[2] Just how strongly the Kaiser resented his rôle is shown by a letter he wrote to Bülow after the Björkö fiasco (Tangier was in March 1905, Björkö in July): "Remember that *you* sent me to Tangier against my will, to win a success for your Moroccan policy. Because you wanted me to in the national interest, I mounted a strange horse in spite of the handicap of my bad arm, and if the exploit came within an inch of costing my life, *you* were responsible. I had to ride between Spanish anarchists because *you* wished it. . . . And now, after I have done all this and much more for you, you want to desert me. . . ."

isolation. Britain, France, Spain, Italy, Russia, and the U.S.A. united in opposing German claims to share the control of Morocco. Bülow admitted that "the Austrian Empire is now our only dependable ally". Holstein's policy had so far failed, but he himself was for going the whole hog against France—making war if necessary. Bülow and the Kaiser were not, and a furious Holstein offered his resignation.[3]

Both the Tangier incident, which he did not wish to stage, and the Björkö treaty, which he was not allowed to conclude, show how little the Kaiser was in command of affairs; yet he was no less grandiloquent or truculent as the years went by. His opinions remained as violent and reckless as before. The margins of his ambassador's reports continued to be filled with such ejaculations as "Bosh!" "Feeble!" "Ass!" "Rot!" "Imbecile!" He still rushed at each new situation with a kind of frenzy. He continued to speak as though he were in supreme command. "Clearly," he wrote of the new British Foreign Minister, "Grey has no idea who is master here and that it is I who rule." And certainly he was far from being a mere cipher. His siding with Tirpitz against Bülow in the Big Navy debate was crucial.

"A child or a madman" had been Holstein's sour verdict. And in 1908 an incident occurred which brought out into the open the whole question of the Kaiser's capacity to rule. He had authorized for publication in the London *Daily Telegraph* an account of interviews and conversations giving his views on Anglo-German relations and a "frank statement on world policy". The English were as mad as March hares, he genially declared. Why did they suspect Germany, their best friend? Did they not know that it was he, the Kaiser, who had saved England from Franco-Russian intervention? That he had personally advised Lord Roberts on how to defeat the Boers? Why could England not understand the essentially amicable intentions of the Germans? In any case, perhaps one day the two countries would be fighting *on the same side* in the Far East.

[3] Even so, Holstein was not finished with; in his retirement he was still sometimes consulted by Bülow. Moreover, he intrigued restlessly against those he supposed to have secured his downfall—in particular the Kaiser's intimate, Count Eulenburg, whose position and good name were lost for ever when Holstein and his associates managed to implicate him in a big homosexual scandal. The Kaiser, scared for his own reputation, did not lift a finger to save his oldest friend, who was—at least in some degree—the victim of corrupt evidence.

Never had quite so many international bricks been dropped at one go. He had succeeded in offending not only the British, but the French, the Russians, the Boers, the Japanese, and most of all his own countrymen. For them it was beyond a joke. How could their impulsive Kaiser be restrained? Had Bülow approved the article? (In fact he had, by an oversight, without troubling to read it first, though this could hardly be admitted publicly.) The Social Democrats had, of course, always criticized the autocracy, but now some patriotic conservatives began to debate whether the Kaiser could be allowed thus to continue to make a fool of himself and the Fatherland. In the Reichstag an angry storm blew up. In the Press weighty articles discussed royal responsibility; cartoons[4] ridiculed the Emperor. There was even talk of abdication. Though William professed not to be disturbed, he plainly was. The underlying sense of insecurity—the reverse face of his blatant self-assertiveness—was temporarily deepened. He retired to bed with cold shivers and hysteria. The Empress reported that he was "quite broken up".

It happened that the *Daily Telegraph* affair coincided with the severest crisis Europe had lived through since 1878. In that year by the Treaty of Berlin the Turkish provinces of Bosnia and Hercegovina had been placed under the suzerainty of Austria, whose southern boundary bordered them. The weakness of Abdul Hamid's Turkey, following the 'Young Turk' revolution of 1908, prompted the Austrian Government completely to take over Bosnia and Hercegovina. A six-months crisis followed (1908–9). It appeared that Russia had secretly agreed to the Austrian annexation, her price being the right of the Russian Navy to use the Dardanelles. Britain and France protested. Serbia protested so violently that the Austrian General Staff were for making war on her there and then. The vital question was, what would Germany do? The Kaiser was annoyed to see any further weakening of the Turkish Empire, where German influence increased every year, and deplored the "frightful stupidity" of the Austrian Foreign Minister Aerenthal. Bülow, however, and the aggressive new German Foreign Minister Kiderlen-Wächter were for forcing Russia, under threat of war, to accept the Austrian annexation without gaining her *quid pro quo* at the

---

[4] One showed old William I pleading for God's forgiveness for his grandson: "After all he is *By the Grace of God*." God replies: "Now you want to put the blame on me."

Dardanelles. The threat succeeded; but again, as when Germany forced the dismissal of Delcassé over the Moroccan question, it was a short-term victory that had been won. The Kaiser, never at a loss for a simile, was able to boast how he had stood beside his Austrian ally "like a knight in shining armour"; but with every new German move the unnatural alliance of Russia, France, and Britain came to seem more natural. Meanwhile the Austro-Serb bitterness continued to fester—and to erupt at last in 1914, when again Germany after some hesitation was found standing behind her Austrian ally and encouraging her fatal aggression.

Bülow was the one Chancellor who had enjoyed the Kaiser's affection and confidence. Smooth, superficially charming, personally unscrupulous, Bülow had always had the right word for the ear of the Kaiser, who for his part liked nothing better than to please "*his* Bismarck". But relations cooled after what the Kaiser regarded as the Björko let-down. Then in 1908 serious arguments arose between Bülow and the Kaiser over naval policy. To Bülow it seemed that Britain and Germany were set on a course pointing dangerously towards collision, and he favoured trying to come to an agreement limiting naval building, provided that Britain in return would engage to stay neutral in a Franco-German war. This was the one topic on which William was almost wholly consistent: no modification was to be made to the German naval programme in any circumstances whatever. Tirpitz eagerly concurred. Bülow accepted his rebuff and allowed the Big Navy policy to roll blindly forward.

> Do you wish [asked the Rumanian Minister of Kiderlen-Wächter in 1911] to be both the leading naval and the leading military power? That would mean world domination. . . . You are heading straight for a war with England.

The *Daily Telegraph* affair completed the estrangement between the Kaiser and Bülow. William was aggrieved and considered that Bülow had first deceived him and then failed to defend him adequately in the Reichstag. An offer by Bülow to resign was withdrawn only when he extracted a promise from William not to make any future political move without his Chancellor's approval. When in 1909 Bülow ran into difficulties with the Reichstag on domestic issues William was only too pleased to see him go. He let it be known that he considered poor Bülow was 'failing' and took imperial pride in pointing out to the King of Württemberg the exact spot where he had given "that lump of dead flesh" his marching orders. Bülow, smarting with fury at his dismissal, took a posthumous revenge. When his self-justifying *Memoirs* were published after his death they bristled with malicious comment.

Bülow's successor, the mild Bethmann-Hollweg, inherited an almost impossible legacy. All the dangers and ambiguities of the German situation remained unchanged: a Socialist Party still growing in numbers; a Reichstag whose powers were largely obstructive; an unpredictable Kaiser still in theory supreme; a cocksure and politically powerful Army; an ambitious Navy with the Kaiser on its side and unwilling to accept any restraint on building; an adventurous overseas policy rapidly cementing an alliance hostile to Germany; a European foreign policy tied solely and unequivocally now to Austria-Hungary, whose aggressive Balkan ambitions seemed certain to involve a war with Serbia, if not also with Russia; a popular Press and public opinion fed, like their counterparts in all the other Powers of Europe great and small, on a narrow jingoistic patriotism; a tradition of diplomacy, not confined to Germany but notably present there, recklessly willing to play its ace card of the threat of war, without any realization of what a twentieth-century war would mean. Bethmann-Hollweg, like Europe itself, was the victim of a fatal combination of circumstances.

Bethman tried, as Bülow had, to come to an agreement with Britain; but he lacked authority, and his hands were tied by the continued insistence of Tirpitz and the Kaiser that Germany must go ahead with her battleships. William's own contribution, behind the scenes, to these abortive discussions fluctuated, as usual, according to his prevailing mood. On his optimistic days he was sure the British Government was ready to negotiate only because of some inherent weakness; Germany must therefore press her advantage and demand the right to join, and thus destroy, the Anglo-French Entente. On his suspicious days all the talk from England became a device to make Germany lower her guard; at such times he listened receptively to the old suggestion that the British might try to 'Copenhagen' his fleet. No concession therefore; Tirpitz was right. Even so, in spite of the inconclusiveness of these negotiations, by 1914 Britain and Germany had arrived unofficially at an agreed 16:10 ratio for naval building.

Between two of the bouts of talks had come the second Moroccan crisis of 1911. Despite their diplomatic rebuff at the Algeciras conference of 1906, the Germans persisted. The French, although they had been offered soothing reassurances concerning the independence of Morocco, had been pressing ahead in colonizing the territory. This was galling to the Germans, whose Foreign Minister Kiderlen now flung down a challenge as risky and dramatic as the earlier Holstein-Bülow demonstration at Tangier. The Kaiser himself had not the slightest interest in Morocco. Let the French pursue their aims there, he calculated; the more troops they were obliged to send, the fewer for guarding the Rhine. Yet he assented when Kiderlen proposed sending a warship to the Moroccan port of Agadir, ostensibly to protect German lives and property but in fact to force the French under threat of war to cede a large slice of French Congo to the Germans. The *Panther* was accordingly dispatched, a gunboat small indeed, but bearing a mission and a name—with its suggestion of springing muscle, its hint of claws and teeth—that went to the head of the German Press and people like strong wine. Again, as in 1905 and 1908-9, war threatened. France looked to Britain for support and received it; both the 'imperialist' Grey and the 'pacifist' Lloyd George made strong ministerial speeches reaffirming the Entente and warning Germany of the consequences of her actions.

Once again the German Government, having forced a crisis, withdrew in time. France was given her free hand in Morocco; in addition she received a strip of German territory in West Africa in return for an extensive but impoverished stretch of French Congo. Kiderlen's 'brinkmanship' had shown little profit and a deal of loss. When he died (late in 1912) he left Germany's foreign policies in a dangerous variety of hands—those of Bethmann, more and more committed to Austria come what might; of the unyielding Tirpitz; of Moltke and the Army chiefs, a state within a state; and of the flotsam Kaiser himself, fearing war with one breath and shouting *Let war come* with the next.

It was in the Balkans that the greatest dangers lay. In 1912 Bulgaria, Serbia, Greece, and Montenegro all declared war on Turkey, swiftly defeated her, and enlarged their territories. A cockahoop Serbia, with Russia's moral support, took what she had for some time been claiming, the port of Durazzo, which gave her access to the Adriatic Sea; and it began to look as if Germany must then and there be dragged into the quarrel by her threatened ally, Austria-Hungary. William wriggled to get off the hook,[5] but Bethmann and Kiderlen soon had him on again; Germany, they insisted, must go to war if Austria did, or else lose her only reliable ally and be forced to fight later from a weakened position.

For a time the threat of European war again receded as Russia withdrew some of her support for the Serbs, who in turn had to withdraw from Durazzo. In 1913 there followed the Second Balkan War, in which Greece and Serbia fought Bulgaria, lately their ally, and wrested from her her Macedonian conquests of 1912. The position of Serbia now took on a double significance: she stood as the only major obstacle, and an uncommonly belligerent one, in the path of Austro-German dominance of the Near East; and since she dreamed of uniting all the Yugoslavs under the rule of Greater Serbia, she posed a threat of disintegration to the Austro-Hungarian Empire—for seven million Yugoslavs lived under the Habsburg flag. Behind Serbia stood Russia, preparing for the war that might come at any moment.

Sometimes the Kaiser persuaded himself that it was inevitable. If Serbia provoked Austria beyond bearing "there comes a time when a Great Power must draw the sword". Like most military romantics of his era, he habitually spoke of war as of some kind of medieval combat. Still the knight in shining armour, he said to the Austrian Foreign Minister:

> You can be assured that I stand behind you and am ready to draw the sword whenever your measures require it. . . . Whatever comes from the Vienna Foreign Office is an order for me.

At other times he felt sure that Russia, uncertain of Britain, would not fight—that Nicky, his good friend and continuing correspondent, would heed his advice. But, more and more, this was like whistling in the dark, and occasionally he recognized it. A man would be mad, he said, not to see that "in Russo-Gaul they are working at high pressure for an early war with us".

These words were written in mid-1914. On June 28th, at Sarajevo in Bosnia, a Serb assassin fired the shot that killed the heir

---

[5] William wrote to his Foreign Office advisers: "I think it is objectionable to oppose Serbia's wishes needlessly. I admit that there are many changes in the Balkans caused by the war which are very awkward and unwelcome for Vienna, but none are so desperate that we should be exposed to war for her sake. . . ."

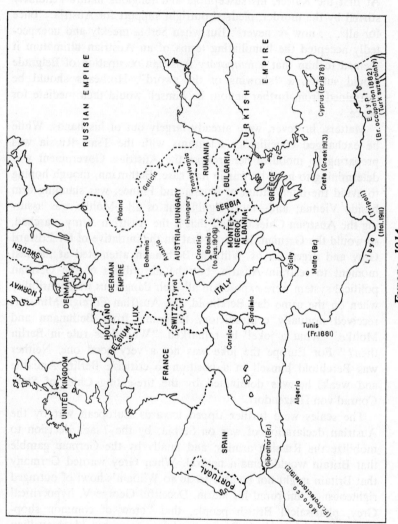

Europe, 1914

to the Habsburg throne and so ushered in the First World War. Austria, already contemplating a war against Serbia, was now given an irresistible chance to settle her hash once and for all. At first the Kaiser, his susceptible and religious nature genuinely stirred by the murder, pledged outright support for Austria: "once for all . . . now or never". But when Serbia meekly and unexpectedly accepted the humiliating terms of an Austrian ultimatum it seemed to him that a *temporary* Austrian occupation of Belgrade would suffice, a "showing of the sword". Hotheads should be restrained from further action; he himself would then mediate for peace.

Matters, however, were already largely out of his hands. While he exchanged conciliatory telegrams with the Tsar, Russia was preparing to mobilize her troops; the Austrian Government was determining to have its war in any case; Bethmann, though hoping to avoid the intervention of Russia and France, was standing firm beside Vienna; and—most signifiicant of all—Moltke was assuring the Austrian Chief of Staff that if the Austrian Army marched, so would the German. It is true that on the initiative of Sir Edward Grey and urged on by William, Bethmann attempted at the last moment to restrain Austria, but the absurdities of the German political system were exposed in all their dangerous irresponsibility when on the same day Berchtold, the Austrian Foreign Minister, received mutually contradictory telegrams from Bethmann and Moltke. "What a joke!' he remarked. "Who does rule in Berlin then?" For Europe the joke was not a very good one. Neither was Berchtold himself in a position to criticize Berlin. Amiable and weak, he was dominated by the fire-eating Chief of Staff, Conrad von Hötzendorf.

The scales were further tipped towards European war by the Austrian declaration of war on Serbia; by the Tsar's decision to mobilize the Russian armies; and finally by the German gamble that Britain would remain neutral. When Grey warned Germany that Britain might not be able to do so William's howl of outraged righteousness mirrored his alarm. Deceitful George V, hypocritical Grey, pharisaical British people, that "crew of common shopkeepers"! Wicked Uncle Bertie, dead four years but Machiavellian beyond the grave, "stronger after his death than I who am still alive"! It was all a diabolical manœuvre of those who had been plotting to encircle Germany. Wailing this hysteria and full of misgivings, William nevertheless allowed himself on the advice of his political, military, and naval chiefs to mobilize German forces and declare war on Russia and France. His last-minute attempt to limit the war to Eastern Europe by persuading the generals not to put into operation the Schlieffen Plan (for an attack on France through Belgium) was brushed aside by men who were very confident of the superiority of their military machine and anxious to seize what Moltke called "the extraordinarily favourable moment". It was as favourable as it would ever be for the naval chiefs too: they had just taken over the use of a Kiel Canal widened to permit the passage of the latest dreadnoughts. So Germany was landed with its "war on two fronts" that Bismarck had laboured to avoid at all costs. The flood of national confidence and military triumphs upon which he had ridden had now burst its banks and was about to carry his successors, and the hapless generation of their sons, to disaster.

On August 4th, the day Britain declared war, the Reichstag unanimously voted the war credits. Henceforth, said the Kaiser, he recognized no parties but only Germans; and the common cause of a patriotic war did serve briefly to make him the people's Kaiser that he had always wished to be. The political and industrial unrest that had been a strong feature of the immediate pre-war years died away temporarily. The Socialists, whose numbers in the 1912 Reichstag had again gone up—there were 110 of them now—were swept up in the wave of war nationalism as the Radicals had been in 1848; they voted with the rest.

But in fact, from the outbreak of the war, the Kaiser grew less and less important. He was the Supreme War Lord, but the conduct of operations was far too delicate and technical to be left in the hands of one so inexpert and unstable. While German armies fought out the most widespread and savage war till then known to history, the Army's chief, though he paid visits to the fronts, stayed for the most part on his estates at Pless or Homburg, insulated from the decision-makers. It pleased the Kaiser, in those moments of fantasy that were necessary to sustain him, to pretend that General Hindenburg (the nation's hero after his triumphs in East Prussia against the Russians) was subject to General Ludendorff, and that Ludendorff in turn took orders from his own Imperial Majesty. The truth was very different, as William recognized in his more realistic moods.

The General Staff tells me nothing and asks me nothing [he complained]. If people in Germany imagine that I lead the Army they greatly deceive themselves. I drink tea, saw wood, go for walks, and from time to time hear that this or that has been done, just as the gentlemen choose.

Of these "gentlemen", the ailing Moltke had soon been superseded by Falkenhayn after the Schlieffen Plan was seen to have failed. (In the early weeks of the war a million men had swung round upon Paris and the French defenders, but were halted at the first Battle of the Marne.) By August 1916 Hindenburg (Chief of General Staff) and Ludendorff (Quartermaster-General) had taken over the direction of the war, and very soon Ludendorff became in effect political as well as military dictator. Bethmann had done what he could to promote a separate peace with Russia and to keep America out of the war by imposing a measure of restriction on the German submarine attacks. After the unprecedented and appalling casualties of 1916—appalling for all the contestants, with the particularly protracted agonies of the Somme and Verdun —Bethmann, with the Kaiser's backing, had indeed tried to end the war. It was not a very realistic attempt—the peace offer did not mention the state of Belgium, still held by the Germans. However, an offer was made, in December 1916, when William presented it to the Pope and the neutrals, together with an introductory effusion from his own pen, in the form of a letter to Bethmann.

Such an action as this needs a Monarch with a conscience, with a sense of responsibility to God, with a sense of duty towards his own people and those of the enemy; one who, not afraid of being misinterpreted, has the will to free the world from its sufferings. I have the courage for this. In the name of God I will risk it. Hurry, Mr Chancellor. Submit the notes to me. Make everything ready.

The old vein of grandiloquence; but nobody was even listening now. Ludendorff was forcing the war on to a new pitch of ruthlessness. (Hindenburg and the Army aristocracy, at the crucial pinch, were under the domination of this socially upstart but professionally most able general.) The Kaiser, losing his last chance to end the war, surrendered tamely to the service chiefs. There was to be all-out submarine war, even upon neutral ships, in order to bring Britain down—regardless of the danger of antagonizing the U.S.A. Warned of this last, the Kaiser responded with fatalism: "It's all the same to me."

Events in 1917 seemed to be justifying Ludendorff. The U.S.A. declared war, but Germany looked as if she might win before American intervention could be effective. The U-boat sinkings came very close to defeating Britain; Russia collapsed; the French Army passed the limits of endurance and mutinied; Italy suffered a débâcle at Caporetto. To the German Army chiefs, therefore, despite the slaughter of their own men and rumblings on the home front as shortages multiplied under the British blockade, it seemed possible that victory might well come in the spring of 1918.

It was all the more necessary to silence the mounting criticism inside Germany. Many left-wingers whose socialism had in 1914 been drowned under the patriotic wave took heart from the Russian Revolution and turned against the war. Erzberger, of the Catholic Centre, dared to get up in the Reichstag and demand a compromise peace. This did not at all shock William. It expressed an attitude not far from his own, and for once the Reichstag earned from him words of praise. But to Ludendorff and Hindenburg all this was, of course, anathema. They forced William to throw over Bethmann, who, following his softness on submarine warfare, had shown a readiness to conciliate the parties of the Left. The next two Chancellors were nobodies. Ludendorff ruled.

A Kaiser who was a back number; an arrogant High Command in the saddle; a Reichstag which voiced growing criticism; at home a disillusioned people running short of food; at the front troops stretched to the utmost limits: victory must come quickly it it were to save the old Germany. It nearly did. Between March and July 1918 German armies broke the long stalemate of the trenches, came near to driving the British into the sea, and for the second time stood on the Marne threatening Paris. The prospects of victory provided a lightning cure for the Kaiser, who had been bogged down in his own trenches of depression. Suddenly he was the old Kaiser again, all bounce and bombast. The victory was won—by Germany over her enemies, by monarchy over democracy, by right over wrong. He began to wonder how best to receive the English surrender: beneath the Imperial flag, with the Englishman kneeling, perhaps? Even when the first checks came (from the British at the final Battle of Ypres, from the French at the second Battle of the Marne, from the Americans along the Chemin des Dames), he continued rushing round Germany, recharged with the old frenzy and melodrama, rallying, so he hoped, civilian morale. But the war was on its last legs. Ludendorff's tremendous onslaught proved to be Germany's last card. From August 1918 onwards defeat crept unmistakably closer day by day. The High Command knew it and put out feelers for an armistice. The Reichstag knew it and were strong enough—at last—to force constitutional changes: parliamentary control of the government and civilian control of the military.

Prince Max of Baden now became the last Chancellor of the Second Reich. Ludendorff, dictator since 1916 by virtue of success, fell by virtue of failure. He was dismissed on October 26th. The question remained, what of the Kaiser? The word "abdication", first heard after the *Daily Telegraph* fiasco in 1908, was now spoken openly and ever more insistently as the armies were rolled back towards the western borders.

In Wilhelmshaven and Kiel the Navy was in mutiny. Bremen and Hamburg fell into the hands of soldiers' and workers' councils. In Cologne the garrison declared for the revolution. In Bavaria the Socialists proclaimed a republic. By the first week of November 1918 Germany was in the throes of a revolution which, although ostensibly socialist, had as its main driving force the overwhelming desire to end the four years' misery of the war. Inevitably, if the régime foundered, its chief figurehead would go under with it.

Tired of kicking his heels in Berlin, William had gone to Imperial Headquarters at Spa, in Belgium. Here the news from the front was bad enough, but from Berlin it was even more ominous—the situation was deteriorating daily; and from the provinces it was positively calamitous. The single crumb of comfort was that the troops in the field were still loyal, and for one last moment of imagined heroism he visualized turning them about, to march back to Berlin and subdue the rebellion. November 8th and 9th were spent in trying, and failing, to persuade Hindenburg and the General Staff to undertake this project. At last Groener, Ludendorff's successor, spoke the awful, the incredible words: "The Army no longer stands behind your Majesty."

By this time in Berlin Chancellor Max of Baden had been overthrown. The voice at the end of the wire was no longer Max's counselling abdication but another saying that the Kaiser *had abdicated* and that the Socialist Ebert had been appointed Chancellor. Worse, mutinous troops were reported to be advancing towards Spa. There was no safety there, or anywhere in Germany.

Anguished by indecision, he eventually resolved to take Hindenburg's advice and make for the Dutch border. Even then he reversed his decision ("They would think I was afraid") before at last stomaching the bitter realities. In the cheerless small hours of November 10th he set down before the world and posterity the justification for his flight. It is distressing to notice how his words here pre-echo the future tirades of Hitler against the "November criminals":

> There remains nothing for me but to leave my army. For almost thirty years I have lived and worked for it, and now, after four and a half years of brilliant victories, it collapses shamefully through the youth at home poisoned and blinded by Jews and Social Democrats. . . .

Self-deceived to the last, he made for Holland. To his shock and astonishment, a lot of people wanted to hang him as a war criminal. Even when he had not figured prominently as a war leader in Germany he had always played in the hate propaganda of the Allied countries a leading rôle as the personification of *furor teutonicus*, the sinister butcher of the cartoons, with the spiked helmet and evil moustaches, and the blood dripping from his hands. Now that the Allies were victorious, and even insisted on the German representative at Versailles signing an acknowledgment of the country's war guilt, it seemed reasonable to some that they should claim the arch-villain's life as retribution for the ten million dead and the incalculable suffering of the war. The pressure did not come merely from the popular Press. Lloyd George's Cabinet in July 1919, having rejected London as "not a very suitable place" for the Kaiser's trial, proceeded seriously to discuss "the relative advantages of Hampton Court and Dover". But in any case the Dutch Government refused to surrender their charge, or even to adopt the next British suggestion that he should be interned in the East Indies. Instead they allowed him to buy a sixty-acre estate at Doorn, where he soon adapted himself to the peaceful life of an elderly country gentleman, with his regular family prayers, his wood-cutting for exercise, his rose-gardens, his visitors, his dogs, his nine motor-cars—but, at last, no uniforms. The ex-Empress Augusta, more shocked than he himself by the Imperial collapse, and further distressed by family quarrels and the suicide of her second son, died at Doorn in 1921, and in 1922 the ex-Kaiser was remarried to Princess Hermine of Schoenaich-

Carolath, a lively widow of thirty-five, with five children. Nobody else liked her, but for William it was a convenient and happy marriage; she brought sunshine, he said, into his house of darkness.

For a long time, dreaming of a restoration, he continued to clutch at every straw. Pained by his continued exclusion from Germany, he strongly resented Hindenburg's failure to speak up in his defence. Although three of his sons became Nazi supporters, and Princess Hermine herself (ambitious to be Empress, said her many ill-wishers) had high hopes of Hitler, William, a strongly religious man, deplored the new barbarism. By the mid-thirties he had abandoned ambition for nostalgia. He need no longer wish, as someone had said he used to wish, to be "the bride at every wedding, the corpse at every funeral". For the first time in his life it was possible for him to live in tranquillity without having to try to impress upon God in heaven, upon his Hohenzollern forebears, or even upon himself that he was masterful and wise and great. On the years that had gone before, Winston Churchill's verdict stands:

> His undeniable cleverness and versatility, his personal grace and vivacity, only aggravated his dangers by concealing his inadequacy.... Underneath all the posing and its trappings was a very ordinary man, a vain, but on the whole well-meaning man, hoping to pass himself off as Frederick the Great.

Table of Events

1859.	Birth of future William II.
1871.	William I becomes Kaiser of Germany.
1888.	Reign of Kaiser Frederick. William II accedes.
1890.	Dismissal of Bismarck. Caprivi Chancellor.
1893–98.	Franco-Russian *rapprochement*.
1894.	Hohenlohe Chancellor. Sino-Japanese War; 'scramble for China' follows.
1895–96.	Armenian Massacres. German overtures to Turkey. (Kaiser's visit, 1898.)
1896.	Telegram to Kruger following Jameson Raid.
1897–1916.	Tirpitz at Admiralty; naval challenge to Britain.
1899.	Bülow Chancellor. Boer War.
1902.	Berlin-Bagdad railway agreement.
1904.	Franco-British *entente*. Russo-Japanese War.
1905.	Tangier episode. Algeciras conference. Abortive Björkö treaty.
1907.	Russo-British *entente*.

1908.	*Daily Telegraph* affair. Crisis follows Austria's annexation of Bosnia.
1909.	Bethmann-Hollweg Chancellor.
1911.	Crisis follows German intervention at Agadir.
1912–13.	Balkan Wars.
1914.	Sarajevo assassination heralds First World War.
1918.	German defeat and revolution. Abdication and flight of Kaiser.
1933.	Nazis gain power.
1941.	Death in Holland.

SELECT BIBLIOGRAPHY

On the whole, recommended books are here limited to those available in English and of not more than moderate length. This means the exclusion of some major sources and authorities, such, for instance, as Srbik on Metternich or the numerous jumbo-sized lives of Napoleon, Lincoln, etc. There is no adequate biography of Thiers in English; of the several in French I have listed two.

General Works of European History
New Cambridge Modern History, vols. 9 (1965) and 10 (1960) (C.U.P).

HEARDER, H.: *Europe in the Nineteenth Century* (Longmans, 1966).

HOBSBAWM, E. J.: *The Age of Revolution (1789–1848)* (Weidenfeld and Nicolson, 1962).

KNAPTON, E. J., and DERRY, T. K.: *Europe, 1815–1914* (Murray, 1965).

MEDLICOTT, W. N. (ed.): *From Metternich to Hitler* (Routledge and Kegan Paul, 1963).

SEAMAN, L. C. B.: *From Vienna to Versailles* (Methuen, 1955).

TAYLOR, A. J. P.: *The Struggle for Mastery in Europe, 1848–1918* (O.U.P., 1954).

THOMSON, D.: *Europe since Napoleon* (Longmans; Penguin Books, 1954).

Napoleon and Thiers
BROGAN, D. W.: *The Development of Modern France* (Hamilton, 1939).

BURY, J. P. T.: *France 1814–1940* (Methuen, 1949).

— *Napoleon III and the Second Empire* (E.U.P., 1964).

COBBAN, A.: *History of Modern France*, vols. 2 and 3 (Penguin Books, 1965).

ELTON, LORD: *The Revolutionary Idea in France, 1789–1871* (Arnold, 1931).

FISHER, H. A. L.: *Napoleon* (O.U.P., 1912).

GEYL, P.: *Napoleon For and Against* (Penguin Books, 1964).

GIRARD, L. (ed.): *Histoire*, vol. 2: 1789–1848, and vol. 3: 1848–1914 (Harrap, 1962).

GUERARD, A.: *Napoleon* (Hutchinson, 1957).

MALO, H.: *Thiers, 1797–1877* (Payot, Paris).

MARKHAM, F. M. H.: *Napoleon* (Weidenfeld and Nicolson, 1963).

MAUROIS, A.: *History of France* (Cape; Methuen paperback, 1960).

POMARET, C.: *Monsieur Thiers et son siècle* (Gallimard, Paris).

RUDÉ, G.: *Revolutionary Europe* (Collins, 1964).

THOMPSON, J. M.: *Napoleon Bonaparte, His Rise and Fall* (Blackwell, 1951).

WOODWARD, E. L.: *French Revolutions* (O.U.P., 1934).

Metternich, Bismarck, and Kaiser William II

CECIL, A.: *Metternich* (Eyre and Spottiswode, 1947).

COWLES, V.: *The Kaiser* (Collins, 1963).

EYCK, E.: *Bismarck and the German Empire* (Allen and Unwin, 1950).

FLENLEY, R.: *Modern German History* (Dent, 1964).

GOOCH, G. P.: *Studies in Diplomacy and Statecraft* (Longmans, 1942).

MARRIOTT, J. A. R., and ROBERTSON, C. G.: *The Evolution of Prussia* (O.U.P., 1946).

NICOLSON, H.: *The Congress of Vienna* (Constable; Methuen paperback, 1946).

PASSANT, E. J.: *A Short History of Germany (1815–1945)* (C.U.P., 1959).

RICHTER, W.: *Bismarck* (Macdonald, 1964).

SCHWARTZ, H. F. (ed.): *Metternich "The Coachman of Europe"* (Harrap, 1962).

TAYLOR, A. J. P.: *Bismarck, the Man and the Statesman* (Hamilton, 1955).
— *The Course of German History* (Hamilton, 1948).

WILSON, L.: *The Incredible Kaiser* (Hale, 1963).

WOODWARD, E. L.: *Three Studies in European Conservatism* (Cass, 1963).

Bolívar

KIRKPATRICK, F. A.: *Latin America, a Brief History* (C.U.P., 1930).

MADARIAGA, S. DE: *Bolívar* (Hollis and Carter, 1952).

PENDLE, G.: *History of Latin America* (Penguin Books, 1965).

TREND, J. B.: *Bolívar and the Independence of South America* (E.U.P., 1946).

Garibaldi

GLADSTONE, E. W., ST AUBYN, G. R., and REES, B.: *The Unification of Italy* (Blackwell, 1955).

HEARDER, H., and WALEY, D. P.: *A Short History of Italy* (C.U.P., 1963).

HIBBERT, C.: *Garibaldi and his Enemies* (Longmans, 1965).

SMITH, D. MACK: *Garibaldi* (Hutchinson, 1957).
— *Garibaldi and Cavour* (C.U.P., 1955).

TREVELYAN, G. M.: *Garibaldi's Defence of the Roman Republic* (Longmans, 1949).
— *Garibaldi and the Thousand* (Longmans, 1948).
— *Garibaldi and the Making of Italy* (Longmans, 1948).

Jackson and Lincoln

AGAR, H.: *Abraham Lincoln* (Collins, 1952).

BASSETT, J. S.: *Life of Andrew Jackson* (2 vols., New York).

BRAGDON, H. W., and MCCUTCHEN, S. P.: *History of a Free People* (Macmillan, New York, 1956).

DONALD, D.: *Lincoln Reconsidered* (Vintage Books, New York).

HOFSTADTER, R.: *The American Political Tradition* (Cape, 1962).

JAMES, M.: *Andrew Jackson; Portrait of a President* (2 vols., Indianapolis).

MORISON, S. E., and COMMAGER, H. S.: *The Growth of the American Republic* (O.U.P., New York, 1962).

NYE, R. B., and MORPURGO, J. E.: *A History of the United States*, vol. 2 (Penguin Books, 1955).

RANDALL, J. G.: *Lincoln the President: Springfield to Gettysburg* (Eyre and Spottiswode, 1956).

THOMAS, B. P.: *Abraham Lincoln* (Eyre and Spottiswode, 1953).

VAN DEUSEN, G. G.: *The Jacksonian Era 1828–1848* (Harper & Row, 1965).

WHEARE, K. C.: *Abraham Lincoln and the United States* (E.U.P., 1948).

Palmerston and Gladstone

CECIL, A.: *Queen Victoria and her Prime Ministers* (Eyre and Spottiswode, 1952).

CONNELL, B.: *Regina v. Palmerston* (Evans, 1962).

ENSOR, R. C. K.: *England, 1870–1914* (O.U.P., 1936).

EYCK, E.: *Gladstone* (Allen and Unwin, 1965).

HAMMOND, J. L., and FOOT, M. R. D.: *Gladstone and Liberalism* (E.U.P., 1952).

MAGNUS, P.: *Gladstone* (Murray, 1954).

MARTIN, K.: *The Triumph of Lord Palmerston* (Hutchinson, 1963).

PEMBERTON, W. B.: *Lord Palmerston* (Batchworth Press, 1954).

SOUTHGATE, D.: *The Most English Minister* (Macmillan, 1966).

WOODWARD, E. L.: *The Age of Reform (1815–70)* (O.U.P., 1962).

Tsar Alexander II

ALMEDINGEN, E. M.: *The Emperor Alexander II* (Bodley Head, 1962).

CHARQUES, R.: *A Short History of Russia* (E.U.P., 1959).

KOCHAN, L.: *The Making of Modern Russia* (Cape, 1962).

KROPOTKIN, P.: *Memoirs of a Revolutionist* (W. H. Allen, 1962).

MOSSE, W. E.: *Alexander II and the Modernization of Russia* (E.U.P., 1959).

PARES, B.: *A History of Russia* (Cape, 1955).

SETON-WATSON, H.: *The Russian Empire 1801–1917* (O.U.P., 1967).

— *The Decline of Imperial Russia* (Methuen, 1952).

UTECHIN, S. V.: *Everyman's Concise Encyclopedia of Russia* (Dent, 1961).

Index